M. J. (Martin John) Spalding

Lectures on the Evidences of Catholicity

M. J. (Martin John) Spalding

Lectures on the Evidences of Catholicity

ISBN/EAN: 9783741142383

Manufactured in Europe, USA, Canada, Australia, Japa

Cover: Foto ©Thomas Meinert / pixelio.de

Manufactured and distributed by brebook publishing software
(www.brebook.com)

M. J. (Martin John) Spalding

Lectures on the Evidences of Catholicity

LECTURES

ON THE

Evidences of Catholicity;

Delivered in the Cathedral of Louisville,

BY M. J. SPALDING, D. D.

ARCHBISHOP OF BALTIMORE.

"But prove all things; hold that which is good."
I. THESS. v: 21.

"Jesus Christ yesterday, to-day, and the same for ever."
HEBREWS xiii: 8.

FIFTH EDITION, REVISED AND ENLARGED.

BALTIMORE:
PUBLISHED BY JOHN MURPHY & CO.
LOUISVILLE ... WEBB & LEVERING.
1870.

TO

ALL THE LOVERS OF CHRIST,

WHO SEEK TO SAVE THEIR IMMORTAL SOULS,

BY ATTAINING TO A

KNOWLEDGE OF THE TRUTH,

AND OBEYING ITS TEACHINGS,

These Lectures

ARE AFFECTIONATELY DEDICATED,

BY THE AUTHOR.

LOUISVILLE, KY.,
FEAST OF ST. ALFONSO LIGUORI, 1877.

Preface to the Third Edition.

The following Lectures, delivered a few years ago in the Cathedral of Louisville, were intended to exhibit, in a plain and straightforward manner, the principal Evidences of the Catholic Church. They are now again offered to the public in a third edition, with the hope that some sincere and candid souls, now wandering amidst the mazes of hereditary error, may be led back by the perusal of them to the bosom of the true Church, from which their fathers in an evil hour separated, to follow after the devices of their own hearts.

To every lover of the Christian Religion it must be apparent, on sufficient examination, that the Evidences which sustain Catholicity are substantially identical with those which establish Christianity itself. The scope of these Lectures is to establish this identity. In point of fact, Catholicity and Christianity were the same thing during the first fifteen centuries of the Christian era; and to every one who will carefully and candidly examine the question in all its bearings, it must become manifest that this identity has continued down to our own day, and that it will continue to the end of time.

The uncertainty of all human things, never perhaps more strikingly illustrated than by the present unhappy condition of our own beloved country, should lead all men to lift their eyes towards heaven, and make them think seriously and inquire diligently concerning the divinely appointed pathway which leadeth thereto.

Time is short, eternity never ending; and "what doth it profit a man, if he gain the whole world, and LOSE HIS OWN SOUL?" While in the religious world all has become unsettled, by the devices of wicked leaders "lying in wait to deceive," and causing men "to be tossed to and fro by every wind of doctrine," and in the political and social world all is short-lived, and withal very unstable and uncertain, we may well adopt the language and use the tender invitation of God's plaintive Prophet: "Stand ye in the ways, and see, and ask for THE OLD PATHS, which is the good way, and walk ye in it, and you shall find refreshment for your souls." *Jer.* vi. 16.

Under these circumstances, a third edition of these Lectures is deemed opportune to the times. The Catholic Church, which for eighteen centuries has nobly battled against all forms of error, and which has consistently sustained Christianity amidst all the vicissitudes of human affairs, has surely a right to have her claims diligently investigated by every lover of the truth, especially by those who have been taught from childhood to protest against her doctrines and institutions. She knows no concealment; she courts inquiry, and is willing to abide its result. All that she asks is, that her principles should be correctly represented, and her claims to be the true Church of Christ be fairly and impartially weighed. She demands no more than this, and surely she could not ask less.

BALTIMORE, *Feast of St. Martin,* 1864.

CONTENTS.

(vii)

LECTURE IV.

THE APOSTOLIC COMMISSION—ITS FULFILLMENT—THE SECOND EVIDENCE OF CATHOLICITY.

LECTURE V.

MIRACLES—THE THIRD EVIDENCE OF CATHOLICITY.

LECTURE VI.

CATHOLICITY AND UNITY—THE FOURTH EVIDENCE OF CATHOLICITY.

LECTURE VII.

SANCTITY—THE FIFTH EVIDENCE OF CATHOLICITY.

LECTURE VIII.

APOSTOLICAL ANTIQUITY—THE SIXTH EVIDENCE OF CATHOLICITY.

LECTURE IX.

INFALLIBILITY OF THE CHURCH—THE SEVENTH EVIDENCE OF CATHOLICITY.

LECTURE X.

TRIALS AND TRIUMPHS OF THE CHURCH — THE EIGHTH EVIDENCE OF CATHOLICITY.

LECTURE XI.

CHURCH GOVERNMENT—THE PRIMACY—THE NINTH EVIDENCE OF CATHOLICITY.

LECTURE XII.

CHURCH GOVERNMENT—THE PAPACY—THE NINTH EVIDENCE OF CATHOLICITY

(CONCLUDED).

LECTURE XIII.

SIX OTHER EVIDENCES.

xii

CONTENTS.

LECTURE XIV.

RECAPITULATION—THE PARALLEL—CONCLUSION.

Becoming little children for Christ's sake—Faith a gift of God, vouchsafed only to the humble—Object of this concluding Lecture—Drawing scattered lights to a focus—Rapid analysis of the evidences contained in the thirteen previous Lectures—St. Augustine's reasons for being a Catholic—Our own still more ample and conclusive—THE PARALLEL between the two lines of reasoning in support of Christianity and Catholicity—Prophecies of the Old and New Testaments—Ancient types and figures fulfilled in the Catholic Church alone—Miracles—Rapid propagation of Christianity—Its beneficial influence on morals—The number of its martyrs—Its stability and permanency—No infidels among Christians in Catholic times—But many now in Christendom—Appeal—Conclusion—Prayer. 417

LECTURES

EVIDENCES OF CATHOLICITY.

LECTURE I.—INTRODUCTORY.

ON RELIGIOUS INQUIRY—ITS OBLIGATION AND DUTIES.

Words of Christ explained—A command and a promise—Both universal in their application—Religious Inquiry—Its obligation—Whence it arises—Religious indifference—Its absurdity—and manifold evils—Latitudinarianism—Exclusive salvation—Sectarianism—What are its causes—and how is it to be remedied?—The principles which should guide Religious Inquiry—and the spirit which should pervade it—Freedom from prejudice—Humility—Persevering prayer—Fenelon—Recapitulation and prayer.

"Ask, and it shall be given unto you: seek, and ye shall find; knock, and it shall be opened unto you. For every one that asketh, receiveth: and he that seeketh, findeth: and to him that knocketh it shall be opened."—St. Matthew, vii: 7, 8.

THESE words, Beloved Brethren, should be heard with the most profound reverence and submission, for they were pronounced by the lips of our divine Lord and Master Himself, when, sitting upon the mountain top, full eighteen hundred years ago, He was instructing the multitudes who eagerly thronged to listen to His divine eloquence. They unfold a principle which, if adopted and fully carried out, would terminate all contentious disputation on the subject of religion, and would render all those who claim to be disciples of Christ brethren indeed, in unity of faith and sincerity of love. They lay down a golden rule, by which

2

all the sincere lovers of Jesus Christ may certainly attain
to the knowledge of His saving truth—and, what is still
more important, may have, at the same time, the strength
and courage to embrace it. May Jesus himself, "who
enlighteneth every man that cometh into this world;" who
is "the way, and the truth, and the life," as well as "the
light of the world," shed His blessed light and grace into
our minds and hearts, that we may know and feel the full
import of these sacred words, and may arrive at the happy
conclusion to which they are so well calculated to lead us !

The words of our Saviour contain two things: a command and a promise—both of them positive in their nature
and general in their application. The command is binding
on all men; the promise is also for all mankind. "Ask,
seek, knock,"—behold the positive command: "it shall
be given to you, you shall find, it shall be opened to you,"
—behold the consoling promise. And that this promise
might be the more cheering and certain of fulfillment, it
is repeated in still stronger and more emphatic language:
"For *every one* that asketh, receiveth; and he that seeketh,
findeth; and to him that knocketh, it shall be opened."

Both the command, and the promise corresponding thereto, are couched in language which increases in force as it
flows on, in a species of climax; so urgent was our blessed
Lord in impressing this important truth upon the minds of
all mankind. "Ask, seek, knock:" *ask* of God the light
and grace which are indispensably necessary to enter with
profit upon the field of Religious Inquiry; *seek* the truth
with sincerity, earnestness, and perseverance, under the
divine light and guidance, turning neither to the right nor
to the left, consulting not with flesh and blood, but pushing
boldly on to the goal; *knock* at the portals of that glorious
temple of truth, when you will be so fortunate as to reach
it; knock and beg with instance for admission into its time-
honored aisles and venerable sanctuary, in which your forefathers worshiped with so much simplicity and earnest faith.
Do all this, and as surely as the promise of the Saviour
God may be relied on, so surely will you succeed in thread-

ing the mazy windings of unbelief, and emerging into the clear light and the blessed day of the truth, when the Sun of Justice will enlighten and warm you with his rays. Then will you be free from the darkness of error, and the bondage of sin; then will you breathe a fresher and more bracing atmosphere; then will you thank God with overflowing hearts, for having broken your bonds, and stricken off your chains; then "you shall know the truth, and the truth shall make you free."*

I. No one, we presume, will venture to deny the obligation and the necessity of Religious Inquiry. This necessity grows out of the very nature of the Christian Religion, the objects which it contemplates, and the importance of its institutions for the happiness of mankind in time and in eternity. A mere glance at these three great characteristics of Christianity will convince every reasoning mind of the obligation in question.

The Christian Religion, in its very nature, is far elevated above all human sciences and concerns. It soars far above the earth with its transient goods, into the regions of a sublimer philosophy, and of a more radiant truth. Like the eagle in his heaven-ward flight, it fixes an undazzled eye upon the bright sun of truth itself, and pauses not in its ascent until it has come within the immediate influence of his orb, and bathed its plumage in his rays. It speaks to us of the creation and end of man; of the early history of the world; of the origin of sin, and its remedy; of the darkness of the human understanding, the blindness of the human heart, and of the causes and remedies of both; of the wondrous scheme of man's redemption by the imperishable love of the Man-God; of God and His attributes; of heaven and its glory; of eternity, with its alternative of final happiness or endless woe. Moreover, it treats of Christ and His holy institutions; of the Church which He established, and commanded all to hear, under the penalty of being reckoned "with heathens and publicans;"† of the ministry He organized to

* St. John, viii, 82.   † St. Matthew, xviii.

teach all nations, and to found His Church every where; of the life-giving sacraments they were to administer; of the manner in which the sinner is to be reclaimed and brought back to God through Christ; of the healing balm to be applied to the hearts of the miserable and down-trodden; of benefits innumerable—of mind, of heart, of body—to be bounteously bestowed on the human race.

Did ever a system of merely human philosophy take so wide, or so sublime a range as this, treat of so many vastly important topics, or appeal with more earnest eloquence to our fullest attention and most careful investigation? As heaven is elevated above earth, as eternity is elevated above time, as God is exalted above man, so is God's truth elevated above man's truth, and God's holy Religion above any human science or system. And if merely human systems of legislation, or crude theories of moral and practical philosophy, devised for the welfare of our race, are deemed entitled to our serious attention during the brief period of their feverish existence on the stage of the world, how much more worthy of our careful inquiry is that one great, divine, and unchanging system of truth, which unfolds principles on which our happiness for time and for eternity depends—discloses relations and duties with which our eternal welfare or misery is bound up! If the things of time awaken so much interest, possess so strong an attraction, and stimulate us so powerfully to action, should not the things of eternity move us still more? Should they not arouse all our dormant energies, and nerve us with courage and vigor for prosecuting successfully an Inquiry fraught with so many important results?

This resolution will be still more strengthened by a rapid glance at the objects contemplated by the Christian Religion. These are no less than the dispelling of the clouds which darken the human understanding by the radiation of a heavenly light, the warming of the human heart by a communication of a genial heavenly heat, and the healing of man's natural infirmities by strength imparted from on high. The truths of Christianity enlighten the understanding, its moral precepts guide and strengthen the will, while its sacraments heal the weakness of the heart, and clothe it with the panoply of heavenly strength and beauty. Thus the whole Christian system is medicinal; its object being to *heal* the evils produced in all the faculties of the soul by the fall of Adam, and to lead man back to God, from whom he had, in an evil hour, strayed away. Its ultimate end and object is to remove from man the greatest of all evils, and to bestow upon him the greatest of all goods; to deliver him from eternal misery, and to crown him with eternal happiness.

And who will say that these objects are not of sufficient value, to entitle the Religion which contemplates them, to the serious study and investigation of every reasonable man? Who will say that man is not bound to inquire into a Religion of so much importance in itself, and in its objects, that to establish it God did not spare His own dearly beloved Son, but sent Him into the world to be buffeted by afflictions and privations, and to become finally the bleeding victim of persecution? Who will dare affirm that we are not bound to inquire into a Religion, to seal which Jesus died on the cross? Look at the bloody cross of Calvary, and at the agonizing form of the great Man-God stretched thereon—count His bruises and His sufferings, and reckon, if you can, the drops of His precious blood which streamed down from every gaping wound, for the sealing of this Religion; and then lay your hand upon your heart, and tell me whether you do not *feel* that a system established at such a cost as this is important enough to merit your most earnest Inquiry!

And yet, alas! religious indifference appears to be the besetting sin of this, our age of boasted enlightenment! We are in earnest about every thing else; it is only in Religion that the coldness and the pall of the tomb have settled around us. This world and its fleeting interests are every thing; the world to come, with its momentous truths and awful because eternal realities, is as nothing. Verily, "the children of this world are wiser in their generation than

the children of light."* Men will run wild on schemes
of speculation for bettering their earthly condition; they
will labor day and night, through a long and feverish life,
to amass wealth, to acquire honors, to taste pleasures, though
all of these things are very uncertain of acquisition, very
fleeting and perishable in their nature, and really inadequate to satisfy the longing of the human heart after
happiness; and yet you cannot awaken in their bosoms a
serious thought on the infinitely more important concern
of Religion! They are keenly alive to every other interest
but that which is the highest and greatest; they labor and
fret to acquire every other boon than the "ONE THING
NECESSARY." O that some inspired prophet of God, with
lips touched with the living coal from God's holy altar, and
with a tongue uttering the burning words of divine eloquence, could traverse the world, and from every highway
and market-place proclaim to the children of men, in a
voice of thunder, the momentous question of our blessed
Lord: "WHAT DOTH IT PROFIT A MAN IF HE GAIN THE WHOLE
WORLD, AND LOSE HIS OWN SOUL?" Then might men be
aroused to a sense of the great importance and absolute
necessity of Religious Inquiry. Then might they be induced to bestow as much attention upon Religion as upon
steam navigation, railroads, magnetic telegraphs, banks,
politics, phrenology, mesmerism, spiritism, and other pursuits and interests which now seem to engross their whole
time and investigation. Alas! for this age of boasted enlightenment, but of real mammonism—of enlightenment in
every thing else more than in Religion!

Nearly akin to this religious indifference is that wide-
spread and popular latitudinarianism, the most current
maxim of which is, that it matters not what religion a man
embraces, or what he believes, provided he be a moral man,
and a good citizen! As if truth and error, light and darkness, were alike agreeable to God! As if He were indifferent whether man believe the truth or a lie! As if Christ

* St. Luke, xvi: 8.

would have poured out His blood to seal His Religion, though indifferent Himself whether mankind embraced or rejected its saving truths! As if a man could be moral and pleasing to God, while rejecting even a portion of His holy truth! Away with such absurdities, if not downright blasphemies, and away with the pernicious principle from which they necessarily flow.

Either Christ left His Religion vague and unsettled in its principles, and, therefore, open to the disputation of men, who were thus left free to receive or reject as much of it as accorded with or was repugnant to their own notions of what is right and true; or He fixed and settled it in every particular, and required the assent of mankind to every one of its truths, as an essential condition of salvation. One or the other of these views you must adopt. You cannot adopt the former without virtually blaspheming Christ, by making Him a weak and unwise legislator, and without flying into the face of His own explicit and solemn declarations to the contrary. He directed His apostles to teach mankind "to observe *all things* whatsoever He had commanded them," *and He laid down the awful penalty of unbelief, without any limitation or restriction whatsoever: " He that believeth not shall be condemned." †

After these plain and solemn declarations of Christ, who will doubt of the necessity of believing ALL things which He taught in His holy Religion? Who will venture to make distinctions, where He made none? Who will flatter himself with the hope of salvation, without feeling morally certain that he believes *all* the doctrines taught by Christ? Is not Christ as much entitled to be believed in what we may choose to call small and unessential things, as in those which we may deem of greater importance? Did not an inspired apostle declare, that "without faith it is impossible to please God?"† And has not another laid down the principle : ‡"He that offendeth in one point (of the law) is become guilty of all?"‖ How then can we expect, my

---

* St. Math. xxviii: 20. † St. Mark, xvi: 16. ‡ Heb. xi: 6. ‖ St. James, ii: 10.

Dear Brethren, to save our souls with either a partial
faith, or an imperfect obedience?   God will have all or
nothing; the whole homage of our understandings, and of
our hearts, or no homage at all.   Let us not, then, deceive
ourselves in a matter so closely connected with our eternal
salvation.   We must not seek to please men, nor to flatter
their pride, but rather to tell the truth as it is in Christ
Jesus, for we shall be judged by the truth.

Do we then say that all who are in error will be necessarily lost?   Not at all.   We judge not men, for God only can
see the heart.   But we do say, that we will all be judged by
the principles just laid down not by ourselves, but by Christ
and His inspired apostles.   God will judge every man
according to the deeds done in the flesh.   Those who are in
error, without any fault of their own—if there be any such—
who have done every thing in their power to find out the
truth, and are disposed to embrace it when ascertained, no
matter at what sacrifice, will not be condemned merely for
being in error.   But those who will not avail themselves of
every opportunity afforded them by divine Providence for
investigating the truth, who are unwilling, or who neglect
to embrace it when ascertained, through selfish or worldly
motives, must not delude themselves with the hope of salvation; for they persist in their errors through their own fault,
and they thus trample upon the blood of that God who died
to establish the truth.   In short, God will judge us all with
justice, according to our lights, graces, and opportunities,
and the manner of our correspondence therewith; and if we
are lost, it will be solely through our own fault.   Hence, if
we value our eternal salvation we are bound to inquire diligently into the great affair of Religion, and not to pause in
our investigation until we have knocked at the door of the
temple of truth, and been admitted into its holy sanctuary.

Religious Inquiry will thus remedy the fatal religious
indifference which is so prevalent, as well as that unhappy
latitudinarianism which is scarcely less dangerous.   But it
will do more: it will greatly check, if it will not wholly arrest
another opposite excess into which the religious mind of the

day is so apt to run. Sectarianism, with its endless divisions
and bitter contentions, with its fiendish pride and selfish
uncharitableness, will disappear, in a great measure, before
the progress of a wholesome investigation of the truth.

The sincere inquirer cannot fail to perceive that pride
and passion are at the bottom of all these unhappy divisions,
and that the only adequate remedy to them is found in
the opposite virtues of humility and self-denial. If he will
look into the inspired volume with a mind open to conviction, he will find that unity of faith is an essential mark
of the truth, and that sects are not the work of God, but
rather of the arch-enemy. He will be forcibly impressed
with the solemn declaration of St. Paul, who, after placing
"dissensions and sects" by the side of "murders and drunkenness," says of them all: "Of the which I foretell you, as
I have foretold to you, that they who do such things shall
not obtain the kingdom of God."* He will listen reverently to the same Paul, when reasoning with the Corinthians against the divisions which had unhappily rent their
church, he asked them emphatically: "Is Christ divided?
Was Paul crucified for you? or were you baptized in the
name of Paul?"† He will ask, can it be that Christ established a hundred conflicting systems of Religion, or that
all those jarring sects which now claim to be the Religion
of Christ are really what they profess to be? And if not,
where is the one, unchangeable, undying truth, originally
taught by Christ, promulgated by His apostles, and handed
down through an uninterrupted series of faithful witnesses
even unto the present day? Is there not such a Religion
as this now upon the face of the earth? If there is not,
then what adequate provision has God made for leading me
to the truth amidst so many conflicting sects? If there is,
then where is that one, old, unchanging Religion? Let me
but find it out, and I will immediately and cheerfully embrace it, no matter if the step should cost me my life; for
"what doth it profit a man if he gain the whole world, and
lose his own soul?"

---

* Galatians, v: 20 21.   † Corinthians, i: 13.

Such are the conclusions to which a healthy Religious Inquiry will lead the sincere lover of truth. It will not fail to open his eyes to the danger and evils of the two fearful extremes between which the religious world is now oscillating: religious indifference, and fanatical sectarianism. Upon the former he will look as a state of apathy, of spiritual death; upon the latter, as a condition of spasmodic and unnatural life, bearing in its bosom the elements of death. And this reflection will explain to him, why it is that these extremes so often meet. The fanatic grows tired of his convulsive life, and at length falls exhausted into the embrace of icy indifference; and the indifferent, on the contrary, terrified and aroused from his torpor by the fitful gleamings of an awful eternity upon his darksome pathway, may be induced, while under the excitement, to throw himself into the arms of fanaticism, though when the fever will be over, and he will have relapsed into his former state of apathy, "the last state of this man is made worse than the first."* The golden mean of truth, embraced with soberness but held with firmness, and remote alike from indifference and fanaticism, is the blessed result of this sincere and earnest Inquiry. The truth, when once ascertained and embraced with earnestness, will arouse the mind into a healthy and permanent activity, which, instead of exhausting, will increase its vigor and life; it will nourish the soul as healthy food does the body, removing the languor left by spiritual hunger, and imparting strength and vigor, without producing over-wrought excitement or intoxication of the brain.

II. But you will perhaps tell me that men do inquire with sincerity and earnestness, and yet that they are not all aroused to a sense of the necessity of Religion, nor brought to unity of religious faith. I admit that these results are not always produced by religious inquiry as it is now sometimes conducted even by men of apparent ability and sincerity; but I maintain that they would most certainly be produced, were there not something radically wrong either in the principles on which

---

* St. Matthew, xii: 45.

the Inquiry is conducted, or in the spirit by which it is directed. Many men inquire into Religion without any distinct idea of what Religion is, and consequently with very indefinite and vague, perhaps wholly erroneous principles, guiding their investigation. They have a certain vague and faintly glimmering notion that Religion is a something divine, intended for the spiritual benefit and eternal happiness of mankind; but they are not quite sure that it is any thing more than a theory, a speculation, a science, or a mental excitement and gush of feeling, accompanied by a persuasion that past sin is forgiven, and the sinner is thus reconciled and confirmed in the friendship of his God. They lose sight of first principles in some favorite, preconceived theory of conversion. They do not apprehend Religion as a positive institution, a system of divine truths, moral principles, and sacraments, *one* in its very nature and essence, accurately defined and clearly marked in all its features, resting for its origin and sanction on the *fact* that GOD HATH SPOKEN, and clearly obligatory in all its parts upon all mankind as an essential condition of salvation. And yet this is the real nature; these are the distinctive characteristics of Christianity.* What Christian will deny this? If so, can we wonder that men, even sincere men, who start out in their inquiry on other principles altogether, should not reach the goal of truth? Their premises are wrong, and if they reason logically, their conclusion must be erroneous.

But there are yet other reasons to explain the fact that seemingly sincere inquirers do not always arrive at the truth. There is often something radically wrong in the spirit of the Inquiry, as well as in the principles on which it is conducted. Many men bring into it their prejudices and their passions, their pride of mind and heart, their defilements of conscience and their bitter uncharitableness; and how can they hope, under the guidance of such a spirit, to reach that blessed truth which is utterly at war with all

---

* This, with some other points alluded to above, will be shown more fully in the next Lecture.

these feelings and sentiments? They begin in the flesh, and how can they hope to end in the spirit? Do they not know that "the sensual man perceiveth not the things which are of the spirit of God; for it is foolishness to him and he cannot understand; because it is spiritually examined?"*

The mind of the religious inquirer, if he would be suc cessful in coming to a knowledge of the truth, should be. 1. Free from prejudice and from passion; 2. Humble; and 3. Addicted to humble and earnest prayer. We will endeavor briefly to develop these qualities, and to point out their utility and necessity.

1. How can a man whose mind is fettered by precon- ceived opinions, expect to attain to a knowledge of the truth, unless he first of all be resolved to break his bonds and to be free? Truth alone, my dearly Beloved Breth- ren, can set us free from the trammels of error; but how can we hope to attain to this blessed freedom of the children of God, if we still fondly cherish our bonds and cling tenaciously to the chains of slavery? How can a man whose limbs are bound with the cords of a voluntary servitude to error or vice, hope to breathe again the pure atmosphere of heavenly freedom, unless, Samson-like, he first burst asunder those cords which hold him captive? In other words, how can a man who is wedded to a favorite theory, and who is resolved not to give it up, whether it be right or wrong, expect to have courage sufficient to embrace a truth which conflicts with that theory? We all know, and we have all felt the force of early prejudice; but our knowledge will be to little purpose, if it do not lead to the determination to war against it, and to sacrifice it, if need be, on the holy altar of truth. No matter how dearly it may be cherished; no matter how closely it may have become intertwined with our minds so as to become almost a part of our very being; if it should have become as dear to us even as was Isaac to Abraham; we must yet be willing to immolate it, at the bidding of God.

* 1 Corinthians, ii: 14.

Early prejudice may be dear, but truth and duty should be dearer; and we have the divine command, that "if our hand or foot scandalize us, we must cut it off, and cast it from us; for it is better for us to enter into life maimed or lame, than, having two hands or two feet, *to be cast into everlasting fire.*"*

The sun is bright in the heavens, but if a cloud pass over his disk, his beams reach us not; though he is not blotted from the heavens, his light is not for us. So if the cloud of prejudice interpose between us and the bright sun of truth, that sun will still be there, nobly careering in the heavens of God, but his blessed light will not shine on us. In the midst of light we will be still in darkness. And tell me not, that this shutting out of the light is not our own fault. Could we not remove the intervening cloud, if we would? Could we not, with the divine assistance, render clear and transparent the atmosphere in which our soul lives and moves? Surely we could. We are free agents, and God, who is the God of light, will never refuse to aid us in dissipating the darkness which envelopes our spirits, if we be only willing to permit Him to shed His light upon us. The man who would shut himself up in his chamber, close all the windows, and then complain that he was left in darkness, would be set down as guilty either of extreme folly or extreme madness. Is not the light gleaming brightly without, enlightening and cheering all who are willing to come under its blessed influence; and why does this churlish friend of darkness persist in closing the avenues to its ingress? May we not say the same of those who obstinately refuse to open the windows of their soul to the light of truth?

The darkness of prejudice is rendered darker still by the indulgence of low and groveling passion. There is nothing which so darkens the chambers of the mind, and renders them so impervious to the light of truth, as the thick fumes of passion—especially of carnal passion, the most vehement

---

* St. Matthew, xviii. 8.

8

and the most debasing of all. A man who wilfully nestles this foul monster in his bosom, cannot hope to see the truth, or at least to embrace the truth. It is too spiritual for his carnal sense; its light reveals too strongly all his moral turpitude; it gleams too terribly through all the dark avenues of his heart, lighting them up in all their ghastly nakedness and deformity. Despising his groveling vices, and yet resolved not to abandon them, the voluptuary shrinks from the heavenly vision, as did Baltassar from that of the terrible hand-writing upon the wall. He is in darkness; and he "loves darkness rather than the light, for his works are evil."* How can such a one as this hope to attain to a knowledge of the truth? And if he should, how will he have the courage or grace to embrace it?

2. No, Dear Brethren, we must not deceive ourselves to our own eternal perdition. We must not persuade ourselves that we are in the light, when really we are in the midst of darkness. But another great obstacle to the entrance of God's light into our souls, is the indulgence of a passion still more dangerous, because less revolting and therefore more insidious in its approaches: a secret and fondly cherished pride of mind and heart. Faith, by which we apprehend the truth, and without which "it is impossible to please God," is,—we must never forget it,—a gift of God which will be bestowed only on the humble. "God rejects the proud, and gives his grace to the humble." This is a cardinal principle of Christianity. In order to be taught of God, we must carefully bring down "every hight that exalteth itself against the knowledge of God, and bring into captivity every understanding to the obedience of Christ."† If we would know the truth, we must humble ourselves, and put on the simplicity and docility of little children, mindful of what our blessed Lord has so emphatically said: "Amen I say unto you, unless you be converted, and become as little children, you shall not enter into the kingdom of heaven."‡

---

* St. John, iii: 19.   † 2 Corinthians, x: 5.   ‡ St. Matthew, xviii: 3.

These, my Dear Friends, are the infallible words of divine wisdom; they contain principles by which we shall be judged, and by which our eternal happiness or misery will be settled. We should examine and embrace them now while there is time, lest we should be struck with their dreadful truth when it will be too late for us to profit by them. No, it is not to the proud man who vaunts his own superior skill in understanding the holy scriptures, who bitterly sneers at others as less enlightened than himself, who piques himself on his superior shrewdness in spiritual things, and who is secretly vain of his influence over others, that the blessed light of truth is vouchsafed; but it is to the humble, to those who distrust their own lights, who seek with humility the light and guidance of heaven, and who are prepared to submit their reason to any authority which will show a divine warrant for its exercise. This proud and captious spirit, this disposition to misrepresent others, and to revolt against all constituted authority which is opposed to self-love and which restrains the pride of opinion; this feeling that we are more enlightened than all the world besides; this embodied dogmatism based on pride and nourished by pride, is not, can not be in conformity with the spirit of Christianity. It is the very antipodes of true Religion; it is rather the spirit of Lucifer than that of Christ. It has ruined millions; it has never saved one soul.

The great and amiable Fenelon, the Catholic Bishop, whose whole life proved that he could not only teach, but practise the purest and the loftiest Christianity, has developed this truth, with his wonted clearness, meekness, and earnestness. I cannot do better than to read his own words—he is writing to a Protestant friend:

"If you truly wish a reform, do not commence outwardly by a sour and haughty criticism; turn your thoughts within; humble yourself profoundly; distrust your own weak light; labor to overcome natural tastes; listen not to the delicacies of self-love; bring down high, proud thoughts; reckon not upon your own courage. If you wish to find

God, enter within your own breast, and listen to His voice in silence; suppress the movements of a bewildered imagination, that you may be occupied in the presence of God, and be enabled to ask of Him the accomplishment of your duties and the correction of your faults. This would be a happy and solid reform, and the more you would do in reforming *yourself* in this way, the less would you attempt to reform the *Church*."*

3. But the great means for freeing the mind from all undue prejudice, for calming down its passions, and disposing it, by a deep humility, for the reception of the priceless jewel of faith, is prayer,—humble, fervent, persevering prayer. We are in darkness; we must pray to God for light to illumine our pathway: He is the great Father of light, and He will not refuse our petition. Weak and miserable as we are, yet are we surrounded by dangers, beset with temptations, buffeted by the passions; let us pray with confidence to Him who is strong, and who is both able and willing to protect us. Perplexed and embarrassed, amidst the intricate windings of the labyrinth of error, to whom can we look for guidance but to Him who is wisdom itself, and who stands pledged to hear our prayer? "If any of you want wisdom," says an inspired apostle, "let him ask it of God, who giveth to all abundantly, and upbraideth not, and it shall be given him. But let him ask in faith, nothing wavering."† And our blessed Lord himself has uttered this emphatic and remarkable promise: "Therefore I say to you, all things whatsoever you ask when ye pray, believe that you shall receive, and they shall come unto you."‡

After all these explicit and consoling promises, made by Him who can not deceive, who will doubt the efficacy of prayer as a means to attain to a knowledge of the truth? "God will have all men to be saved and to come to the knowledge of the truth,"§ says the inspired Paul; and can we doubt that He will hear the fervent prayer, put up by

---

* Fenelon's Letters on the Church.   ‡ St. Mark, xi: 24.
† St. James. 1: 5, 6.   § 1 Timothy, ii: 4.

the humble heart, for the inestimable gift of faith? Why, then, are we in error, when God is so willing to lead us to the truth, if we will only ask Him to do so, and submit ourselves entirely to His guidance? What excuse can we offer at the dreadful bar of God, for straying from the truth, when we have so easy a means as this for emerging from our errors? Let us reflect well upon this while we have yet time; our salvation may depend upon it.

"Prayer," says Fenelon, "would put an end to all disputes. Happy are the men whom vanity does not make jealous of their liberty, who distrust their own light, and who are often recollected in prayer before God, in order to be guided by His grace. If the true spirit of prayer shall enter into your heart and take possession of it, you would find the treasure concealed in the earth; you would taste the hidden manna; you would not fear to be poor with your spouse, nor would you feel the want of any real good; you would perceive His omnipotence and His infinite love extended over you. If you will not believe me, try it; you will see. Be not wanting towards God, and He will not be wanting towards you."*

Yes, my Dear Friends, Fenelon was right; God will not be wanting on His part, if we are not wanting on ours. His goodness is infinite, and His mercies are above all His works. If we will let Him lead us to the knowledge of the truth, He will take us by the hand and conduct us thereto; if we will permit Him to save us, He will most certainly do so. If we be only free from prejudice, and humble of heart; if we pray humbly, fervently, with unwavering confidence, with perseverance, He will most assuredly bestow upon us the gift of saving faith, and will guide us unto eternal salvation. No one will be lost, but through his own fault. May I not then address you in the language which the prophet of old once addressed to the people of God: "Why will ye die, O house of Israel."† When Christ died for you on the cross; when God stands pledged in His holy word to hear your

---

* Fenelon's Letters on the Church.　　† Ezekiel, xviii: 31.

8 *

earnest petitions, why will you, through lethargy, negligence, or malice, not obtain or lose the precious gift of faith, and with it the glittering prize of life eternal?

Too long, Dearly Beloved Brethren, have we neglected the saving injunction to pray; let us neglect it no longer. "Ask, and you shall receive; seek, and you shall find; knock, and it shall be opened unto you. For *every one* that asketh, receiveth; and he that seeketh, findeth; and to him that knocketh, it shall be opened." Let us pray daily, pray with humility and fervor, and then will God's light shine around you; then will we all learn the truth, and the truth shall set us free; then will we all meet in the unity of faith; and being one on earth—one in faith and one in charity—we shall be all blended in glorious unity in heaven. May God grant it, through Jesus Christ! Amen.

LECTURE II.

God earnestly desires the salvation of all mankind — And has provided sufficient means of salvation for all — His goodness and mercy — Grace and free-will — Why some are saved and others lost — Saving truth — Contained in the Religion of Christ — State of the world before its establishment — Pagan philosophy powerless — Man a slave — Freed only by the Christian Religion — Its nature, properties, and objects — Theory of fundamental and non-fundamental doctrines — Christianity rests on a *fact* — Summary evidences of this fact — Leading characteristics of the Christian Religion — Four great guiding principles developed — Will heathens be saved? — Recapitulation — The Church — Its nature, office, and purpose — Object of these Lectures — Importance of the investigation — Prayer.

" I desire, therefore, first of all, that supplications, prayers, intercessions, and thanksgivings, be made for all men: for kings, and for all who are in high stations, that we may lead a quiet and peaceful life, in all piety and chastity: for this is good and acceptable in the sight of God our Saviour, who will have all men to be saved, and to come to the knowledge of the truth." — I TIMOTHY, ii: 1, 2, 3, 4.

THE inspired apostle of the gentiles, my Beloved Brethren, desires that we should pray for all men, of every station in life, of every country, tongue, and caste on the face of the earth; for men, for women, for children, for kings and subjects, for princes and beggars, for all mankind without any exception whatsoever. And the reason he assigns for this wish is well worthy our most serious consideration, as it unfolds to us a cardinal principle of the Christian Religion. In thus endeavoring to promote, as far as in us lies, the salvation of all men, we do but follow the example, and co-operate with the warmly cherished desire of "God our Saviour, who will have all men to be saved, and to come to the knowledge of the truth." There is no exception of persons with God; there is no restriction to His all-embracing benevolence; there are no bounds to His goodness, no limits

31

to His mercy; He loves all mankind, without shutting out
any from His expansive charity; his sun shines alike upon
the just and the unjust; and His own divine Son, in whom
He is well pleased, entering fully into the spirit of His
Father, bounteously poured out His heart's blood on the
cross for the salvation of all the children of Adam, whether
born before or after His first advent into the world.

This will of God to promote the salvation of all mankind,
is both sincere and active: that is, He really and truly
wishes that all the children of Adam should enjoy an eternal happiness in the life to come; and as an evidence that
this wish is not barren or inoperative, He has provided all
with the means which are necessary to enable them actually to attain salvation if they will. Whosoever wishes an
end, wills also the means necessary for securing that end;
otherwise the wish were not real or sincere. Therefore,
it is manifest that God has actually provided all mankind,
without any exception whatsoever, with all the means
necessary to enable them to secure eternal life; and therefore, if any are lost, it is through their own fault only, and
not through any deficiency on the part of God. It is
because, with every opportunity and means to save their
souls placed within their reach, they obstinately either neglect or reject this proffered help, and thus rush headlong to
their own perdition.

And there is no doubt whatever, my Dear Brethren, that
the most bitter and heart-rending thought that now tears
with anguish the souls of those who are unhappily lost forever, is this simple, but painful reminiscence: I could have
been saved, and behold I am lost; God loved me with an
eternal love, He sent his own beloved Son to save me by
dying on the cross for my redemption: He provided for me
in abundance the means of salvation; I might have been
saved, but I am lost eternally through my own fault!

God has done every thing that is necessary, on His part,
to save our souls; but He will compel none into heaven
against their own will. He places before us the glittering
prize of immortality; He enlightens our minds, warms our

hearts, moves our wills, to make us ardently desire it, and to enable us to secure it, if we will; but He will not award it to us, unless we faithfully co-operate with His grace, learn and embrace His truth, and reduce to practice whatever He has commanded. He created us without our co-operation, as St. Augustine says, but he will not save us without our co-operation. We are blind, we are weak, we are incapable of doing any thing of ourselves, as of ourselves; but He stands pledged to help us, and to listen to our humble supplication for mercy and assistance; He will smile down from heaven upon our feeble efforts, even as a father smiles upon the exertions of the little child who is beginning to walk; and, with far more efficient tenderness than the earthly parent, He will strengthen the tottering weakness, and prevent the fall, of His helpless children who confidently and lovingly look up to Him for light and guidance.

Salvation, then, is clearly the result of two distinct agencies: the grace of God, and our own free will. Of ourselves we can do nothing; "we can do all things in Him that strengtheneth us."* God did not make us mere *automata*, to be guided by Him blindly, and without our own co-operation; but He was graciously pleased to make us free agents, or, as the holy Scriptures express it, "to place us in the hands of our own counsel,"† and, after proffering His grace, make it depend measurably on ourselves whether we would be saved or lost eternally. Thus, free will in man, and the necessity of grace from God, are both amply vindicated. Man can not glory against God, because he can do nothing towards securing his salvation without God; and God can not be charged with injustice towards man, because He proffers to all, without exception, whatever grace is necessary for salvation.

This is the golden mean of truth, between the mere humanism of Pelagius, who ascribed every thing to free will and denied the necessity of divine grace, and the

---

* Phillipians iv: 13.   † Ecclesiasticus, xv: 14.

C

horrid predestination of Ca.vin, who gave every thing to grace, and nothing to free will. By this principle alone can we triumphantly vindicate the justice of God, both in rewarding the good and in punishing the wicked.

But what are the means provided by God for the salvation of all mankind, and where are they to be found? The apostle sufficiently indicates this in the text, when he says, "God our Saviour will have all men to be saved, and to come to the knowledge of the truth." The knowledge of the truth, then, is the primary means appointed by Almighty God for the salvation of "all men;" and as He wishes that all men should be saved, so He also necessarily wishes that all should come to the knowledge of the truth. But He could not wish the latter, without, at the same time, providing means by which all men might, if they would, actually come to a knowledge of the truth; therefore, it is a clear logical inference that He has provided such means; and hence, that those men who have not come to a knowledge of the truth, and are therefore lost, must ascribe the fault to themselves, not to God.

The truth, the knowledge of which is to prepare mankind for salvation, is contained in that divine RELIGION which Christ established, and for the confirmation of which He died upon the cross. Man had fallen from the high estate of righteousness in which he had been constituted at the moment of his creation; he had become the willing victim of error and vice; his noble nature, stamped originally with the divine image, had sadly deteriorated—had sunk down to the lowest depths of moral degradation. It still bore, indeed, some plain lineaments of that original resemblance to the Deity; the faculties of the soul were not annihilated; the understanding had still its light, but that light was faint and clouded by error; the memory still fulfilled its office of treasuring up the past, but it did so very imperfectly, and seldom recalled deeds of virtue, or instances of the divine goodness; the will was still free in its choice between good and evil, but it had become weak and almost powerless against the violent assaults of inward concupiscence and external temptation. In a word, man's nature was grievously wounded, not wholly destroyed; it was dangerously sick, not yet dead; it needed a remedy to heal its multiplied infirmities, to clothe it with strength, and to raise it up again to God.

Four thousand years had elapsed since the fall of man, and the evils which pressed upon his weakened nature had become daily more and more aggravated. Error and vice had overspread the earth, and had rendered its habitation darksome, its very atmosphere pestilent. Man sat down contented, a willing slave of his passions, "in the region of the shadow of death." From the farthest off India in the east, to the pillars of Hercules in the west; from the burning sands of Africa in the south, to the remotest Scandinavia in the north, a dark cloud, lighter in some places, heavier in others, was brooding, like a pall of death, over the whole human race. The polished Greeks and the stern Romans boasted alike of their light and of their brilliant achievements; but they forgot that their light itself was darkness, and that their martial deeds were stained with blood. The poetical and imaginative Greek had originated and built up a highly wrought and colossal system of mythology; and the more practical Roman had borrowed all its absurdities, and was content to worship in all its polluted shrines. Rome, the mistress of the world, as St. Leo the Great well remarks, thought that she could boast of her superior religion, when she had really become enslaved to the errors of all other nations, by associating the motley divinities of her conquered provinces with her own, in her gorgeous religious ceremonial.

This system of paganism, thus recognized and adopted by the two most polished and civilized nations of antiquity, openly patronized every species of error, and boldly deified vice itself. In the name of reason, it basely prostituted reason to the vilest and most groveling purposes; and all this under the pretence of serving God! Pride and rapine were worshiped in the person of Jove, the dread thunderer of Olympus, and the prince of the gods; drunkenness was

adored in the person of Bacchus; lust, in that of Venus;
and war, rapine, and bloodshed, in that of Mars. From
reeking altars, erected on the high places and in the magnificent temples of the most splendid cities, there arose continually the smoke of sacrifice in honor of all these foul,
yet deified, impersonations of vice in every loathsome and
disgusting form. Nor was this confined to the ignorant
and the debased multitude; the greatest, the most enlightened, and the most powerful men of pagan times, also
shared, to a greater or less extent, in those impure orgies.

Philosophy, indeed, sometimes sent forth a faint and
doubtful ray of light through this heavy and universal
darkness; but philosophy proved utterly powerless for the
enlightenment of the world. It promised much, but effected
nothing. It had beautiful sayings on its lips, but it was
rotten at heart. The pagan philosophers did not agree
among themselves, even in matters of vital importance;
they had little weight of authority to persuade others.
Nor, in fact, do they seem to have cared much about propagating their principles, or making proselytes beyond a mere
handful of immediate disciples. They even sometimes pur-
posely wrapped up their meaning in mystery, and pretended that they had learned a wisdom which was not for
the common people; that they, indeed, were above the gross
errors of the age, but that these were quite good enough for
the ignorant multitude. They disputed on every thing,
from the smallest insect on the earth to the nature of the
gods themselves; they agreed on almost nothing, and did
not appear even to put much confidence in their own conclusions, still less to be solicitous about impressing them
upon the minds of others. They taught the most atrocious
errors without shrinking or remorse; and, as Cicero says,
there was no absurdity, no matter how gross, which one or
another of them did not maintain. Even the best of them
often held the most dangerous principles. Socrates sacri-
ficed a cock to Esculapius on the eve of his death; Cicero
advocated vanity and lying; Epictetus and Cato patronized
suicide; and the great Plato himself openly plead for a

community of wives. Such men could not cure the evils of mankind, or regenerate the world;—in fact they never even dreamed of doing so. They sadly needed healing and regeneration themselves, and they knew not the remedy for the manifold evils which were heavily pressing on themselves;—how could they hope to heal or regenerate others?

The Jewish Religion, that of the chosen people of God, was confined to one small corner of the globe; all the world besides was sunk in vice, in error, in moral degradation. Human nature was corrupt and vitiated to its very heart's core. "From the sole of its foot to the top of its head, there was no soundness therein; wounds, and bruises, and swelling sores; they were not bound up, nor dressed, nor fomented with oil."* Man, with a heart swollen with pride and rotten with vice, was delivered up to a reprobate sense. He had trusted to the light of mere unaided reason, and he saw the frightful abyss to which it had led him; but he saw it without a shudder! He was blind, and he knew it not; he was a slave, bound hand and foot, and he willingly embraced his fetters, and, whilst he heard their dismal clanking, still fondly flattered himself that he was free!

Such was the deplorable condition of mankind at the first dawn of Christianity. After fallen man had been left to his own resources for four thousand years, in order that he might find out, by his own sad experience, his innate powerlessness and utter inability to avoid evil and to do good of himself; God was pleased, when the fullness of time was come, to look down in mercy upon him from His high throne in heaven, and to send His only begotten and well-beloved Son to raise him up from the degradation of error and vice, to heal his multiplied wounds, to brighten up once more His own partially defaced image in his soul, and to guide him safely to heaven. Man had fallen, had become a slave:—to elevate him again to his original position in the scale of creation, the Son of God became man, and shared in all his infirmities, sin only excepted, and to

---

* Isaiah, i: 6.

4

strike the manacles of slavery from his hands, He himself vouchsafed to become a slave. Such were the results contemplated by the ineffable mystery of the Incarnation; such the unutterable love which prompted it. God became man, that man might be raised up to a participation of the divinity; God humbled Himself that man might be exalted.

"The Word was made flesh and dwelt amongst us,"* that He might be "the true light which enlighteneth every man who cometh into this world." †   All other teachers had been tried, and they had failed to lead man into the path of truth; all other lights had proved faint, uncertain, and deceptive; this heavenly Teacher, and this divine Light alone could remove all man's errors, and point out to him with unerring certainty the way to heaven. Human teachers had grievously misled him; a divine Teacher was indispensably necessary. None other could have the power to verify the declaration made by this One: "And you shall know the truth, and the truth shall make you FREE."‡ Man had all along panted for freedom: but until now he had been deluded with its mere shadow. Now, at length, he was to be FREE indeed; and his Liberator was to be the Truth taught by the infallible lips of TRUTH Himself incarnate. All the trammels of his enslaved soul were to fall off at the magic touch of Truth; its clouds and its mists were to vanish before the rising Sun of justice; and, breathing once more the pure and invigorating atmosphere of paradise, it was again to exult "in the liberty of the glory of the children of God."

The RELIGION of Christ was to accomplish this glorious regeneration. It was the great work of the GOD MADE MAN, the end and aim of His mission to mankind, the embodiment of His own infinite wisdom, the impregnable fortress of His truth on earth, the focus from which His light was to radiate over the world, and, at the same time, the school of heavenly liberty. Nay, more: it was a kind of second incarnation of the Word, or of the personal wisdom of the

---

* St. John, 1: 14.   † St. John, 1: 9.   ‡ St. John, viii: 32.

eternal Godhead; an incarnation which was to be permanently visible on earth, even after its divine Author would have Himself ascended to heaven. Had Christ left us no permanent revelation of the kind, His appearance in the flesh would have been like that of some brilliant meteor that shoots athwart the gloom of night, which would have startled and astonished mankind for a moment, only to leave them in deeper and more palpable darkness than before.

From the *objects* contemplated by the Religion of Christ, we may readily infer its *nature*. Designed as an adequate and divine remedy to all the complicated ills of humanity, it was essentially medicinal in its character. But the medicine, to be adequate, must be adapted to the disease which it is intended to heal; therefore, the Christian Religion must have contained in itself an effectual antidote to all the maladies of afflicted human nature. These maladies, as we have already intimated, pervaded and vitiated all the faculties of the human soul—the will, the memory, the understanding; therefore the remedy should be equally extensive. The understanding had been vitiated by error; therefore the remedy should provide the antidote of truth. The will had been weakened by sin, and misguided by false principles; therefore the remedy should provide the strengthening influence of heavenly grace, as well as the safe guidance of a sound morality. The memory had forgotten God, and had been filled with images of this earth; therefore the remedy should lead it back to God, and train it to think on heavenly things. Thus, by a reasoning *a priori*, we would be naturally led to expect three distinctive elements in the Christian system: intellectual or doctrinal truths, moral principles, and certain external ordinances or institutions embodying both, and imparting to the recipient the strengthening and vivifying influence of grace. In other words, we would naturally expect to find doctrines, morals, and sacraments with sacrifice, as the essential part of the system itself; and, on the part of those who wish to come under its influence and to be benefitted by it, the implied correlative obligations of faith and obedience. And accordingly, upon a closer examination, we find that this is precisely what constitutes the essential nature of the Christian Religion.

This divine Religion embraces all that Christ taught and his apostles promulgated; nothing more, nothing less. It is divine in all its parts; and those principles which man, in his mere human wisdom or pride might consider the least important portions of it, rest upon precisely the same divine authority as those which he might feel disposed to pronounce essential and fundamental. Take away but one of its principles or elements, and you destroy the integrity, and mar the divine harmony, of the whole system; add but one foreign element, and you mingle with the pure and refined gold of God's truth the vile dross of human wisdom or error. Woe to him who thus attempts impiously to add to, or to subtract from, this master-work of the divine Wisdom; woe to him, who, like Oza of old, dares put forth his sacrilegious hand to stay this ark of God, under the pretext that otherwise it might totter and fall; let him beware of Oza's terrible punishment!* The Christian Religion is like a golden chain, which reaches from earth to heaven, and binds both firmly together; woe to him who severs even one of its sacred links, and thereby destroys the connection.

Nothing can be more certain, than that Christ required mankind to receive His whole Religion, just as it came from His hands, with all its doctrines, all its moral principles, and all its sacramental and sacrificial institutions. In His farewell address to his apostles, He solemnly commanded them to teach "ALL THINGS whatsoever he had commanded them;"† and He, at the same time, pronounced

---

* All know that Oza, whose chief fault seems to have been a want of confidence in God's ability or wish to protect His own work, was suddenly stricken dead for his temerity in irreverently extending his hand towards the ark. See II Kings, (in Protestant version II Samuel,) Chapter, vi.

† St. Matthew, xxviii: 20.

the terrible sentence of eternal condemnation on those who would disbelieve even ONE of all those things: "he that believeth not, shall be condemned."* On another occasion, He declared that salvation could be attained only by keeping ALL the commandments: "if thou wilt enter into life, keep the commandments."† His inspired apostle James has so interpreted this declaration: "now whosoever shall keep the whole law, but offend in ONE point, is become .guilty of ALL."‡

Where divine inspiration makes no distinction, how dare we make any? When Christ and His apostles required us, under the penalty of eternal condemnation, to receive *all*, what safety is there to us in receiving only a part? How absurd, then, and how dangerous is that theory,—now become so fashionable in certain quarters,—which draws a line of distinction between what it is pleased to designate *fundamental* and *non-fundamental* doctrines; the former of which are essential and must be believed by all who would be saved, the latter non-essential and may be received or rejected at will, without thereby endangering salvation! As if Christ established, or required His apostles to teach any thing that was not essential to salvation! As if He would have poured out His blood on the cross, to seal a system, many parts of which were after all not necessary! As if His authority were not as great and deserving of as much respect in what may appear to our weak reason as small things, as it is in those which we apprehend as great and important! As if, in a word, Christ himself or His inspired apostles had made or authorized this distinction, whereas the precise contrary is apparent both from their words and from their actions!

This and many similar theories, which have been broached at different times by persons claiming to be Christians, are all predicated upon a totally false view of Christianity. The Religion of Christ is virtually regarded by these misguided men as a fine drawn theory, a beautiful

---

* St. Mark, xvi: 16. † St. Matthew, xix: 17. ‡ St. James: ii. 10.

4 *

speculation, a sublime system of philosophy, to be received and developed by each man according to his own natural light; rather than as a *positive* institution, practical in its very nature and in its bearing upon mankind, and resting for all its principles and its whole character on a simple but impressive fact,—GOD HATH SPOKEN; and the inference from this fact,—let the earth be silent and obey! Yet, there cannot be the slightest doubt that this is precisely the nature of Christianity. This system of Religion is just what Christ made it; neither more nor less. It is a divine, not a human institution. In inquiring into it, we should not ask, what human reason and human philosophy would have it to be, but what Christ actually made it, when He established it for the guidance of mankind. Once we have ascertained the fact, that God hath spoken so and so, all our investigations should cease, and speculation should give place to reverent obedience. All other methods of inquiry are fallacious and cannot fail to mislead; because they are all based upon a view radically erroneous.

The fact that God hath spoken to us through His Son Jesus Christ, and that the Christian Religion, as established by Him, is the expression and embodiment of that speaking,—the outspoken word of Him who is the WORD OF GOD MADE FLESH,—is freely admitted by all who claim to be Christians; and it is moreover demonstrable by a mass of evidence which no reasonable mind can resist. A long chain of prophecies, extending from the very creation of the world to the birth of Christ, and growing clearer and more explicit as they approximate towards the latter event;—uttered at different times, under different circumstances, by different individuals, without any combination or collusion whatever; some of them general, others particular: all find their complete fulfillment in this great fact, and they can find it no where else. Miracles the most prodigious and astounding;—the sudden healing of the sick, the raising of the dead to life, a control over the elements and the laws of nature, and finally, the grand miracle of miracles, the resurrection of Christ Himself from the dead on the third day in spite of the power and vigilance of His enemies; all these miracles performed, too, not in a corner, but in public places, in the open light of day, and in the face of doubting and perverse enemies: these are the manifold seals of God stamped upon the divine mission of Christ, and upon the truth of His Religion. The chain of evidence is complete and irresistible, when we reflect on the nature of the Religion itself;—its innate purity, its elevation above the senses, its opposition to the most cherished passions, and its happy effects in reforming and civilizing the world. Its wonderful propagation over the whole earth, by instruments, humanly speaking, utterly inadequate to the work, and in the face of a terrible opposition from all the great, powerful, and learned of the world, and in spite of its principles essentially conflicting with all that had been hitherto so warmly cherished by mankind as important to personal comfort, and as closely intertwined with national greatness; in the face of a colossal system of paganism which bestrode the earth, and was intimately blended with the political institutions of every people; of a fierce, avaricious, and powerful priesthood, of a proud and inflated philosophy, of a turgid and grandiloquent rhetoric; finally, of a vast and all-powerful empire, which governed the world with a rod of iron, and rose up, at ten different times, with all its combined and terrible energies, to crush this apparently feeble and helpless system: the complete and final triumph of Christianity, in spite of all this combined opposition, and the final rearing of the glorious cross in triumph over the pinnacles of fallen Roman greatness, after the world had been drenched with the blood of thousands and tens of thousands of Christian martyrs;—this incontestable fact alone proves the divinity of the Christian Religion. This is the greatest miracle of all; and, as St. Augustine remarks, the proud philosopher who would still remain incredulous after all this, and who would yet persist in saying that the world was converted without miracles, is guilty of a glaring logical inconsistency and self-contradiction, by admitting a

greater miracle than that which he professes to reject.
For the world converted without miracles, under the circumstances above indicated, would be the greatest miracle
of all.

But we are not here reasoning with infidels, so much as
with fellow-Christians. We are not here inquiring *whether*
God has spoken through Jesus Christ, but *what* He has
spoken; what truths He taught; what Religion He established; what church He founded to maintain and propagate
this Religion? This is the momentous inquiry upon which,
with the grace of God, and your kind indulgence, Beloved
Brethren, I propose to enter at some length in the following
Lectures. We are all deeply and vitally concerned in the
result of this investigation; and I may be allowed to entreat
your patient attention to the facts and evidences which I
shall endeavor to lay before you on this all-important
subject.

But, in order that our inquiry may lead to a satisfactory
conclusion, we must enter on it with certain clear ideas in
regard to the real nature and great characteristics of that
Religion which we propose to find out and to embrace, for
the salvation of our immortal souls.

In the preceding portion of this Lecture, I have endeavored to lay down certain facts, and to unfold certain
truths which I think you will have had little difficulty
in admitting. The remainder of it will be devoted to
the development of some other great principles of the
Christian system, to which, I feel confident, you will have
as little difficulty in yielding your assent. As these great
truths constitute the foundation of all our future investigations, and as they will often be referred to in the sequel as
already established, I request your undivided attention to
them. Without mutually agreeing beforehand on some such
general guiding principles, we would be as much bewildered
in our future attempts to follow the path which leads to the
sacred goal of truth, as would be the traveler who should
attempt to cross a vast wilderness without guide, compass, or land-mark; or as the mariner, who should make the

effort to cross the ocean without the usual appliances of navigation.

I think, then, that no Christian—and such only do I address at present—will be disposed to controvert any one of the four following principles, or facts—which I will first state, and then briefly explain, in the order in which they will occur:

FIRST PRINCIPLE.—Christ established, and could have established, BUT ONE RELIGION.

SECOND PRINCIPLE.—He did not leave, and could not have left, this one Religion vague and unsettled in all, or in any of its parts; but He must have clearly defined and fixed all its component elements, both in themselves, and in their signification and application to mankind.

THIRD PRINCIPLE.—He did certainly require all mankind to embrace this one Religion, as thus settled and defined by Himself, under the awful penalty of eternal condemnation.

FOURTH PRINCIPLE.—He must have made it so plain, both in itself, and in the means which He furnished for ascertaining it, and distinguishing it from all other systems, that no doubt could be left in regard to it, in the mind of the sincere inquirer, disposed to embrace all the opportunities in his power to come to the knowledge of the truth, and thereby to save his soul.

A few remarks on each of these principles will convince you—if you are not already convinced—not only of their soundness, but of their vital importance in the investigation upon which we propose to enter, and in the result of which we are all so deeply interested.

1. THE FIRST PRINCIPLE—that Christ did establish, and could have established but ONE RELIGION—is self-evident, and therefore needs no proof. It is as intuitively certain as that there is but one God, and that there was and is but one Christ. St. Paul so apprehended it when he said, so briefly but so expressively: "One Lord, one Faith, one Baptism;"* that is, as there is but one Lord in the Chris-

* Ephesians iv: 5.

tian system, so there can be, in the very nature of things,
but one Religion established by Him as the object of faith,
and but one baptism, as an external means of becoming
initiated into the body of those who profess this one faith.
If Christ established more religions than one, they either
agreed among themselves in all their parts, or they were
contradictory, at least in some of them. If the former, then
where was the necessity for such a multiplication of identical
principles under different forms, and where the wisdom of
Christ in distracting mankind with such seeming diversity,
but real unity? If the latter, then what becomes of the
truth of Christ? and who could be expected to embrace a
Religion which is but a compound of warring elements and
of self-contradictions? Truth is one and consistent; error
is multiform and self-contradictory ; and to say that Christ
established more than one Religion, is really to deny Christianity itself, by uttering palpable blasphemy against its
divine Author.

2. THE SECOND PRINCIPLE—that Christ clearly defined,
and fully settled His religion in all its parts—is, perhaps,
not less manifest and self-evident. It necessarily follows
from the admitted fact, that the Christian Religion is not a
human, but a divine institution, established for the salvation
of mankind. Once you grant this, you must either say that
Christ defined it in all its parts, or that He, through a
settled purpose, left it in many things vague and indeterminate. If the former, then you grant all that I ask, and I
need say no more. If the latter, then I ask you to reconcile
your assertion with the infinite wisdom of Christ, and His
devoted love for mankind. Is it consonant with His wisdom to have left His work but half done? Was the divine
light which guided Him ever doubtful or uncertain? Is He,
the Incarnate Wisdom of God, to be put on a level with
those human philosophers who propounded systems half
certain, half doubtful, always vague and ill-defined? If so,
then away with the idea that Christianity is divine in all
its parts, and that its author is God! Discard this notion;

cease to be Christians, and put Christ at once on a level with Socrates, Plato, and Aristotle!

Again, I ask you, is it conformable with the infinite and boundless goodness of Christ, to suppose that He established a Religion *for the salvation of mankind*, and yet studiously left many of its parts vague and doubtful, so that it would be almost impossible for sincere men to ascertain them with any thing approaching to certainty? Could He have left the way to heaven, which it was His special mission to point out to the world, so very obscure and uncertain? If so, then He tantalized mankind with a promise of salvation which He never intended to fulfill! To say this, were unmitigated and horrible blasphemy. Therefore, if you believe that He was both infinitely wise and infinitely good, you are compelled, of logical necessity, to admit the principle above laid down, namely: that Christ did not leave His own master-work half done, but made it clear and well defined, so that all might be able to know what it was and is.

3. THE THIRD PRINCIPLE—that Christ required all mankind to embrace His one Religion, as settled and defined by himself, under the penalty of eternal condemnation — is equally undeniable as the two preceding ones. It necessarily follows from the very genius and purpose of Christianity, and from the character of its divine Founder. If men could go to heaven without embracing His Religion, then where was the necessity, and what was the object of His mission to earth, and of the Religion which He came to establish! Why did He insist so much on the necessity of a belief in, and a practice of His heavenly system? Why did He, in His farewell address to His apostles, pronounce the awful sentence of eternal condemnation on all those who would not believe "all things whatsoever He had commanded them to teach?"* Why did He endure so many privations and sufferings, and at length die on the cross to establish and confirm this Religion? Why did His apostles,

---

* Compare St. Matthew xxviii, with St. Mark xvi, as above cited.

clothed with His authority and filled with His spirit, brave death in a thousand forms, and gladly lay down their lives for this Religion, if, after all, it was not *necessary* for the salvation of man? Why did such vast numbers of martyrs willingly pour out their blood like water for this faith, if it was not obligatory on men? Why, in a word, is so much interest felt for this Religion by all Christians, even by those who would be disposed to question these principles, if it is not viewed by them as essential to the happiness of mankind for eternity.

4. THE FOURTH PRINCIPLE—that Christ made His Religion plain, and provided means by which all sincere inquirers might easily and certainly ascertain it, come to the knowledge of the truth, and thereby save their souls — is a logical corollary from the third just established. How could Christ have required all men to embrace His Religion, unless He had, at the same time, provided them with ample means for ascertaining it with certainty? Would it have been just to impose the penalty of eternal damnation upon those who would reject a system, for a certain knowledge of which sufficient means had not been provided by its divine Author? Would it have been just to consign the bulk of mankind to endless perdition, for the sin of not having embraced what they had no adequate means of ascertaining? The bare idea is revolting in the extreme, and it implies a horrid blasphemy—that God will punish His creatures eternally for what they could not have avoided! What Christian is prepared to think or to say this? And yet it must be said, unless you admit the principle for which I here contend.

You ask me what then will become of those to whom the gospel was never preached? The question is reasonable and opportune, and I confess that it is difficult to answer it with certainty. Nor does my present position require me to solve this difficulty. The principles I have laid down are certain and self-evident, even though I should not be able to meet the objection with a satisfactory answer. I am addressing Christians to whom the gospel has been

preached, not pagans who have not enjoyed that privilege.
And I leave it to you to decide, whether the principles
above indicated are not evident and true, even though we
should not be able to ascertain how far they are applicable
to pagans, or whether they are applicable to them at all.
God only can know this, because He alone can judge the
hearts of men, and He alone can decide whether and how
far, they are culpable for rejecting or not receiving His
truth. Two things, however, we do know with certainty
on this subject: first, that God will not condemn any one
eternally without wilful and grievous fault on his part; and
second, that all shall be judged according to their works,
weighed by the lights, opportunities, and graces they have
severally received. God only can decide on all this, because He alone can be fully acquainted with the whole
cause. We leave the judgment to him; but, at the same
time, we must admit His truth in all its length and breadth,
as well as in its full application to ourselves to whom it has
been preached; and we must tremble for our own responsi-
bility before Him. St. Paul lays down this principle of the
divine judgment, when, speaking of the pagan nations, he
says that they shall be judged by "the law written in their
hearts, their consciences bearing witness to them, and their
thoughts within themselves accusing them, or else defend-
ing them, in the day when God shall judge the secrets
of men, by Jesus Christ."* This is all that revelation
says on this difficult question; and it is enough for us
to know, that we will be judged by a much higher standard,
on the principle that "unto whomsoever much is given, of
him much shall be required:"† for, as our blessed Lord says,
"that servant who knew the will of his Lord, and hath not
prepared, and did not according to His will, shall be beaten
with many stripes, but he that knew not and did things
worthy of stripes, shall be beaten with few stripes."‡
Such then, my Beloved Brethren, is the nature, such are
the leading characteristics of the Religion which Jesus Christ

---

* Romans, ii: 15.   † St. Luke, xii: 48.   ‡ Ibid. xii: 47, 48.

established for the salvation of men. What I have hitherto
said, and I hope proved to your satisfaction, may be
summed up in a very few words. The Religion of Christ
is a *divine* institution, embracing all that Christ taught,
whether by His own lips or by those of His inspired apostles, neither more or less, and depending for its nature and
its principles solely upon His will, and not upon human
ingenuity or speculation; it is a divine system which rests
upon a Fact,—that God hath so and so spoken to us,
through His Son, Jesus Christ, and upon the principle necessarily inferred therefrom,—that our inquiry should not go
beyond this fact, but should yield to conviction and obedience so soon as this will be once ascertained; and finally,
it must necessarily be *one*, must have been clearly defined
and fully settled by its divine Founder, must be obligatory
on all, and consequently must be easily ascertainable by all.
No Christian, I presume, will be disposed to question any
one of these facts or principles.

To preserve this divine Religion, and to transmit it
unchanged and entire to the latest posterity, Christ established and organized a CHURCH. The holy Scriptures proclaim this fact on almost every page of the New Testament,
and all Christians admit it, how much soever they may differ in their opinions on the nature, prerogatives, and powers
of this Church.

As it is not my purpose, at this preliminary stage of the
investigation, to lay down any principle, or to make any
statement, which our adversaries might be disposed to controvert, I will here content myself with defining the Church
"an external, organized body or society of men, professing
the one true Religion of Jesus Christ." No reasonable
Christian can object to this definition. It embodies the ele-
mental principles and primary notions which every one has
of that institution. A merely invisible and wholly spiritual
Church, is a fiction, an absurdity. It has never had an actual
existence in history; according to the very nature of things,
it never could have existed. Had Christ established His
Church for the benefit of angels, it might have been an in-

visible institution; as he established it for men, it was
necessarily an external and visible body, else it could not
have been adapted to their condition and wants, and could
not have answered the purpose for which it was appointed.
For how could men be held together in the bonds of a
society which they could not see, and whose voice they
could not hear? How could an invisible Church preserve
and securely transmit to posterity the one Religion of
Christ? Are not all the means which Christ himself appointed, with a view to enable it to discharge these offices,
external and visible? How could an invisible Church
preach the gospel to every creature, administer the sacraments, make an external profession of faith, convert sinners, and exercise discipline upon offenders? And yet, as
all must admit, Christ imparted to His Church all these
powers.

Man is composed of two distinct parts blended into one
individual—body and soul; and the Church of Jesus Christ,
to be fully adapted to his wants, must likewise necessarily
consist of two distinct corresponding elements, intimately
united and harmonizing with each other—the external
and the spiritual. The RELIGION of Christ is the soul, the
CHURCH is the body united with this soul. On the day of
Pentecost, Christ infused into the body of His Church, already organized, the Holy Spirit, and "it was thus made
into a living soul." Destroy either of these essential elements, and you destroy the individuality of the Church,
just as the individuality of man would be destroyed by
the removal or destruction of either the body or the soul.
In each case, the conjunction of both elements is essential
to the individual. In man, death alone can sever the
union; in the Church there is no death, so long at least as
this world will last, and the union is, therefore, as lasting
as time itself.

While on earth, Christ gathered together a body of disciples; He organized them into a regular society, by select-
ing from them officers composed of two distinct orders—
the twelve apostles and the seventy-two disciples; He im-

parted to these, especially to the apostles, the power of binding and loosing, of forgiving sins, of preaching the gospel, of administering the sacraments, of punishing offenders by casting them out among heathens and publicans; while on the great body of the disciples He enjoined the duty of hearing, of being taught, and of obeying. Thus the society of His followers was naturally distributed into two classes—that of teachers and that of the taught. No one will question this fact, which is as clear as any thing else in the entire gospel history. St. Paul asks emphatically, "Are all apostles? Are all prophets? Are all teachers?"* And, in another place, he clearly lays down this same principle: "And some, indeed, He (Christ) gave to be apostles, and some prophets, and others evangelists, and others pastors and teachers, for the perfection of the saints, for the work of the ministry, for the edification of the body of Christ."†

It is plain, then, my Dearly Beloved Brethren, that the Church which Christ established was organized—precisely like every other visible society on earth—by the distribution of its members into officers and subjects, with special powers and duties assigned to each. The specific nature of the organization in all its details, depends wholly and solely on the will of Christ, not on our own individual notions or peculiar theories of government. We must accept the Church precisely as Christ organized it, not as our crude and earthly ideas of order and polity would have it to be. The Church, like the Religion of which it is the divinely constituted guardian, is based upon a fact—Christ so established and so organized it—and we are not at liberty to go beyond that fact in our investigations.

From what I have said, it follows that the Church is marked by precisely the same qualities as the Religion which it contains, as the casket does the precious jewel. Like that, it is essentially one; it is clearly defined in all its parts and principles; it is obligatory upon all; it may be easily ascertained by all. Whoever would possess the

---

* I Corinthians, xii: 29.   † Ephesians, iv: 11, 12.

Religion of Christ, must find out the Church, must go to the Church, must be taught by the Church, and must hear and obey the Church. The Church is the living, and breathing, and speaking organ, by which, and by which alone, Christ holds communication with the world, and manifests His truth and His will to mankind. The Church is HIS BODY, of which He Himself is the great HEAD. You can not sever the head from the body, without depriving the latter of life; and you can not sever the Church from Christ, its Head, because both are essentially full of life, and both are essentially and divinely united; and "whom God hath united, let no man put asunder."* If you would, then, be a member of Christ, you must be a member of His body, the Church; He recognizes none other. All members severed from that body are cut off from all communication with the Head, and are, therefore, lifeless. "No one can have God for his Father, who has not the Church for his Mother," is an adage as true as it is ancient.†

Such, then, is the nature—such is plainly the office of the Church. And, as we value our eternal salvation, we are all bound to inquire diligently into this momentous question: which is the one true Church of Christ; and having ascertained which is that Church, we are all bound to enter it, and to hear its voice; to believe what it believes, to reject what it rejects, and to practice what it commands; to listen to its teaching as to that of Christ Himself, of whose truth and will it is the living and authoritative interpreter.

All this, my Beloved Brethren, I will endeavor, with the divine grace, to unfold more fully in the following Lectures, in which I will lay before you a number of facts and arguments tending to show which, among all the claimants to that high honor by which the religious world is now distracted, has really the best founded title to be considered

---

* St. Matthew, xix.

† It is as old as the age of St. Cyprian, who flourished about the middle of the third century.

the one, original, and only true Church of Christ. Whatever may be your own peculiar religious views or prejudices on the subject, I earnestly entreat your attention to the Evidences which I will endeavor to spread before you. In the language of the inspired apostle, I beg you "to prove all things, but to hold that which is good."*

How great soever may be your own feeling of opposition to the venerable Church of your forefathers, as well as of mine, you are bound, in common fairness and justice, to hear what she has to offer in her own defense. You have been taught to protest against her; you are surely bound to inquire seriously whether your protest be well grounded. If, after all the clamor that has been raised against this time-honored Church during the last three centuries, it should still turn out that she is now and always has been, the one true Church of Christ, what answer would you make at the bar of Christ, when He will ask you in judgment for the reason of your protest against her authority, and of your refusal to hear and obey her voice? You should look to this while it is yet time. Time is short; eternity never ending. We will be judged, not by the errors and prejudices of our early education, but by the unvarying standard of God's eternal truth; and our doom once pronounced by the lips of Christ, will be irrevocable, eternal. "What doth it profit a man, if he gain the whole world, and lose his own soul?"†

May Almighty God, who "wills that all men should be saved and come to the knowledge of the truth," grant us His heavenly light and guidance, that we may all learn the truth, embrace it, no matter at what sacrifice, and thereby save our immortal souls, for which Jesus Christ died on the cross! Amen.

_____

* I Thessalonians, v: 1.   † St. Matthew, xvi: 26.

LECTURE III.

THE APOSTOLIC COMMISSION — THE RULE OF FAITH — THE
FIRST EVIDENCE OF CATHOLICITY.

The commission — Its general scope — Its objects most difficult of attain-
ment — Its four distinctive characteristics — It embraces two things —
The argument stated — Its positions evolved — Division of the subject —
The inquiry narrowed down to a simple question of fact — The Rule
of Faith — The Protestant and Catholic Rules stated — Strong presump-
tive evidence against the former — Its positive difficulties — The scrip-
tural arguments in its favor examined — A popular theory exploded —
The inspiration, canon, version, and interpretation of the Bible — What
is faith? — Can an act of faith be made consistently with the Protestant
Rule? — The vicious circle — Scriptural proofs of the Catholic Rule —
Both rules tested by the four great principles laid down in the previous
Lecture — Recapitulation — The conclusion reached — THE FIRST EVI-
DENCE OF CATHOLICITY.

*"And Jesus coming, spoke to them (the apostles) saying: all power is given to
me in heaven, and in earth. Go ye, therefore, and teach all nations; baptizing
them in the name of the Father, and of the Son, and of the Holy Ghost; teaching
them to observe all things whatsoever I have commanded you; and behold, I am
with you all days, even to the consummation of the world."—St. MATH. xviii:
18, 19, 20.*

*"And He said to them: Go ye into the whole world, and preach the gospel to
every creature. He that believeth and is baptized, shall be saved; but he that
believeth not, shall be condemned."—St. MARK, xvi: 15, 16.*

*"And He said to them again: Peace be to you. As the Father hath sent me,
I also send you."—St. JOHN, xx: 21.*

ENTERING, my Beloved Brethren, on the investigation of
that most important of all questions — which, among all the
Christian denominations now existing on the face of the
earth, is the one, original, true Church of Christ?—I take as
my starting point, the farewell address of our beloved Lord
and Master to His apostles, before He was taken up into
heaven. Already had He sealed the great work of our redemption with His own precious blood shed on the cross;
already had He triumphed gloriously over death by His

(55)

resurrection. And now, about to return to the bosom of that Father who had sent Him on His divine errand of mercy to the world, He turns His eyes to those dear disciples whom He had raised to the apostolate, and He imparts to them the Commission to convert the whole world to His Religion, and to make all mankind His humble followers.

Wonderful to relate, He commissioned eleven poor Jewish peasants or fishermen,—one of the original twelve had already turned traitor and betrayed his Master,—men without human learning, without wealth, without worldly influence or natural eloquence, without any human qualifications whatever for the undertaking,—to do what? No less than "to teach all nations," to "preach the gospel to every creature," to confound the learned philosophers and rhetoricians of Greece and Rome, to silence the oracles, to destroy the impure orgies of paganism, and to plant, on the ruins of a gigantic idolatry, which then governed the world, the glorious and unsullied banner of the cross! And more wonderful still, this Commission was fully and faithfully executed by them, obstacles humanly insuperable were overcome, the world was actually converted, heathenism was made to give way to Christianity; and we are now, after the lapse of full eighteen centuries, reaping the blessed fruits of that change!

A Commission, which thus exercised so potent an influence on the destinies of the world, is surely deserving of our most serious consideration. What, then, are the most striking circumstances or features of this last solemn charge of Jesus Christ to the first incumbents of the ministerial office? I will endeavor briefly to state and unfold them.

The first feature that strikes us in the Commission, is the fact, that our blessed Lord was pleased to choose frail men as instruments for executing His purpose of converting the world. He might have converted it Himself, without the intervention of secondary causes; one single ray of that "Light, which lighteneth every man who cometh into this world," gleaming and flashing across the world, would have been sufficient to light up its darkness, to dispel all mists and errors from the human soul, to reveal the hideous deformity of paganism, and powerfully to attract men to the truth. But this light would have been too bright and too dazzling for mere human eyes; mortal man could not have seen Christ in all His glory, and have lived; and it was meet that he should be addressed and won over to the truth by men naturally weak like himself, but all powerful when clad in the armor of God and the panoply of heaven.

Such a method was much better adapted to the condition of mankind, and it left man's free will wholly unimpaired in its choice between good and evil. God, as I have already said, will compel no one into heaven; He will award the crown to those only who will have fought the good fight, and will have finally triumphed over error and sin, with the assistance of His freely proffered grace strengthening the natural weakness of their free will. The truth is clear enough to enable us to see it, if we will but open our eyes, look attentively for it, and humbly implore the divine light to assist us in our inquiries; it is not bright enough to flash conviction into our minds, whether we will or not; else there would be no merit in faith. These and similar considerations may serve to explain to us the very remarkable fact, that our divine Saviour made comparatively very few converts Himself, but left the conversion of the world mainly to His apostles and disciples. He sowed the seeds and watered them with His blood; they were to reap the harvest! He took the labor, they were to receive the honor of converting the world;—but they were to lay their crowns at His feet.

The next prominent feature in the Commission is this, that it was unlimited as to space, as to persons, and as to time. It was as wide as the world, as universal as mankind, as lasting as time. It reached from one end of the earth to the other, it embraced all the children of Adam of every country and clime, and it looked forward to all coming generations even to the end of the world. Nay, it had a retrospective, as well as a prospective influence and action.

For those who lived and died before the redemption, which it was meant to proclaim and apply, could be saved only by faith in the good things to come. "There is no exception of persons with God;" "God wills all men to be saved and to come to the knowledge of the truth;" and Christ died for all the children of Adam, without any exception whatsoever. Other commissions might expire with the object for which they were given; this could never expire, so long as the world lasted or there were men to be taught and to be saved; for this was precisely the object which it contemplated.

The third feature in the Commission, is the circumstance, that the Saviour imparted full and ample powers to the apostles for its complete accomplishment. He made them His ministers plenipotentiary to the world; their credentials were stamped with the broad seal of His own omnipotence. He sent them clothed with the powers with which He Himself had been invested by His heavenly Father; and He tells them so plainly and explicitly: "All power is given to me in heaven and in earth; go ye, *therefore, &c.*," "As the Father hath sent me, so I also send you." They were to preach, to teach, to baptize, to do all the acts necessary for the full and permanent establishment of Christianity every where; and He would be with them and in them, guiding and assisting them, enlightening their minds, confirming their purpose, and sanctioning their acts, "ALL DAYS, even to the consummation of the world."

Closely connected with this, is the fourth quality of the Commission. Christ intended and willed that all the substantial powers with which He then clothed His first body of ministers should descend to their regular and lawful successors in the ministerial office, to the very end of time. There is, there can be no doubt of this whatsoever. The Commission was to last till "the consummation of the world;" and it could not do so, at least it would become utterly powerless and barren of all effect, unless it should continue to be invested with all the substantial powers which it possessed at the beginning. I say *substantial powers;* for it might, and probably would happen, that, amid the changes which circumstances might induce, the exercise of those original plenipotentiary powers would be variously modified, without their being, however, themselves substantially diminished or changed. Under the extraordinary circumstances in which the first body of Christ's ministers were placed, some extraordinary powers and privileges,—such as personal infallibity and unlimited individual jurisdiction in point of persons and space, seemed to be required by the emergency. The men who, under Christ, were to lay the foundations of the Christian Religion, were very properly clothed with these personal privileges, in addition to the substantial powers of the ministry, which latter were to descend unimpaired to their successors. It would be the province of the latter merely to continue to the end of time the glorious work begun by the former;—to govern and preserve the Church which they had founded, and to transmit unchanged the precious deposit of the faith received from their hands.

No reasonable Christian will, I think, be disposed to question the truth of this position. To say that the substantial powers of the ministerial office were to cease with the death of the last of the apostles, would be in effect the same thing as to assert that Christ died only for those who lived in the apostolic age, and that He made no adequate provision for the less favored generations which were to come afterwards. It would be, moreover, to falsify the plainest language of the Commission itself, and set limits where it sets none whatever. Nay more; it would effectually cut off, at the very source, all the powers of the ministry, claimed and exercised by Christians of all denominations at the present day. Once you admit this novel and strange theory, where is the proof that Christian ministers of any denomination have *now* the power to preach, to baptize, or to do any of the other acts of the original ministerial office instituted by Christ? You cannot appeal to the words of the Commission, for you have virtually nullified the Commission, by limiting it to the apostolic age. To what other authority will you then appeal for evidence? I know of none other; for all others presuppose and are based upon this. This theory manifestly strikes a mortal blow at the Christian ministry, and therefore undermines the very basis of Christianity itself.

It is, then, clear from the very nature of the Commission itself, and from the words in which it was given, that the will and intention of Christ was, to have His Religion taught and established in the whole world and among all mankind, and to have it maintained, and progressively extended, to the very end of time, by means of a ministry authorized by himself, clad with ample powers derived from Him; which ministry and which powers were to be substantially kept up and maintained in regular uninterrupted succession to the end of the world. This is the plain and obvious meaning of the Commission; this is the interpretation which the whole Christian world unanimously put on it, for the first fifteen hundred years of the Christian era; there is no other interpretation worthy of its end and scope, or compatible with its plainest language. All other explanations of it are narrow, inconsistent, and contradictory; all others strike at the very essence of the Christian ministry, at Christianity itself.

Besides the features already indicated, and some others to which I may have more appropriate occasion to advert hereafter, the Commission embraces two things, both of which are worthy our most serious reflection; because they both lie at the very foundation of the Christian system, and furnish us likewise with a key for ascertaining which is the one true Church of Jesus Christ. These two things are: the *object* of the Commission itself, which was the conversion of the world to Christianity; and the *means* by which, according to the intention of Christ, this object was to be accomplished.

The argument is this:

The Church which has fulfilled the Commission according to its letter and its spirit,—which has actually converted the world, and by the precise means and in the precise manner ordained by Christ,—must be the one original Church

which He founded, and with which he promised to be all
days even to the consummation of the world.

But the Roman Catholic Church alone has done all this:

Therefore the Roman Catholic Church alone is the original Church of Christ.

The first, or major proposition, is certain, and it needs no
proof. At least it is so far certain, that no Church which
has not fulfilled the Commission, and in the manner ordained
by Christ, can lay claim to be the true Church of Christ;
unless, indeed, you are prepared to say, that Christ gave the
Commission to His Church, and yet did not mean that his
Church should execute it according to His command! If
there be a church which has fulfilled the Commission, in
accordance with both its letter and its spirit, there is, then,
very strong presumptive evidence, that this Church is
identical with that established by Christ; and if it farther
appear, that this Church alone, and no other, has fulfilled
it, and in the manner indicated, the presumptive evidence
grows into a conclusive argument; unless you say, that
Christ either did not, or could not keep His word, and have
His Commission executed according to its letter and its
spirit.

All, then, that I am bound to prove, in order to make the
argument complete and irresistible, is the second or minor
proposition, which contains three distinct assertions: first,
that the Roman Catholic Church has fulfilled the Commission
by actually converting the world to Christianity; second,
that she alone has done this; and third, that she has done it
by the precise means and in the precise manner ordained
by Christ. The proofs of these three propositions will open
before us a field as vast as it must be interesting to every
lover of Christianity; the whole field, in fact, of theology
and of Church history. The third proposition involves a
matter of principle and of theology; the first and second,
questions of fact and of history.

The subject is so extensive, that I cannot hope to do any
thing like justice to it in one Lecture; hence, with your kind
indulgence, I will treat it in two successive discourses, the

6

first of which will be devoted to the development of the
third proposition, or the question of principle. As this lies
at the basis of the other two, the nature of the argument
requires that it should be treated first.

I solicit your calm and undivided attention; and I entreat
you, in the name of Jesus Christ, who died for our salvation,
and who fervently wished with His last breath that we
should "all be saved and come to the knowledge of the
truth," that you enter with me on the inquiry with an
humble prayer to heaven for light and grace, without which
all our efforts to find out and to embrace the truth were
vain and unproductive of any happy result.

What, then, were the means ordained by Christ for the
fulfillment of the Commission by the conversion of the
world? Though the answer contains an important and fundamental principle, embodying no less than the RULE OF
FAITH established by Christ, yet it rests, like every thing
else in Christianity, upon a fact;—upon the will, intention,
and positive act of Christ himself. Two antagonistic principles are advocated on this subject; the one by the Protestant sects, and the other by the Catholic Church. The
former maintain, that the means ordained by Christ for the
conversion of the world and the maintaining of Christianity
to the end of time, is to be found in the bible alone, as
understood and interpreted by each individual Christian for
himself; the latter holds, that it originally consisted, and still
consists, primarily and mainly, of authoritative preaching
and oral teaching by an authorized and duly commissioned
ministry, to whom belongs of right, by the will and intention of Christ himself, the keeping and interpretation of the
written word itself. The Protestant has a ministry and a
preached word, but he holds that this is a secondary institution, that the written word is the primary, and, in fact, the
only infallible means ordained by Christ for coming to the
knowledge of the truth, and that each individual Christian
is bound to hear and obey the preached word, only so far as,
according to his own private lights and judgment, it is conformable to the sense which he puts upon the bible: the

Catholic receives and reveres the bible as the inspired word
of God, in all its parts; but in its interpretation he distrusts
his own private lights, whenever they conflict with the
lights of the Church, the authorized teaching of which he
feels bound, by what he believes to be the express command
of Jesus Christ, to hear and obey, and to the decision of
which in all matters of doubt and controversy he feels it to
be a positive, divinely imposed obligation, to submit his
individual judgment.

Now, both of these principles cannot be, at the same time,
true and divinely established; for they are contradictory
and mutually exclude each other. I am willing to abide by
this simple test of the great question that lies back of it,—
which is the true Church of Christ? If the Protestant Rule
of Faith be that which was established by Jesus Christ,
then the Protestant is right in his opposition to the Church
of all ages and of all nations; if the Catholic Rule of
Faith, on the contrary, be the one ordained by Christ, then
the Catholic Church alone is the true Church of Christ.

The question, as I have already intimated, though involving an important principle of theology, yet rests on a plain
matter of fact. To solve it, we must appeal to the will and
intention of the divine Founder of Christianity, who certainly understood its true genius and character, and was
alone competent to lay down and establish a Rule of Faith.
Let us, then, see what Christ said and did on this subject;
and also what His inspired apostles, taught by himself and
the best acquainted with His will and intention, said and
did. This is a line of argument adapted to the lowest capacity; because it goes back to first principles, begins at the
beginning, and treats of a question of fact to be settled by
evidence.

1. And first, if Christ had intended that the world should
be converted solely or mainly by writing, is it not probable,
to say the least, that He Himself would have written something? Yet, it is a well known fact that He never wrote
one single word in His whole life. One or two fragments,
formerly ascribed to His sacred pen by a few unskillful

critics, are now universally rejected as spurious.* All Christians, Protestants as well as Catholics, now admit that He never wrote any. thing. He *preached;* He never *wrote.* During the years of His public ministry, He was wholly engaged in oral teaching; He never once gave the slightest intimation about writing.

2. What is yet more remarkable, he often commanded his apostles and disciples to teach, to preach; He never once uttered a syllable to them about *writing.* There is no record of any such command from one end of the new testament to the other. And yet there would certainly have been at least some faint intimation of it, had such a command ever been given; especially had the sacred writers been persuaded of the Protestant principle,—that writing was to be the primary means for fulfilling the commission to teach all nations. Protestants certainly have no right to assert the existence of any such command; for, according to their own Rule, they cannot travel beyond the record, and the record is wholly silent on the matter. One of the sacred writers of the new testament,—St. John,—indeed, tells us, that he was commanded to write out some divine messages to the seven Churches of Asia, and also a particular heavenly vision, which he saw;† but this solitary exception does not impair the force of the argument, nor materially serve our adversaries. For, besides that this happened more than sixty years after the ascension of Christ into heaven, it is confined to a very small portion of a very mysterious and awfully prophetic book; it does not embrace much that is doctrinal, but rather contains a mere warning; and, what is yet more to the purpose, it does not even hint that the object of this writing was to lay down a complete and primary Rule of Faith.

---

* As, for example, his alleged epistle to Agbarus, mentioned and given in full by Eusebius in his Church history: Book 1. ch. 18. Eusebius says, that he translated the document from the Syriac original in the public archives of Edessa. *Ibid.* page 44, of the American Translation.

†Apocalypse, or Revelations, chaps. i, ii, iii, and chap. xix: 9.

3. With this single exception, not one of the sacred writers of the new testament says any thing from which we are led to infer that Christ ever meant or intended that His Religion should be taught to the world and handed down to posterity chiefly and primarily by means of writing. Had such been the persuasion of the apostles, would they not all have left us some writings to transmit to us their testimony to the doctrines of Christ? Had they neglected to do so, they would certainly have been grievously wanting to a most sacred duty imposed upon them by the Commission. Yet we find that only five out of the twelve,—reckoning St. Mathias in the place of Judas,—are recorded to have written any thing at all. And three out of these five,—St. Peter, St. James, and St. Jude,—have left us nothing more than brief epistles, written under particular circumstances, and for special reasons. More than half of the new testament was written by inspired men, who were not among the apostles to whom the Commission was addressed by our blessed Lord.* If the Protestant Rule of Faith be the true one, and that which Christ intended to establish in giving the Commission, we are forced to say one of two things: either that those to whom it was addressed did not so understand it, or that, having so understood it, more than half of them utterly failed to comply with either its letter or its spirit! What Christian is prepared to say this?

4. Again, had such been the original intention of Christ, would not the sacred writers have taken some pains to furnish us with a full and connected account of the doctrines and institutions of Christianity? Would they not, somewhere at least in their writings, have given us a regular and complete summary of the Christian faith, and told us what tenets it was indispensably necessary for all Christians to hold, if they would secure the salvation of their souls? Had they understood the mind of Christ as our dis-

---

* The Gospels, according to St. Mark and St. Luke, The Acts, and the Epistles of St. Paul, were written by inspired men, who were not among the apostles to whom the Commission was addressed.

senting brethren now profess to understand it, they would most assuredly have done something of the kind, else they would have been sadly deficient in the discharge of a most sacred duty solemnly imposed upon them by their divine Lord and Master. Yet they nowhere profess to do this. They nowhere inform us, that it was their design to present a full and perfect synopsis of the principles constituting the Christian Religion. They seem, on the contrary, to have written by accident, or under the influence of particular circumstances, rather than with any settled purpose of telling us all that a Christian should know and believe in order to be a real and thorough disciple of Christ. They wrote at different times, in different places, and without any apparent mutual understanding that what was pretermitted by one should be supplied by another.

The four Gospels, for instance, contain a very brief summary of a few among the many things which Christ said and did, chiefly during his public life. The first three of the Evangelists,—St. Mathew, St. Mark, and St. Luke—often relate the same things, and almost in the same words. The last of them,—St. John,—supplies us with a great many additional details on the same subject; but how very meagre is even his account of the public life of Christ! How very condensed are his reports of the discourses of that Saviour, upon whose bosom he was wont to lean, as the beloved disciple! Does he furnish us with an account of one hundreth part of what his dearly beloved Master said and did? In the very last verse of his Gospel, which was also, in point of time, the last sentence of inspiration that was penned by any writer of the new testament, he himself tells us as much, and in the most emphatic language: "But there are also many other things which Jesus did; which, if they were written every one, the world itself, I think, would not be able to contain the books that should be written."*

---

* St. John xxi: 25. The gospel of St. John was written at Ephesus about the close of the first century, the last of all the books of the new testament. See also St. John xx: 30, 31.

Even if St. John had not left on record this plain and unequivocal testimony, we might easily gather from the gospel
accounts themselves, that they do not profess to give us any
thing more than a few very brief hints and sketches of the
doctrine and life of Christ.   How little, for example, do any
of them all tell us concerning what Christ said and did
during the forty days intervening between His resurrection
and His ascension, when "He appeared (to the apostles), and
spoke of the kingdom of God?"*   Those were days full of
interest and pregnant with instruction to the world; for it
was then chiefly that Christ fully unfolded the principles,
and instituted the sacraments of His holy Religion.   Even
a very brief and comprehensive account of what occurred
during that short period, would have filled a volume probably much larger than the whole new testament.   The evangelists all write with a studied brevity; far from intending
to relate every thing, they appear to have almost entirely
confined themselves to such things as would be best calculated to persuade the world of the divine mission of Jesus,
and to induce men to believe in Him: and St. John states
this purpose in the most explicit language.†   This end once
secured, they knew that the believer would be disposed to
receive implicitly every thing which Christ had taught, and
that he would have ample means for fuller instruction in the
ordinary teaching of those to whom Christ had intrusted
this special Commission.

What has been said of the four Gospels, is still more
strikingly true of the other books, composing the new testament.   I have not time to dilate upon them all; but a
mere glance at their contents and scope is sufficient to convince any impartial man, that they are mere historical
sketches or incidental disquisitions on particular subjects,
specially adapted to the times in which they were severally
written, or to the wants of the persons to whom they were
respectively addressed.   They presuppose, rather than furnish, a full knowledge of the Christian system.   The Acts

* Acts i. 8.   † St. John xx. 30, 31, *sup. cit.*

of the apostles, after the twelfth chapter, are little more
than a brief chronicle of the missionary labors of St. Paul:
they tell us little of the other apostles; they do not state
where most of them labored or died; they break off suddenly, without even informing us of what St. Paul himself
did during the last years of his life; they evidently leave
more unsaid than they say. The Epistles of St. Paul and
those of the other apostles, were mere letters of advice
written to meet particular emergencies, to solve special
doubts, or to convey instruction on particular points on
which information was specially needed: some of them were
addressed to particular persons, on subjects of a private
nature. They were manifestly intended to be merely re-
membrancers of the doctrines already fully unfolded by
preaching, or as supplements to the preached word. St.
Paul often refers to his oral teaching; as, to select one
out of many instances, when he bade the Thessalonians
to "stand firm, and to hold the traditions which they had
learned whether by word or by his (previous) epistle."*

5. From all these considerations it is manifest, that the
sacred writers did not compose the various inspired tracts
which make up the new testament with any settled purpose
to give us a complete and connected summary of the Christian doctrines and institutions; and that, consequently, they
did not write under the impression that, according to the
will and intention of Christ, any such written summary was
absolutely necessary. To gather the whole Christian doctrines from their writings, you must take a passage here and
another there; you must separate them from their connection and generalize their meaning; you must explain what is
obscure in one by what is plain in another; and after having
gone through all this patient labor, you must put those
passages together in a certain order, and must even supply
some things upon which the new testament is almost wholly
silent, before you can hope to have arrived at a full understanding of the Christian doctrine. This is a task mani-

_____

* II Thessalonians, ii: 14.

festly above the capacity of the great bulk of mankind,
besides that it requires more time and study than is allowed
by the necessary avocations of most men. Is it to be thought
that Christ instituted a Rule of Faith which, He well knew,
it would be morally impossible for the vast majority of mankind to apply? Would it have been just in Him, to require
of all men an unconditional belief in all His doctrines, under
the penalty of eternal damnation, while, at the same time,
He instituted a Rule according to which it would be next to
impossible for them to ascertain with certainty what He
had really taught?

6. Yet more; had it been the design of Christ that the
Bible, as understood by each individual Christian for himself, should contain His whole Religion and be the only Rule
of Faith and practice, would not the sacred writers, fully
aware of such intention, have taken special pains to write
out every thing so plainly that no one, even the most dull
and ignorant, could be mistaken in the interpretation?
Most assuredly. And yet, is such the case? If the sacred
writers are so very plain, why is it that our Protestant
brethren, who profess to understand them so thoroughly,
have given to the world so many contradictory systems
of Religion, all professing to be derived from the Bible? If
the Bible is so very plain, why do they not all understand it
alike? Is it a mass of contradictions, like the religious
creeds said to be extracted from its sacred pages? If the
Bible contains but one religion, divine and harmonious and
one in all its parts, where is the safety in a system of interpretation which draws a hundred warring creeds from its
various books? Is it not plain to the lowest capacity, that
ninety-nine out of these hundred conflicting faiths, at least,
must be wrong and spurious, and that one only of them, at
most, can be right? And therefore, that the Protestant,
according to his own showing, has at least ninety-nine
chances to be wrong, to one to be right; whereas, if the
Catholic Church be right, he is infallibly wrong? There is
no escape from this difficulty. There is no possibility of
reconciling the alleged clearness of the scriptures with the

many conflicting religious systems built up on their supposed meaning.

Tell me not, that the Bible is plain, at least on all points
necessary for salvation; and that the differences of interpretation among Protestants regard only unimportant tenets.
If those doctrines upon which our dissenting brethren differ
among themselves are so very unimportant, why do they
constitute the basis of denominational distinctions? Why
divide the unity of the Church for matters so trivial? Why
set up church against church and altar against altar; why
rend the seamless garment of Christ; why tear His mystical
body into fragments, for articles which, after all, every one
is free to receive or reject without thereby incurring the
divine displeasure? It is plain, that those who hope to
escape from the difficulty by this answer, do not themselves
practically believe in its soundness; else, instead of organizing a hundred conflicting communions, they would certainly all coalesce into one.

Again, have not the most learned men, those who were
well acquainted with the original languages in which the
Bible was written, and who were thoroughly versed in oriental manners, customs, and literature, to which allusion is
constantly made in its sacred pages, been nevertheless often
sadly puzzled to arrive at its original meaning? Have not
men equally learned, equally pious, equally sincere, often
pronounced very different opinions on the meaning of the
same passages? Did not the early German Protestants, for
instance, give as many as two hundred different interpretations of one single text, the plainest, perhaps, in the new
testament,—"This is my body?" And such being the case,
how can the unlearned hope to arrive at the real meaning
of the sacred text?

Let us hear what St. Peter says on this very subject:
"As also our most dear brother Paul, according to the
wisdom given to him, hath written to you; as also in all
his epistles, speaking in them of these things: IN WHICH
ARE SOME THINGS HARD TO BE UNDERSTOOD, WHICH THE UN-
LEARNED AND UNSTABLE (the bulk of mankind) WREST, AS

ALSO THE OTHER SCRIPTURES, TO THEIR OWN PERDITION.''*
There are then, many passages of the sacred scriptures, embodying doctrines, too, essential to salvation, which are hard to be understood, and which many wrest to their own perdition. This testimony strikes a mortal blow at the Protestant Rule of Faith. Another testimony of the same apostle completes the evidence against its truth: "Understanding this *first*, that no prophecy of scripture is made *by private interpretation*."† •

7. You will, perhaps, object, that it is incompatible with the wisdom and goodness of the Holy Ghost, who inspired the sacred scriptures, to have left them obscure, at least in matters of importance for salvation; and you will state your argument in this form: if the scriptures are not plain enough to be understood by the most ordinary capacity, it is because the Holy Ghost either could not, or would not, speak plainly; but it were little short of blasphemy to say either of these things.

I answer, that this is little better than a shallow sophism it takes for granted the very thing in dispute, and supposes that the Holy Ghost meant to make the scriptures the sole Rule of Faith, as interpreted by each individual for himself, apart from all Church authority. This is plainly a begging of the question. The Holy Ghost made the scriptures plain enough to those who would seek to expound them, not by private interpretation, which St. Peter rejects, but by the clear and unmistakable light thrown upon them by the public teachings of those to whom Christ intrusted the commission to "preach the gospel to every creature." With this authorized commentary, every thing in them would become plain enough; without it, many things would remain uncertain and obscure. The new testament was to be received as a divine commentary on, and a supplement to, the public or oral teaching of the first inspired incumbents of the ministerial office appointed by Christ Himself; and, in matters of doubt, they were to be consulted, and after them their

---

* II Peter, iii: 15, 16.   † *Ibid.* i: 20.

successors in the same office; and their exposition was to be received as authoritative and definitive.

This is manifest from various passages of the new testament itself. Thus St. Paul, writing to the Corinthians, clearly intimates that he had not taught them every thing, but had confined himself to those elements of Christian knowledge which were adapted to their weakness: "Howbeit, we speak wisdom among the perfect . . . . . but we speak the wisdom of God in a mystery. . . . . . And I, brethren, could not speak to you, but as carnal. As to little ones in Christ, I gave you milk to drink, not meat; for you were not able as yet: but neither indeed are you now able; for you are yet carnal."* Thus again, in the same Epistle, he plainly says, that he had not written every thing concerning the holy eucharist and public worship, but that he would afterwards supply the deficiency by his oral teaching: "And the rest I will set in order when I come."† In the most sublime of all his Epistles, the one to the Hebrews, he intimates the same economy, when, speaking of Melchisedech, he says: "Of whom we have great things to say, and hard to be intelligibly uttered: because you are become weak to hear."‡ In all this, the apostles did but follow the example of our blessed Lord Himself, who was wont to speak to the multitudes in parables hard to be understood, but which He took particular pains fully to explain to His apostles and disciples, that they might be thereby fully qualified to become the instructors of the people. To them He said, when they inquired into the motive of this His mode of procedure: "Because to you it is given to know the mysteries of the kingdom of heaven; but to them (the people) it is not given . . . . . Therefore I speak to them in parables: because seeing, they see not, and hearing, they hear not, neither do they understand."‖ Had Christ intended to make the people the interpreters of His Religion, apart from the oral teaching of

---

* I Corinthians, ii: 6, 7, and iii: 1, 2.   ‡ Hebrews, v: 11.
† I Corinthians, xi: 34.   ‖ St. Math. xiii: 11, 13.

His ministry, His conduct on this and other similar occasions is wholly inexplicable.

Nor can we, in this hypothesis, explain the answer made by the learned and pious Jewish eunuch to the deacon Philip, when the latter, finding him engaged in reading Isaiah, ventured to ask him : "thinkest thou that thou understandest what thou readest?" To which the eunuch answered: "How can I, unless some one show me ?"* Even the apostles and disciples themselves, though they enjoyed for so long a time the company of the Son of God and had been taught by His lips, yet were dull of comprehension, and did not understand the meaning of the ancient scriptures, until He Himself, after his resurrection, "beginning from Moses and the prophets, had expounded to them, in all the scriptures, the things which were concerning Him;" and "had opened to them the Scriptures."† And it was only after the descent of the Holy Ghost upon them on the day of Pentecost, that their minds were fully enlightened on a subject so difficult of comprehension.

The self-same principle runs through all these and many other passages of the sacred volume: namely, that the Bible was intended to be plain in all its parts only to those who were specially taught by Christ Himself, or by those whom He had taught and specially commissioned to unfold its sacred meaning in doubtful points to others. In matters of obscurity and difficulty, the faithful were under the necessity of consulting those who had been regularly authorized "to teach all nations." This principle is the pivot upon which the whole scriptural system turns. It is the great luminous center from which radiates the light that dispels its obscurity and clears up its doubts. Without it, the whole scope and genius of scriptural meaning becomes uncertain, if not wholly unintelligible to the mass of mankind.

8. Without this clear light, thrown upon the new testament by the public oral teachings of the Christian ministry,

---

* Acts viii. 80, 81.   † St. Luke xxiv. 27, 82.

7

how could the early Christians have become acquainted
with many things in the Christian religion, concerning
which its sacred pages are either wholly silent, or speak
only in the most obscure language? How else could they
have learned the transfer of the obligation of keeping the
Jewish Sabbath or *seventh* day of the week, to Sunday, or *first*
day of the week? This change was certainly made by the
authority of Christ, or by that of His apostles promulgating
His will; and yet the new testament says nothing from
which it may be necessarily inferred, or even inferred at all.
How else could they know that the ceremony of washing
feet, so strongly enforced both by the example and the apparent command of Christ, was not an obligation on all
Christians, or even a sacrament of the new covenant?*
How else could they know, that infants were to be baptized,
or that baptism administered by heretics was not to be renewed by authorized ministers? How else could they know
that the obligation of "abstaining from blood and things
strangled," so clearly inculcated by the apostolic Council of
Jerusalem among "the things necessary," was not intended
to be as permanent in the Church as that of "abstaining
from fornication," with which it is associated in the same
connection?† And upon what authority, other than that of
the Church expounding the scriptures, do our dissenting
brethren know and believe all these and many other things
of a similar kind, which most of them nevertheless receive
as well as ourselves.

9. Again, if the new testament, as understood by private interpretation, was intended to contain all the doctrines
and institutions of the Christian Religion, and in so plain a
manner that no one could be mistaken as to their meaning,
number, and character, will our adversaries have the goodness to tell us whether they mean to assert this of any one

* See St. John, chapter xiii. As far as the mere language of scripture
is concerned, how is any one to know that this ceremony was not as obligatory as the Lord's Supper itself?

† Acts, xv: 28, 29.

of its many books taken separately, or of all of them taken together? If the former, then which of those books contains all that is necessary? And if any one of them does contain all this, where is the utility or the necessity of the others? If the latter, then pray where is the evidence for the fact? Do any of the sacred writers inform us, that their own writings, in conjunction with the rest, were intended to contain every thing appertaining to the religion of Christ? If so, where is the testimony? Our brethren, who profess to receive nothing that is not based on a clear scriptural warrant, have surely no right to assert any thing as of divine institution which is not founded upon such evidence. Is there any thing, even in the general tenor and complexion of the various books composing the new testament, which would lead us to believe, that all the sacred writers, taken together, meant to unfold to us the entire Christian system? From what we have already said on the subject, the presumption lies rather on the other side; at least there is certainly no proof of the alleged fact in the book itself.

10. The scriptural testimonies, which our separated brethren are in the habit of alleging to prove their position, are certainly not to the purpose. They regard the old testament only, and our present question is mainly in reference to the new.

The testimony of our Saviour: "Search the scriptures, for you think in them to have life everlasting: and the same are they that give testimony of me;"* even if it was meant to imply a command or an exhortation, and not a reproof or a mere declaration of a fact,—as is more probable from the original Greek and the whole context,—is certainly confined to those prophetical portions of the old testament which regarded the coming and divine authority of the Messiah.

So also the famous passage of St. Paul, in his second epistle to Timothy: "All scripture divinely inspired, is profitable to teach, to reprove, to correct, to instruct in justice;

* St. John v: 39.

that the man of God may be perfect, furnished unto every
good work,"* is manifestly limited to those scriptures
which Timothy "had known from his infancy," and does
not at all regard the new testament, a great portion of
which was not yet written.   Besides, St. Paul says, that
those scriptures were *profitable*, not that they were sufficient or contained every thing necessary to salvation: as
they certainly did not, even according to the judgment of
Protestants themselves.   Who among the latter is prepared
to say, that the old testament alone suffices to instruct us in
the Christian Religion ?   It may, indeed, "instruct us unto
salvation," as it did Timothy, but only "through the faith
which is in Christ Jesus."†

The same remark may be made in regard to the "noble
Bereans," who "daily searched the scriptures, whether
those things were so."‡   St. Paul had quoted the old scriptures to prove the divine mission of Jesus Christ; and it
was natural enough that the Bereans, who were as yet Jews
and not believers in Christianity, should seek to verify the
quotations.   Had they been Christians, and still doubted
the preaching of St. Paul, they would certainly have been
more deserving of censure than of commendation for their
conduct, even according to the principles of our opponents
themselves.

11. You will, perhaps, tell me, that so long as the inspired
apostles were upon the earth, their oral teaching, which
was infallible, was to be received as an authoritative commentary on the written word; but that, after their death,
the early Christians were deprived of this resource, and had
nothing left to guide them in the path of Christian truth
and duty except their writings.

I know that this theory is fashionable enough now-a-
days; but it is not, for all this, the more defensible or true.
Where is the evidence that the original mode of teaching
all nations, established by Christ himself, was to be changed
after the death of those to whom the Commission was given?

---

*II. Timothy, iii: 16, 17.   † Ibid, 15.   ‡ Acts, xvii: 11.

This mode was clearly in possession, and it could not be superseded but by an express divine warrant. Where is the proof that such a warrant exists? Had Christ said to His apostles: you must preach and teach so long as you will live, but you must take care to commit the whole substance of your preaching and teaching to writing, as I intend that these writings, as understood by each individual for himself, shall, after your death, become the only Rule of Faith: then, indeed, the theory would be made out. But Christ said nothing of the kind. He clearly intimated the contrary, when He said that this original mode of teaching all nations was intended by Him to continue, sanctioned by His divine presence and assistance, "all days, even to the consummation of the world." The burden of proof is upon our adversaries; and they should surely prove the alleged change in the established method of God's teaching by a clear testimony of the record itself, their only Rule of Faith. But the record is not only silent on the subject of the alleged change, but its obvious meaning clearly implies the contrary.

12. Besides, is it at all probable, that Christ intended that this change should really take place? Even if there were no express testimony on either side of the question, is it not highly probable, to say the least, that no such change was ever contemplated by Christ? Is it probable that our divine Lord who "was God and changed not," would have authorized so speedy a change in one of His primary and most cherished institutions? Did He not, as God, clearly foresee, that His followers who would live after the apostolic age, would be in much greater need of pastoral instruction and guidance, than those who would be imbued with the principles of His Religion by His own inspired apostles? Would not doubts and controversies arise among them, which could be settled in no other way than by authoritative oral teaching?

Did he not also foresee what proved to be the fact, that the books of the new testament would be scattered over the whole world, in the different churches to which they were

7 *

respectively addressed, or for which they were written, and
that they would not be collected into one volume for three
entire centuries after His ascension? And that if He constituted them the only Rule of Faith and practice, all His
followers, during this long period, would be entirely and
necessarily shut out from all means of ascertaining the principles of His Religion? Did he not know, that even for
many centuries after this period, not one in a thousand of
His disciples, would be able to read those sacred documents,
even if they should be so fortunate as to have access to
them? And did He not also foresee, that the art of printing would not be discovered for full fourteen centuries
after the date of the Commission, and that as a necessary
consequence, not one in ten thousand of His followers would
be able to possess the sacred volume? Did He not, finally,
clearly know beforehand all the innumerable and discordant interpretations which those adopting that volume
as their only Rule of Faith, and expounding it by their
own private judgment, would put upon even its plainest
language?

Being God, He certainly foresaw all this; and being a
God infinitely wise and infinitely good, He surely could not
have intended to establish a Rule subject to so many difficulties, and absolutely impossible of application by the vast
majority of His followers. Had He done so, he would have
made no adequate provision for the wants of men, and
would have, on the contrary, rendered it next to impossible
for the bulk of mankind to ascertain with any certainty the
real tenets of His holy Religion.

13. These are some of the many insuperable difficulties in
the way of the Protestant Rule of Faith. But there are
others if possible, yet more striking and insurmountable.
We have space merely to glance at a few of the most obvious.

And first; if the scriptures, especially those of the new
testament, be the only Rule of Faith, and contain *all* that is
necessary to be believed, they should surely furnish us with
satisfactory information and proof in regard to the important previous question,—whether they are themselves,

inspired in all their parts: but they tell us no such thing. There is not one passage from St. Matthew's Gospel to the Apocalypse, which gives us this essential information, and we defy our adversaries to produce any such testimony. But even if they could produce it, there would yet be something wanting to the evidence; for it might still be objected, that the book could not bear testimony to its own inspiration, as that testimony might not itself be inspired. We might, indeed, presume that whatever was written by any one of the apostles to whom Christ had specially promised his assistance, was and is inspired; but, as we have already said, much more than half of the new testament was not written by them, but by others to whom there is no evidence, at least on the record itself, that any such promise was ever made. How, for example, can any one prove from the new testament itself, that St. Mark and St. Luke were inspired? Thus, then, there is manifestly a most important link wanting in the chain of evidence furnished by the Protestant Rule.

The second great difficulty in the way of the Protestant Rule, is that which regards the canon, or the authentic list of those books of the new testament which are to be received as divine. The book itself certainly contains no such catalogue, nor is there any thing in it which gives us even a hint by which we might be guided to a correct conclusion in a matter of such vital interest. Yet the canon certainly does involve a question of faith; and if the Bible be the only Rule of Faith, it is a fundamental question: for how can we be guided by a Rule, until we first ascertain what composes the Rule? Therefore, here too, the alleged Rule is obviously incomplete, and it says nothing whatever on an article essential to its very existence.

How is this article to be settled? Plainly by evidence outside of the record, and, of course, wholly independent of the Protestant Rule; by the oral teaching of the early Church, handed down to us by tradition—that is, by the Catholic Rule. Even Protestants are compelled to fly to this only resource for determining the canon; but, in doing so, they act inconsistently with their great fundamental principle, and virtually admit that their Rule is wholly inadequate.

This question of the canon is as difficult as it is important. For more than three centuries after the birth of Christianity, serious doubts were entertained, in many parts of the early Church, concerning the canonicity of various books of the new testament, which our opponents *now* agree with us in admitting: such as the Epistle of St. James, the second Epistle of St. Peter, the Epistle to the Hebrews, the second and third of St. John, the Epistle of St. Jude, and the Apocalypse, or Revelations; besides several smaller portions of some other books, as the history of the adulteress in the eighth chapter of St. John's Gospel, a portion of the last chapter of St. Mark, and the passage in the twenty-second chapter of St. Luke, which treats of the bloody sweat of our Lord. The doubt arose chiefly from the peculiar condition of the Church, which was then grievously persecuted, and was often unable to convene councils to examine into this and other matters; and also from the fact already alluded to, that most of the books of the new testament were as yet scattered over the world, and some of them were therefore almost wholly unknown in many churches.

But so soon as the Church emerged from the catacombs into the full light of day, in the fourth century, her pastors set about the great work of collecting together all the scattered books, and of determining which were canonical and which were not. By her solemn verdict, rendered in various councils, many books which had been previously circulated to greater or less extent, and had been viewed by some as inspired writings of the apostles or disciples, were set aside as spurious or uninspired, and those only were pronounced genuine which we now receive. Among those thus set aside, we may reckon the following: the gospel according to the Hebrews, the gospel according to the twelve apostles, the history of the Infancy of Jesus Christ, the epistle of St. Barnabas, the acts of St. Paul and St.

Thecla, the Shepherd, or Pastor of Hermes, the two epistles of St. Clement, and many others.*

Now, amidst so many serious difficulties in the way of settling the canon, which existed even at that early day when the means of arriving at the truth were so much more abundant than they are at present, how is a Protestant, at this remote period, to satisfy his mind that a correct conclusion was then arrived at, unless he virtually admit that the Church was guided in the matter by the light and assistance of the Holy Ghost,—which would be plainly to abandon his own Rule of Faith, and to adopt ours? This difficulty never has been, and, I suppose, never will be solved, by those who contend that the Bible is the only Rule of Faith, and that nothing is to be believed which is not found recorded therein. The Protestant cannot prove the canon without abandoning his Rule of Faith, and virtually admitting Church authority.

The third difficulty in the way of the Protestant Rule is not less serious. How can a Protestant feel certain that he has a true version of the Bible? The Bible can give him no information whatever on this most important question; and yet, if he have not a true version, he has not the true word of God, and therefore cannot even begin to apply his Rule. The Bible was not certainly written in English, nor in any other modern language, but in Hebrew and Greek; and the Protestant translation into our vernacular, was not made by inspired men, but by men who were not only fallible, but were known to have often grievously mistaken the meaning of the sacred text. Thus there were no less than four successive Protestant translations of the Bible into English, previous to that of King James: Tindal and Coverdale's, Mathews,' Cranmer's, and the Bishops' Bible;† all

---

* There is much contest among the learned about an epistle which many suppose, from a passage in the epistle to the Colossians, to have been written by St. Paul to the Laodiceans. It seems certain, however, that the one which is now exhibited as such is spurious.

† See on this subject, Hallam's "Introduction to Literature," etc., vol. I. p. 201. American edition.

F

of which were, however, subsequently rejected by English Protestants as notoriously corrupt, and, therefore, not a true representation of the word of God. King James's translation fared little better at first. Protestant ministers, in great numbers, openly proclaimed its utter unfaithfulness; and even after it had undergone various corrections, it still retained, and retains to this day, many mistranslations, in matters, too, vitally affecting doctrines.* This has been triumphantly proved more than once; nor have the proofs ever been satisfactorily answered. In this state of things, how is the English or American Protestant to know with certainty, that he has a faithful translation; or, which is the same thing, that he has really the word of God, and not a mere counterfeit?

To determine the matter to his full satisfaction, the Protestant should be thoroughly acquainted with Hebrew and Greek, with ancient history, with oriental manners and customs; and, being well furnished with all this various knowledge, he should devote a long lifetime to a critical examination of the principal translations which have been made at different times, and should carefully, patiently, and impartially weigh the reasons on both sides of every mooted question; and even then he might arrive at an incorrect conclusion, as many men equally learned and sincere have done before him! Where there is so great a diversity of opinion among the learned, even those of his own religious sentiments, he cannot safely or consistently receive on trust the opinion of any one in particular; for this might mislead him into fatal error. Nor can he accept, without examination, the opinion of his own particular sect, or even of all the sects; for he holds that they, one and all, may deceive him, because they, too, are fallible. Besides, this would be plainly traveling out of the record, and thereby violating his Rule.

Placed in these straits, how is the candid Protestant to feel assured that he has a true version, or the word of God

---

* For more details on this point, see the last Lecture in this course.

in its original purity and integrity? And if he cannot be assured of all this, how is he to apply his Rule, and of what practical use is it to him?

But suppose all these difficulties settled, there is yet another equally formidable, which never can be solved by the Protestant Rule; but which must yet be settled before the Protestant can feel any certainty that he is following the word of God. Amidst so many conflicting opinions as to the real meaning of the Bible, how is the sincere Protestant inquirer to determine which is the true interpretation? Others may be right, and he may be mistaken; and if he is mistaken, he is really not following the word of God, but his own fancy only. With so many chances against his being right in his interpretation, how can he, without pride or presumption, think that all others have erred, and that he alone, with much less learning, and perhaps piety, on his side, has attained to the truth? The Bible has really only one true and legitimate meaning; but the Protestant Rule, regularly applied, has put upon it hundreds of contradictory interpretations; therefore the Protestant Rule stands self-convicted of having grievously perverted and fatally wrested the word of God; and, therefore, of being totally inadequate for the purpose of safely guiding mankind unto a knowledge of the truth.

14. From what I have hitherto said, it is manifest, my Beloved Brethren, that a Protestant cannot consistently make a true ACT OF FAITH. He may very sincerely and honestly entertain *opinions*; but, with so many insuperable difficulties staring him in the face, he cannot have *faith*, properly so called. For what is faith? St. Paul defines it thus: "Now faith is the *substance*[*] of things hoped for, the *conviction*[†] of things that appear not."[‡] That is, according to the clear import of the original, faith is the firm and unshaken basis of all our future hopes, a full

[*] In Greek, Ὑπόστασις,—*subsistence* or *basis, substance, a certain persuasion.* Hederici Lexicon.

[†] Ἔλεγχος, or *Elenchos,—an argument, a conviction of the mind.* Ibid.

[‡] Hebrews, xi : 1.

and unwavering conviction of those things which are not known by the senses, but by the positive and unerring revelation of God. Now, I ask, how can the Protestant Rule, beset as it has been shown to be, with difficulties innumerable and insurmountable, be a firm and unshaken basis of future hope; how can it induce a firm and unwavering conviction of truths revealed? What is, in ultimate analysis, the basis of a Protestant's hope and faith? It is plainly his own private judgment, avowedly the most fallible thing in the world, and, among Protestants especially, the fruitful source of almost innumerable contradictions.

I know that Christian faith may have two distinct but connected elements; the divine and the human, the supernatural and the natural. The latter consists in the firm persuasion of the mind as to the fact that God has spoken, which persuasion may be induced, to a greater or less extent, by the examination of the evidence bearing on this fact; the former consists of a ray of heavenly light flashed into the soul, confirming its conviction of the truth, removing all its doubts, and, by the unction of divine grace, sweetly inclining it to believe unhesitatingly on the authority of God. Mere natural or human faith will never save us; and we cannot have, or even begin to have, supernatural faith without the gift of God. Even the human element in its highest degree, is plainly wanting in the analysis of Protestant faith; where is the evidence that the divine element is not also wanting?

I know that God may, and often does, bestow the saving gift of divine faith upon the unlearned, the simple-minded, and humble, who have not had the opportunity, or have not the ability, fully to examine the evidences of Christianity; but where is the evidence that he has ever promised to bestow it upon those, whose leading principle is to reject the teaching of the Church, and to trust solely to their own private judgment; who "are carried about by every wind of doctrine;" and who often doubt of those very truths of which they profess to be most firmly persuaded, and even take credit to themselves for superior liberality, in allowing that they may possibly be wrong, and that those who differ from them may possibly be right? Faith essentially, and in its very nature, excludes all doubt. Hence it follows, by a logical inference from what has been said, that a Protestant, who is consistent in following out his Rule, may have *opinion*, more or less strong, but not Christian *faith*. And yet St. Paul assures us, that, "without faith it is impossible to please God."* Let our separated brethren look to it in time!

15. You will, probably, tell me, that the Catholic Rule too is pregnant with difficulties and beset with doubt; because a Catholic is forced to prove the scriptures by the infallible Church, and the infallible Church by the scriptures, thereby reasoning in what is called a vicious circle. This objection has been raised and answered about a thousand times already; and I hope to answer it again at some length in the proper place, when I shall have to treat of the infallibility of the Church. Meantime, it is sufficient for our present argument to offer these two plain remarks: first, in reasoning with Protestants, who admit the scriptures, but deny the Church, it is surely competent for us to quote the former to prove the latter, though, in reasoning with an infidel, the course to be pursued would be different; second, we can surely prove the scriptures independently of Church authority, at least as well and as conclusively as can our separated brethren, and therefore, apart from the authority of the Church, we occupy on this subject at least as high ground as they do.

16. In a subsequent Lecture, I trust I shall be able more fully to convince you that this objection is a mere quibble; that the Catholic rests his faith on the solid and immovable rock of that Church which Christ solemnly commanded him to hear and obey; and that consequently, if he err, he errs by the express command of Christ himself. And, in fact, is it not manifest from the evidence already alleged, that the Catholic Rule of Faith is precisely that which Christ in-

---

* Hebrews, xi: 6.

8

stituted, and which His inspired apostles adopted for the
spread of the gospel? Are not the words of the Commission
plain and conclusive on this subject? "Teach all nations,"
"preach the gospel to every creature,"—what could be more
plain and explicit than this language? Consult all the
parallel passages in the four Gospels; turn to all the apostolical writings; run over the whole new testament; and
you will not find one syllable about any intention of Christ,
that the world should be converted by writing.

But you will find precisely the contrary asserted, over
and over again, and in the clearest and most unquestionable
language that even inspiration itself could employ. Thus,
St. Paul, speaking in general on this very subject,—of the
means ordained by Christ for the conversion of the world,
lays down the identical principle for which we are now
contending, in the following strong and emphatic language:
"How then shall they call on Him in whom they have not
believed? Or how shall they believe in Him of whom THEY
HAVE NOT HEARD? AND HOW SHALL THEY HEAR WITHOUT A
PREACHER? AND HOW CAN THEY PREACH, UNLESS THEY BE
SENT?.... FAITH, THEN, COMETH BY HEARING; AND HEARING
BY THE WORD OF CHRIST."* Faith, then, cometh by hearing,
and not by reading; it cometh by hearing the preached
word of Christ from a minister duly authorized and sent by
Him, through the legal channel of the ministry established
by Himself, and designed to be perpetuated in regular suc-
cession to the end of time. Such is plainly the doctrine of
St. Paul, and therefore of Christ who sent St. Paul.

St. Paul lays down the self-same principle in another
place, where he is likewise speaking of the ministerial office
in its most ordinary relation to the Christian Religion; a
relation which, according to the will of Christ, it must sustain to the very end of time. "And some, indeed, He gave
to be apostles, and some prophets, and others evangelists,
and others pastors and teachers, for the perfection of the
saints, for the work of the ministry, unto the edification of
the body of Christ: TILL WE ALL MEET IN THE UNITY OF

---

* Romans, x: 14, 15, 17.

FAITH, and of the knowledge of the Son of God, unto a perfect man, unto the measure of the age of the fullness of Christ. That we may not now be children, tossed to and fro, and carried about with every wind of doctrine, in the wickedness of men, in craftiness by which they lie in wait to deceive."* That is, Christ established a regularly organized ministry, for the purpose of teaching all men, by preaching the gospel, the self-same principles of faith, in order that all might be led to unity of faith, and that none might be led astray by the false teaching of cunning and wicked men, unauthorized to preach, "who lie in wait to deceive" the unwary. If the passage mean any thing, it clearly means this, and if it means this, it plainly annihilates the Protestant Rule, and sets up the Catholic.

I might produce many more passages of a similar import from the new testament, all going to establish the same principle; but the fear of trespassing too long upon your time compels me to confine myself to one more, taken from St. Paul's sublime Epistle to the Hebrews. "Remember your prelates," says the apostle of the gentiles, "who have spoken to you the word of God; considering well the end of their conversation, imitate their faith. Jesus Christ yesterday, to-day, and the same for ever. BE NOT CARRIED AWAY WITH VARIOUS AND STRANGE DOCTRINES."† That is, listen to the teaching of your pastors, or, as he adds a little afterwards: "Obey your prelates, and be subject to them, for they watch as being to render an account of your souls:"‡ imitate their faith; remember that the truth taught by them is one and unchangeable, even as Jesus Christ himself is; and take heed, lest you be carried away by new and strange doctrines. This is precisely what the Catholic Rule enjoins.

17. In the last Lecture, you will remember that I laid down four principles, as embodying the great characteristics of Christianity. Those principles being once admitted,—and no Christian can reject them,—it is evident that a Rule

* Ephesians, iv: 11, 12, 18, 14.   † Hebrews, xiii: 7, 8, 9.   ‡ Ib. xiii: 17.

of Faith which is conformable to them and carries them out
in practice, is that established by Christ; at least, it is intuitively certain, that no Rule which is incompatible with them
can possibly be that which was instituted by the Saviour.
Let us briefly apply this test to the two Rules of Faith
under consideration ; and I am willing to abide the result.

The first principle is, that Christ established but one
Religion. Now the Catholic Rule necessarily leads to a
belief in one religious system; whereas the Protestant Rule,
both in its theory and in its practical operation, must as
necessarily lead, and has actually led, to more than a hundred contradictory creeds. The second principle is, that
Christ has clearly settled and defined this one Religion in
all its parts. The Catholic Rule does the self-same; the
Protestant Rule leaves Religion vague, undefined, a crude
mass of floating and ever changing opinions, and its followers are accordingly "tossed to and fro, and carried about
by every wind of doctrine." The third principle is, that
Christ made this His one Religion obligatory, in all its
parts, on all mankind. The Catholic Rule enforces this
same doctrine; the Protestant Rule cannot carry it out,
even if it would, for it cannot tell its followers, with any
thing like certainty, what that Religion really is, or what
are its essential doctrines. The fourth principle is, that
Christ established means by which all men might easily
and safely learn what are the real principles of His one
Religion. The Catholic Rule is also easy; for all men,
however simple and unlearned, can hear and obey the
preached word : the Protestant Rule is extremely difficult,
and utterly impossible of application to the vast majority
of mankind, who either cannot read, or have not sufficient
leisure to read, or have not the capacity to understand
what they read, especially when they are bewildered by so
many conflicting systems alleged to be all derived from the
word of God, as read, examined, and understood by men of
learning and sincerity who have adopted this mode of
arriving at the truth.

18. I view it, then, as fully demonstrated, nay, as almost

self-evident, that Christ did not establish, and could not, in
conformity with the genius of His Religion, have possibly
established, the Protestant Rule of Faith ; but that He did,
on the contrary, clearly institute the Catholic Rule. For
the former Rule there is no evidence whatever in the Bible
itself; it is based upon an assumption wholly unwarranted
by the principles therein repeatedly and explicitly set
forth ; it is clearly, if not avowedly, opposed to the original
means of propagating the gospel ordained by Christ and
reduced to practice by His apostles and first disciples ; it is
not, even now, adapted to the wants of the vast majority of
mankind, and during the first fourteen hundred years, before the invention of printing, it was utterly impossible of
application ; it has split up the one original Religion of
Christ into a hundred warring sects, and has thereby disgraced the Christian profession, and aimed a mortal blow at
Christianity itself; it fosters pride of opinion, it is opposed
to the humility of the gospel, and it encourages rebellion to
the authorities established by Christ, with solemn command
that all should hear and obey their teaching; it is utterly
powerless in its attempt to prove the inspiration, to establish the canon, to ascertain the true version, or to fix upon
the real meaning of scripture; it has been the fruitful
source of a wide-spread infidelity, which was almost wholly
unknown in Christendom until it sprung into existence, and
unsettled the ancient faith by its proud and captious spirit ;
it has spread anarchy and confusion over the Christian
world, has left nothing but ruins in its course, has set up
altar against altar, and Christian against Christian, and has
done nothing but mischief; it is not, therefore, it cannot be,
the Rule of Faith which was established by Christ.

It, in fact, makes Christ less wise than the merest human
legislator; for the latter always takes care to have a speaking authority—legislatures and judicial tribunals—to decide
on the meaning of the law, and to settle controversies; well
knowing that, without such a system, society could not be
kept together, or even exist for a single year.

We must clearly seek the true Rule of Faith elsewhere;

8 *

in that venerable Church of all ages and of all nations, which, like Christ, its Founder, has, everywhere and at all times, spoken the self-same language, taught the same faith, been the same "yesterday, to-day, and for ever." We can find it nowhere else. This rule is consistent with itself, it obviates all the difficulties above set forth, it is adapted to the wants of all mankind, it fosters humility, it establishes unity of faith, it firmly sustains the whole Christian system, it is eminently conservative in its character and tendency, it is worthy the wisdom of Christ, it is conformable with the whole genius of Christianity, and it can, moreover, plead an express and solemn institution of the Saviour.

The argument based on what we have hitherto said, may be thus stated: that Church is the one true Church of Christ which alone adopts the Rule of Faith established by Christ, and which alone receives and fully carries out the means which He Himself ordained, when delivering the apostolical Commission for teaching all nations and converting the world to His Religion; but the Catholic Church alone does all this, as we have shown; therefore, the Catholic Church alone can claim to be the one true Church established by Christ. THIS IS THE FIRST EVIDENCE OF CATHOLICITY.

This argument will receive additional weight from what I hope to establish in the next Lecture; in which, if you will honor me with your attention, I hope to satisfy you on the question of fact,—that the Catholic Church alone has fulfilled the Commission, by actually converting to Christianity all the nations which have ever been so converted.

May God, in his infinite goodness and mercy, and through that boundless love which prompted Him to give His own dearly beloved Son for our redemption, vouchsafe to shed His light into our souls, to dispel our carnal darkness, to teach us the truth, and to bestow upon us the sweet unction of His grace, without which we cannot hope to be able to embrace the truth, even if we should be so fortunate as to ascertain it with certainty. May He grant, that we may "all meet in the unity of faith," and that we be not any longer "tossed to and fro by every wind of doctrine!"   Amen.

LECTURE IV.

THE APOSTOLICAL COMMISSION—ITS FULFILLMENT—THE SECOND EVIDENCE OF CATHOLICITY.

The argument stated—Two facts to be proved—The first fact—Summary
history of Protestant Missionary Societies—Their estimated income—
Number of bibles and tracts published—Number of converts made—
Paucity of result—Dr. Wiseman—The American Board—The mission
at the Sandwich Islands examined—And that of Oregon—Reasons for
the failure of Protestant missions—The great cause of this failure—
Catholic missions—A cavil met—The conversion of the world progressive—Conversions of nations during the early ages—An objection answered—Progressive conversion of the Northmen—Missions of the
middle ages—And of the sixteenth century—Reaction of the reformation—The losses through it more than retrieved by Catholic missions—
Modern Catholic missions—Great leading feature of Catholic missions
of every age—Reflection—Parallelism—The conclusion reached—The
second evidence of Catholicity.

*" Go ye, therefore, and teach all nations; baptizing them in the name of the
Father, and of the Son, and of the Holy Ghost; teaching them to observe all
things whatsoever I have commanded you: and behold, I am with you all days,
even to the consummation of the world."*—ST. MATH. xxviii: 19, 20.

*" He that is not with me is against me: and he that gathereth not with me,
scattereth."*—ST. MATH. xii: 30.

IN the last Lecture, my Dearly Beloved Brethren, I trust
that I showed you what was the original means ordained
by Jesus Christ for the conversion of all nations, and that
the Roman Catholic Church alone has adopted this means,
and fully entered into the spirit of the Apostolical Commission. In the present, I shall endeavor to show, that she
alone has actually fulfilled the Commission, by the conversion to Christianity of all the nations which have as yet
been converted from paganism. If I can once establish this
great fact, the argument based upon it is as obvious as it is
irresistible. It is simply this:

Christ willed and intended that the world should be converted to His Religion by His one true Church, through the
means which He Himself instituted for this purpose:

But the Roman Catholic Church alone has done all this:

(91)

Therefore the Roman Catholic Church alone is, or can be, the one true Church of Jesus Christ.

The first, or major proposition, is evident from the words of the Commission itself, as well as from what has been already said; * and it will not, I think, be denied, even by our adversaries themselves. The second or minor proposition, besides the question of principle which we have already discussed,† embraces two assertions, which we must now prove: first, that the Protestant sects have not converted any of the nations from heathenism to Christianity; and second, that the Catholic Church has converted *all* of them that have ever emerged from the darkness of paganism into the light of the Christian Religion. These two propositions, like all others involving facts, are to be established by historical evidence; and I propose now to furnish that evidence in regard to each of them in succession.

The whole argument being thus narrowed down to a plain question of fact, the development of it becomes comparatively easy; and I am willing to rest its whole merits upon the historical testimony bearing on the subject.

I. PROTESTANTISM HAS NEVER CONVERTED ONE SINGLE NATION FROM PAGANISM TO CHRISTIANITY.

The evidence for this assertion is manifold and conclusive. It will be unfolded in the following considerations, which will go far to show what Protestantism has *attempted* but *failed* to do in this respect.

1. Protestantism came into the world full fifteen hundred years too late to be able to fulfill the commission for converting the nations to Christianity. For long centuries before it had sprung into existence, this glorious work had been successfully going on, under the auspices of that Church against which it afterwards reared the standard of revolt. It could, then, lay claim to none of the laurels already won in this wide battle-field of the world, over which the cross of Jesus had been erected in triumph by other hands than its own, and by men possessing a faith from which it dis-

---

* In the last Lecture.   † Ibid.

sented. This consideration proves that it was *utterly impossible* for Protestantism to execute the Commission.

2. It cannot be denied,—and I most cheerfully make the admission,—that our dissenting brethren of various denominations have lately manifested a most laudable zeal for the conversion of the heathen nations. A rapid glance at the various efforts they have made at different times for this purpose, must satisfy every impartial mind, that they have not lost sight of this object, nor been sparing of continued and organized exertions for its accomplishment. During the last fifty years, in particular, millions of money have been cheerfully contributed, tens of millions of bibles, testaments, and religious tracts, have been printed and circulated, and thousands of missionaries have been sent out by the various Protestant missionary societies. The following brief statement will enable us to form some conception of the almost incredible efforts made by these societies for the enlightenment of heathen nations.

3. Shortly after the rise of Protestantism,—as early as the year 1536,—the Calvinistic church of Geneva organized a society for converting pagan nations : but we know little of its history; and it seems to be admitted on all hands that its efforts proved wholly abortive, and that it was in consequence very soon discontinued. From this date to the beginning of the last century, a period of more than a hundred and sixty years, the various Protestant sects appear to have lain wholly dormant on this subject; to have been content to remain quietly at home, and let the heathens shift for themselves. It was only in the year 1701, that the first Protestant missionary "society for the diffusion of Christian knowledge" was organized in England, under the royal auspices and with a royal charter. This was soon followed by the "society for the propagation of the gospel in foreign parts ;" and by another of a similar character, established in Denmark, by king Frederick IV., in 1706. But it is pretty generally admitted, that these various missionary establishments were conducted with little activity and still less success, during nearly the whole of the last century.

With the close of the last and beginning of the present
century, a new and much brighter era of Protestant missionary effort opens upon our view.* In the year 1792, was
established the "Baptist Missionary Society;" which was
followed, in 1795, by the "London Missionary Society," and
the "Scotch Missionary Society." In 1800, the English
"Church Missionary Society" came into full and active
operation; and it was very soon followed by a great variety
of similar associations, both in England and America, among
which the most wealthy and influential, perhaps, is the
"Bible Society," both on account of its thorough organization and its wide-spread ramifications. We may say, in
general, that, during the last fifty years, the missionary zeal
of our dissenting brethren has received a new impulse, and
has been brought into fuller and more active development.

4. Let us now see what means these various societies have
had at their command, in order that we may be able to form
some idea of what we might suppose should have been their
probable success in the work they all aimed at accomplishing. And we shall see, that if they failed, it was not certainly for want of zeal, of liberality in contributing, or of
men who were willing to enter the missionary field. They
succeeded in enlisting in their favor the wealth and learning
of the first men in England, in America, and on the continent of Europe. Of the vast resources at their command,
we may form some conception from the fact, that, in 1824,
it was publicly boasted, that, in England alone, *one thousand
pounds a day* were contributed for the conversion of the
heathen! Taking this as the basis of our calculation, we
may set down the annual receipts in England at three
hundred and sixty-five thousand pounds, or about one million eight hundred thousand dollars! Adding the annual
receipts of the American societies, which fall little short of
half a million of dollars, and taking into the account the

---

* For these facts, and for some of those that will follow, I am indebted
to the learned, accurate, and moderate Dr. Wiseman, who had access to
the original documents, and who has nearly exhausted this subject. See
his sixth Lecture.

amounts yearly contributed by the various Protestant societies of France, Switzerland, Germany, and Northern Europe, we will probably be rather below than above the mark, in estimating the annual receipts of all the Protestant missionary societies throughout the world, for many years past, at TWO AND A HALF MILLIONS OF DOLLARS. But, for fear of exaggeration, let us take two millions as the average annual receipts of the last forty years; and we will find that, during this period alone, not counting what had been previously contributed, the total amount reaches the astounding sum of EIGHTY MILLIONS!!

5. The English Bible Society alone, up to the year 1835, had printed more than nine millions of bibles and testaments; and the American more than six millions; making the total number, up to that date, more than fifteen millions! Add those which have been since printed, and also those published on the European continent; and it will not, perhaps, exceed the truth to say, that the whole number of bibles and testaments printed, up to the present date, does not fall far short of TWENTY-FIVE MILLIONS! I say nothing of the almost innumerable religious tracts which have been printed and circulated by the various Protestant societies during the same period.

It is much more to our present purpose, to inquire into the number of missionaries which these various societies have kept constantly in the field, in various parts of the world. At a very moderate estimate, this number may be set down at four thousand;* that is, at about four times as many as the Catholic Church is in the habit of employing annually. These missionaries receive large annual salaries, varying from five hundred to a thousand dollars to each, with an additional allowance for their wives and children. They thus enter the field abundantly furnished with all the comforts of life, and with all the resources that money can

---

* A scientific Journal, Le Nouveau Journal Asiatique, (vol. ii. p. 82.) estimates the number at five thousand; but I prefer to be rather under than above the mark. Those of America are included in the estimate given in the text.

ensure. While on this subject, I may as well mention, that the Catholic missionaries usually receive from the Propaganda, or from other Catholic societies, the very moderate annual allowance of from one hundred to one hundred and fifty dollars only, and that frequently they do not receive even this.

6. Eighty millions of dollars,—twenty-five millions of bibles and testaments,—four thousand missionaries annually employed, and under the most favorable auspices;—these are the enormous means wielded by those active and colossal Protestant missionary societies, which have hitherto attempted to fulfill the commission, by the conversion of the heathen world to Christianity. Surely, if their labors had been attended with the blessing of God, they would have been crowned with the most complete success.

But what are the actual results of all this magnificent enterprise? They may be summed up in two words: those societies *promised* much, but have really *accomplished* nothing, or almost nothing; even according to their own showing! Their annual reports exhibit a long list of moneys expended, of bibles and tracts distributed, of missionaries sent forth, of fields white for the harvest, of bright hopes and anticipations for the future; but they tell us of few converts made, and never once stimulate the zeal and liberality of their members, by presenting the simple fact, that *a whole nation* has been converted to Christianity from heathenism! And yet they would surely have done this, had it been in their power. Many of the missions have been wholly abandoned as hopelessly fruitless; others are in a very languishing condition; others again present brighter hopes, but really little better prospects of success.

Most of the converts are among those who are attached, as servants or otherwise, to the various missionary stations; others, as in the East Indies, are often found among the wives or children of the English soldiery; and many of them relapse into paganism so soon as the missionaries withdraw, or as they return to live among their own people. In general, it may be set down with safety, that not one permanent convert has been made for every ten thousand dollars expended!

Dr. Wiseman has fully established all this, and much more besides, of the same kind, from the annual reports of the English missionary societies themselves, and from the statements of Bishop Heber and other Protestant travelers or missionaries. My present plan does not allow of the copious details which he has given on the subject; and I must refer you, for the facts and specifications, to his sixth Lecture.*

7. But I can not refrain from briefly alluding to the history and results of Protestant missions in a very interesting portion of the world, of which Dr. Wiseman does not treat. The Oriental countries, comprising all the Asiatic territory bordering on the Mediterranean, from the borders of Egypt to Constantinople, have been for many years past a favorite field for Protestant missionary labor. How has this field been cultivated by Protestant missionaries and with what success? We have the most ample and satisfactory testimony, by recent Protestant travelers themselves, that this mission has turned out, like the rest, a complete failure. This fact is fully vouched for and clearly established by Dr. Madden, in the following remarkable passage, taken from the first volume of his Travels in the East:†

"It is in vain to delude ourselves with the notion that we are contributing to the civilization of the East, by the fashion of our zeal, 'the conversion of the heathen.' The knights-errant of Christianity, indeed, pervade every corner of the kingdom. The Scriptures have been translated into a hundred *mutilated* tongues; and vast sacrifices of money and truth have been made in the cause of Eastern proselytism.

"To convert, it is thought, is to civilize: in my apprehension, to civilize is the most likely method to convert.

---

* "Wiseman's Lectures" may be found in all our Catholic bookstores in the United States.

† Travels in Turkey, Egypt, Nubia, and Palestine, &c.; by R. R. Madden, M. D. In two volumes. Vol. i., p. 174, seqq. Edition, London, 1838.

Our missionaries have been totally unsuccessful, for they
commenced at the wrong end of religious education. They
relied too much on the abstruse dogmas of the Church, and
too little on the mild doctrines of Christianity for persuasion. The Turk had to digest the Trinity before he was
acquainted with the beautiful morality of the gospel. The
Greek had to abjure the errors of his creed before he was
initiated into the advantages of a purer worship. The
Catholic had to listen to the defamation of his creed before
he was convinced of a more rational Religion; and if they
were so successful as to shake him in his faith, he had then
to decide whether he would be a Methodist, or a Presbyterian, or a Calvinist, or an English Protestant, or a German Lutheran; for our missionaries in Egypt and Syria are
of as many conflicting sects. But such is the obstinacy of
the perverse Arabs, who prefer walking 'in the darkness
and shadow of death,' rather than receive the light we fain
would force upon them, that when they are reproved, they
have the audacity to say, '*We have the faith which our fathers
followed, and we are satisfied with it.*'

"A temporal provision has sometimes produced a temporary change, but this is rare; for the conversion of a
Musselman would necessarily consign the convert to the
grave; but if, in secret, a proselyte be made, the event,
under the magnifying lens of 'the Missionary Herald,'
makes a flourishing appearance. 'The Conversion of the
Heathen,' heads a chapter; the Evangelical reviewers
chuckle over 'the triumph of the cause,' and John Bull pays
another year's subscription to support 'the *Truth*.' A Jew
here, whom the Rev. Joseph Wolff 'left impressed with the
truths of Christianity,' showed me a splendid copy of the
scriptures, which that gentleman had given him: I was
astonished to find the New Testament had been torn out;
I begged to know the reason; the man acknowledged to
me that he had torn out the New Testament after Mr.
Wolff's departure. I accompanied one of the missionaries
to the synagogue, who, in the middle of the worship, commenced distributing tracts. I saw some of them thrown

down; others were deposited, without a regard, on the forms: surely the zeal was indiscreet which for any purpose disturbed the performance of religious duties; and assuredly a Hebrew missionary would have been roughly handled by the beadle of St. Paul's, had he intruded himself, on the Sabbath, between the congregation and their God, to distribute controversial pamphlets. In alluding to the many supposititious conversions that abound in Mr. Wolff's book, I impugn not that gentleman's veracity; but I have good reason to know that he and his enthusiastic brethren have been grossly imposed upon by the needy and the vile."*

8. It may, perhaps, be more interesting to my present hearers, to learn the results of Protestant missionary societies nearer home; and to be reminded of some recent facts on the subject with which Dr. Wiseman could not furnish us. During the month of May, our various religious and missionary societies generally hold anniversary celebrations in the city of New York. On these interesting occasions, reports are presented and read on the actual condition, future prospects, and past results of each society. These reports are drawn up by men connected with the societies themselves, and are, of course, as favorable and as glowing as possible. I have before me an abstract of the report made in May, 1845, by the "American Board of Commissioners of Foreign Missions;" and I think no one can peruse it without being forcibly struck with the great disproportion between the means employed and the results obtained.

---

* Similar testimony, though in language much more cautious and guarded, is borne to the fact by a more recent, and an equally unexceptionable witness, a Protestant clergyman, and a countryman of our own— Dr. Durbin, of the Methodist denomination. I have not room at present to furnish extracts from his late work in proof of this; but the book is in the hands of our reading community generally, and hence I will be content with a few references. See his "Observations in the East," vol. ii. p. 111. 296, 297, &c. The passages may be seen collected together and examined in a Review of the work, published in the United States Catholic Magazine, No. for August, 1846; republished in my Miscellanea.

In spite of the manifest effort made by the Commissioners
to keep up the missionary zeal and to awaken the liberality
of their constituents, one may see, at a glance, the sad
paucity of result which has attended their labors during the
forty-six years of their organization. They tell us of "a
great door opened" in different places; of fields white for
the harvest; of their missionaries in Syria "enjoying the
confidence of the people;" of their bright anticipations in
regard to Greece and Africa;—"that the land of classic
story and song will, *one day*, become vocal with the songs
of Sion and the story of the cross, and that not Ethiopia
alone, but all Africa will *speedily* stretch forth her hands,
unto God." They tell us of printing presses in full operation, of schools opened, of immense sums expended in various places, of bibles and tracts distributed almost without
number; but, if we look for the great and ultimate practical result of all these missionary resources — converts —
we shall be sadly disappointed. Upon this vital subject
they observe a studied silence, or deal in vague generalities,
leaving their readers to their own conjectures. This looks
very suspicious, to say the least; for surely they would
have spoken of their converts had they made any worth
the mentioning. There is, by the way, a remarkable same-
ness of tone and language in all these annual reports; they
all promise much for the *future*, but say little about the
actual results in the way of converts obtained in the *past;*
they seem to be always beginning to do, and never ending
in doing any thing worth boasting of.

9. True, they do not fail to tell us, and with evident self-
complacency, of the converts made by their missionaries in
the Sandwich Islands, the number of whom they estimate
at twenty-two thousand. As our dissenting brethren, when
pressed to show us one single nation or tribe converted
from idolatry to Christianity by their missionary societies,
generally point with pride to the Sandwich Islands, it may
not be inappropriate to dwell at some length upon this
subject.

I will not deny that they have there made many converts,

at least many nominally such. And it would be, indeed, remarkable if they had not, when we consider the long time they have been cultivating this field, the very large amount of money they have expended on it,—estimated by "Zion's Herald," a few years ago, at considerably more than six hundred thousand dollars;—and above all, when we consider the favorable circumstances under which they first entered on this mission. The native princes of those Islands, struck by the superior civilization of the white traders who had settled among them for commercial purposes, and panting to learn the arts by which their distinguished visiters had been enabled to attain this superiority, themselves earnestly, and of their own accord, petitioned for missionaries; and they are the first people within our knowledge of whom history states any thing of the kind.* Missionaries were accordingly sent out to them by the Protestant societies, chiefly by those of the United States; and under the very auspicious circumstances which attended their entrance upon the mission, their efforts were at first crowned with much *apparent* success. The natives came to hear their preaching in great numbers, and the schools were numerously attended by the young of both sexes.

But the event did not correspond with the brilliant anticipations founded upon this flattering beginning. The islanders soon found, that, instead of parental instructors, who would generously labor to civilize them and to teach them the way to heaven, they had really brought in, in the persons of the missionaries, imperious taskmasters, who lorded it over them with a rod of iron, both in church and state. Their legitimate princes dwindled down into mere subservient tools of their new teachers. A union of Church and state was soon brought about, and religious conformity,

* A similar circumstance is related of the Nez Perces Indians of the Rocky Mountains, who sent delegates to St. Louis for Catholic missionaries, but this was at a subsequent period. See "Letters of Father De Smet."

9*

embracing the obligation of attending public worship on
Sundays, was rigidly enforced by a code of pains and penalties.   Their ancient liberties were gone; their beautiful
Islands had been subjugated, not converted.   Their numbers, too, had decreased from 400,000, at which they were
estimated when the whites first visited the islands, to
110,000; * and the decrease still went rapidly on, so as
to threaten their final annihilation.

The traveler Kotzebue states, that he saw with his own
eyes, the natives driven into the Protestant meeting-houses
with sticks. †   The chief of the American Protestant missionaries, the Rev. Mr. Brinsmade, was appointed American
consul; and he and his reverend brethren had the ear of
the king and queen, and held almost supreme control over
the Islands.   So severe and intolerable was the yoke imposed upon the natives by their new religious protectors;
so great was the increase of civil feuds and quarrels among
them, that one of the princes, who had been among the
first converts, disgusted with the state of things, actually
prepared an expedition to emigrate from his own country!‡

And what was the moral influence on the natives, of the
gospel as preached to them by the Protestant missionaries!
Did they become more virtuous or less vicious; did they rise
or fall in the scale of civilization?   If my limits permitted
the necessary details, I could here spread out before you a
whole volume of such evidence as even you would not be
disposed to reject, all going to prove that the moral condition
of the natives was almost as bad after their alleged conversion as it had been before.   I could even show, by the testi-

---

* This statement is made by "Zion's Herald," an authority which will
not be questioned.

† See his "Second voyage around the World," quoted by Dr. Wiseman,
Sixth Lecture, *sup. cit.*

‡ Dr. Wiseman states this and other similar facts, on the following Protestant authority: "Voyage of H. M. S. Blonde to the Sandwich Islands,"
London, 1827; "the Quarterly Review," vol. xxxv., p. 400, and lxx., p.
609; Toole, "Account of nine months' residence in New Zealand;" and
Kotzebue, as above stated.

mony of many among the missionaries themselves, contained in their letters published in this country, and by other
accredited evidence, that the simplicity of the Islanders was
changed into craftiness and treachery, and that vices of a
most disgusting nature became much more common among
them than they had ever been before. From the same
sources I could establish the fact, that the missionaries
themselves quarreled on the subject of slavery and other
matters, and that some among them in consequence retired
in disgust from the mission.

I could, moreover, confirm all this, as well as what I have
previously stated, by the testimony of two secular papers
published on the spot by intelligent Protestants,—the
"Sandwich Island Gazette" and the "Hawaii Spectator,"
which prints established, by evidence that could not be resisted, the important fact, that the whole mission had turned
out a complete failure. Copious extracts from them were
published some years ago in many of the American news-
papers; and it would lead me too far to repeat them here.

But I must mention one undoubted fact which speaks a
volume on the subject. In April, 1833, the king published
an edict by which the natives were to be thereafter left free
to neglect or to attend Protestant worship at will. So soon
as a forced attendance was no longer enjoined, the new converts abandoned the meeting-houses almost in mass, and
returned, with frantic ardor, to their once prohibited heathen sports! Many of the missionaries complain of this
sad defection in their letters published in this country.

I wish I could stop here; but there is yet a darker shade
to the picture. The Protestant missionaries were not content with imposing upon the natives, for a number of years,
the intolerable yoke of a forced religious conformity, but
they disgraced themselves with the crime of persecution.
The first Catholic missionaries, three in number, reached
the Islands in 1826; and their labors were soon crowned
with the most complete success. But after two or three
years they were forcibly driven from the Islands, at the instigation of the *American* missionaries, who had themselves

come from the boasted land of *freedom!* Other Catholic missionaries who visited the Islands in 1837, met with the same
unchristian treatment. They were placed in a rickety
vessel, wholly unseaworthy, and were thus compelled to
leave the field of their labors.

After their sudden and constrained departure, a most unchristian and inhuman persecution was carried on against
the converts they had made. According to the testimony
of the two local Protestant journals above referred to,
Catholic women and children were condemned to carry
burdens and to work on the public highways, like condemned criminals! The cruel sufferings they endured for
the *crime* of having listened to the Catholic missionaries,
and the additional circumstance that those sufferings were
inflicted at the instigation of *Christian* missionaries, natives
of a free Republic, and in the nineteenth century, would
seem almost incredible, were not all these facts vouched for
by eye-witnesses of undoubted veracity.

The Catholic missionaries who had been last expelled,
were natives of France, and the French government resolved to reinstate them, on the ground that their expulsion
had taken place against the laws of nations. Captain La
Place was sent out for this purpose in a French frigate, and
he succeeded in accomplishing his enterprise, and in com-
pelling the local authorities, under the surveillance of the
missionaries, to grant free toleration to Catholics;—for he
asked nothing more in their behalf. This fact presents to
our view a curious commentary on the boasted liberality of
Protestants, and the alleged intolerance of Catholics in the
nineteenth century. It points our attention to Protestant
missionaries openly advocating and carrying out principles
of persecution, and to a Catholic government standing forth
the champion of religious liberty!

What now ensued in the Sandwich Islands may serve to
show us the boasted stability of the Protestant converts
there made, as well as the relative success of the Catholic
and Protestant modes of securing conversion. In less than
five years after this act of free toleration, ninety Catholic

chapels were erected in the Islands, three thousand children were in regular attendance in the Catholic schools, and fourteen thousand converts were made! These are remarkable, too, for their industry, honesty, and progress in civilization, according to the testimony of travelers of undoubted veracity. Catholicity is now evidently rapidly gaining the ascendency in those Islands, while Protestantism is as certainly on the decline.

From all these undoubted facts, it may easily be gathered, that the Sandwich Islands are the last place in the world to which Protestantism should point with complacency, as to a field where its missionary labors have been crowned with success, and blessed by Almighty God with an abundant harvest of souls.

10. Still less can Protestants boast of their missionary success in Oregon, another field which their organs not long since proclaimed as already "white for the harvest." Here, too, their missions for the conversion of the Indians promised much at first, and at last ended in nothing. The Methodist mission, which, in 1840, *promised* to convert the entire country, was suddenly broken up in 1844, when all its extensive property was sold, and its ministers were dismissed.* Captain Wilkes had already borne ample evidence to its utter barrenness of all success; while he, at the

---

* The American religious public was highly amused and edified by the perusal of a letter written some years ago by sister Susan Gary of the Methodist mission in Oregon. The letter is dated "William Fleetalts, July 24, 1844," and is addressed to Mrs. Lane. We refer to it, because it is a pretty good specimen of this species of correspondence. She thanks her sister in New York for a present of "preserved meats and sardines," and adds: "I do not know how I could have been comfortable without them." Speaking of the young females who had been sent out by the Society, she admits that the object for which they came,—the instruction of the Indians,—had failed, but says; "they are unwearied in well doing. I have become acquainted with three of the females who came out single, *but married since their arrival.* They have married well, and will be as useful, and I think much more so, than if they had remained single." She says also, that some pious young gentlemen would have married, had they not concluded " to wait for the right one to come!"

same time, had spoken in the highest terms of the brilliant success which had crowned the Catholic missions.*

But while the Protestant missions of Oregon, notwithstanding the large amounts expended on them, have thus proved a signal failure, the Catholic missionaries in the same country, with little other means at their command than prayer, zeal, and the blessing of God, have made, in a very few years, more than six thousand converts among the Indians, have erected fourteen churches, founded one college for young men, and two flourishing female academies. With sixteen zealous missionaries in the field, this flourishing mission bids fair to bring into the one fold all the hundred and ten thousand Indians who dwell in different parts of that territory.†

11. From the facts and evidence thus far exhibited, I think, my Dear Brethren, you will agree with me in the opinion, that the Protestant missions, notwithstanding the immense outlay of money and other signal advantages with which they were undertaken and prosecuted, have proved singularly barren and fruitless, even in those countries where they at first promised the most brilliant success. How are we to explain this strange phenomenon? There must surely be something wrong somewhere; else this gigantic missionary enterprise would not have been thus doomed to failure, after having been commenced and carried on with so much labor and at so great a cost. The signal failure of Protestant missionary effort may be traced to a combination of causes, which, taken together, may sufficiently explain what might seem otherwise wholly inexplicable.

---

* See his "Exploring Expedition," vol. 4, p. 822, and Ibid. p. 850, 1, 2. Also Ibid. p. 815. Speaking of the boasted Protestant mission at Willamette, he says: "About all the premises of this mission there was an evident want of attention required to keep things in repair, and an absence of neatness that I regretted to witness. We had the expectation of getting a sight of the Indians on whom they were inculcating good habits, and teaching the word of God; but with the exception of four Indian servants, we saw none since leaving the Catholic missions." Ibid p. 851, 2.

† For these details, see the Catholic Almanac for 1846, in which there is also an interesting paper on Oregon.

Among these causes may be enumerated, to* worldly a spirit among the missionaries, connected with a too great reliance on money and mere worldly means for converting the heathen nations; and the additional circumstance that the missionaries are, for the most part, married men, whose zeal is cramped, and whose efforts are often wholly paralyzed by the continued solicitude necessarily consequent on the care of a family. A married missionary cannot undergo the labor, nor expose himself to the dangers, which one that is single might fearlessly endure and encounter. Even some of the missionary societies are beginning to perceive this, and to prefer single men for foreign missions.*

While on this subject, I will relate two or three characteristic incidents. The Rev. Mr. Kidder, lately sent out to Brazil by the Methodist missionary society, to distribute bibles and to make converts among the Roman Catholics of that empire, tells us himself, that he was compelled, by the sudden death of his wife, abruptly to break off his mission,—at the very moment too that he had learned the Portuguese language and prepared himself to be useful;—and to return forthwith to the United States, in order to preserve the life of an infant child.† Thus also, we read in a late number of the "New York Observer,"‡ that the Rev. Mr. Shuck, for many years a missionary in China, was compelled to return to the United States, in order to attend to the education of his children, whom he could not find it in his heart to rear up among heathens! And in the same standard Protestant print, I recollect to have read, some years ago, a lengthy article, written with a view to show the expediency of married missionaries returning from their respective fields of labor after a certain number of years, for the same purpose of providing for the Christian education of their offspring.

Another reason why Protestant missions among the

* Thus, a Synod lately held in Connecticut took precisely this view of the case, and enacted accordingly.
† "Sketches of Brazil," vol. ii. p. 352, 3.
‡ In a number for January, 1846.

pagans are so very fruitless, may be the fact, that they are conducted by men of different denominations, who preach different doctrines, and thus bewilder the minds of those to whom they address the gospel truths. The poor heathen idolaters, on finding their religious teachers thus quarreling among themselves, and preaching contradictory systems of Religion, are apt to answer them as the famous Seneca chief Red Jacket is reported to have answered the Protestant missionaries under similar circumstances; which was substantially as follows:—I have held a talk with my people, and our talk to you is this: go home, and agree among yourselves about the talk you are making to us, then come back, and we will listen to you.*

Still another reason may be found for the failure, in the complex and inverted method the Protestant missionary is compelled to employ in his instruction of the heathen people. He must first tell his simple-minded hearers, that Christ established a Church, and died on the cross to seal the truth of its doctrines with His blood; then that His Church became corrupt and continued so for many centuries, until some men were specially sent by God to restore it to its original purity; and, if he be entirely honest, he should next add, that, in carrying out the work of reformation, those men sent by God sadly disagreed among themselves, and gave to the world, instead of the old Religion, a hundred new but jarring creeds. If the simple heathen can understand all this, he is much shrewder and wiser than the great majority of intelligent Christians. The Catholic missionary, on the contrary, begins at the beginning, and tells a plain, straightforward, unvarnished, and consistent story, which the pagan can readily understand and easily appreciate.

But the principal reason of the almost total failure of Protestant missions among heathen nations, is undoubtedly to be found in the fact, that they do not attempt to convert

---

* See the splendid work on the Indians, by Col. McKinley and Judge Hall—Life of Red Jacket—which I quote from memory, not having the work before me.

the world *by the means* which Christ originally ordained, but by others of more recent origin, and of their own devising, upon which *He* never pronounced a blessing, and to which He never promised success. Protestant missionaries do not rely so much upon *preaching*, as upon the distribution of bibles and tracts, which not one in a thousand of the heathens can understand or even read; they are not *sent* to preach by those who are the heirs of the men that first received the commission to teach all nations; they act not in communion with the one Church of all ages and of all nations, and therefore, they act not in concert with Christ who is the great Head of that Church. He had said: "He that is not with me, is against me; AND HE THAT GATHERETH NOT WITH ME SCATTERETH:"—and the failure of Protestant missionary enterprise is a remarkable commentary on this saying.

How, in fact, can men hope for success, who labor not for unity, but for the perpetuation and propagation of disunion and sectarianism? Can a general lawfully fight for his country with a view to extend its territory by conquest, without a regular commission to this effect from its executive, duly delivered and properly authenticated? Did he attempt to do so, would he not be branded as a rebel, and would not his acts be disavowed? And how can a Christian undertake, with any prospect of success, to extend the dominions of his spiritual country, the Church of Christ, without a legitimate commission from the regularly constituted authorities of that country? "HOW CAN THEY PREACH UNLESS THEY BE SENT?" As a late eloquent writer* has well remarked, the Church is the spouse of Christ, and the only fruitful mother of his children, and those who have disavowed her and separated themselves from her household, are doomed to a perpetual sterility; or, as St. Cyprian had said before him, as early as the third century, "no one can have God for his Father, who has not the Church for his mother."

11. ALL THE NATIONS WHICH HAVE EVER BEEN CONVERTED FROM PAGANISM TO CHRISTIANITY, HAVE BEEN SO CONVERTED BY THE CATHOLIC CHURCH.

---

* De Maistre.

Let me now briefly invite your attention, my Beloved Brethren, to what the Catholic Church has done for the conversion of the world,—the great object contemplated by Jesus Christ when He gave the Commission, and the one nearest and dearest to His heart. If I prove to you, that the Catholic Church has executed that Commission, by constantly promoting and actually securing the conversion of all the nations who have ever passed from paganism to Christianity, I will have completed the basis of my argument, and furnished you with one more conclusive evidence that the Catholic is the only true Church of Christ. I hope to establish this proposition by incontrovertible historical testimony; though the subject is so vast, that I can hope to do little more at present than to glance rapidly at its most prominent facts and features. I shall, however, allege no fact that is not indisputable, and which is not admitted even by our adversaries themselves.

1. And first, to preclude the possibility of cavil, let me state,—what every one at all conversant with Church history will know to be an undoubted historical fact,—that the Greeks and Latins were united in one Catholic Church in communion with Rome during the first eight centuries and a half of the Christian era, until the period of the Greek schism brought about by Photius towards the middle of the ninth century; and even, with the exception of a few years of interrupted communion, for two centuries later, until the final consummation of that schism in the eleventh century, under Michael Cerularius, bishop of Constantinople. Bearing this important fact in mind, it is manifest that all the nations which were converted from paganism to Christianity during all that long period, whether converted through the agency of the Greek or the Latin branch of the great Catholic Church, were really brought to a knowledge of the truth by the operation of the very principle for which I am now contending. It matters not for our argument, whether the missionaries who acted as agents of divine Providence in bringing about this conversion, were sent immediately and directly by Rome; or acted under the broad

seal of a commission tacitly sanctioned and approved by Rome, because legitimately derived from the proper authorities in the Catholic Church which was in communion with Rome.

2. Another important consideration must be carefully borne in mind. According to the original intention of Christ, the Conversion of the Nations to His Religion was not necessarily to take place all at once, but was to be, or at least might be, *progressive*. As the Saviour himself expressed it : " Penance and the remission of sins was to be preached in His name among all nations, beginning at Jerusalem."* Making Jerusalem their starting point, the apostles and their successors in the holy ministry, acting under the ample powers bestowed by the original Commission given to them by Jesus Christ, were to preach the gospel successively to all nations; and Christ had promised "to be with them" preaching and teaching, and to crown their labors with success, " all days, even to the consummation of the world."

3. The stupendous progress of Christianity during the first three centuries, notwithstanding the appalling and, humanly speaking, insurmountable difficulties which resisted its propagation, and threatened it daily and hourly with annihilation, is well known and fully recognized by all. Not more than twenty-four years had elapsed since the date of the Commission, when St. Paul could boldly assert, in the face of the whole world, that the magnificent prophecies of the old testament concerning the universal dominion of the Christian Religion, were already on the eve of being completely fulfilled: "But I say; have they (the nations) not heard? Yes verily, their sound (of the apostles)· went over all the earth, and their words unto the end of the whole world." † And, in the same epistle, he could, even at that early date, utter these words of eulogy in regard to the Roman Christians: "First I give thanks to my God through Jesus Christ for you all ; *because your*

---

* St. Luke, xxiv: 47.   † Romans, x: 18.

faith is spoken of in the whole world.''   As Eusebius informs
us, the apostles divided out the whole world among them,
and traversed it like conquerors, bearing every where with
them, and planting in triumph, the glorious banner of the
cross; and all of them, except St. John, who was proof
against martyrdom, watered it with their own heart's blood.

The second and third centuries present to our view the
cheering prospect of a still wider extension of Christianity.
The blood of the martyrs, which during this period flowed
like water, was, in the language of Tertullian, a fruitful
seed† cast upon the earth, which took deep roots, grew
luxuriantly, and produced abundant fruits.   For one Christian struck down in the ranks of this ever increasing army
of the Lord, a thousand new champions sprang forth, armed
for the contest, and prepared to lay down their lives for
Christ.   "We are but of yesterday," says Tertullian to the
authorities of pagan Rome, "and we have overspread your
empire.   Your cities, your islands, your forts, your towns,
and your assemblies,—your very armies, wards, companies,
tribes, palaces, senate, and forum, swarm with Christians.
We have left nothing but your temples to yourselves."‡
"Now the various tribes of the Getulians and Moors, in all
parts of Spain and Gaul, and amongst the Sarmatians, Daci;
Germans, and Scythians, and the territories of the Britons,
which were inaccessible to the Romans, are subject to the
religion of Jesus Christ;"§—is the public testimony of the
same energetic writer.

The same consoling truth is attested by other cotemporary writers.   Thus St. Justin, Martyr, says: "There is no
race of men, whether Greeks or barbarians, or of whatever
other denomination, amongst whom prayers and Eucharist
are not offered up to the Father and Maker of all things, in
the name of Jesus crucified."|| And St. Irenæus not only
bears evidence to this result, but clearly points to *the means*
by which it was brought about: "As the sun is one and the

* Romans i: 8.   † Sanguis Martyrum, semen Christianorum.
‡ Apologet. c. 37.   § Contra Judæos, c. 7.
|| Dialog. cum. Tryphone.

same in the whole universe, so also the faith, disseminated throughout the whole world, is kept with great care one and the same: for, though in the world there is a variety of languages, yet the *virtue of tradition* is the same in Germany, Spain, Gaul, Egypt, and Lybia. The light of THE PREACHING of the truth every where shines and enlightens all men who are willing to come to a knowledge of the truth!" *

4. For long centuries had pagan Rome been extending her conquests, and it was only by slow degrees that she finally became the mistress of the world. The march of Christianity was much more rapid, and its conquests were much more extended and permanent. With giant strides it suddenly overstepped the boundaries of the Roman empire, and, planted the cross in triumph among nations over whose heads the Roman eagles had never floated. Sprung from heaven, and established by Him to whom "all power was given in heaven and on earth," it claimed and received the whole world for its inheritance. Pagan Rome had risen up in her colossal strength to crush it under her iron heel; but pagan Rome was made to bite the dust, and the divine system which she had endeavored to annihilate at its very birth, was destined to sway the destinies of the world. The cross of Jesus, long despised and down-trodden by the rulers of the earth, was destined to surmount the highest pinnacles of the Roman monuments, and to glitter, as a priceless ornament, in the coronals of Roman emperors and empresses. God had so willed it, and all human opposition melted away before *His* lofty purpose. The "Lion of the tribe of Juda" conquered; Constantine became a convert to Christianity; the Church, hitherto opposed and persecuted, came forth from the darkness of the catacombs into the full light of day, and dazzled the world by the brilliancy of her worship, and the richness of her temples, and the splendor of her ceremonial.

5. But she was not content to have been thus crowned

---

queen of imperial Rome; she panted for new conquests;
she could not be at rest so long as one single nation remained without her fold, buried in the darkness of paganism.   Two more nations were added to her wide dominions
in the fourth century—the Ethiopians and the Iberians—
the former dwelling in the heart of Africa, and the latter
along the borders of the Euxine Sea. St. Frumentius, consecrated bishop of the Ethiopians by that great champion
of Catholic orthodoxy, St. Athanasius, and acting under the
authority of a commission regularly given by the holy
Catholic Church, finally succeeded in bringing that people
into the great Catholic fold;* while Catholic bishops, sent
out from Constantinople at the instance of the great Constantine, and armed with similar powers from the Church,
were blessed with like success among the Iberians.† .

6. The succeeding centuries present to us the same consoling prospect of nation after nation successively entering
into the Catholic fold, under the *preaching* of apostles *sent
forth* by the Catholic Church, teaching her doctrines, and
acting in her communion. But before I proceed farther in
the very rapid sketch allowed by the limits of the Lecture,
I must first meet an objection of some apparent plausibility,
which may be alleged against the principle for which I am
now contending. It is asserted, that many nations were
converted to Christianity, especially among the northern
tribes, by the Arians, in the fourth and fifth centuries; and
that the Nestorians, at a later period, also made many similar conquests in the heart of Asia.‡ The missions under
the auspices of these sects, you will say, were certainly not
sanctioned by the Catholic Church, from whose communion
they had been justly excluded. How are we to explain this
fact? Is it not, at least, an exception to the general principle above laid down? I think not.

* See Ludolphus — Historia Ethiopiæ — and Fleury —Histoire Eccle-
siastique, L xi., o. 88.
† Fleury, *Ibid.* c. 89.
‡ For many facts on this subject, see Mr. Newman's late learned work,
"Essay on the Development of Christian Doctrine," ch. v.

It is not at all certain, that Ulphilas, the original apostle of the Goths, was infected with Arianism when he first preached to them the gospel of Christ, about the year 370: it was only in 375, after the nation had probably already embraced Christianity, that he and his converts turned Arians, in order to please the emperor Valens, and to obtain from him a grant of lands within the borders of the empire. Once infected with the Arian heresy, the Goths spread the infection among the kindred tribes of the north, partly by appealing to their self-interest and innate hatred of Rome, which had always proved the strongest bulwark of Catholicity; and partly through the extension of their conquests by force of arms. This method of propagating their heresy certainly had no affinity with that established by Christ, and as certainly presents no valid argument against our position. Besides, these spiritual conquests were not permanent; they were doomed to the fate predicted by the Saviour of all mere human enterprises: "Every plant which my heavenly Father hath not planted, shall be rooted up."* The Arian Goths and Vandals were soon re-converted to Catholicity; and Arianism, which had received its birth in a corner of Africa, was destined to find also its tomb in Africa, two centuries later. All vestiges of it disappeared with the extinction of the Vandal kingdom founded in Northern Africa by the ferocious Huneric.

The case of the conversions alleged to have been made by the Nestorians is more difficult. But, besides that there probably exists much exaggeration as to their extent and durability, we must not fail to bear in mind that those heretics professed the Catholic faith in every thing but one or two points, chiefly of a speculative nature; and that they had at least *valid* orders, if they had not a *lawful* mission from the Catholic Church. Our dissenting brethren of the present day cannot surely look to them for a precedent in the work of successful conversion of heathen nations, unless they be disposed to believe as they believed.

---

* St. Matthew, xv: 13.

The spiritual conquests of the Nestorians, whatever might have been their original extent, have all vanished centuries ago; and the sect itself has almost disappeared with them. Their case, then, presents but another remarkable fulfillment of the declaration of Jesus Christ above recorded; and it cannot be pleaded, any more than that of the Arian Goths and Vandals, as a valid objection to the principle which I am now advocating.

7. After the pagan empire of Rome in the West had fallen under the shocks of successive invasions by the northmen in the fifth and following centuries, the Church arose, clad in new splendor, amid its ruins, and extended forth her arms for new spiritual conquests. In the great panorama of Church history, we behold the new dynasties established all over Europe by these ferocious conquerors, entering successively into the ever extending fold of Catholic Christianity. Not a century elapsed from the fifth to the eleventh, that was not signalized by the conversion of one or another of those nations of the North, to which all the kingdoms of modern Europe owe their origin. And it is a remarkable feature in all these progressive conversions, that they were accomplished, *in every instance*, not only by apostles regularly sent by the Roman Catholic Church, but, almost without an exception, by missionaries sent *directly* by Rome. Thus, they all furnish us with ample evidence sustaining the truth of our principle in all its bearings.

In the early part of the fifth century, Ireland was converted by St. Patrick, sent out by Pope Celestine I.; and, towards the close of the same century, the Franks were converted, with their king Clovis, by St. Remigius, bishop of Rheims. At the close of the following century, England was converted by St. Augustine and his forty monks, sent out by Pope St. Gregory the Great. In the seventh age, St. Kilian, commissioned for this purpose by Pope Conon, converted the Franconians; St. Swidbert, and St. Willibrord, the Frislanders, the Brabanters, the Hollanders, and the lower Germans; and St. Rupert, the Bohemians. In the eighth, St. Boniface, the great apostle of Germany, received his mission from the hands of the second Pope Gregory, and, with St. Virgilius and other colleagues, converted the Hessians, the Thuringians, and the Bavarians; and extended his spiritual conquests into another portion of Friesland, where, in 755, he suffered a glorious martyrdom, together with fifty-two of his apostolical co-laborers.

The good work went steadily on in the ninth century. St. Gallus preached the gospel among the Swiss. St. Adalbert carried the gospel into Prussia; and St. Ludger, afterwards bishop of Munster, into Saxony and Westphalia. About the year 830, St. Anscarius, archbishop of Hamburg and Bremen, after having converted a great number of the Danes to Christianity, penetrated into Sweden, and planted the cross in triumph amidst the most remote fastnesses of the Northmen. The course of spiritual conquest moved eastward as well as northward. Two holy brothers, Saints Cyril and Methodius, acting under the sanction of Pope John VIII., extended the kingdom of Christ into Slavonia, Moravia, and Russia, and made a convert of Michael, king of the Bulgarians.

Their labors were continued by other apostolical men in the tenth century, which witnessed the almost complete conversion of the Muscovites, the Gothlanders, and the Poles, and the yet farther extension of the gospel into Denmark and Sweden. In the beginning of this century, the first Normans embraced the faith, with their valiant king Roland; and at the commencement of the eleventh, the Hungarians came into the Christian fold, with their sainted king Stephen.

Thus was Christianity firmly and permanently established among all the different tribes and families of the north who had crushed the Roman empire in the west, and had built up their new dynasties amidst its crumbling ruins. The Northmen conquered the Roman eagles; but the cross of Christian Rome conquered the Northmen. For two centuries and more, the inexhaustible North had poured forth invading army after invading army, who had carried

the tide of conquest to the farthest South,—to Italy, to
Sicily, to Spain, to Africa; for five centuries afterwards, a
counter tide of a far more glorious, because a bloodless and
stainless conquest, continued to roll in the opposite direction, from south to north; nor did it cease until its waters
had washed away the defilements of those fierce and truc-
culent destroyers of the ancient empire in the laver of regeneration. Pagan Rome had been the goal of all those
barbarian incursions, as well as the glittering prize at
which they all aimed; Christian Rome became the center
of the counter current of spiritual conquest;—the radiating
point of the new civilization which broke upon the dazzled
vision of the conquerors themselves. "The Germans," says
even the prejudiced and fanatical D'Aubigné, "had received from Rome that element of modern civilization, the
faith. Intruction, legislation,—all save their courage and
their weapons, had come to them from the sacerdotal city.
Strong ties had, from that time, attached Germany to the
papacy." *   It is a beautiful sight thus to behold Christian
Rome repaying evil by good, requiting the most atrocious
insults and injuries by the free bestowal of the greatest and
most lasting blessings. †

8. Did the narrow limits of this Lecture allow of the
necessary details, I might very easily show you, my Beloved
Brethren, how during the twelfth and following centuries
down to the sixteenth, the limits of the Church were gradually extended; how the work of conversion constantly went
on in those various countries of northern Europe into which
the gospel had been successively introduced, until scarcely
an infidel remained in all those vast regions; and how, not
satisfied with its conquests in Europe, the fearless and untiring missionary zeal of the Catholic Church penetrated
into the very heart of Asia and Africa, following, and even

---

* History of the Reformation. Book i: p. 78, 9.

† For the facts above given, and many others of the same kind, together with copious details of a most edifying and consoling character,
see that excellent work, "Catechism de la Perseverance," in 8 vols. 8vo.,
vols. v, and vi: and Church historians *passim.*

frequently anticipating the progress of exploration and discovery, announcing the glad tidings of salvation wherever
any prospect of success presented itself, and often, too,
where no such prospect existed.

It would furnish us with a most interesting and consoling subject of reflection, to trace the missionary labors of
the Franciscans and Dominicans in Asia, as far even as the
country inhabited by the great Khan of the Tartars, during
the thirteenth and following centuries; to relate the number
of those devoted men who willingly laid down their lives
for the truth during this memorable period; to recount the
great number of converts they every-where made; to show,
in a word, how well they profited by all the discoveries
made in those regions by Marco Polo and other intrepid
Italian travelers and navigators, and how much they added
to the amount of information Europe already possessed in
relation to them. But I should be endless, were I to enter
into all these details. Besides, it is unnecessary for the
present argument to do so; those topics are already familiar
to all the readers of Church history, and there exists no
doubt whatever in regard either to the facts themselves, or
to the important feature by which they are all alike marked; I mean, the circumstance, that all those glorious missionary enterprises were originated by Rome, and were
carried on by men who had received their mission from the
Roman Pontiffs.*

9. The sixteenth century at length dawned upon the world,
the harbinger of a revolution which was destined to shake
religious society to its very center, and to threaten its
almost total disorganization, if not annihilation. Christian
Rome wept, as she saw many of those nations of the North,
to which her missionaries had first announced the gospel of
Christ, violently wrested from her bosom; by men, too, who
had been reared under her own fostering care, but who had

---

* See, among the ecclesiastical historians who furnish all the evidence
on this subject, *Becchetti*—Storia Ecclesiastica—a continuation of Cardinal Orsi's Church History. Seculo xiii, xiv, &c. Also, Fleury, Bercastel,
and Rohrbacher.

abandoned her altars, and had boldly raised the standard of revolt against her time-honored authority. The reformation, so called, robbed her, in a few short years, of many of those spiritual conquests which she had been engaged for centuries in making and consolidating, at the price of the labor and blood of so many among her most devoted missionaries.

Nay more; a new invasion of the Northmen threatened to roll back the tide of conquest to her very gates, and to bury herself beneath its angry waters. For nearly fifty years, her very existence seemed to be in danger; "the princes" of the north "raged against her and the people meditated foolish things;" they said they "would break her bonds and cast off her yoke:" but "God who dwelleth in heaven, laughed at" their puny efforts!* The reaction came; the "great defection" ceased to extend its ravages; and even many who had been thoughtlessly carried away by its first enthusiasm, in their cooler moments re-entered the Catholic pale. Austria, Bavaria, Bohemia, and several of the minor German States, which had at first bid fair to swell the ranks of the opposition, finally took their stand on the side of conservative Catholicity; they subsequently consoled the Church by their steadfastness in the ancient faith, and even proved her most valiant champions in this the hour of her greatest peril.†

What is more remarkable still, when so many of her own children had revolted against her at home, Rome turned to the gentiles, and directed her missionary zeal towards those heathen nations in the extreme east and in the extreme west, inhabiting countries which had just been discovered by the enterprise of her navigators. It would appear, indeed, that divine Providence at this period specially watched over her preservation and her extension to all the nations of the earth, with the conversion of which Jesus

---

* See Psalm ii: 1, 4.

† For Protestant testimony on this important feature in the history of the reformation, see Ranke, "History of the Papacy," &c., ii: 46, seqq., and Hallam's "Introduction to Literature," &c., i: 272, seqq.

Christ had specially charged her. At the very time that the reformation was raging most in Europe, her St. Francis Xavier and his apostolical associates converted millions of heathens to her faith in Hindostan, in the East Indies, and in Japan, in the far East; and her Olmedos, her Las Casas, and her other devoted missionaries, brought tens of millions of the Mexican and South American aborigines into her vast and ever extending fold, in the far West. In Mexico alone, according to the statement of Torribio, an eye-witness and one of the missionaries employed in the good work, the number of converts from idolatry made during the first twenty years after the conquest was estimated at twenty-nine millions.*

Thus, the Catholic Church became more extended after than she had been before the reformation; and her losses in Europe were more than compensated by her gains in Asia and in America. How can this singular fact be explained on any other principle, than by admitting that Christ was with her "all days," according to His own solemn promise, and that He watched over her safety and threw around her the panoply of His own strength, to enable her still to discharge the commission "to teach all nations?" We can explain it in no other way, without doing violence to the plainest principles of reason and of Christian philosophy. To say that it was the result of mere chance, would be worse than paganism itself.

10. I might continue this rapid and necessarily imperfect sketch even down to the present day, and show you the actual extent, the vital energy, and the brilliant success of Catholic missions in all parts of the world. I might point you to the splendid conquests made among the North American Indians by the early Jesuit missionaries;† and more recently by Father De Smet and his indefatigable asso-

---

* See Prescott's admirable "Conquest of Mexico," vol. iii: p. 267. The historian thinks this account exaggerated, but he does not prove that it is so. He deals rather in conjecture than in facts on this subject.

† For abundant details on this subject, the American reader is referred to the third volume, ch. xx., of Bancroft's United States.

ciates.* I might direct your attention to our missionary
success in China during the last two centuries and a half,
often in the face of a most bloody persecution, and of obstacles, humanly speaking, wholly insuperable; as well as to
the brighter prospects for the future in that empire, now
that the iron wall of separation, which had for long centuries shut out the celestial empire from the "outside barbarians," has been broken down by the English cannon.

I might prove to you that, with means apparently wholly
inadequate to the enterprise of converting the world, with
much less money and much fewer missionaries† than the
Protestant societies, our efforts for converting the heathen
have every-where been crowned with a success as complete
as that of our adversaries has been slender.‡ I might show
you flourishing Catholic colonies springing up under the
auspices of Catholic missionaries sent out by Rome, in Al-
geria, in New Holland, in New Zealand, and in all the principal Islands of Oceanica. But these details would lead me
too far; besides that Dr. Wiseman has already preoccupied
the ground. I refer those who wish for more ample information on a very interesting subject, to his seventh Lecture.

11. Surveying the ground thus far passed over, you can
not fail to have remarked a most singular feature which
has usually distinguished Catholic missionary enterprise in
every successive age. I refer to the *striking and prominent
fact* of Church history,—that the most remarkable and extensive conquests to Catholic Christianity were generally
made against all human probability, and at times when the
Church seemed to be in the greatest danger herself, and to
be threatened with total destruction, both from within and
from without. Thus, the rapid propagation of the gospel
during the first three centuries, took place in spite of the
herculean efforts made by the all-powerful and all-conquer-

* See Father De Smet's published work, and also his more recent letters
published in most of our Catholic papers.

† Dr. Wiseman estimates that the total number of missionaries annually
sent out by the Roman Propaganda does not exceed *ten.*

‡ See, for ample details on this subject, the "Lettres Edifiantes," and
the "Annales de la Propagation de la Foi," both published in France.

ing Roman empire to crush the Christian Religion at its
birth, and in the face of ten general persecutions, which
drenched the whole empire in Christian blood. Thus also,
the conversion of the Ethiopians and of the Iberians, in
the fourth century, took place precisely at the time when
Arianism was rending the bosom of the Church, waging
against her children a most fierce and bloody warfare, and
actually chanting her hymns of triumph over the boasted
annihilation of her orthodoxy.*

Thus again, when the northern hordes had spread desolation over the face of the Church; when she had to weep
over the death or dispersion of her children, the desecra-
tion or destruction of her temples, the burning of her libraries, and the seeming prostration of all her hopes; when a
new deluge was sweeping over the earth, burying beneath
its angry waters all that was best and brightest in Christendom;—at this very moment of her greatest desolation, God
bade her dry up her tears shed amid the ruins of His holy
sanctuary, gird on her spiritual armor, re-enter with renewed spirits and hopes the wide field of the nations, and
march on to new and brighter conquests than had ever,
perhaps, before signalized her glorious career. Thus, likewise, when the reformation came with its numerous and
wide-spread defections from her ranks, God opened to her
zeal a much wider field of conquest, bade her rise up in the
beauty and strength with which her divine Founder had
clothed her; and, like a giant awaked from slumber and
prepared with renewed energy to run his race, to stretch
forth her vigorous arms to the farthest East and to the
farthest West, and to grasp, in one hand America, and in
the other the Indies!

Thus, finally, when the French revolution broke over her,
like a terrible storm, destroying the lives of her priests, or
driving them into exile, dragging her venerable chief Pon-

---

* Ingemuit orbis, et se Arianum esse miratus est — "the world groaned,
and wondered at its having become Arian" — is the well known saying
of St. Jerome, in reference to the grievous fraud practiced on the Fathers
of the Council of Arimini by the unprincipled Arian bishops Ursacius
and Valens.

tiffs into captivity, pillaging her churches, or desecrating
them with the foulest orgies, breaking down her altars, and
scattering to the winds the ashes of her sanctuaries; when
every thing boded ruin and annihilation, and her enemies
were shouting their *io triumphes* amidst the ruins they had
caused; when Voltairism seemed on the eve of being substituted for Christianity; then it was, precisely, that the
Church manifested the most unconquerable energy; then it
was that, under the Providence of her ever watchful Head,
she not only retrieved her losses at home, but, through the
zeal of her exiled ministers, scattered far and wide over the
surface of the earth the fruitful seeds of new and glorious
conversions among the nations without her pale.

12. Who, that seriously reflects but for one moment on
these astonishing and thrilling incidents in her protracted,
various, and eventful history, will be disposed to ascribe all
these prodigies to mere contingency, or blind chance?
What Christian philosopher can seriously entertain the
thought, that her preservation and wonderful extension, in
the midst of all these reverses, can be accounted for on
merely human principles, and without supposing any divine
interposition?

One of the strongest and most persuasive evidences of
Christianity, is found in the remarkable and evidently
supernatural propagation of the Christian Religion, during
the long and bitter persecutions of the first three centuries;
and in the final triumph of her principles over the Roman
empire itself. I have here alleged, in a series of indisputable facts, a chain of evidence of precisely the same nature,
but much more ample and extended. I have endeavored
to extend the self-same argument to the universal history
of Catholic Christianity, at all times and in all places; and
I trust, my Dear Brethren, that I have shown an exact parallelism to it in the cases presented by the different ages,
both as to the means employed and the results obtained. Is
not the inference plain and irresistible?—that the Catholic
Church and Christianity are identical in principle and
essence, as they certainly were in point of fact during the

first fifteen centuries of Christian history. Or, is an argument valid to prove Christianity, and not valid, though even more striking and ample, to prove Catholicity?

The argument in favor of Catholicity, based upon what I have thus far proved, becomes still more cogent, and, in fact, conclusive, when we take into consideration the other parallel chain of facts already established in the preceding part of this Lecture, all going to prove that Protestantism did not at all fulfill the Commission to teach all nations, because, it did not convert a single nation from paganism to Christianity.

I have thus, I trust, my Dear Brethren, established by the clearest evidence the two facts required to be proved in the syllogism with which I set out at the commencement of this Lecture. The conclusion reached by that argument must then, necessarily, be admitted;—that the Catholic Church alone can claim to be the one true Church of Christ.

THIS IS THE SECOND EVIDENCE OF CATHOLICITY,—which is supplemental to the first.

But I hope to place this argument in a still clearer light in the next Lecture, when, if you will favor me with your attention, I trust to show that the progressive fulfillment of the Commission was in all ages accompanied and comfirmed by miracles, the sure evidences of the divine presence and approval, and the unquestionable seal of God himself impressed on the truth of the doctrines announced. This will constitute the Third Evidence of Catholicity.

May God grant to us all His holy light and grace, without which we cannot hope either to come to a knowledge of the truth, or to have the courage and strength necessary to embrace it when ascertained! May Jesus Christ, who died for our salvation on the cross, and who sincerely wishes that all men should be saved by coming to the knowledge of the truth, be Himself our Guide and our Teacher by His Holy Spirit, that we may all meet in the unity of the faith here, and may hereafter be permitted to join that mighty throng of the redeemed, who reign for ever with Christ in heaven! Amen.

11 *

APPENDIX TO LECTURE IV.

ON THE SANDWICH ISLANDS MISSION.

LEST any one should think that I have done injustice to the Protestant missionaries who have been laboring for so many years in the Sandwich Islands, or that I exaggerated aught in pronouncing the mission a complete failure, I will here give a few extracts from a very interesting work, published a few years ago in this country, and written by an intelligent American Protestant traveler. The work is entitled: "TYPEE, a peep at Polynesian life during a four months' residence in a valley of the Marquesas, &c.; by Herman Melville. New York; Wiley and Putnam, 1846." 1 vol. 12mo. pp. 325.

The author was an eye-witness of the facts he relates; and being a Protestant himself, it is not to be supposed that he cherished any feelings of prejudice against the Protestant missionaries of Polynesia. His testimony is the more valuable as it is recent, and affords us accurate information on the moral and religious condition of those Islands. *

In the preface to his publication, the author thus states his motives for giving to the world certain facts in regard to the Sandwich Islands mission:

"There are a few passages in the ensuing chapters, which may be thought to bear rather hard upon a Reverend order of men, the account of whose proceedings in different parts of the globe—transmitted to us through their own hands—very generally, and often very deservedly, receives high commendation. Such passages will be found, however, to be based upon facts admitting of no contradiction, and which have come immediately under the writer's cognizance. The conclusions deduced from these facts are unavoidable, and in stating them the author has been influenced by no feeling of animosity, either to the individuals themselves, or to that glorious cause which has not been always served by the proceedings of some of its advocates."—p. 8, 9.

He fully admits, and attempts to account for, the late rapid decrease in the population of the Sandwich Islands, in the following passage:

"It is to the looseness of the marriage tie that the late rapid decrease of the population of the Sandwich Islands and of Tahiti is in part to be ascribed. The vices and diseases introduced among these unhappy people, annually swell the ordinary mortality of the Islands, while, from the same cause, the originally small number of births is proportionally decreased. Thus the progress of the Hawaiians and Tahitians to utter extinction is accelerated in a sort of compound ratio."—p. 246.

He deplores the utter wretchedness of the inhabitants, and traces it to what he deems its true source, in the following strain:

"How little do some of these poor Islanders comprehend, when they look around them, that no inconsiderable part of their disasters originates in certain tea-party excitements, under the influence of which benevolent looking gentlemen in white cravats solicit alms, and old ladies in spectacles, and young ladies in sober russet gowns, contribute sixpences towards

---

* I believe that many of the passages which I shall proceed to quote have been expunged from later editions of the work!

the creation of a fund, the object of which is to ameliorate the spiritual condition of the Polynesians, but whose end has almost invariably been to accomplish their temporal destruction.

" Let the savages be civilized, but civilize them with benefits, and not with evils ; and let heathenism be destroyed, but not by destroying the heathen. The Anglo-Saxon hive have extirpated paganism from the greater part of the North American continent; but with it they have likewise extirpated the greater portion of the Red race. Civilization is gradually sweeping from the earth the lingering vestiges of paganism, and at the same time the shrinking forms of its unhappy worshipers.

"Among the Islands of Polynesia, no sooner are the images overturned, the temples demolished, and the idolaters converted into *nominal* Christians, than disease, vice, and premature death, make their appearance. The depopulated land is then recruited from the rapacious hordes of enlightened individuals, who settle themselves within its borders, and clamorously announce the progress of the truth. Neat villas, trim gardens, shaven lawns, spires and cupolas, arise, while the poor savage soon finds himself an interloper in the country of his fathers, and that too on the very site of the hut where he was born."—p. 247, 250.

After speaking of the manner in which the poor natives are robbed, in the name of Religion, of their lands, and deprived of their usual means of subsistence, so as to be brought to the very verge of starvation, he continues :

" But what matters all this? Behold the glorious result: The abominations of paganism have given way to the pure rites of the Christian worship,—the ignorant savage has been supplanted by the refined European. Look at Honolulu, the metropolis of the Sandwich Islands! A community of distinguished merchants and self-exiled heralds of the Cross, located on the very spot that twenty years ago was defiled by the presence of idolatry. What a subject for an eloquent Bible-meeting orator! Nor has such an opportunity for a display of missionary rhetoric been allowed to pass by unimproved!—But when these philanthropists send us such glowing accounts of one half of their labors, why does their modesty restrain them from publishing the other half of the good they have wrought! Not until I visited Honolulu, was I aware of the fact that the small remnant of the natives HAD BEEN CIVILIZED INTO DRAUGHT-HORSES, AND EVANGELIZED INTO BEASTS OF BURDEN. But so it is. They have been literally broken into the traces, and are harnessed to the vehicles of their spiritual instructors, like so many dumb brutes!"—p. 251.

He draws the following graphic sketch of an exhibition of the kind, setting forth the thorough degradation and brutalized condition of the natives, brought about by the missionaries themselves; and though it is somewhat long, we can not refrain from giving it entire. It will be perceived that the heroine of the incident is no less a personage than a missionary's wife!

"Among a multitude of similar exhibitions that I saw, I shall never forget a robust, red-faced, and very lady-like personage, a missionary's spouse, who day after day, for months together, took her regular airings in a little go-cart drawn by two of the Islanders, one an old gray-headed man, and the other a roguish stripling, both being, with the exception of the fig-leaf, as naked as when they were born. Over a level piece of road this pair of *draught* bipeds would go with a shambling, unsightly trot, the

youngster hanging back all the time like a knowing horse, while the old
hack plodded on and did all the work.

"Rattling along through the streets of the town in this stylish equipage,
the lady looks about as magnificently as any queen driven in state to her
coronation.   A sudden elevation and a sandy road, soon, however, disturb
her serenity.   The small wheels become imbedded in the loose sand,—the
old stager stands tugging and sweating, while the young one frisks about
and does nothing; not an inch does the chariot budge.   Will the tender-
hearted lady, who has left friends and home for the good of the souls of the
poor heathen, will she think a little about their bodies, and get out and
ease the wretched old man until the ascent is mounted?   Not she; she
could not dream of it.   To be sure, she used to think nothing of driving
the cows to pasture on the old farm in New England; but times have
changed since then.   So she retains her seat, and bawls out, 'Hookee!
hookee!' (pull, pull.)   The old gentleman, frightened at the sound, labors
away harder 'than ever; and the younger one makes a great show of
straining himself, but takes care to keep one eye on his mistress, in order
to know when to dodge out of harm's way.   At last the good lady loses all
patience; 'Hookee! hookee!'—and rap goes the heavy handle of her
huge fan over the naked skull of the old savage; while the young one shies
to one side, and keeps beyond its range.   'Hookee! hookee!' again she
cries—'hookee tata, kanaca!' (pull strong, men)—but all in vain, and she
is obliged in the end to dismount, and, sad necessity, actually to walk to
the top of the hill!

"At the town where this paragon of humility resides," he adds, "is a
spacious and elegant American chapel, where divine service is regularly
performed.   Twice every Sabbath, towards the close of the exercises, may
be seen a score or two of little wagons ranged along the railing in front of
the edifice, with two squalid native footmen in the livery of nakedness
standing by each, and waiting for the dismissal of the congregation to
draw their superiors home."—p. 251, 252.

This is, indeed, a sad picture of the utter wretchedness and debasement
to which the poor Sandwich Islanders have been reduced, by the very men,
too, who are for ever boasting of having already converted them to Christianity, and taught them the refinements of civilized life!   Such treatment
as this is well calculated to disgust the Island savages with Christianity,
as well as with their Christian instructors.   Instead of converting and
humanizing the natives, the missionaries must have suffered no little themselves from their contact with them; else, how can we explain the hard-
heartedness which induces their gentle spouses, who probably were patterns of womanly kindness in America, to practice such wanton cruelty
towards their fellow-men at the Sandwich Islands as the above picture
manifests?   The case of the missionary's wife does not appear to be a
solitary one, but rather a specimen of what is now deemed fashionable life
among the converted and civilized Sandwich Islanders!

Mr. Melville justly draws the following inference from what he saw with
his own eyes, while sojourning in those Islands:

"There is something apparently wrong in the practical operations of
the Sandwich Islands mission.   Those who from pure religious motives
contribute to the support of this enterprise, should take care to ascertain
that their donations, flowing through many devious channels, at last effect

their legitimate object, the conversion of the Hawaiians. I urge this, not because I doubt the moral probity of those who disburse these funds, but because I KNOW THAT THEY ARE NOT RIGHTLY APPLIED. To read pathetic accounts of missionary hardships, and glowing descriptions of conversions, and baptisms taking place beneath palm-trees, is one thing; and to go to the Sandwich Islands, and see the missionaries dwelling in picturesque and prettily furnished coral-rock villas, while the miserable natives are committing all sorts of immorality around them, is quite another."—p. 253, 254.

I might furnish many other extracts from the pages of the same author, in which he speaks incidentally of the doings of the Protestant missionaries at the Sandwich Islands, and throughout those of Polynesia. But I will confine myself to one or two more passages taken from an appendix to the work, which was written to vindicate Sir George Paulet for the temporary occupancy of the Sandwich Islands in 1843, and for his conduct while administering the government in the name of the British crown.

It appears that the worthy missionaries and their agents in the United States, had placed the whole matter in an erroneous and utterly false light; and Mr. Mélville undertakes to set it right before the American people. The cause of the displeasure of the British government was the refusal of the authorities at the Islands to offer any explanation for alleged ill-treatment of British residents, or to enter into any treaty by which they might be protected for the future.

Mr. Melville thus speaks of those persons who then had the ear of the king, and secretly directed his councils:

"High in the favor of the imbecile king at this time was one Dr. Judd, a sanctimonious apothecary-adventurer, who, with other kindred and influential spirits, was animated by an inveterate dislike of England. The ascendency of a junta of ignorant and designing Methodist elders in the councils of a half civilized king, ruling with an absolute sway over a nation just poising between barbarism and civilization, and exposed by the peculiarities of its relations with foreign states to unusual difficulties, was not precisely calculated to impart a healthy tone to the policy of the government."—p. 321, 322.

During the five months that Sir George Paulet held authority in the Islands, scenes of gross and universal immorality and iniquity were revealed, which the missionaries had taken special care to keep concealed from their American friends and patrons. Sir George's awful exposure of them in this respect probably brought down upon his devoted head the misrepresentations and calumnies with which our Protestant *religious* papers teemed at the time, and which Mr. Melville seeks to refute in the appendix. The missionaries had induced their weak and yielding tool, the king, to re-enact the old Blue Laws of Connecticut, and these laws were actually in force when Sir George Paulet reached the Islands! The fines upon licentiousness brought an immense income to the government, which thus fattened upon vice! This was, indeed, Mr. Melville assures us, the principal source of revenue!—p. 323.

The events which occurred at the Islands, when the British rear-admiral

I

Thomas visited them towards the close of 1848, and when he ceded them
back again to the local authorities, speak volumes in regard to the boasted
conversion, morality, and civilization of the Islanders. The king Kam-
mahamaha III. was again solemnly proclaimed sovereign of the Islands;
and a scene of rioting and debauchery took place on the joyous occasion,
such as we have seldom read of in the annals of the most brutalized heathen
country under the sun!

"Royal proclamations in English and Hawaiian were placarded in the
streets of Honolulu, and posted up in the more populous villages of the
group, in which his majesty announced to his loving subjects the re-estab-
lishment of his throne, and called upon them to celebrate it by breaking
through all moral, legal, and religious restraint, for ten consecutive days,
during which time all the laws of the land were solemnly declared to be
suspended. Who that happened to be at Honolulu during those ten memorable days will ever forget them! The spectacle of universal broad-day
debauchery, which was then exhibited, beggars description. The natives
of the surrounding Islands flocked to Honolulu by hundreds, and the crews
of two frigates, opportunely let loose like so many demons to swell the hea-
thenish uproar, gave the crowning flourish to the scene. It was a sort of
Polynesian Saturnalia. Deeds too atrocious to be mentioned were done at
noonday in the open street, and some of the Islanders caught in the very
act of stealing from the foreigners, were, on being taken to the fort by the
aggrieved party, suffered immediately to go at large and retain the stolen
property—Kekuanoa (the governor) informing the white men, with a sar-
donic grin, that the laws were 'hampa'—(tied up.)

"The history of these ten days reveals in their true colors the character
of the Sandwich Islanders, and furnishes an eloquent commentary on the
results which have flowed from the labors of the missionaries. Freed
from the restraints of severe penal laws, the natives almost to a man had
plunged voluntarily into every species of wickedness and excess, and, by
their utter disregard of all decency, plainly showed that, although they
had been schooled into a seeming submission to the new order of things,
they were in reality as depraved and vicious as ever."—p. 325.

Such being, from the testimony of an unexceptionable eye-witness, the
wretched moral condition of the Sandwich Islanders, and such their brutal
degradation in the scale of civilization, was I not right in saying, in the
preceding Lecture, that they had not risen either in civilization or in
morals, under the teaching of the Protestant missionaries? Might I not
even have said—what these startling facts clearly prove—that the Sandwich Islands mission, so much extolled by our Protestant religious press,
has really turned out, not only the most complete failure, but also the
greatest imposition that was ever practised on the pious credulity of a
generous and confiding religious public? Had I said this, I would have
been fully borne out by the facts of the case. The very name of the Sandwich Islands should make every sincere and candid Protestant Christian
blush for his missionaries stationed there, and cause him to acknowledge
at once the utter powerlessness of Protestantism to convert a single nation
from heathenism to Christianity.

LECTURE V.

MIRACLES.—THE THIRD EVIDENCE OF CATHOLICITY.

Text explained — Miracles a sure criterion of truth — Various definitions of a Miracle — Those of Hume and Locke exploded — That of Bishop Hay adopted — How to distinguish a true Miracle — Four principles to guide us — The issue between Catholics and Protestants — Has the age of Miracles ceased? — Objections and cavils met — Presumptive evidence for the continuation of Miracles — Positive evidence — The testimony on the subject sifted — And found to possess all the characteristics of truth — The process for the canonization of saints analysed — Its slowness and extreme rigor — Incident— Miracles of St. Francis Xavier examined and vindicated — Objections against them answered— The argument resumed — Conclusion — Third evidence of Catholicity.

"And He said to them : Go ye into the whole world, and preach the gospel to every creature. He that believeth and is baptized, shall be saved; but he that believeth not, shall be condemned. And these signs shall follow them that believe : in my name they shall cast out devils ; they shall speak with new tongues ; they shall take up serpents ; and if they shall drink any deadly thing, it shall not hurt them ; they shall lay their hands on the sick, and they shall recover. . . . . But they going forth preached every-where: the Lord co-operating with them, and confirming the word with signs that followed."— St. Mark, xvi: 15, seqq.

Such, my Beloved Brethren, is the language employed by one of the inspired evangelists, in the account he furnishes us of the Commission given by our blessed Lord to His apostles, to preach the gospel, and to establish His holy Religion every-where throughout the world. You see that the solemn promise of miraculous powers accompanies the Commission itself; that, in the view of our Saviour, Miracles were to be to His first appointed heralds of the truth the seals of their apostleship, and the conclusive evidence to the world that their mission was derived from God, and was sanctioned by God; and that, accordingly, their preaching was every-where followed and confirmed by miraculous signs and wonders. It is evident, then, from the words of Christ, that Miracles were to be the constant accompaniments of that preaching by which the heathen nations were

(131)

to be brought to a knowledge of Christianity, as well as one
of the principal and most effectual means of bringing about
their conversion. If the language of Christ imply not all
this, it implies nothing.

It is agreed on all hands among Christians, that Miracles
are a certain criterion of truth, and that the system in
favor of which they are wrought must be true and divine.
Hence they are invariably put forward as among the most
palpable, the most brilliant, and the most conclusive evidences of Christianity, by all Christian writers of every
shade of religious opinion who have ever entered the lists
with the infidel. Christ himself constantly and confidently
appealed to this species of evidence as decisive and unanswerable, to establish His own divine mission.

Thus rebuking the Jews for their incredulity, he says:
"But I have a greater testimony than that of John. For
the works which the Father hath given me to perfect; the
works themselves, which I do, give testimony of me that
my Father hath sent me."* Thus again: "Jesus answered
them: I speak to you and you believe not: the works that
I do in the name of my Father, they give testimony of
me."† In another discourse, He declares the Jews wholly
inexcusable for their unbelief, on the ground that they had
witnessed His wonderful works: "If I had not done among
them the works that no other man hath done, they would
not have sin: but now they have both seen and hated both
me and my Father." ‡

As I am at present treating, not with infidels who deny
Christianity, but with brother Christians who differ from
me as to its nature or where it is to be found, it will not be
necessary for the argument to dwell at any great length on
the nature of Miracles, and on their conclusiveness as
proofs to establish the truth of any particular system. Still
a few preliminary remarks on this branch of the subject may
be of service, for better understanding and appreciating
the line of argument upon which we are about to enter.

_____

* St. John, v: 36.   † St. John, x: 25. See also St. John, xiv: 11, 12.
‡ St. John, xv: 24.

This appears the more necessary, as in this age cf boasted progress in science, of animal magnetism, spiritism, and Mormonism, the minds of men are often sadly bewildered as to what really constitutes a Miracle, properly so called, and what are the *criteria* by which the true may be distinguished from the false.

The infidel Hume flippantly defined a Miracle, "a *transgression* of a law of nature by a particular volition of the Deity, or by the interposition of an invisible agent." He used that word *transgression* with the captious intent of implying that a Miracle was inconsistent with the wisdom and immutability of purpose of the Deity, and therefore impossible.

Locke's definition is scarcely less objectionable. It is this: "a sensible operation which exceeds the capacity of the spectator, and which he *believes* to be contrary to the course of nature, and judges to be divine." From this definition it would follow, that what would be a Miracle to the ignorant might be a very natural phenomenon to the learned; and thus that all miraculous occurrences might be viewed with distrust and suspicion.

Christian theologians have also given somewhat different definitions of miracles. But most of them agree in the substance, and differ merely in the views they respectively take of the subject. Some limit the definition to those extraordinary occurrences which evidently transcend the powers of all created nature, whether corporal or spiritual, and which are therefore referable to a direct and immediate agency of the Deity. This seems to have been the view of that deep and penetrating Christian philosopher, St. Thomas Aquinas.* Others make the definition more comprehensive, so as to embrace what is above the power of corporeal nature or of men, but not above that of spiritual intelligences of a higher order. The advocates of this opinion, among whom appears the brilliant name of Bene-

* Pars I. Quæst. cxiv. art. 4.— *Summa Theolog.* He, however, in the same passage, refers to a secondary order of Miracles performed by spirits inferior to the Deity.

12

dict XIV.,* draw a line of distinction between those wonderful events which manifestly can have God alone for their
immediate Author, and those which do not clearly and
obviously transcend the capabilities of angels. The former
they denominate *absolute* Miracles, or Miracles in the strictest sense of the term; the latter *relative*, or Miracles in a
larger sense, and less properly so called.

Bishop Hay, in his learned and philosophical work on
Miracles, coincides with this view, and gives the following
definition, which I shall adopt: " an extraordinary effect
produced in the material creation, either contrary to the
known laws of nature, or beyond the usual course of nature,
above the abilities of natural agents, and performed by
God, or by His holy angels."†

The principal difficulty in the way of distinguishing a
true from a false Miracle lies in our ignorance of the precise
innate powers possessed by the spiritual creation in relation
to the things of this world. That angels and demons are
gifted with a more acute perception and a higher order of
intelligence than man, is universally conceded; that they
possess the power to do things above the capacity of man,
appears equally unquestionable. But whatever may be the
extent of their powers over the material creation, it is
entirely certain, from the very first principles of natural
theology, that they are entirely subordinate to the Deity,
and under His complete control in their actions; and that
they can do nothing without His positive will or permission.

This principle solves a difficulty which would be otherwise insurmountable. By the broad light which it throws
upon the entire subject, we are enabled to lay down the

* De Servorum Dei Beatificatione, &c., Lib. iv. A splendid work, which
exhausts the subject. We shall have occasion to refer to it in the sequel.

† Hay on Miracles; vol. 1. p. 21, American edition. He fully develops
this definition, and investigates the nature, instruments, authority, and
criteria of Miracles, throughout the first ten chapters of his solid and well
reasoned work. The work was undertaken as a supplement to the weak
arguments of Dr. Middleton, who had entered the lists with the infidel
Hume. It has been lately republished in this country.

following practical rules for distinguishing a true from a
false Miracle; and as these rules are admitted by all Christians, with whom alone our present argument lies, it will
not be necessary to do more than merely to state them.

1. God cannot, under any circumstances, work a Miracle
in order to patronize error.

2. Neither can He permit a created agent to do so, under
circumstances in which it would be impossible to discover
whether the Miracle performed be a true one or not.

3. God cannot permit a created agent to perform a
relative Miracle, even known to be such, to patronize falsehood, under such circumstances as would inevitably lead
men into error.

4. If God sometimes permits evil spirits to perform a
relative Miracle, he must furnish us with ample means to
discover the delusion.*

I might extend and apply these principles, but this would
lead us much too far, besides that it is not called for by my
present object. It is sufficient for us to admit and know,
that whenever a Miracle is performed in the name of God,
in order to prove a doctrine said to be revealed by Him,
and not manifestly repugnant to His attributes or to sound
morality, and under such circumstances, too, that no means
are left us for ascertaining that it is not a true Miracle;
then we are necessarily bound to infer that it is from God,
either immediately, or through the agency of some spiritual
being acting with His sanction; and that the doctrine in
favor of which it is operated is therefore divine.

By the light of these principles, we are enabled, at a
single glance, to detect the satanical origin of those prodigies alleged to have been performed for the support of the
atrocious errors and impure worship of ancient paganism,
even if we could not prove that they were the effects of
natural causes unknown only to the ignorant. And by
the same test we are able fully to vindicate the Miracles
wrought in favor of the true Religion, whether under the
old or the new dispensation.

---

* See Bishop Hay, On Miracles, *sup. cit.*

Having premised these general remarks, I come now at
once to the main question at issue between us and the
adversaries of the Catholic faith on the subject of Miracles.
If I be able to establish by indisputable evidence, as I trust
I shall, that Miracles have been operated in all ages of the
Church, from the birth of Christianity to the present day,
in favor of the Catholic Religion ; then will I have furnished, in behalf of the latter religious system, precisely the
same character of proof, as the Christian apologist alleges
in support of the Christian Religion itself.

Our opponents have all along perceived this ; and hence
ever since the date of the reformation, so called, they have
without an exception, fallen back on the position,—that the
age of Miracles has long since ceased. They all agree in
advocating this opinion. To the arguments of Catholics in
favor of the continuance of Miracles in every successive age
down to the present day, they respond in different ways,
but more generally by ascribing all alleged Catholic Miracles to the agency of Satan. This is the theory adopted
by the Centuriators of Magdeburg in their ecclesiastical
history ; by John Calvin, in the preface to his Institutions ;
by Osiander, in his explanation of the Miracles wrought by
St. Bernard in the twelfth century ; and by Whitaker, in his
response to the argument of Bellarmine, based on the
Miracles of St. Francis Xavier.

Whatever else may be said of this theory, it is certainly
not original. The Arians of the fourth century, according
to the testimony of St. Ambrose and St. Augustine, adopted
it in order to account for the notorious and wonderful Miracles wrought by the relics of St. Gervase and St. Protase
in the presence of all Milan ; and a much more ancient
precedent is found in the gospel itself, were we read that
the Scribes and Pharisees ascribed the Miracles of our
blessed Lord Himself to "Beelzebub, the prince of devils!"*
Our adversaries can certainly plead very ancient, if not
very reputable authorities, for their favorite mode of solving

* St. Math. ch, xii.

the difficulty presented by Catholic Miracles. The Pharisees did not, because they could not, deny the *facts*; and therefore were they compelled, either to believe in Christ, or to broach some theory by which they might explain away the difficulty presented by His wonderful miracles. They chose the latter alternative; and, in doing so they have found followers among the disciples of Christ himself!

If by the received adage,—the age of Miracles has ceased, —it be intended only to mean, that miraculous gifts have ceased among those who have left the Catholic Church, I admit its truth to the fullest extent. But if the adage imply the absolute and total cessation of miraculous powers among the disciples of Christ, conclusive evidence may be alleged to prove that it is a mere assumption, to evade a difficulty otherwise wholly insurmountable.

The leading writers on this subject among the numerous denominations opposed to Catholicity, seem themselves to feel the straits to which they are necessarily reduced by the advocacy of this principle. If you ask them to inform you definitely when it was that Miracles ceased, they will be probably much puzzled for a satisfactory answer. Some will say, that they ceased after the full establishment of Christianity, at the close of the first five centuries of the Church; as if, forsooth, more nations were not converted from paganism to Christianity, after than before that period; and as if Miracles, which were deemed necessary for the conversion of the nations during the first five centuries, were not at least equally necessary for a precisely similar reason and emergency during the ages which followed! Some, again, will limit the miraculous gifts to the first three centuries, during which alone, they assume, the Christian Religion continued pure;—as if Miracles were not even more necessary to convert men in an age which, as they allege, was more corrupt in faith and practice, and therefore much more in need of a miraculous interposition of Heaven to lead it back to the truth, and to reform its morals!

Others, again, will tell you that the age of Miracles passed away with the apostles, to whom miraculous gifts were

12 *

meant to be confined; while others, pushing their skepticism still farther, assert with Dr. Middleton, that no Miracles are to be received as authentic but those recorded in the Bible itself;—as if the very last book of the Bible that was written, did not explicitly inform us, that many of the Miracles of Jesus Christ Himself were not mentioned by the sacred writer. The infidel Hume advanced but one step beyond the position assumed by his *Christian* antagonist Middleton, when he denied the existence of Miracles altogether, and maintained that no amount of human testimony, no matter how cumulative, could be sufficient to convince any reasonable man of facts which he viewed as flagrant "transgressions" of the natural law established by God himself!

Against all these various and discordant theories, Catholic writers have always asserted, with entire unanimity, the existence and continuation of Miracles throughout all the ages of the Church, from the apostolic days down to the present time. They do not, indeed, pledge themselves to a belief in all the miraculous occurrences which have ever been related to have taken place; but they agree in maintaining, that, while the judicious critic may be disposed to make all proper allowance for exaggeration or pious credulity in particular cases, he cannot, without violating all the laws of evidence, refuse credence to those numerous miraculous facts scattered throughout the various ages of Church history which are supported by a sufficient amount of unexceptionable testimony.

Miracles, they maintain, are to be examined and established just as other historical facts. If the evidence for them be deemed sufficient, they are to be received; if it be not considered satisfactory, after a mature examination, they may be rejected, or at least be set down as doubtful. The Church authorities have examined and decided juridically on those only which have come up in the process of the canonization of saints; and these are comparatively very few in number. In regard to all the rest, the Catholic is perfectly free in his judgment; he may receive or reject them according to his appreciation of the evidence in their favor.

It is important to bear this distinction constantly in mind; as the chief staple of our adversaries in their arguments against Catholic Miracles, is found in the attempt to cast suspicion or ridicule on doubtful or not sufficiently attested occurrences of the kind, some of which rest upon mere hearsay, or on pious legends framed for instruction and edification. Even if the Catholic should be willing to give up all Miracles of this sort, his adversaries would not have gained their point; for there would yet remain another and a very numerous class, against which such objections would be wholly out of place.

Another popular mode of attacking the continuation of Miracles to the present day in the Catholic Church, consists in the asking of present and palpable proof on the subject. You maintain,—says the Protestant objector, with an air of triumph, addressing the Catholic,—you maintain that miraculous powers still exist in your Church; prove the truth of your assertion by the performance of a Miracle before my own eyes: then will I believe you. We might answer such an adversary just as our blessed Lord answered the Pharisees and Sadducees 'on a precisely similar occasion. " They asked Him to show them a sign from heaven : but He answered and said to them :.... A wicked and adulterous generation seeketh after a sign : and a sign shall not be given them, but the sign of Jonas the prophet. And he left them and went away." * No one could infer from this refusal of our Saviour to gratify the insidious curiosity of his enemies, that He had not miraculous powers ; so no one can infer that the Church of the present day has not the same gifts, from the fact that her ministers do not or can not operate Miracles under all circumstances.

We do not at all maintain, that Christ gave to His Church the power of working Miracles at will and on all occasions, whether there existed sufficient reason for its exercise or not ; but only under those circumstances in which weighty

---

* St. Math. xvi: 1—4. A similar instance is found in the refusal of Christ to work a Miracle in order to gratify the vain curiosity of Herod.

reasons connected with the glory of God and the salvation of men, might render it necessary or expedient. Christ Himself worked Miracles only on such occasions as these; and surely His Church could not be expected to do more.

The whole controversy, then, between us and our adversaries on the subject of Miracles, is narrowed down to the investigation of a question based on a plain historical fact, to be examined, like all other facts, by the weight of testimony :—Have Miracles wholly ceased, or have they continued through all ages of the Church down to the present day ? Is there, or is there not, sufficient historical evidence for their continuance ?

We Catholics maintain that there is; and I will now endeavor briefly to lay before you some of the principal reasons we produce in support of the position. I solicit your undivided attention, as the issue which depends upon this inquiry is one of vast and vital importance to us all; being nothing less than the dicision of that momentous question, which is the true Church of Christ?

1. And first, in support of our proposition, we allege the argument of analogy, based upon· what we know from the inspired writings to have been the constant economy of God in the religious government of mankind. Open the books of the old and of the new testament, and you will find upon almost every page accounts of Miracles operated by God in behalf of His people. In every great emergency, whenever it was necessary or expedient to warn, to protect, to teach, or to chastise, we find the hand of God extended in miraculous interposition.

This feature of the divine government pervades the whole history of God's chosen people under the ancient dispensation, from the time that Abraham was miraculously called, down to the wonderful mission of John the Baptist; it reaches back into the patriarchal age, even far beyond the deluge; to the time when our first parents walked with God in the earthly paradise. It extends forward into the period of the new testament, and manifests itself on almost every page of its sacred records. Christ established His divine mission by the working of Miracles; His apostles and disciples did the same, under His eye and by His positive direction; and after His ascension, they continued to exercise the same miraculous powers. The first preaching of the gospel in Jerusalem after the day of Pentecost, was accompanied and rendered effectual by the miraculous healing of the lame man at the gate of the temple, by Peter and John ;* the very shadow † of Peter, and the aprons and handkerchiefs‡ of Paul, were the instruments employed by God for signal manifestations of divine power; Paul converted the proconsul Sirgius Paulus by striking with sudden blindness Elymas the magician :§ — in a word, the gospel was introduced and every where established by Miracles.

Shall we say, that God has, in later ages, changed His usual mode of action towards mankind; a mode which He had constantly adopted during more than four thousand years? Is God in the habit of changing His purpose, or His ordinary and long established manner of making Himself and His will known to men? Or has He been, and is He still more sparing of divine interposition in favor of Christians, than He had been in behalf of the Jews? If such a change has really taken place, there must surely be some sufficient reason to account for it, as well as some incontestable evidence to prove the fact. In the absence of such a reason and of such evidence,—and none worthy the name has ever been alleged as we shall soon see,—we would be naturally inclined to expect a continuance of the same divine economy in favor of Christianity throughout its entire history.

2. This reasoning *a priori* is strongly confirmed by the positive declarations of Jesus Christ Himself, who is surely an accredited witness on the subject. Had He intended that Miracles should cease at any particular period, He would certainly have said so in plain language, or He would, at least, have given some faint intimation of such intention. Did He do so? Not at all. But He did precisely the

---

* Acts, iii.   † Acts, v: 16.   ‡ Acts, xix: 12.   § Acts, xiii: 10–12.

contrary. As we have already seen, He imparted to His apostles the general power of working Miracles, in immediate connection with the commission to preach and to convert the nations; and as this latter was to continue "all days even unto the consummation of the world," so also was the former. What right have we to affix a limitation, either as to time or place, where Christ not only set none, but positively excluded any, as plainly as language could convey this meaning? Might we not, by the same whimsical canon of interpretation, limit the commission itself either to the apostolic days, or to some particular period thereafter?

The evidence derived from the language of Christ, for the perpetual continuation of miraculous gifts, is even stronger, perhaps, than that for the unlimited continuance of the commission to preach, to baptize, and to convert all nations. Mark how emphatic, and how general, are the words contained in these two parallel texts: "Amen I say to you, that *whosoever* shall say to this mountain: Be thou removed, and be thou cast into the sea, and shall not stagger in his heart, but believe that whatever he shall say shall be done: *it shall be done for him.* Therefore I say to you, *all things whatsoever* you ask when ye pray, believe that you shall receive, *and they shall come unto you.*"*—"Amen, amen, I say to you, he that believeth in me, the works that I do he shall do also, AND GREATER THAN THESE SHALL HE DO: because I go to the Father."†

From such passages as these, not modified, much less explained away, by any thing found elsewhere in the New Testament, we are surely warranted in the belief, that, according to the original intention and the positive promise of Jesus Christ, Miracles were to continue among His disciples unto the very end of time. The presumption in favor of this opinion is so very strong, that it cannot be overcome but by the strongest and most incontestable evidence to the contrary; which evidence has never been produced, and never can be produced.

---

* St. Mark, xi: 23, 24.   † St. John, xiv: 12.

3. But we have another strong presumptive evidence in favor of the continuance of Miracles, founded on the principal object to promote which miraculous gifts were originally imparted to the Church. These were manifestly granted for the conversion of the nations to Christianity; but this conversion was to be progressive in time, and it was to go on steadily until the consummation of the world; therefore, the accompanying gift of working Miracles was to continue for the same period. History proclaims the fact asserted in the second or minor proposition, as I have already shown;* and Christ, who was God, clearly foresaw that such would be the case; therefore the conclusion is irresistible. We cannot, in fact, well conceive how a heathen nation could be converted without Miracles; for as St. Augustine remarks, its conversion without their intervention would be the greatest Miracle of all.

4. Moreover, the unanimous and positive testimony of all Christian history proclaims the fact for which I am contending, establishes it beyond all possibility of cavil, and impresses the seal of the highest moral certainty on a conclusion, which we were already prepared to admit on the cogent presumptive evidence hitherto alleged. Dr. Middleton himself admits that the testimony in favor of the existence of Christian Miracles in all ages is clear and unanimous; but he gets over the difficulty thence arising, by discarding the evidence altogether as inconclusive!

In doing so, the learned Protestant champion practically adopted the very principle on which his infidel opponent, Hume, rejected all testimony of the kind, both human and divine; the only difference is, that he did not carry the principle so far, and was therefore not so consistent. Still he was much more consistent than those Protestant writers, who limited the continuance of Miracles to the first three or to the first five centuries of Christianity; for he was not compelled, like them, to receive the testimony of one age, and to reject that of another immediately succeeding, and at least equally strong and conclusive. Nay, it is a prominent

* In the preceding Lecture.

feature in this department of Church history, that the farther we advance, the fuller and more cogent becomes the evidence in favor of miraculous interpositions. What Mr. Brook, an English Protestant writer,* says in substance— that nothing but the force of truth could have induced the unanimous consent of the Fathers who wrote during the first three centuries, in attesting the existence of Miracles— may be applied, with still greater force, to the testimony of the ages which followed.

As our adversaries are thus compelled to admit the fact of the testimony, and of its extension through all ages of Christian history, I am saved the necessity of establishing its existence. All that I have to do is to sift the evidence, to show that it has all the characteristic marks of truth, and all the qualities requisite for inducing moral certainty. This will be an easy task. By a very rapid analysis, it will appear that the testimony has all the conditions which even the most skeptical could demand as a preliminary of belief.

5. The first thing into which we usually inquire in examining moral evidence, is the nature of the facts which it attests. Are they of such a character as to come fairly under the legitimate province of human testimony? Are they, for example, external, plain, and palpable to the senses? Could the witnesses be morally certain of their existence? It is manifest, that the miraculous occurrences in question had all these qualities. They consisted of plain and palpable external acts, coming fairly within the range of the senses, and even riveting their special attention, by the additional circumstance that they were new and startling exceptions to the usual course of nature. Men would be much more likely to mark them, and to remember them well, than they would facts of daily occurrence. And the witnesses would surely be entitled to as much credit in relating them, as far as regards the nature of the facts themselves, as they would be in narrating ordinary events.

A witness would be as deserving of credit in narrating

---

* Quoted by Bishop Hay, On Miracles, ch. xv.

the resurrection of a dead man which he witnessed with his own eyes, as would he or another of equal veracity in relating the death of the same individual; for both facts are obviously equally palpable, and may be ascertained with the same facility. The same men who witnessed the death of Lazarus, witnessed also his resurrection; and their testimony is entitled to equal credit in both cases. Unless we admit this principle, we strike a mortal blow at the evidences of the Miracles recorded in the New Testament itself, and may as well subscribe at once to the opinion of Hume against all Miracles.

6. The next thing we naturally inquire into, is the character of the witnesses for veracity. Here we occupy a high and proud position. The men who attest the continuation of Christian Miracles were the ornaments of the ages .in which they respectively lived and wrote. They were men of high station and of eminent learning and sanctity, conspicuous for their fervent religion and their unwavering love of truth. They are justly entitled to the reverent appellation which they are in the habit of receiving even from their enemies,—Fathers of the Church. They trembled at the very shadow of falsehood; they taught, with St. Augustine, that under no circumstances whatever was a Christian allowed to prevaricate from the truth, no matter how trivial was the nature of the untruth, or how great the motive for giving it utterance, even if it were to preserve life or honor.* They proclaimed with St. Sulpitius Severus:† "I would rather be silent than utter an untruth." They declared with St. Justin, that they would rather sacrifice life itself than assert a falsehood.‡ They were men who cheerfully went to the stake, rather than betray their conscience by declaring that they believed what they really rejected. Some of them were confessors, some were martyrs of the truth. Surely such witnesses are entitled to the fullest credit.

---

* St. Augustine—ad Consentium, c. x. † In Vita S. Martini.
‡ Apologia.
18 K

7. Again: they not only simply narrate the miraculous occurrences in question, but they often solemnly pledge their veracity to the truth of them, and even take God to witness that they are making no misstatement. Thus Origen, in the third century, calls upon the name of God to attest the truth of his narrative in regard to Miracles wrought by the Christians of his day;* thus also does Palladius in his Lives of the Fathers of the desert, and St. Sulpitius Severus in his Life of St. Martin of Tours. A later instance of this is furnished by Geoffroy in his Life of St. Bernard, in the twelfth century.† He relates the Miracles operated by the saint, on the authority of several highly respectable witnesses—the Bishop of Constance, two abbots, two monks, and three other clergymen—who were his almost constant companions, and who all solemnly averred the truth of what they stated even with the sacred form of an oath. We have another example of this belonging to the close of the fourteenth century. The blessed F. Raymond, was the confessor of St. Catharine of Sienna, and he wrote her life, in which, after having stated that he at first doubted the truth of many among the wonderful heavenly gifts which God had bestowed upon her, he calls God to witness the truth of what he narrates. Unless, then, we suppose all these grave witnesses to be perjured men, we are bound to admit the truth of their statements.

8. But, perhaps, they may have been mistaken, or they may have received their facts on mere hearsay. Let us see. In the five cases just mentioned, the narrators assure us that they were either themselves eye-witnesses of the facts, or that they received them from those who were such. Thus, Origen states that he had seen with his own eyes many such Miracles performed by the Christians of his time; and he adds, that he might have related many more had he not been apprehensive that the enemies of Christianity would not believe him.‡ The same may be said of most of those witnesses upon whose authority we receive

---

* Contra Celsum.   † Vita S. Bernardi, Lib. vi.   ‡ Contra Celsum.

the Miracles wrought in the succeeding ages. The great champion of orthodoxy in the fourth century, St. Athanasius, gives us a lengthy account of the Miracles by which God had attested the sanctity of His servant St. Anthony; and he assures us that he saw many of those things himself, and learned others from eye-witnesses of unimpeachable veracity.*

In the same century, St. Paulinus relates many Miracles performed by St. Ambrose of Milan before his own eyes; and St. Ambrose† and St. Augustine‡ both tell us, with great positiveness and some minuteness of detail, of the wonders wrought in presence of all Milan on occasion of the discovery and translation of the relics of the holy martyrs saints Gervase and Protase. The great St. Chrysostom attests that the cross was the instrument for performing many public and notorious Miracles in his own time.§ St. Paulinus was himself an eye-witness of the Miracles of St. Felix.‖ Theodoret states that he had himself seen many great Miracles performed by the monks, and in particular by St. Simeon Stylites, who was probably still living when he wrote his history.

St. Augustine relates, at considerable length, the signs and wonders which astonished all northern Africa on occasion of introducing into that country the relics of St. Stephen, the first martyr; and he adds, "we ourselves were present and beheld them with our own eyes."¶ Speaking of the miraculous cure of two men who had visited the shrine of St. Stephen at Hippo, he says the fact was so notorious, that the whole city was witness to its truth, and that no one durst deny it.**

Thus, we see that the writers who record the miraculous facts in question, were not only cotemporaries, but were themselves, in most cases, eye-witnesses of what they relate;

---

*Prefatio in Vitam S. Antonii. † Epistol. 2. ad Sororem Marcellinam.
‡ Confessiones lib. 9. c. 7.   § Opp. tom. 7, p. 852, quoted by Bishop Hay.
‖ Poema, 28.
¶ Nos interfuimus et oculis adspeximus nostris—De Civitate Dei, Lib. xxii. c. 8.   ** Ibid.

therefore we cannot reasonably suppose that they could have been easily mistaken.

9. There is still another consideration which adds great weight to their authority. In many cases, there is a remarkable concurrence of testimony of witnesses living in different parts of the world, and writing independently of each other;—a circumstance which strongly corroborates the evidence. Thus, the Miracles of saints Gervase and Protase at Milan, alluded to above, are attested by saints Ambrose and Augustine, the former of whom wrote in Italy, and the latter in Africa.

But there is one remarkable miraculous fact belonging to the fifth century, in support of which there is a concurrence of testimony that is conclusive. The Arian king Huneric carried on in Africa a most fierce and relentless persecution against the Catholics who believed in the divinity of Jesus Christ. Among the many acts of wanton cruelty of which he was guilty, one was to apprehend a number of Catholic confessors and to have their tongues cut out by the roots, because they persisted in refusing to blaspheme Christ, by denying His divinity. But wonderful to relate, these men continued to speak and to praise Christ without tongues! For this Miracle we have the solemn testimony of many cotemporary writers of unimpeachable veracity. Æneas of Gaza* assures us that he saw those confessors with his own eyes, that he heard them speak, and that, having examined their mouths, he found that they had not even the vestiges of a tongue. Another cotemporary, Victor of Vite, challenges his adversaries to repair to Constantinople, where they would find one of those confessors, named Reparatus, who spoke without a tongue in presence of the entire court of the emperor Zeno. And Procopius, the Greek historian, accordingly tells us in his history, that he himself saw them in Constantinople, and witnessed the Miracle.

10. It appears, then, that our witnesses of Miracles not only confidently relate the facts as having been seen by

---

* Dialogus inter Theophrastum et Arithæum.

themselves, but also as confidently appeal to their most bitter adversaries to attest the truth of their assertions. Did these enemies dare deny the truth of the facts? No, they could not. Sometimes, indeed, they attempted to account for them, as the Pharisees had attempted to account for the Miracles of Christ, and as the heathens of the first three centuries had explained away the Miracles of the early Christians;—by ascribing them to magical practices. But the facts themselves they durst not impugn; they were too public and notorious.

Occasionally the infidels and heretics were struck dumb with astonishment, and trembled with fear at the sight of those prodigies; sometimes again, their hostility was soften- ed, and they were converted to the truth. Thus, while some of the leading Arians of Milan ascribed the Miracles of saints Gervase and Protase to magical incantation, others better disposed were led by them to embrace the Catholic faith. The tyrant Huneric, according to the testimony of Victor of Vite, was greatly alarmed at sight having been restored to a blind man by the prayers of St. Eugenius, bishop of Carthage; but he dared not deny the fact with which the whole city was well acquainted. In the twelfth and thirteenth centuries, large bodies of heretics were con- verted to the true faith by means of Miracles, the truth of which they could not impugn, and the force of which they could not but feel. It was thus that St. Bernard succeeded in converting so many of the Henricians at Toulouse, and St. Dominic so many of the Albigenses in the south of France.

11. There is still another circumstance which strongly inclines us to believe in the truth of the miraculous occur- rences in question. Those who were invested with the miraculous gifts above attested, were men as eminent for their humility and modesty, as they were for their piety and sanctity. They made no ostentation of their wonderful works; they sought not human praise; they adopted none of the arts of the juggler and mountebank for arresting attention and conciliating faith. They did not claim mi-

13 *

raculous powers on all occasions, nor did they attempt to put them in requisition for trivial purposes. In all this, they closely followed the example of Christ and of His apostles. Whenever they wrought Miracles, it was for promoting the glory of God and the salvation of souls; they did not attempt to do it otherwise than by humbly invoking God's aid through fervent prayer; and to Him alone they gave all the honor and glory thence accruing. They even shrank from public observation, and sought to conceal from the eyes of men the extraordinary gifts with which they had been invested. St. Cyril of Jerusalem exhorts those to whom God had vouchsafed such gifts, to be humble;* and St. Gregory the Great, in his correspondence with St. Augustine, the apostle of England, gives him similar advice.

12. Finally, in addition to all the arguments thus far alleged in support of the credibility of the Miracles related to have occurred in different ages of the Christian Church, I may mention the fact, that those prodigies were often commemorated by public monuments erected on the spots at which they were respectively performed. This practice has been more or less common among Christians, from the earliest ages to the present time. The woman of the gospel, who had been healed by touching the hem of our Saviour's garment, erected a statue at Thebais to commemorate the event; and Eusebius, who tells us that he saw this monument with his own eyes, also informs us of the additional fact that the early Christians were in the habit of erecting oratories and other monuments over the tombs of the martyrs, in order to commemorate their virtues, as well as the signal Miracles which had often marked their exit from this world. † To the operation of a similar principle are we to ascribe the numerous sanctuaries and places of devout pilgrimage erected in subsequent centuries, especially during the middle ages.

---

* Homilia de Paralytico.

† St. John Chrysostom mentions, as a notorious fact, that many were healed by anointing themselves with oil from the vials which ancient piety used to suspend near the shrines of the martyrs. Opp. Tom. vii. Sermo 82.

13. Thus you see, my Dear Brethren, that all the motives of credibility combine to convince us that Miracles have been wrought in all ages of Christianity. The nature of the facts attested, the character of the witnesses for veracity, their opportunities to ascertain the facts, their solemn appeals to God to attest the truth of what they state, the concurrence of testimony in favor of the same miraculous events, the confident appeals made to enemies, the signal conversion of many among the latter brought about by those occurrences the truth of which they could not doubt, the humility and sanctity of the men who were the instruments employed by God for operating those prodigies, the publicity and notoriety of many of the alleged facts, and the practice of erecting public and permanent monuments to perpetuate the memory of them: these are the principal features of the cumulative testimony produced to prove the continuation of miraculous gifts throughout all the ages of the Church. All these evidences, too, do but carry out the general purpose and plan of God in the government of His people in all ages, from the very beginning of the world down to the full establishment of Christianity; and they are but a natural commentary on the words of Christ, while they contain a complete fulfillment of His solemn promises.

What reasonable man, then, can repudiate evidence possessing all these combined characteristics of truth? Where is the dependence to be any longer placed on human testimony, if it be lawful to reject the very highest order of it on mere conjecture, prejudice, or suspicion? Consistency requires, that we either reject human evidence altogether, and thus fall into a universal skepticism, or that we attach full credit to this highest department of it in favor of the unlimited continuation of Miracles.

14. But let us suppose, for the sake of argument, that nine-tenths of the miraculous facts attested by such witnesses as those above indicated, are either doubtful or spurious; let us make a most liberal allowance for mistakes, misrepresentations, or the exaggerations of a heated fancy;

let us even suppose that there is not more than one well
authenticated Miracle for each century, instead of the many
attested in Church history; still, even in this case, our
argument loses little of its force: for it would yet appear
that Miracles have been wrought in all ages, which is all
that we contend for. One undoubted Miracle alone, operated to prove a religious system, is quite sufficient to establish its truth beyond the possibility of cavil; for one Miracle
alone would afford ample evidence of the divine sanction,
which could not be given to falsehood. And surely, out of
the many Miracles mentioned in Church history, we may
succeed in establishing at least *one;* and this is all our
argument absolutely demands.

15. There is still another species of evidence of a very
high order, bearing chiefly on the Miracles wrought in the
Catholic Church during the last three centuries, which is
particularly worthy of our most serious consideration. I
refer to the most rigid judicial process which precedes the
canonization of saints in our Church. This process was at
all times marked by the greatest care in the weighing of
testimony and in the examination of facts, even from the
first time* that it was adopted by the Church as a necessary preliminary to the public declaration and veneration of sanctity in a particular individual. But, during the
last centuries, its forms have become much more complex
and difficult. The great and enlightened Pontiff, Benedict
XIV., in a special work on the subject,† enters at great
length into all the details and forms of the judicial investigation in question, and develops the principles by which it
is usually governed throughout its various stages. No one
can peruse his work without coming to the conclusion, that
if any error should exist in the result reached, it is surely
from no want of time and patience and rigid scrutiny in
conducting the investigation. No civil tribunal, whether

---

* Probably about the close of the tenth century. See Palma — Prælec-
tiones Hist. Ecclesiast.

† See SS. Beatificatione et Canonizatione.

in ancient or in modern times, has ever taken, or now takes, so much pains to arrive at the truth.

16. Space fails me to enter into a minute account of all the formalities which attend this most remarkable judicial process. Hence I must limit myself to a very rapid analysis, which I present under the following heads!*

1. The investigation runs through a period of no less than FIFTY YEARS after the death of the reputed saint!

2. The first thing that is done, is the preliminary inquiry conducted on the spot where the saint lived and died, by the diocesan bishop with the assistance of a court organized according to all the forms prescribed. This proceeding is conducted in writing, and must be marked by at least ten essential formalities, among which the principal are: that the witnesses must all be of unexceptionable character, that they must be examined on oath and apart from each other, and that their testimonies both *pro* and *con*, as well as those of all other persons who may know any thing of the matter, must be taken down and countersigned by the one who conducts the cross examination in presence of the bishop, as well as by the witnesses themselves.

3. After this preliminary examination has been completed, and the bishop has pronounced judgment thereon, a neat and well authenticated copy of the proceedings is sent by a special courier to the Congregation of Rites at Rome; the original papers being preserved under seal in the diocesan archives. In these papers it is not permitted to insert any extra-judicial information of any kind whatsoever.

4. The authentic copy, after it has reached Rome, is deposited in the archives of the Congregation in charge of the apostolic notary, where it must remain TEN YEARS, before the seals can even be broken, or any action can be had in the premises.

5. During this long period, however, many important

* Those who may wish to see a full and elaborate exposition of the laws which are observed in the Canonization of Saints, are referred to Bishop Hay "On Miracles," ch. xv.

circumstances are carefully examined at Rome: such as, whether the public renown of the reputed saint has meantime increased or diminished; whether there arise any serious doubts in regard to his sanctity; and whether his writings, if any, will bear the test of rigid orthodoxy.

6. Should there remain a serious doubt on any of these subjects, the case is at once dismissed; should the result be favorable, after the lapse of the ten years, the Pope is petitioned by the Congregation of Rites to issue a special commission for the *commencement* of the cause. The commission is empowered to proceed to the diocese of the reputed saint, to organize a new court of local bishops, of whom the diocesan must be one, to open and examine the original papers there deposited, and to pronounce upon them, as also upon all the objections raised by the "solicitor of the faith."*

7. Should this second examination on the spot result favorably, the new papers containing a full account of the entire proceedings, are again sealed and sent to Rome by a special courier sworn to the faithful execution of his commission.

8. Finally, after the lapse of at least fifty years from the death of the alleged saint, the last mentioned proceedings of the diocesan court are carefully examined, both in their substance and in their formalities; the whole matter is fully discussed in three successive extraordinary Congregations in presence of the Pontiff; and now it is only that the process may be said to have fairly begun!

9. Two things are invariably required that the judicial examination may result even in the beatification† of the Saint: first, that it be proved by unequivocal testimony, beyond all possibility of cavil, that God has wrought in his favor at least three Miracles; and second, that these Miracles bear the twofold test of philosophy and religion, and be

---

* Often popularly called "the devil's advocate."

† There is this difference between the *beatification* and the *canonization* of saints, that the former is local in its effects, while the latter is more solemn and extends their veneration to the whole Church.

proved to be real, and such only as God could be the Author of, or could at least sanction.

Every one must see, at a glance, that a tribunal thus organized, taking so much pains to arrive at the truth, and occupying so much time in the investigation, can scarcely go astray in its final decision. The Roman courts have ever been remarkable for their extreme slowness and caution, for the rigor of their scrutiny, and for the consequent accuracy of their judgments: none merits this eulogy more than that which is ordered for the canonization of saints. The very least circumstance, the slightest want of formality in the preliminary proceedings, the smallest doubt remaining on the subject, will ensure an unfavorable issue to any cause. Various facts might be adduced in proof of this. I will here mention but one incident of the kind.

An English Protestant gentleman was present at one of the sessions of the Roman Congregation of Rites, in which the evidences in proof of a Miracle were discussed, as well as the principle whether the alleged occurrence was really miraculous. The proofs of both positions appeared to him so strong and conclusive, that, on leaving the court room, he remarked to a friend, that if the evidence were equally cogent in all cases of canonization, he would not object to submit to the decision of Rome in the premises. But what was his surprise on learning subsequently that the proofs he had deemed so conclusive were rejected as wholly insufficient!

17. Such, then, my Dear Brethren, is the rigid scrutiny through which alleged miraculous occurrences have to pass, before our Church will consent to pronounce upon their truth as facts, or their reality as Miracles. Such is the fiery ordeal through which, not merely the virtues, but also the Miracles of all our canonized saints for many centuries past have had to pass; and if they have bravely stood this test and come out unscathed, they were surely sustained by the very highest species of human evidence. If we bear in mind, that a saint cannot be canonized in the Catholic Church without conclusive proofs of at least three undoubt-

ed Miracles, operated through his agency or to attest his sanctity, we may form some idea of the great number of Miracles which have been juridically established, on the most ample testimony, during the last three centuries.

To say that all these Miracles are spurious, would amount to a repudiation of all moral evidence, and would lead us to the very verge of universal skepticism. And yet a Protestant should disprove not only one but all of them; for if he concede that even· one was wrought in favor of our doctrines, he must necessarily grant that these are true, because sanctioned by the clearest evidence of the divine approval.

Dr. Middleton himself admits this, when he says: "it is a maxim, which must be allowed by all Christians, that, whenever any religious rite or institution becomes the instrument of Miracles, we ought to consider that rite as confirmed by divine approbation."* Hence, we are not to be surprised if our adversaries employ every effort to disprove Catholic Miracles, even those which are the best attested. It is for them, as for us, a vital question; one upon which depends the final decision of the momentous inquiry,—which is the true Church of Christ?

18. The Miracles of St. Francis Xavier, the great apostle of the Indies, present a case exactly in point. He reared in triumph the banner of Catholicity in the farthest Indies, at the very time that Luther and Calvin were endeavoring to tear it down in Europe. It is admitted, on all hands, that the success of the reformation, so called, was not at all ascribable to Miracles; while it is alleged, on the strongest possible evidence, that Xavier's remarkable success in converting the heathens of India, was mainly owing to the performance of them.

That he was a man of eminent sanctity, of unquenchable zeal, of undaunted courage, and of devoted heroism, is freely admitted even by Protestant writers of eminence; such as Carne, Sir James McIntosh, the Rev. Dr. Palmer of

---

* Quoted in the appendix to the Life of St. Francis Xavier, p. 448, Amer. edit.

Oxford,* Baldæus, Hacluyt, Tavernier, † Stephens, Buchanan, and many others. That his virtues were signalized
by miraculous gifts, is fully attested by all the writers of
his life, by the universal opinion of all the eastern nations
among whom he labored,—Jews, Mohammedans, Pagans,
and Christians,—and by the testimony of hundreds of
sworn witnesses examined during the process of his canonization. Thus Hacluyt says: "The modern histories of
India are filled with the relations of the excellent virtues
and miraculous operations of that holy man:"‡ and Tavernier, after having spoken of him in terms of the highest
eulogy, says that "he may justly be called a new St. Paul,
and the apostle of India."§

St. Francis Xavier, was placed in precisely the same condition as the apostles, in regard to the people to whom he
preached the gospel. He was legitimately carrying out the
commission originally intrusted to them for "teaching all
nations;" his preaching was attended with a success similar to that which had crowned theirs; he was also an heir
to their virtues and to their zeal;—why, then, should it
appear strange that he had similar miraculous powers?
These had been divinely promised to the apostles and to
their successors in fulfilling the commission, "even unto the
consummation of the world;" and without them the world
could never have been converted to Christianity:—what
sufficient reason can be assigned for denying that the promise of Miracles was fulfilled in Xavier? Surely we would,
on the contrary, naturally expect to find those gifts in him;
and it is impossible to explain his wonderful success on any
other hypothesis.

But, as I have already intimated, we have positive evidence, wholly unexceptionable and unanswerable, to establish the existence and truth of his Miracles. Xavier died

---

* See their testimonies in the Preface to the Life of the Saint.
Amer. edit.

† See Life of the saint: p. 437, 438. Amer. edit.

‡ Navigations, Voyages, and Discoveries, vol. ii. part xi. Quoted in
Life, &c., p. 438. § Ibid.

14

at Sancian, a small island near the coast of China, on the
2d of December, 1552. His body was placed in a large
Chinese chest filled with quick-lime in order to consume
the flesh, and it remained in this condition for two months
and a half. At the close of this time it was found fresh and
entire, of a rosy and natural color, and exhaling a sweet
fragrance; and on a wound being inflicted on it by a brutal
sailor, the blood flowed freely. The quick-lime was re-
placed in the chest, and the body was removed to Malacca,
where it remained interred during the scorching heat of the
ensuing summer and fall, when it was removed to Goa, and
placed in the Church of St. Paul, on the 15th of March,
1554.

The grave was again opened on the 17th of December,
1556, when the body was found still entire, of a natural
color, covered with a healthy moisture, and without the
least offensive smell. Nearly two hundred years later, in
1744, the same wonderful phenomenon was witnessed on
the occasion of a public visitation made to the relics by the
archbishop of Goa and the marquis of Castello Nuovo, by
order of John V., king of Portugal; and to this very day
this same prodigy continues.

How are we to explain this on merely natural principles?
How explain it, particularly, in such a climate as that of
the East Indies, were putrefaction and dissolution invariably ensue almost immediately after death? Learned
physicians, who have thoroughly examined the body, have
pronounced its preservation under such circumstances a
decided Miracle.

But this is not all. During his mission in India, his
preaching was every-where marked with miraculous manifestations. The blind saw, the lame walked, the sick were
suddenly healed, the dead were raised to life; nay more,
the very elements obeyed his voice, and the mysterious
future was revealed to his searching glance. After his
death, these prodigies were rather increased than diminished. They were not done in a corner; they were witnessed by thousands and tens of thousands of spectators.

They were not reported by friends alone, but also by his most bitter enemies. The Bonzas of Japan seriously deliberated on the proposition to enroll his name among those of their gods, and were prevented from carrying their project into execution only by the indignant rebuke of the humble apostle himself. A similar incident is related of St. Paul and St. Barnabas, in the Acts of the Apostles; and, in fact, whoever peruses with attention and impartiality the life of St. Francis Xavier, cannot fail to remark the striking parallelism between his life, character, and Miracles, and those of the great apostle of the gentiles.

Upon what evidence do all these miraculous facts rest? Were they received on mere hearsay or popular partiality. for his memory? Not at all: but they rest on the testimony of hundreds of persons of every shade of religion, scattered over all parts of the Indies where he had preached the gospel; on that of witnesses who saw those prodigies with their own eyes, and some of whom had received personal benefit from their performance; of witnesses, in fine, sworn to tell the whole truth, and whose depositions were carefully taken down on the spot, only four or five years after the death of the saint, and were authenticated according to all the forms of law. All this was done by the commission of learned men and jurists appointed for this purpose by Don Francisco Baretto, Viceroy of India, in conformity with a decree issued by John III., king of Portugal, bearing date March 28, 1556.

The judicial documents transmitted to Portugal by this commission, were immediately forwarded by the Portuguese court to the Roman Congregation of Rites, where they were sifted according to all the rigorous forms of law, of which I have above given a brief synopsis. Nearly seventy years were consumed in this judicial scrutiny, notwithstanding the ever increasing fame of the saint, and the constant entreaties of the Portuguese court to have the matter expedited. The bull for his canonization was issued only on the 6th day of August, 1623, almost seventy-one years after the death of the saint. This instrument sets forth, at considerable length, the numerous Miracles wrought by the saint, both in life and after his death, and it insists particularly on the well established fact that several persons had been raised from death to life by his prayers.

If all this, and much more of the same kind which might be said on the subject, be not sufficient to establish the fact that at least some Miracles were wrought by St. Francis Xavier, I really know not the force of human evidence, or under what circumstances one may rely on it with safety.

The force of the evidence is not diminished, but is rather greatly enhanced, by the manifest futility of all the objections which have been raised against it by a few Protestant writers of some learning and ability. I have not space to go at present into a full account and refutation of these difficulties; nor is it at all necessary. Dr. Milner has scattered to the winds all the false assertions and transparent sophisms of Dr. Douglas, bishop of Salisbury in England, and of the Rev. Mr. Grier; who, with others that followed them and copied their objections, had ventured to deny the truth of Xavier's miracles. *

Suffice it to say, that the merely negative argument brought forward by these objectors, from the alleged silence of the saint on the subject of his miraculous gifts, is met by a letter of his to St. Ignatius,† in which he expressly, though modestly, claims those gifts, and relates a miraculous cure which he had lately performed on a dying woman, and which had caused the conversion of an entire village: that their assertion to the effect that his Miracles were performed in the far east, and that no investigation of them was made, and no account published on the spot, but only in Europe and many years afterwards, is met by the facts above given, which prove the assertion to be wholly ground-

---

* See Dr. Milner's End of Controversy, and his Vindication of it, in answer to the Rev. Mr. Grier. A brief synopsis of the arguments on both sides may be found in an appendix to the Life of the Saint, American edition, p. 441, seqq.

† Epistolæ S. Francisci Xav. Lib. I. Ep. 4.

less: that their reasoning upon some passages in the saint's correspondence, in which he laments that he did not know the languages of all the nations to whom he preached the gospel, is wholly inconclusive against his having had, at any time or on any occasion, the miraculous gift of tongues; for the simple reason, that none of his biographers ever asserted, nor do the acts of his canonization declare, that he always had this gift, but only on a few special occasions; and that, finally, the pretended testimony of the Rev. Joseph Acosta* against the verity of the saint's Miracles, turns out to be nothing more than a mere regret at the comparative fewness of the Miracles wrought by the Jesuit missionaries thirty or forty years after his death, and is, moreover, triumphantly met by an explicit declaration of Acosta, that "signs and wonders, too numerous to be related, accompanied their preaching in the East and West Indies, even in his own times; and that of the blessed Master, Francis, a man of an apostolic life, so many and so great Miracles are related by very many, and these suitable witnesses, that such wonders are scarcely related of any other, save of the apostles."†

These are literally all the objections which have been brought against the Miracles of the saint; and I put it to every impartial man to say whether they are not most futile, and whether they have not been most triumphantly answered.‡

---

* In his work,—De procuranda Indorum salute,—published in 1589.

† Lib. II. c. 10—work above quoted. "Convertamus oculos in nostri sæculi hominem, B. Magistrum Franciscum virum apostolicæ vitæ; cujus tot et tam magna signa referuntur per plurimos eosque idoneos testes, ut vix de alio, exceptis apostolis, (talia) signa legantur." The translation of this passage in the text of the appendix to the American life of St. Francis is very deficient.

‡ I might here refer to many miraculous events of recent occurrence, both in Europe and in America. Every one remembers the sensation created some years ago by several wonderful cures effected through the prayers of Prince Hohenlohe. Among many of this kind, I may refer to that of Mrs. Mattingly in the city of Washington, a full account of which, with all the evidence bearing upon it, was published at the time by the

Our argument, then, fairly drawn out, fully sustains the
position, that Miracles have been wrought in all the successive ages of the Church, and as fully warrants the inference necessarily flowing therefrom,—that the Catholic
Church is the true Church of Christ. No Protestant church
even claims those miraculous gifts promised by Christ;
therefore, if they exist at all, they certainly belong to the
Catholic Church alone, and, as a necessary consequence,
she alone is, or can be, the true Church.

This conclusion can be escaped in only one of two ways:
either by denying the existence of Miracles in all successive
ages of Christianity,—and then all human testimony must
be repudiated, and nothing in human transactions remains
any longer certain; or by denying that Miracles are sufficient *criteria* of divine truth, or conclusive evidences of the
divine sanction to any religious system,—and then one of
the most brilliant and irresistible evidences in favor of
Christianity itself is given up, and the infidel is left to
triumph. Either the Catholic Church, then, is the only
true Church of Christ, or there remains nothing certain
either in history or in Christianity.

THIS IS THE THIRD EVIDENCE OF CATHOLICITY.

In my next Lecture, if you will favor me with your
attendance, I will endeavor to point out to you a fourth
evidence, not less striking and conclusive, founded upon
some of the primary characteristics impressed on the
Church by her divine Founder himself.

May God grant, my Dear Brethren, that we may bring to ·

---

late bishop England. She was of a highly respectable family and of
unblemished character. Her disease was of a most inveterate chronic
nature; it had baffled the skill of the best physicians; and her cure was
sudden and instantaneous. It occurred, too, during the session of Con-
gress, and was vouched for by witnesses of unimpeachable character,
both Protestant and Catholic. The fact is indisputable, and its miraculous character certain. In fact, I know of no attempt ever having been
made to refute the abundant evidence and conclusive arguments spread
out in bishop England's publication. Our adversaries seem, on the contrary, to have been greatly puzzled for an answer, and to have permitted
an event so extraordinary to pass by almost unnoticed.

the investigation of truths so closely interwoven with our eternal destinies minds free from all undue prejudice; minds and hearts humble, docile, and pleading fervently by persevering prayer for the divine light and assistance, without which all our feeble efforts for ascertaining or unfolding the truth were wholly unavailing. May God vouchsafe us this boon, through Jesus Christ our dear Lord and Saviour! Amen.

LECTURE VI.

CATHOLICITY AND UNITY. — THE FOURTH EVIDENCE OF CATHOLICITY.

Recapitulation — The truth plain — But often obscured by passion and prejudice — Necessity for distinctive characteristics or marks of the true Church —Their qualities developed —Those assigned by Protestants examined — The Church visible — Her marks palpable — Those of Catholicity and Unity inferred from the words of the Commission — Each of them threefold—That of Catholicity established by the prophecies of the Old and the testimonies of the New Testament — Unity essentially connected with Catholicity—Application of these marks as tests of the true Church —The question simplified —A popular objection answered — Relative extension and numbers of the Catholic Church and of all dissenting communions —The tree and its branches — Religious statistics —Test of Unity— No Unity out of the Church — Number of Protestant sects —Divisions and sub-divisions—A necessary consequence of Protestant Rule of Faith—A quibble answered — General council of Protestant sects—And one of the Catholic Church —A picture of Catholic Unity—The College of Propaganda —The conclusion reached —The fourth evidence of the Church — Striking facts of early Church history —The Church of all ages and of all nations.

" Go ye, therefore, and teach ALL NATIONS, *baptizing them in the name of the Father, and of the Son, and of the Holy Ghost; teaching them to observe* ALL THINGS *whatsoever I have commanded you ; and behold, I am with you* ALL DAYS, *even to the consummation of the world."*—ST MATH. xxviii: 19, 20.

" And other sheep I have that are not of this fold: them also I must bring ; and they shall hear my voice; and there shall be made ONE FOLD AND ONE SHEPHERD.— ST. JOHN, x: 16.

THE Commission given by our blessed Saviour to His apostles, fulfilled both in its substance and in its manner;— all the nations taught of God, and entering one by one into the ever-extending fold of Christianity;—stupendous Miracles in each successive age, following and confirming the preached word:—this is the ground which we have thus far gone over together; these are the first three evidences of Catholicity which I have so far endeavored to lay before you. I propose now, with the assistance of God and your kind indulgence, my Beloved Brethren, to proceed to the development of other evidences, growing out of these, equally convincing, and, perhaps, even more striking; of

(164)

evidences adapted to every capacity, clear as the light of day, and such as no one, no matter how unlearned or how slow of intellect, can fail to understand and appreciate.

There can be no doubt, that Jesus Christ made His Religion plain, and that consequently He placed the decision of the great and all important question,—which is the true Church,—within the reach of every sincere and well disposed inquirer. The question has, indeed, been not unfrequently obscured by prejudice and passion, the fumes of which have so darkened the mirror of the mind, that it could no longer reflect fully and fairly the image of the truth. The veil of misrepresentation and sophistry, raised by crafty men "lying in wait to deceive,"* has often interposed to conceal its real merits and the true issue; and the truth-loving and simple-minded Christian has thus been often sadly bewildered by the array of contradictory claims based upon conflicting arguments. Yet the truth itself is plain enough, and it is easily discoverable by those who, distrusting their own lights and fervently imploring those of heaven, are disposed to pursue the investigation with proper humility, diligence, prayerfulness, disinterestedness, and courage.

Thus the sun is clear and conspicuous in the heavens; the clouds which sometimes flit across his disk do not blot it out from the firmament; these soon pass away, while he is still there; and all who will consent to open their eyes may be illumined by his rays. So is it precisely with that blessed light of Religion, which "enlighteneth every man that cometh into this world."† All may easily see it, by simply opening the eyes of their mind, and by chasing away, with the divine aid, the interposing clouds of prejudice which sometimes conceal its brightness from the beholder.

We have already seen,‡ that Christ taught and established but one Religion; that He fixed and defined it in all its parts; that He made the belief and practice of it, as thus defined,

---

* Ephesians, ch. iv.   † St. John, i: 9.   ‡ In the first Lecture.

obligatory on all men; and that, consequently, He must
have furnished all with the means necessary for ascertaining it with ease and certainty. As He founded but one.
Religion, so also, in the very nature of things, He could
have established but one Church, for the guardianship,
preservation, and faithful transmission of this one Religion
to the end of time. This we have also shown.

Upon this one Church, established for this very purpose,
He must have impressed certain great distinctive characteristics or MARKS, by which it might easily be recognized by
all, and clearly distinguished from every other society, and
more especially from every other which might falsely claim
to be the one original Church. Had He not done this, He
would have left His work incomplete, and would not have
made any adequate provision for the salvation of men. His
blood would have streamed from the cross all in vain; His
ardent love for mankind would have been frustrated of its
purpose; we would still have been left in the darkness of
doubt and uncertainty; and our very salvation would have
been in jeopardy: for, in this hypothesis, it would have been
impossible for us to ascertain with certainty which is the
Church of Christ. All men were bound "to hear the
Church," under the awful penalty of being cast forth with
"the heathen and the publican;"* and yet they would have
been deprived of a means indispensably necessary for discovering where this Church is to be found.

Merely human legislators have taken special care to stamp
certain distinctive features on the governments which they
respectively originated; a monarchy has characteristics by
which it may readily be distinguished from an aristocracy
or a democracy:—and are we to say that the divine Founder
and Legislator of the Church had less wisdom and foresight
than they; and that His greatest work, the masterpiece of
His wisdom and the fruit of His tears and of His blood,
came from His hands less distinctly marked, and, therefore,
less fully developed and less perfect, than the necessarily

* St. Math. xviii: 17.

imperfect institutions of merely human skill and sagacity? God forbid, that we should cast any such imputation as this on the wisdom of the WORD MADE FLESH.

It is, then, unquestionable, that Christ must have impressed some such distinctive marks on His Church. And all that we have to do in order to discover which is the true Church, is to investigate what these characteristics are, and to which of all the many claimants to be the Church of Christ at the present day they really belong. This is no difficult undertaking. The line of inquiry which it traces requires no abstruse reasoning, no great mental acumen, no profound learning; the most simple-minded, the veriest little child in Christ, may pursue it with ease and safety, and with a well-grounded hope of reaching the goal of truth to which it certainly leads.

It is not so with the investigation through the distinctive marks of the true Church as usually set forth by the divines among our dissenting brethren. These are: the unadulterated preaching of the word, the legitimate administration of the sacraments, and, according to some, the enforcing of a wholesome church discipline. The inquiry into these alleged distinctive characteristics is really more difficult than that into the great question itself lying back of them, —which is the true Church? It opens before us a field without either boundaries or landmarks; instead of shedding new light upon the great problem to be solved, it only embarrasses it with a multiplicity of new issues, and thereby increases the difficulty it was intended to solve. It is certainly more difficult to ascertain which is the sound doctrine, which are the true sacraments, what constitutes their legitimate administration, and in what consists a wholesome discipline, than it is to discover which is the true Church in which all these things are taught and observed.

But you will say, there is the Bible in which all these points are clearly and distinctly set forth, so that every well disposed person can easily discover them, and thereby ascertain with certainty which is the true Church.

If these characteristics are so very plain in the Bible,

why is it, that those who read this sacred book with equal
sincerity and learning, fail to see them in the same light?
Why are there so many different and contradictory systems
of sound doctrine, of legitimate administration of the sacraments, of wholesome dicipline, all alleged to have been
taken from the same Bíble?   Why is it, that every denomination of Christians, that has ever arisen in the world, has
framed a different system in all these particulars, and has
insisted upon it as the only one really warranted by the
written word?   Is a line of inquiry thus plainly leading to
contradictory results either easy or safe?   Can it be, that
Christ left no other means than this for ascertaining which
is His Church?   Had He left no other, He would not have
defined His Religion, but would merely have handed it
over to the disputation of men; He would not have made
adequate provision for leading mankind to a certain knowledge of the truth, to seal which He shed His precious blood
on the cross; but He would, on the contrary, have left them
" to be tossed to and fro by every wind of doctrine,"—the
mere sport of their own exuberant fancies, and of the crafty
false teachers who " lie in wait to deceive."

The truth is, my Beloved Brethren, the Marks of the true
Church, as assigned by Protestants, are no Marks at all.
They involve the very question in controversy; they assume as already settled, what is in dispute; they are not
distinctive, because they may be applied, and they have been
applied, to a hundred jarring sects, all alike claiming to be
the one true Church; they are not plain and palpable,
because they involve principles which are invisible, hidden,
and difficult of discovery; they are above the capacity of
the unlearned, who constitute the bulk of mankind; and
they necessarily embarrass even the learned, and have actually led these to contradictory conclusions.   They present,
then, no adequate means for ascertaining which is the true
Church; they bewilder even the believer himself; and to
the unbeliever they afford no clue for emerging from the
labyrinth of doubt into the clear light of truth.   Therefore
they are not, they cannot be, the distinctive characteristics

impressed by Christ upon His Church, for the purpose of
leading mankind to a certain knowledge of it; and we must
seek these Marks elsewhere, if we would find them at all.

. It is no difficult task to ascertain these Marks, and to
point them out. They are so conspicuous that they are unmistakable. They stand forth as clearly traced on the face
of the Church, as do the distinctive features on a man's
countenance. Nay more; the blessed light of heaven shines
strongly upon them, and causes them to be revealed in such
boldness and distinctness of outline, "that he who runneth
may read."

. They flow from the original nature and constitution of
the Church herself as she came forth fresh from the hands
of her divine Founder; they are as inseparable from her
essence as they are distinctive of her character; they can
co-exist with no other institution; they have shone forth,
plain and palpable, through all the long centuries and eventful vicissitudes of her history. Age has not obscured their
brightness; the breath of persecution and the clouds of
sophistry have not tarnished their brilliancy, nor dimmed
their luster. They are as visible as is the Church herself;
they have not sought concealment, but have been proclaimed from the house-tops; nay, they have stood forth,
as beacons of light, on the top of the mountains, and have
guided the nations in safety to the house of God established
thereon, according to this magnificent prophecy of Isaias:
"And in the last days, the mountain of the house of the
Lord shall be prepared on the top of the mountains, and
it shall be exalted above the hills; and all nations shall
flow unto it."* No one who is not strangely perverse or
wilfully blind can fail to see them, and to recognize, at a
glance, the Church to which they belong.

The sincere Christian inquirer, who stands with Christ on
the elevated position from which He delivered His farewell
address to His apostles containing the commission,—who
listens reverently to the words of solemn import which
then fell from His sacred lips,—who takes with him a pros-

* Isaias, ii: 2.

pective view of the future existence of His Church,—who
compares the language then employed with that employed
by Him on other occasions in which He more fully developed
the same principles; cannot fail to ascertain what are those·
distinctive characteristics of the true Church, and cannot be
embarrassed in their application. Christ was a Prophet,
and He was God. As a prophet, His more than eagle
glance took in the future developments and destinies of His
Church even unto the period of His second coming; as
God, He could not be baffled in His purpose, nor fail in
fully carrying out all His intentions.

With the light of these principles, let us examine, for a
moment, some of these distinctive Marks, as gathered from
the words of the Commission, and from the other passage
from St. John, which I have quoted as my text. We find, in
the former, that our blessed Lord commanded His apostles
to teach "ALL NATIONS," to teach them "ALL THINGS, whatsoever He had commanded," and to continue their teaching
"ALL DAYS, even to the consummation of the world." He
set no limitation whatsoever, whether of place, or of time,
or of doctrine; His Church was to embrace the whole world,
to teach all truth, and to endure through all time. It was
thus to be marked by a triple CATHOLICITY; a Catholicity
of extension and numbers, a Catholicity of doctrine, and a
Catholicity of duration. Hence, if the forecast of Christ
was not deceived, or if His intentions were not frustrated of
their effect, we are bound to consider this threefold Catholicity as an essential and distinctive mark of His Church.
If such be not the case, then was Christ neither God nor
even a true Prophet; and His Religion, far from realizing
His expectations, has turned out a complete failure.

Again, in giving the Commission, Christ certainly intended that His apostles should all teach precisely the same
doctrines, should all administer the same sacraments, and
should all combine in organizing into one united body or
society all the nations to whom they were to announce the
gospel. He did not give different commissions to different
apostles, but He gave but one to them all, couched in one

form of language, and conveying but one definite meaning. He did not instruct them to administer different baptisms, but only one, as a means of initiating their converts into the one religious society which they were to found and establish. The apostles could have understood His words in no other way.

Had there been left any room for doubt on their minds as to the real meaning of those words, the explicit declarations of the Saviour on other occasions would have removed all shadow of uncertainty. They had already heard their divine Lord and Master uttering this emphatic and prophetic language: "And other sheep I have that are not of this fold: them also I must bring; and they shall hear my voice; and there shall be made ONE FOLD AND ONE SHEPHERD." What body is more thoroughly one and united than a sheepfold? What fitter emblem of a perfect and indissoluble unity? What more suitable type of perfect docility to the voice of the shepherd? Such a thing as division or schism is impossible in a sheepfold. Divide the flock, and both segments are restless and unsettled until they be united again.

Therefore, the apostles could not but have regarded UNITY as another essential and distinctive characteristic of the Church. Like the other attribute, Catholicity, Unity was to be threefold in the objects which it embraced: Unity in doctrine and in its external profession; Unity in worship and in the reception of the sacraments; Unity in the body and in the government which was to keep the body united.

Thus we see, my Dear Brethren, that, abstracting for the present from the consideration of other qualities of the Christian Church, Catholicity and Unity, as just explained, are certainly to be reckoned among its essential and distinctive characteristics. No one can deny this without impugning the most positive declarations of Christ, and virtually implying, either that He did not Himself comprehend the import of the plainest language, or that He was willing to mislead others as to their meaning.

But there are also many other passages both of the Old

and of the New Testament, which shed a still clearer light upon this subject, and remove all possibility of doubt or cavil.

And first, in regard to Catholicity. The prophecies recorded in the Old Testament, from the time that the promise first went forth that the woman should crush the serpent's head,* down to the coming of Christ, were all unanimous in foretelling the unlimited extension of the Christian Church. To Abraham it was said: "and in thy seed shall ALL THE NATIONS of the earth be blessed;† and the same promise was subsequently renewed to Isaac and to Jacob. In the memorable prophecy made by Jacob on the eve of his death, it was foretold of the Messiah: "and He shall be the EXPECTATION OF NATIONS."‡ This same magnificent promise was re-echoed through all the long ages of anxious expectation which preceded the advent of the Saviour. The royal prophet, penetrating with the glance of inspiration through the dark shadows of the future, saw it already fulfilled in the subjection of all nations to the dominion of Him who was to spring up "a flower from the root of Jesse;"§ and he heard the eternal Father thus addressing His beloved Son: "Ask of me, and I will give thee THE GENTILES for thy inheritance, and the UTMOST PARTS OF THE EARTH for thy possession."‖

The prophet Isaias, as we have already seen, beheld, in advance, "ALL NATIONS flowing to the house of God prepared on the top of mountains, and exalted above the hills."¶ Filled with joy and gladness at the glorious prospect thus opened before his prophetic vision, he broke forth in this magnificent canticle of triumph: "Arise, be enlightened, O Jerusalem: for thy light is come, and the glory of the Lord is risen upon thee . . . . : . And THE GENTILES shall walk in thy light, and kings in the brightness of thy rising. Lift up thy eyes round about and see: all these are gathered together, they are come to thee: thy sons shall come from

---

* Genesis, iii.   † Genesis, xxii: 18.   ‡ Genesis, xlix: 10.

§ Isaias, xi: 1.   ‖ Psalm, ii: 8.   ¶ Isaias, ii: 2.

afar, and thy daughters shall rise up at thy side. Then shalt thou see and abound, and thy heart shall wonder and be enlarged, when the multitude of the sea shall be converted to thee, and the strength of THE GENTILES shall come to thee."*

All the prophets bore evidence to the same glorious characteristic of the Christian Church. The last of them, whose prophecy is recorded in the Old Testament, says: "For from the rising of the sun, to the going down, my name is great among THE GENTILES; and IN EVERY PLACE there is sacrifice and there is offered to my name a clean oblation; for my name is great among THE GENTILES, saith the Lord of Hosts."†

If this prophetic language mean any thing, it clearly implies that, whereas the Jewish Church was confined to one nation and people, the Christian was to extend to all nations; and that hence Catholicity of place and numbers was to be one of the distinctive characteristics of the latter dispensation.

The explicit declarations of the New Testament throw the clearest light on this conclusion, and render it entirely certain. The apostles were commanded to preach the gospel "to all nations, beginning at Jerusalem."‡ On the refusal of the Jews to hear their voice, they were bidden to turn to the gentiles. A special heavenly vision unfolded this intention of God to the mind of St. Peter; and St. Paul was miraculously converted and called to be, in a special manner, the apostle of the gentiles. The sound of the apostles went forth into the whole earth; and St. John, in his vision of the heavenly Jerusalem, saw there assembled "a great multitude which no man could number, of all nations, and tribes, and peoples, and tongues, standing before the throne, and in sight of the Lamb, clothed with white robes, and palms in their hands."§

This unlimited extension of Christianity was, in fact, a

* Isaias, lx: 1, 5. † Malachy, 1: 11.
‡ St. Luke, xxiv: 47. § Apocalypse, vii: 9.
15 *

necessary consequence of its very nature and purpose.
Christ willed "ALL MEN to be saved and to come to the
knowledge of the truth;"* and His inspired apostles proclaimed that they could not be saved without embracing
His Religion and becoming His disciples: "There is salvation in no other: for there is no other name under heaven
given to men, whereby we must be saved."† The inference
is plain and irresistible. If Christ sincerely willed the salvation of all mankind, and if no one could be saved without
entering His Church and therein calling upon His name; it
necessarily follows, that He must have taken effectual means
so to extend the boundaries of His Church, that all men
might be enabled to enter into it, if they would.

Salvation was, indeed, a free gift of God; He would in-
fringe on no one's free will; He would compel none to be
saved whether they would or not: still He must have placed
in the hands of all men this necessary means of salvation;
and He could not have done so without extending His
Church to all nations. But from the very nature of the
case, and from the settled purpose of Christ not to violate
man's free will, this extension was to be morally, not phy-
sically, universal; and it was, for the same reason, to be
progressive, not instantaneous. The Church was to be, in
progress of time and morally speaking, every where; it was
not necessarily to exist at the same time in every part of
the earth, or to reckon among its members all the children
of men. This latter result could not have been secured
without a violation of that free will which God had bestowed upon mankind, and which it was not the purpose of
Christ to destroy or even to trammel.

This universal diffusion of the Church cannot be even
conceived, without Unity among all its component parts.
A Church rent into discordant fragments;—some professing
one set of dogmas and some another, some worshiping in
one way and some in another, some adopting one mode of
government and some another;—would no more constitute

*1 Timothy, ii: 4.   †Acts, iv: 12.

a Catholic or universal Church, than all the different governments of the world, with their various and jarring elements, can constitute one general government. A religious society, to be universal, must necessarily be every-where the same; must profess the same principles, adopt the same worship, be obedient to the same external government.

Catholicity and Unity thus stand or fall together. A society may be, indeed, One without being Catholic; it cannot, in the very nature of things, be Catholic without being One.

The pages of the New Testament every-where proclaim this truth in the most distinct and emphatic language. In addition to the passages already quoted, I may observe, that all the types employed by our Saviour and His inspired apostles to indicate the distinctive character of His Church, essentially denote the necessity of Unity. A household, a kingdom, the house of God, the body of Christ, the vine and the branches, the sheepfold,—what else do they all indicate but the closest Unity? Does not Christ himself tell us: "Every kingdom divided against itself shall be made desolate; and every city or house divided against itself shall not stand?"* Did not St. Paul, on hearing of the schism which had rent the Church of Corinth, ask emphatically: "Is Christ divided? Was Paul crucified for you? Or were you baptized in the name of Paul?"† Does he not, in the same epistle, describe the Church as the body of Christ, in the following remarkable passage: "For as the body is one and hath many members; and all the members of the body, whereas there are many, yet are one body; so also is Christ; for in one spirit we are all baptized into one body, whether Jews or Gentiles, whether bond or free; and in one spirit we have all been made to drink?"‡ And does he not, in his epistle to the Ephesians, written while he was a prisoner of the Lord at Rome, proclaim the same truth, when he exhorts them to be "careful to keep the unity of the

*St. Matthew, xii: 25.　　　　　† 1 Corinthians, i: 13.
‡ Cor. xii: 12, 13.

Spirit in the bond of peace," and tells them that there is
but "one body and one spirit; ..... ONE LORD, ONE FAITH,
ONE BAPTISM?"*

Does he not every-where brand schism and division as
an atrocious evil, which strikes at the very root of Christianity? Does he not "beseech" the Romans "to mark them
who cause dissensions and offenses contrary to the doctrine
which they had learned, and to avoid them?"† Does he
not reckon "dissensions and sects" with "murder and
drunkenness" in his enumeration of the works of the flesh;
and does he not utter this terrible sentence in reference to
all of them: "Of the which I foretell you, as I have foretold to you, that they who do such things shall not obtain
the kingdom of God?"‡

What do all these and many other declarations of the
same kind, which my limits compel me to omit, signify,
unless that Unity is an essential characteristic of the Christian Church? Had it not been so, would Jesus Christ have
prayed so fervently for his disciples, that "they might be
one," even as He and the Father were one?§ Would this
truth have been so often and so emphatically insisted on by
the sacred writers? Are we to say that all their repeated
declarations on the subject amount, after all, to nothing?

We are then necessarily led to the conclusion, that, according to the intention of Christ and that of His inspired
apostles, Catholicity and Unity, each threefold in its objects, were made essential and distinctive attributes of the
Christian Church, to co-exist with it in all time, and to be
its inseparable characteristics. And, this truth being once
admitted, all that the sincere inquirer has to do, in order to
find out which is the true Church of Christ, is to apply
them as tests to the various Christian denominations which
now lay claim to that glorious title. The denomination
which bears the test, is, by the fact, proved to come up, so
far at least, to the lofty type of the Church as established

* Ephesians, iv: 3, 5.   † Romans, xvi: 17.
‡ Galatians, v: 20, 21.   § St. John, xvii: 11, 22.

by Christ and His apostles; the denomination or denominations which will not bear the test, are necessarily excluded from the list of lawful claimants. These can not be the Church of Christ, because they are not stamped with the distinctive features and marks which He impressed upon His Church:—they are not even good counterfeits, for these would preserve at least a striking resemblance of traits with the original.

In order that the applications of these tests may not be embarrassed with too many issues, I may observe, that of the threefold Catholicity of the Church, I shall have to devote a separate Lecture to that in regard to time, when I shall have occasion to prove that the Roman Catholic Church alone can justly lay claim to antiquity and apostolicity; and that the species of Catholicity which regards universality of doctrine would open before us too wide a field for the scope contemplated in this Lecture. Suffice it at present to remark, in reference to this species of Catholicity, that the Roman Catholic Church alone, of all the Christian denominations in Europe or this country, claims to be unchangeable in her doctrines, and to adhere with tenacity to the entire deposit of faith as sanctioned by Church authority, and handed down from past generations. Other Christian societies have changed, and must necessarily change in their faith; hence, if they ever held the whole doctrine of Christ, they do not hold it now, and *vice versâ*. The only species of Catholicity, then, which remains to be considered, is that of extension and numbers.

So also, in regard to Unity, as I intend to devote a separate Lecture to the unity of government and of the body, I shall of course confine my view at present to the other two kinds; those of faith externally professed and of outward worship.

Thus the whole question which is now before us, is narrowed down to the investigation of a very plain and striking fact: which of all the denominations of Christians now on the face of the earth, and each claiming to be the true Church of Christ, is really distinguished by the cha-

M

racteristics of Catholicity and Unity, or which comes the nearest to universal extension in point of place and of numbers, and to a perfect unity in point of faith and of worship? I shall endeavor to answer this question by successively applying each of the two tests just named, first to the churches separated from the Roman Catholic, and then to the Roman Catholic itself.

But before entering upon the application, it may be well to answer a popular objection which is often urged with an air of triumphant complacency by our adversaries, and which, if valid, would prove that the whole reasoning of the present Lecture is inconclusive. We are gravely told, that universality and unity are no certain tests of truth; because they may co-exist, and have often, in fact, co-existed with error, as in the cases of Paganism and Mohammedanism.

I might deny that either of these two systems is marked by the characteristics in question. They are, indeed, wide-spread, and count vast numbers of followers; but they are wholly unknown in Europe and in many other parts of the world; besides that, like all other forms of error, they are split up into a hundred warring sects. That this latter assertion is true of Paganism, no one will deny; that it is equally true of Mohammedanism, every one knows who is at all conversant with the history of this abominable imposture.* The objection, then, rests upon an assumption unfounded in fact, and therefore it falls to the ground of itself.

But suppose, for a moment, that the assumption is true; still, even so, the objection would really prove nothing.' It is entirely beside the matter at issue. The controversy is not between Christianity and Paganism or Mohammedanism; but between different denominations of Christians, each

---

* See the learned "Introduction to Sale's Koran,"• from which it appears that Mohammedanism is divided into two great parties, each of which numbers four principal sects, which are again subdivided into a great many smaller ones, all very exclusive, and bearing to one another a deadly polemical as well as political hatred.

claiming to be the one true Church of Christ. I do not say that Catholicity and Unity are *absolute* tests of truth; but I maintain, for the weighty reasons above alleged, that they are *relative* tests among Christians, wholly conclusive in deciding among them which is the true Church. Christ stamped these characteristics on His Church; therefore no Church, which has them not, can by possibility be His Church. This is the argument, the force of which is obviously not impaired by the objection.

I. CATHOLICITY.

1. It requires no great amount of knowledge or penetration to perceive that none of the communions separated from the Roman Catholic Church is marked by this attribute; and that it cannot be predicated even of all of them put together. The Greek church has it not; for the Greek church is confined to a small part of Asia and Europe, and it is found nowhere else. At the very highest computation, it reckons, including the Russian church, not more than fifty millions of members, not much more than one-sixth of the entire Christian population of the world.

No single Protestant denomination, not even the Lutheran, which is the most numerous, can count half so many followers; therefore no single Protestant denomination can certainly claim to be Catholic. Besides, each of the Protestant sects is mainly confined to a comparatively small territory of Christendom, beyond which it is scarcely known at all. Lutheranism exists chiefly in northern Europe and Germany, and it has but a few feeble and scattered colonies in the United States. Calvinism, in all its various modifications, is found only in a small portion of Germany, in Switzerland, in Holland, in France,* in Great Britain and a few of its colonies, and in the United States. Anglicanism does not show itself except in Great Britain and her dependencies, and in our own Union. The same may be

---

* Where, as in Germany and elsewhere, it has for the most part dwindled down into Unitarianism and rationalism, that is, almost undisguised infidelity!

said of the Methodists, Baptists, and other minor denominations. As to the members of these various sects found in other parts of the world than those indicated, they are few indeed, and scarcely worth reckoning. To say that either of them is Catholic, would be almost as absurd as the assertion that these United States are the whole world, or that Kentucky is the whole United States!

But, perhaps, all of them taken together may form the Catholic, or universal Church. Perhaps they are all branches, which constitute, in the aggregate, the wide-spreading tree of Christianity, planted by Christ and watered by His blood. Let us see how plausible is this very fashionable modern theory of the Church. The branches of a tree are united together by adhering to one common trunk, from which they all derive their nutriment. Now, as this theory, if I understand it aright, likens the true Church of Christ to a tree, of which the different denominations dissentient from Rome constitute the branches, it is natural to inquire which is the common trunk to which they all adhere, from which they all derive their nourishment and life, and in which they are all united? Is there any original, common, parent church, to which all these discordant denominations are attached? The only one of the kind which can be imagined, is the Roman Catholic Church; but they all agree in protesting against this Church ; and, if this be the common trunk, they are manifestly, and by their own avowal, cut off from it, and are therefore lifeless.

It will not do to say that the trunk is Christianity. But what Christianity? This is the very point in dispute. It will not do to say that it is Christ Himself, the great invisible Head of the Church.—"Is Christ divided?" Does it fall far short of blasphemy to say, that Christ is the trunk which gives out the vital sap to a hundred heterogeneous branches, all of different and even opposite character and development? Is this a suitable emblem of His Church? Does it not amount to saying, in fact, that Christ, who "is the way, and the truth, and the life," is indifferent to truth and falsehood, and that He smiles alike upon a hundred contradictory systems? In such an hypothesis, what becomes of His attributes of sanctity and truth?

But let us suppose, for a moment, that this difficulty is solved; can it still be made out that all the Protestant denominations collectively, considered, do form, or can form, the Catholic or universal Church? According to the very highest estimate which can be made, their total number does not exceed sixty-five millions, or a little more than one-fifth of Christendom; but, according to the calculation of Hassel and other recent geographers, their real number ranges between fifty and sixty millions. Let us take sixty millions as the nearest approximation to the truth, and I feel confident that I am rather above than below the mark. This number comprises the total population of Protestant countries, as well as all those who are not Catholics in those Christian countries where different religious sects are found mingled together. It embraces not only Unitarians and Universalists, who are very numerous in many places, but also deists, free-thinkers, and persons of no religion whatever, who are found in still greater numbers. Take our own country as a specimen. It is estimated from official returns lately published in the American Almanac, that more than one-half of our adult population over twenty-one years of age belongs to no religious denomination whatever! In Protestant Great Britain, the religious statistics exhibit a similar result. Protestantism in France is but an empty name; the vast majority of the mere handful who are there enlisted against the Roman Catholic Church have already passed over to Pantheism, or to other systems of unbelief which are any thing rather than Christianity. In Germany and Switzerland the case is the same, if it be not even worse. We have the testimony even of the fanatical D'Aubigné himself, that, in these two fatherlands of Protestantism, "the majority have passed ever to the standard of rationalism, or the religion of men." *

In general, then, we may deduct at least one-half for deists, indifferentists, and rationalists; and this deduction

* History of the Great Reformation; vol. 1. Pref. p. 9.

16

will certainly not be too great, if we include in it the Universalists and Unitarians. The total number of "evangelical" Protestants is thus ascertained not to exceed thirty millions, or about one-tenth of the whole Christian population of the world. Can so small a fragment as this justly claim to be the Catholic or universal church? I think not.

Add to this number the fifty millions of Greek Christians,* and the sum total,—eighty millions,—will not still reach to one-third of all Christendom; so that even with every possible allowance, the dissenters from Rome, all taken together, cannot rightly claim to be the Universal Church. Therefore they have not an attribute which is essential to, and distinctive of, the true Church of Christ; then, they cannot evidently be that true Church, as we have seen.

2. Therefore, we must seek this Mark of Catholicity somewhere else. Where shall we find it, but in the Roman Catholic Church? If it be not found here, it can be found nowhere; and we are driven to the assertion that the true Church of Christ has disappeared altogether from the face of the earth!

But is the Roman Catholic Church morally universal in extension, and comparatively universal in numbers? Surely it is. Is there a single quarter of the globe in which you will not find large bodies of Roman Catholics? In Europe, there are nearly one hundred and twenty-nine millions; in Asia, about three millions; in Africa, about one million; in America, considerably more than twenty-seven millions; in Oceanica, more than three millions. In the heart of the Chinese Empire, on the borders of the Caspian Sea, along the waters of the Ganges and Euphrates; in the very heart of Africa and at its extremities; in the farthest Islands of Oceanica; on the banks of the Amazon, the La Plata, the Mississippi, and the St. Lawrence; every-where in the whole

---

* The Greek Church agrees with the Roman Catholic in all doctrinal points except two: the supremacy of the Pope and the procession of the Holy Ghost; and in regard to the latter of these, all evangelical Protestants dissent from the Greeks and agree with us. Of this I may speak more fully hereafter.

habitable globe, Roman Catholics are found in greater or less numbers, but always in large, well-organized, and consistent bodies. Whither, then, will you go to escape from the boundaries of the Roman Catholic Church? The sun never sets on her wide-spreading dominions; she is literally everywhere. At least, she is certainly much more universally extended, and therefore much more Catholic, than any or all of the Christian sects opposed to her; and this fact, which no one can deny, is all that is necessary for our argument.

In point of numbers, the Roman Catholic Church is, from what I have already said, as strictly universal as she is in point of extension. She does not, indeed, embrace in her communion the majority of the whole human family; but she certainly does embrace the vast majority of Christendom. Even counting the Greeks with the Protestants, she reckons at least twice their total number of followers. Some have estimated the number of Catholics at two hundred millions, others at one hundred and eighty; the most moderate calculation makes it exceed one hundred and sixty millions.* After all due allowance will have been made for the infidels and indifferentists, who, in some Catholic countries—as in France—are counted in the total number, I think the last named computation may be considered as not far from the truth. But, according to any calculation which can be made, it will always appear that our Church has a vast numerical Catholicity over all dissenters, taken together; which is all that our argument requires us to prove.

II. UNITY.

1. The Protestant sects, taken even in the aggregate, do not, as I hope has been sufficiently established, constitute the Catholic or Universal Church; that they cannot possibly constitute it, must be apparent even to the most superficial thinker. They have no bond of union, no common faith, no common worship, no common government; they are

* The estimate made at Rome, a few years ago, from statistical returns, more or less complete, makes the number 160,842,084. It is very probably below the mark; it was next to impossible that all the returns should be full. Malte Brun's estimate is some millions higher.

disjointed fragments which never can coalesce into one
body.   All the various projects for bringing about a re-
union, which have been successively tried by the wisest
and best men in the various Protestant communions, have
resulted in the most signal failure.   There are seeds of dis-
sension in the very bosom of the Protestant system, which
daily bring forth before our own eyes the bitter fruits of
new sects and divisions.   Older sects declining and dying
away; newer ones springing up amidst their ruins; the
latter again frittered away by internal dissensions, and in
a few short years sharing in their turn the fate of their
predecessors: — these have been the ordinary phases of
Protestantism during the three centuries of its fitful existence.   It is powerful for destruction, but utterly powerless
even for self-preservation.

It has no conservative principle to restrain the strong
radical spirit which hurries it on to division and ruin.   The
strong arm of the state may, indeed, imperfectly and for a
brief period, stay its downward tendency, by throwing
around its weakness the panoply of civil protection; but
decay is at its very heart-strings, and no human power can
avert its doom.   What is modern Protestantism on the continent of Europe, where it is universally upheld by the
state, but the mere shadow of its former self;—its youthful
vigor and enthusiasm gone, its energies wasted by division,
its very life almost extinct!

The reason of all this is very plain.   Our blessed Saviour
has sufficiently unfolded it, when He declared: "Every
plant which my heavenly Father hath not planted, shall be
rooted up."*   "Every kingdom divided against itself shall be
made desolate: and every city or house divided against itself
shall not stand."†   Divisions and subdivisions have ever
been the heritage and the plague-spot of Protestantism.

How many Protestant sects are there now in the world?
It would be difficult to answer this question with any thing
approaching to accuracy; because the number is varying

---

* St. Matthew, xv: 13.   † St. Matthew, xii: 25.

almost every day. Since the commencement of the reformation, Protestantism has given birth to more than two
hundred, perhaps to three hundred, jarring sects; making
about one new one for each year of its existence. Its fruitfulness has been really amazing. More than half of its
offspring have, however, already hastened to the tomb; and
many of those sects which yet survive, already manifest
symptoms of speedy dissolution, and must, in the nature of
all things merely human, soon share the fate of their predecessors.

It is not, perhaps, an exaggeration to say that the actual
number of Protestant sects in the world reaches to at least
one hundred! These all profess different religious creeds,
and all adopt different systems of worship. Taken in the
aggregate, they differ on almost every thing; from the divinity of Jesus Christ and the eternity of hell's torments,
down to minor points of worship or church discipline.
They carry on a bitter warfare with one another in regard
to their tenets; and even the same denomination is often
found divided into two or more conflicting parties. The
high and low-church parties in the Episcopal church, the
old and new-school parties in the Presbyterian, the old or
regular, and the reformed or Campbellite parties in the
Baptist, the northern and southern parties in the Methodist
—to say nothing of many other minor subdivisions—are all
cases in point, and familiar to every one in this country.

How are all these bitter controversies settled? They are
not settled at all. Every attempt to settle them results in
a new division. The utmost union of which Protestantism
is capable, consists in an agreement to disagree! And that
it is not often capable even of this, appears from the bitter
denunciations and uncharitable exclusiveness which so often
mark sectarian warfare.

The Protestant rule of faith necessarily leads to all these
unhappy results. So long as every one is told that his own
private judgment interpreting the Bible is to be the only
judge of controversy, so long will religious division be perpetuated. The only circumstance that surprises me, is, that
16 *

there are not even more sects among Protestants than there really are; for, with this principle legitimately carried out, there should be as many creeds as there are individuals. This logical result is prevented only by the restraining influence of established creeds enforced by church organization and discipline;—a restraint which is manifestly at war with the principle itself.* With such a principle as this constantly at work within its bosom, no civil society could exist one month; its organization would be broken up by internal divisions, and its body would be rent into fragments. Can we wonder, then, that precisely the same cause should produce results equally disastrous to Protestantism?

Can it be, my Dear Christian Friends, that a system thus fraught with perpetual changes and divisions, a system with a cardinal principle universally received and acknowledged which necessarily originates and perpetuates schisms, is that true Church of Jesus Christ upon which He stamped the distinctive features of Catholicity and Unity? Can it be, that the one Catholic Church of Christ is nothing more than a mere aggregation of discordant and contradictory sects; another tower of Babel, remarkable only for its confusion of tongues? I can never believe it, nor can any reflecting Christian.

Tell me not, that the Protestant sects all agree in substantial and fundamental doctrines, and differ only in matters of minor importance. If so, why do those points of difference constitute the basis of denominational distinctions? And why do not all the Protestant sects bury their controversies and coalesce at once into one church? Their not having been able to do so, notwitstanding the efforts so often made for this purpose, proves conclusively that

---

* Protestants are beginning to open their eyes to this glaring inconsistency. The reformers, or Campbellites, a growing sect in the western portion of our Union, started out with the declaration that all creeds are incompatible with the received Protestant principle of private judgment. Their Protestant adversaries seem to be much embarrassed by their arguments on this subject.

the points on which they differ are not deemed, even by themselves, of minor importance; and that the assertion upon which the objection is founded, is not credited by those who make it, and therefore falls to the ground of itself. So long as Protestantism will continue to exhibit the features which have constantly marked its countenance for the last three hundred years, so long will it be utterly *impossible* for it to claim the title of the *One Catholic* Church of Christ.

A general council composed of delegates from all the Protestant denominations on the face of the earth, assembled with a view to settle the difficulties of Protestantism, would indeed present a most curious spectacle. There would be almost as many opinions as heads; and in support of all of them, no matter how contradictory, numerous passages of the holy Scriptures would be quoted by their respective advocates with an air of triumph. At least a hundred different and contradictory systems would be thus extracted from the Bible, which yet obviously contains, and can contain, but one Religion! When the debate would be over, and the vote would be taken on any particular point of doctrine, how discordant would be the voices that would be heard to ring through the council chamber! What uproar of ayes and noes! Confusion would become worse confounded; and the council would result in nothing but an increased bitterness of sectarian wrangling. Such would be the inevitable result of a general council of Protestantism.*

2. How very different, my Dear Brethren, would be the spectacle presented by a council composed of delegates from all parts of the Catholic world! There would, there could be, no difference of opinion in regard to a single doctrine of the Catholic faith; if put to the vote, every one of them would be carried unanimously, and without one dissenting voice. The delegate from China would agree with the delegate from America; the delegate from Europe and Africa would agree with the delegate from the farthest

* The great Protestant Convention of London, held a few years ago, exhibited this result, if no other.

off island of Oceanica. There would be no "IT is and IT is NOT," but one unanimous "IT IS"* would swell through the council hall. There might, indeed, be some difference of opinion in matters not defined by the Church, and in disciplinary decrees; there could be none whatever in regard to articles of faith. In all these points the delegates would agree with an entire unanimity.

And the same precisely may be said in regard to the Unity of worship. The Chinese would bend down reverently before the same holy altar as the African, the European, and the American; his priests would offer up and adore the same Holy Victim of sacrifice; they would even be all clad in the same priestly uniform, and would adopt the same language in the public worship of the Church. The Catholic may travel from one end of the world to the other; he may pass to the antipodes; and every-where he will recognize the same time-honored ceremonial, kneel at the same altars, and feel that he is completely at home.

Even if he should notice in some places a difference of rite, of priestly uniform, and of language in the public service,—as, for instance, in the Oriental Churches in communion with Rome,—he would not be shocked by the diversity; for he would know and feel that the faith and the substance of the worship is the same, and that the diversity is allowed because it is hallowed by antiquity. Thus the Catholic alone can be a citizen of the world; he knows no country; all climates, and governments, and tongues, and castes, are alike to him; he is every-where AT HOME, because he every-where finds Catholicity the self-same.

Whence this astonishing Unity? How happens it that, while all the merely human elements in the civil and social condition of mankind are marked by diversity and subject to change, Catholicity alone is every-where the same, and every-where unchangeable? Whence comes this wonderful phenomenon, but from God himself? Does it lie within the

† II Corinthians, 1: 18, 19.

range of human power to bring about a unanimity so very remarkable? And who will not say, that the finger of God is surely here? This wonderful Unity can be explained on no other principle. The world, in all the annals of its history, has presented no similar phenomenon growing out of mere human agencies; it is contrary to the tendencies of human nature, which, unless restrained by some superior power, necessarily lead to diversities incompatible with Unity.

There is at Rome a college for the education of young Catholic missionaries,* which presents the rare spectacle of more than a hundred youths from the four quarters of the globe and the islands of the sea, speaking collectively from fifty to sixty living languages; of youths of different castes and colors, of different political prejudices;—different in all else but in Religion, in which they all agree with one heart and one soul. Protestantism has boasted much of its missionary enterprise; it has signalized its zeal by expending millions of money for the conversion of the heathen; and yet has it never once even attempted to rear an establishment like this. It seems to *feel* that the attempt would be utterly vain and fruitless; it knows its total want of the divine principle of Unity, and it therefore wisely abstains from the effort to present any striking type of what it has not.

The two tests of Catholicity and Unity have been thus successively applied to the Protestant and the Roman Catholic Churches; and I leave it to you, my Dear Brethren, to decide to which of them these distinctive features of the true Church of Christ really belong. You cannot hesitate for a moment in determining this question; you must have been already convinced by your own good sense and reflection, that the Roman Catholic Church alone can lay any reasonable claim to the possession of these characteristics.

The inference from this fact is necessary and irresistible. Christ constituted these attributes of Catholicity and Unity

---

* That of the Propaganda, founded by Pope Urban VIII.

the essential and distinctive marks of His Church; the Roman Catholic Church alone possesses them; therefore, the Roman Catholic Church alone can reasonably claim to be the Church of Christ.

This is the fourth evidence of the Catholic Church.

In the two following Lectures I hope to present you with two others founded upon characteristics of a similar nature with those which I have just endeavored to unfold, and, perhaps, equally striking and conclusive in favor of the Catholic Church. .

But before I dismiss you this evening, indulge me yet for a few moments, while I glance rapidly at some prominent facts in early Church history, which will go far to confirm the conclusion we have already reached in this Lecture.

To even the most superficial reader of ecclesiastical history it must be manifest, that the Catholic Church of the present day occupies precisely the same position in regard to all the sects which have risen up in opposition to her, and wields against them the very same weapons of argument, as did the avowedly true Church of the first centuries against the sects which then went out from her and *protested* against her doctrines. Then, as now, all the dissentient sects, while perpetually quarreling among themselves, could find no other basis of union than that of opposition to and hatred of the Church which reckoned the great body of Christians among its faithful children. Then, as now, the name *Catholic* was distinctive of the One true Church of Christ, and this name was awarded to her even by her most bitter enemies.

In the fourth century, says the learned Dr. Newman, "the Meletians of Africa united with the Arians against St. Athanasius; the Semi-arians of the Council of Sardica* correspond with the Donatists of Africa; Nestorius received and protected the Pelagians; Aspan, the Arian minister of Leo the emperor, favored the Monophysites of Egypt; the Jacobites of Egypt sided with the Moslem, who are

---

* Probably he meant *Syrmium.*

charged with holding a Nestorian doctrine. It had been so from the beginning: 'They huddle up a peace with all every-where,' says Tertullian,* 'for it makes no matter to them, although they hold different doctrines, so long as they conspire together in their siege against the thing, Truth.'"†

In the same century, St. Cyril of Jerusalem gives the following advice to the young candidates for baptism whom he was instructing:

"If ever thou art sojourning in any city, inquire not simply where the Lord's house is,—for the sects of the profane also make an attempt to call their own dens houses of the Lord,—nor merely where the Church is, but where is *the Catholic Church?* For this is the peculiar name of this holy body, the mother of us all, which is the spouse of our Lord Jesus Christ."‡

In the beginning of the following century, the great St. Augustine, writing against the sect of the Manichees, enumerates, among the reasons which retain him in the Catholic Church:

"The very title *Catholic,* which, not without cause, hath this Church alone, amid so many heresies, obtained in such sort, that, whereas all heretics wish to be called Catholics, nevertheless, to any stranger who asks how to find a Catholic Church, no one would dare to point to his own conventicle or house."§

Who does not see in these passages a most striking portraiture of what now-a-days daily takes place under our own eyes? The jarring sects who oppose the Catholic Church "huddle up a peace among themselves," as did their predecessors in the second century; but only when it is a question of attacking the Catholic Church. This is almost their only bond of union, as it was of the ancient heretics. While they greatly ambition the title *Catholic,* yet they dare not

---

* In the second century.

† Newman — "Essay on the Development of Christian Doctrine." p. 118. The subject is learnedly handled and ably developed in this remarkable work, by one among the most learned men of the present day.

‡ Catecheses, xviii.   § Contra Epistol. Manich. 5.

seriously appropriate it to themselves, else strangers to the
assumption would be led astray by the name, and would
flock to that Church, which, by universal usage and consent,
wears the title, and which alone deserves it.

This glorious name has in fact ever belonged of right to
the great united body of Christians in communion with
the See of Rome; it has, in all successive ages, from the
apostolic days downwards, been viewed as distinctive of
this Church in her relative position toward all opposing
sects; it has ever been the touchstone of true Christianity.
The sects have never been able to appropriate it to themselves. The name *Catholic* constituted a compendious description of Christianity from the earliest ages of the
Church.

"And it had been recognized as such from the first; the
name or the fact is put forth by St. Ignatius, St. Justin,
St. Clement; the Church of Smyrna, St. Iræneus, Rhodon,
or another, Tertullian, Origen, St. Cyprian, St. Cornelius;
the martyrs, Pionius, Sabina, and Asclepiades; Lactantius,
Eusebius, Adamantius, St. Athanasius, St. Pacian, St. Op-
tatus, St. Epiphanius, St. Cyril, St. Basil, St. Ambrose,
St. Chrysostom, St. Jerome, St. Augustine, and Facundus.
St. Clement uses it as an argument against the Gnostics,
St. Augustine against the Donatists and Manichees, St. Je-
rome against the Luciferians, and St. Pacian against the
Novatians."*

Thus, My Dear Brethren, we not only agree with the
whole Catholic world of the present day in the same faith
and the same worship, but also with the Church of the
earliest ages in wearing the name *Catholic*, and in claiming
the prerogatives ever and universally acknowledged to be
attached to that venerable name. Ours is thus plainly the
Church of all ages as well as of all nations. She occupies
now precisely the same commanding position in regard to
all the sects, as she did in her brightest days. Her vigor
has not declined with her years. She knows no old age.

---

* Newman, *ibid.* p. 119.

She is yet "without spot or wrinkle," fresh and blooming as when she first came forth from the creative hands of Christ. Never before was her pale so widely extended as it is now; never before did it embrace so many members. She is more Catholic now than she ever was. A Catholic of the present day may still say, with St. Pacian of the fourth century, — "CHRISTIAN IS MY NAME, CATHOLIC MY SURNAME.*

May God grant, in His ever abounding mercy, that we may all see these truths in the same light in which our holy ancestors saw them; and that attracted by the surpassing loveliness and beauty of the Church, we may all find out, and enter into this "ONE FOLD OF THE ONE SHEPHERD." Amen.

---

* Epist. ad Sympron.

LECTURE VII.

SANCTITY.—THE FIFTH EVIDENCE OF CATHOLICITY.

The Nicene Creed — Holiness a mark of the true Church — In what it
consists — It does not exclude scandals — Scriptural evidence — Holiness applied as a test — Tendency of distinctive Protestant doctrines —
Standard of Holiness among Protestants — Their ascetical works — Care
for the poor—The *fashionable* church—Picture of a Protestant church
— And worship — Religious instruction — Protestant sacraments — The
"holy *sabbath*"—Influence of private interpretation, justification by
faith alone—predestination, and other doctrines—Aversion to mortification—Practical fruits of Holiness—Protestant saints—Character of the
reformers — Moral and religious condition of Protestant countries —
Statistical facts — Catholic Standard of Holiness — Influence of Catholic
doctrines — Morals — Worship—And sacraments — Every want of man
amply provided for — Objection from imputed immorality— St. Augustine's answer— The Roman Pontiffs — Excommunicating sinners —
Merciful spirit of the Church — Treasures of ancient Sanctity— Modern
Catholic saints — Love for the poor—Hospitals and asylums — Heroic
charity — Protestant and Catholic missionaries compared — A tacit
tribute to Catholic Sanctity — Sisters of Charity — Conclusion — Fifth
evidence of Catholicity.

*" Husbands love your wives, as Christ also loved the Church, and delivered
Himself up for it, that He might sanctify it, cleansing it with the laver of water
in the word of life; that He might present it to Himself a glorious Church,* NOT
HAVING SPOT, NOR WRINKLE, NOR ANY SUCH THING; BUT THAT IT SHOULD
BE HOLY AND WITHOUT BLEMISH."—EPHESIANS, v: 25, 26, 27.

IN the last Lecture, my Beloved Brethren, you will recollect that I endeavored to develop two of the great distinctive characteristics of the Christian Church,—Unity and
Catholicity,—and to prove to you that they are found in no
other Christian denomination now on the face of the earth
than the Roman Catholic. The necessary inference from
this fact was, that this alone was the true Church of Christ.
In the present Lecture and the following one, I will proceed,
with the divine grace and with your indulgent attention,
to confirm this conclusion still farther, by inviting your consideration to the two other distinctive Marks of the Church,
plainly laid down in the holy Scriptures, and recognized
as such by all Christian antiquity. The Nicene creed, as
more fully explained in the second general council held at
(194)

Constantinople in the year 381, professes to believe "in One, Holy, Catholic, and Apostolic Church." Hence I have still to speak of the attributes of Holiness and Apostolicity, and to unfold the argument based upon them in favor of that venerable Christian society, which more than one hundred and sixty millions of your Christian brethren firmly believe to be the true Church of Christ.

The field which these two subjects will open before us, will be as ample as it will be interesting to the Christian inquirer; while the result of the investigation,— the discovery of the true Church of Christ,— is the one which of all others should be dearest to the Christian heart. I beg you to dismiss all pre-conceived opinions on the subject, to enter upon the investigation with calmness and impartiality, and, as a necessary preliminary to success, on its very threshold, to breathe an humble prayer to heaven for divine light and grace.

There can be no doubt, my Dear Brethren, that Sanctity is an essential and a distinctive Mark of the Church, necessarily growing out of her very origin and nature, and intimately connected with the ends for which she was established. The Church is a *divine* institution; she is the work of the great Man-God, the masterpiece of His infinite wisdom and holiness; and she was established for promoting the glory of God and the salvation of mankind. Her origin is most holy, her objects are most holy; and therefore must she be herself holy. Viewing her in the light of a divinely established and therefore adequate instrument for promoting the salvation of men, her doctrines, her moral principles, and her sacramental ordinances, must necessarily possess two qualities: first, they must contain in themselves all that is requisite and suitable for the blotting out of sin, the bestowal of grace, and the full carrying out of the atonement; and second, they must be practical in their influence on men, producing at all times abundant fruits of Holiness. In other words, the Church must be holy in all her institutions; and she must have been conspicuous, in all ages of her existence, for the holy lives of

many among her members; so conspicuous, that all men
might by this Mark, in combination with the others, easily
recognize her, and distinguish her from all other societies.

I say, *of many among her members;* for it is certainly not
a necessary consequence of Sanctity, considered as a distinctive characteristic of the Church, that all those who
belong to her outward communion should be distinguished
for holiness of life. There was a Judas even among the
twelve who were trained to piety under the eyes of Jesus
Christ Himself, and who were destined to become His instruments for sanctifying the world. Our blessed Lord
foretold that scandals should come; and He contented
Himself with pronouncing a wo upon the authors of them:
"Wo to the world because of scandals. For it must needs
be that scandals come; nevertheless wo to that man by
whom the scandal cometh."* Human nature is corrupt
and prone to evil; the Church was instituted to remedy
this corruption, and to lead mankind to holiness; but she
was to discharge this heavenly office chiefly by moral
suasion and by the winning attractives of divine grace,
without infringing the free exercise of free will. Men were
to be earnestly invited to holiness, not compelled to embrace it; the boon of sanctification and salvation was to be
freely tendered to all, none were to be constrained to receive it, whether they would or not.

There was to be cockle as well as good grain in the field
of the Church; and it was the will of the divine Husbandman that "both should grow until the harvest" of the
general judgment, lest those who would seek "to gather up
the cockle should root up the wheat also together with it."†
Jesus Christ himself ate and drank and associated with the
publicans and sinners, while He severely rebuked the hypocrisy of the self-righteous Pharisees, who censured Him
for this merciful condescension to human weakness. He
had no words of harshness for the adulteress and for poor
Magdalene; He denounced, with all the strength and energy

---

* St. Matt., xviii: 7.   † St. Matt., xiii: 29, 30.

of His divine eloquence, the sanctimoniousness of those
who wore long faces, uttered long prayers at the corners of
the streets that they might be seen by men, boasted of
their high reverence for the sabbath, and bitterly sneered
at others reputed less holy than themselves.*

I dwell upon this consideration, because it is essential to
a right understanding of Holiness considered as a characteristic of the Church; and because those who have not
paid sufficient attention to the merciful character and conduct of Jesus Christ, as every-where set forth in the gospel,
are in the habit of entertaining very erroneous ideas on this
subject. They conceive that the Church is necessarily
composed only of the holy and the elect, and that publicans
and sinners should be excluded from its saving influences,
as objects of loathing and totally unworthy of the Christian
profession. They seem to vaunt the superior holiness of
their own peculiar church organizations in this respect, and
thereby virtually censure the conduct of Christ himself, as
did the Pharisees of old. Surely the Church is not more
holy than her divine Founder; and if His holiness was not
sullied by contact with sinners, neither is that of His
Church by a conduct growing out of a similar spirit of
divine mercy and condescension. In fixing the standard of
Holiness, as a distinctive Mark of the Church, we must look,
not so much to the current notions of the day, as to the
words and example of Christ; and then we cannot go astray.

From the remarkable language of my text, it appears
that St. Paul viewed the Church as the chaste and immaculate Spouse of Christ, whom He loved with an abiding and
effectual love, for whom He delivered Himself up to death,
that He might sanctify her by His own precious blood, and
might thus "present her to Himself a *glorious* Church, *not
having spot, nor wrinkle, nor any such thing;* but that she
should be *holy and without blemish.*" This beautiful description of the Church corresponds with that presented by the
divine Spouse of the Canticles, when, charmed by her sur-

* For the woes pronounced against the Pharisees, see St. Matthew,
ch. xxiii.

17 *

passing beauty and loveliness, he breaks forth into such
exclamations as these: "One is my dove; my perfect one is
(but) one;"* "Thou art all fair, O my love, and there is
not a spot in thee!"† It also tallies perfectly with the
favorite illustration of St. Paul, when he represents the
Church as the body of Christ, of which He is the Head;—
"And (God) hath made Him Head over all the Church,
which is His body, and the fullness of Him who is filled all
in all;"‡—as also with the description of the Church as
the "house of God,"§ and as the "kingdom of heaven."||

Surely, my Dear Brethren, the Church which is described
under all these striking figures must be Holy, of the holiness of Christ Himself. Would He permit the purity of
His own dearly beloved Spouse, for whom He shed His
blood, to be sullied by any defilement? Would He suffer
His own body to be filled with uncleanness and to fester
with disease? Would He take so little care of His own
household or kingdom, as to allow it to be contaminated
by wickedness? Were He thus heedless of His own, He
would not be the all-wise, and all-holy, and all-powerful
Man-God, that all Christians unanimously hold Him to be:
He would certainly be deficient in one or the other, or in all
of these attributes. He would, by the fact, cease to be God,
and His Church would cease to be divine.

From what has been thus far said, I hope you will all
agree with me in the belief, that Holiness is an essential and
distinctive attribute of the true Church of Christ; that this
Sanctity is not incompatible with the existence of sin and
scandals among the members of the Church; and that it
consists in bearing constant witness against all wickedness,
by means of a holy *doctrine* divinely adapted to the sanctification of men, and of a holy *practice* conspicuous in the
virtuous lives of *many* among the children of the Church in
all ages. Such being the principles which are to guide us
in our inquiry, all that we have to do, in order to ascertain

* Canticles, or Song of Solomon, vi : 8.   † Ibid. iv : 7.
‡ Ephesians, i : 22, 23. See also Colossians, i : 18; and I. Corinth., xii.
§ I. Timothy, iii : 15. || St. Matt. xiii : &c.

which is the true Church, is to examine calmly and before God, which of all the Christian denominations now on the face of the earth really possesses this essential Mark of Holiness: that is, which has the most holy doctrines, and which has produced the most abundant fruits of holiness in the lapse of ages. I propose to go into this comparison at some length, and to rest the case upon its merits. I shall, however, to simplify the investigation, confine myself to the Roman Catholic and the Protestant denominations, and leave out the Greek and Oriental churches, which agree with the Roman Catholic in all those doctrines and usages to which I shall have occasion to refer.*

I. And first, let us examine what are the claims to Sanctity of doctrine and of practice put forth by our dissenting brethren, and how far those claims warrant the belief, that any or all of their many conflicting denominations really possess the attribute of Holiness, stamped by Christ upon His true Church, as distinctive of its character. Have the peculiar doctrines of Protestantism any special adaptation to the promotion of Sanctity; have they really produced saints worthy the name? For three centuries those principles have been exerting their legitimate influence on large masses of Christian population; and surely we should now be able to look back, and estimate aright their tendency in the practical development of Holiness.

It is deemed almost unnecessary to remark, that, in pursuing this line of investigation, I mean no disrespect whatever to Protestants, much less do I intend wantonly to wound the feelings of those who sincerely and conscientiously dissent from the Catholic Church. I hope to conduct the inquiry in no invidious or uncharitable spirit, and

---

* Dr. Durbin, in his "Observations on the East," vol. ii., fully confirms the truth of this remark. The Marks which the Greek and Oriental churches manifestly want, are, Unity and Catholicity. They are divided into a number of sects, and even the orthodox Greek Church is split into two segments, the Russian and the Constantinopolitan: while they are all confined to one quarter of the world. These deficiencies are decisive against their claim to be the true Church.

with proper Christian candor and fairness. Cheerfully do I admit, that our Protestant brethren exert themselves, in their own way, to promote piety, and to inculcate certain principles of morality among their followers; and that they number among their various denominations many men distinguished for talent, learning, zeal, and for religion as they understand it, as well as for all the civil and social virtues.

But still, for all this, I cannot think that their distinctive doctrines possess any features peculiarly conducive to Holiness and vital piety, or that their influence has ever produced many persons conspicuous for Christian Sanctity, according to the meaning of this term as laid down in the gospel. Some of you may probably think that I am wrong in this opinion, and that the expression of it is an evidence of prejudice and illiberality, rather than of Christian candor; but, at least, you will do me the justice to listen patiently and attentively to the reasons I shall have to produce in its support. I may tell you in the language of that bold man, whom not a few profess so much to reverence—"Strike, but hear!"*

1. In regard to the moral tendency of Protestant doctrines, I must necessarily be very brief, and must confine myself to general remarks. And first, is the standard of Holiness among our dissenting brethren in this country very elevated? What, according to the notions more generally current among them, constitutes the essence and highest grade of Sanctity? Is it retirement from the world, contempt for the world, a trampling upon riches, upon honors, upon pleasures, the cherishing of a meek and lowly spirit, a watchfulness over the movements of a corrupt heart? Is it self-denial, mortification, and self-sacrifice for the love of God and of the neighbor? Is it "a crucifixion of the flesh with its vices and concupiscences," a triumph over pride and self-love, and a union with God by perpetual prayer?

I know that some of these things are occasionally recom-

---

* Luther.

mended from the Protestant pulpit;—but are they sufficiently insisted on? Is not much more attention paid to merely external propriety of conduct, and to an avoiding of those things which may shock public decorum? Would it not almost appear, that a grave and serious countenance; a decorous walk among men; justice and fairness in dealing; a shunning of intemperance and profanity; a careful avoidance of amusements and plays in themselves innocent, but liable to abuse; a keeping of the *Sabbath* with a special silence and solemnity; and such external observances, constitute the principal features in Protestant godliness? Is it not true, at least, that these are the things which are the most striking, and of which you hear most among Protestants? They may be all, indeed, very good in their own way;—and far be it from me to censure them as evil in themselves;—but do they go far enough? Do they really reach the heart, heal its infirmities, and turn it to God? I fear not.

In a word, does not the Protestant system tend to improve and decorate the outward rather than the inward man; and to make a man a good citizen rather than a good Christian? And do not our dissenting brethren, while they censure the Catholic Church for attending too much to outward forms and observances, really fall themselves into the very defect which they ascribe to us without any sufficient reason?

2. Where, in fact, is the evidence of any peculiar spirituality in the Protestant denominations? Is it to be sought in their books of spiritual instruction and of devotion? But what books of the kind have they produced of any solid merit?

Is Bunyan's "Pilgrim's Progress" fit to be named even in the same day with Thomas A. Kempis' "Following of Christ," or with his "Garden of Roses and Valley of Lilies?" Are the spiritual works of Jeremy Taylor at all comparable with those of Fénelon and of St. Francis de Sales? Has Protestantism ever produced any thing like the "Spiritual Combat" of Lawrence Scupoli? Any thing like the spi-

ritual writings of Cardinal Bona, of St. Buonaventúra, of
St. Vincent of Paul, of St. Ligouri, and of a hundred other
Catholic ascetical writers? How very meager, how inani-
mate, how utterly devoid of spiritual simplicity and pathos,
are the ascetical works in most repute among our separated brethren; and, on the other hand, how rich, how deep
in feeling, how eloquent in a divine unction, how varied
and attractive, how exhaustless in number, are writings of
the kind among Catholics! Many enlightened Protestants
have candidly acknowledged our vast superiority in this
respect; and it is a consoling tribute to Catholic piety, that
some of our spiritual books, such as the Following of
Christ,* are often found in Protestant families.

3. Among the evidences of His divine mission which
Christ gave to the disciples, was this: "That the poor have
the gospel preached to them."† Now, I do not say that the
gospel is never preached to the poor among our separated
brethren; but every candid observer will admit that, at
least among many of their denominations, the wealthy are
much more sought after and more cared for than those who
are deficient in this world's goods. Who are usually the
most respectable and the most influential members in the
various Protestant Churches? Who are generally elevated
to the rank of deacons and elders? Who occupy the first
seats? Who manage the concerns and control the destinies
of the denomination? Are they not most generally the
rich and the influential in society? Do not these often
claim, as a sort of right, the principal influence in church
deliberations and enactments? Is not the pastor himself,
often made to feel their influence? Does he dare rebuke
their vices with the same freedom and boldness as he does
those of the poorer members?

Again, who cause the principal dissensions and divisions
in the Protestant Churches? Is it not usually the richer

---

* Abridged, however, and sadly mutilated in some of its most beautiful
parts.

† St. Matthew xv: 5.

members, whose *dignity* is not sufficiently respected, or
whose opinion is neglected in the administration of affairs?
Christ pronounced a blessing upon the poor, and denounced
a wo against the rich:—do our separated friends imitate
His example and copy His spirit in this respect? *He*
said; "It is easier for a camel to pass through the eye of a
needle, than for a rich man to enter into the kingdom of
heaven:"* do not many of the Protestant denominations
in our midst practically annul this declaration, by promising heaven to the rich on easier terms than they do to
the poor? Is not this palpably and lamentably true?†

4. Is it not, moreover, more or less customary among
Protestants, especially in our cities, to inquire which is the
most respectable and *fashionable* church? Where it is that
those who move in the first ranks of society are in the habit
of meeting for worship? Where it is, that one may hope
to hear the most popular preacher, and to meet the most
fashionable circles? And, on the contrary, are you not
often shocked at seeing the bitter sneer curl upon the lips,
and on hearing the withering and unchristian taunt thrown
out against particular churches frequented only by the poor,
the ill-dressed, and those who are held in contempt by the
world? What is all this but sheer pride and worldly-mind-
edness? Does it betoken aught of the spirit of Christ?
Aught of the unearthly character of His gospel? Does it
not, on the contrary, give evidence of a disposition to unite
the service of God with that of mammon, though Christ
proclaimed that these two services are wholly incompatible:
"You can not serve God and mammon?"‡

5. Enter, for a moment, into one of our *fashionable* Protestant Churches on the day set apart for public worship;
cast a glance at the interior of the edifice, and at the de-

---

* St. Matthew, xix: 24.

† As will be shown a little later, the Catholic Church does not neglect
the poor, nor pay inordinate court to the rich, in her heavenly ministra-
tions. We think all candid persons will be prepared to admit this.

‡ St. Matthew, vi: 24.

portment of the congregation ; mark all the phases of the
service:—is there any thing there that strikes you as peculiarly impressive and stimulating to piety? Is there any
religious symbol, to remind you of heavenly things? Is
there an altar, before which you may bend down in reverent awe and devotion? Is there any sacrifice to remind
you of that of Calvary, and to appeal to your hearts with
a touching and divine eloquence, that you too should offer
up to God, in unison with it, the sacrifice of an humble and
contrite heart? Is there any fragrant incense, filling the
house of God with its sweet odor, and curling up to heaven,
a fit emblem of the Christian's prayer? Do you there *feel*
that you are really in the house of God ; and are you even
tempted to break forth into the fervent exclamation of the
patriarch, when he awoke from his mysterious vision on
Mount Sion : "How terrible is this place! Truly this is
none other than the house of God, and the gate of heaven!"*

Alas! My Brethren, you can feel therein none of this reverent awe : the magnificent Christian temple has dwindled
down to a mere lecture-room ; its Sanctity has fled ; it has
become a place for elaborate *preaching*, rather than the
house of prayer;—the house of man rather than the house
of God.

The congregation accordingly enter and leave it with
their hats on ; they engage in conversation on indifferent,
perhaps on worldly subjects, until the very commencement
of the service, and immediately after its close ; they recline
on comfortable and well cushioned seats, more adapted for
the purpose of ease and luxury than for that of prayer;—in
a word, the spirit of reverence and religious awe is gone
for ever. The fine arts, too, have been banished from God's
holy temple ; and, along with them, the beautiful feelings
and heavenly associations which they naturally inspire.

Nay more; God himself has been banished from His own
house, or if He still exist in it, it is only as in other places
where His presence is equally manifested. Christ no longer

* Genesis, ch. xxviii.

dwells bodily in the midst of His people; His real presence in the holy sacrament has been denied; and the holy sacrament itself is accordingly no longer kept in the churches. Unlighted altars, or rather no altars at all, unstoled priests, undecorated walls, total barrenness of all religious association, a cold and lifeless service;—these are the things that freeze your very soul, and make you almost feel that you are in a temple under a fearful interdict of Heaven, rather than in a lawful Christian church.

6. And in what does the Protestant worship itself consist? Has it any thing that is peculiarly striking and impressive? One or two hymns sung, and often not in the best taste; a prayer delivered or read from the desk, wearing the appearance more of an "eloquent" address to the congregation than of an humble petition to Heaven, and listened to by the people, some in one attitude and position of face and some in another; then a sermon, followed by another chant; and all closed by another prayer like that just named :—these are the most prominent features of the more ordinary worship, in which the Lord's Supper is not administered. And, I now ask you, is there any thing specially elevating and impressive in all this? Is prayer a sufficiently prominent element of the service? Is the heart sufficiently appealed to? Is the practice of secret prayer especially, or the worship in spirit and truth, enough insisted on? Is the influence of the worship such as to cause the soul to sink down in humble adoration and annihilation before the dread majesty of God? Has it any feature of awfulness or of sublimity in its whole composition?

7. Again, do the bulk of Protestants really understand the nature, and have they any very definite ideas of the real principles of Christianity? They frequently talk, indeed, of conversion to God, of "getting Religion," of change of heart, of the redeeming blood of Christ; but have they, withal, any full or adequate conception of the true nature and real extent of the Christian doctrine? Are they carefully taught the details of the Christian system, the beautiful harmony of its various parts, the influence of the

18

Trinity, of the Incarnation, of the Atonement upon its other doctrines;—in a word, the full length and breadth and depth of the whole gospel dispensation?

Do not those revivals, for instance, which are so much insisted on by almost all the modern Protestant sects, depend quite too much for their success on mere nervous and animal excitement, created by fearful denunciation of hell's torments against sinners, and by other appliances of a like nature? Is it in conformity with the Sanctity of Christianity thus to insist more upon the motive of fear than upon that of love? Are the converts made in those revivals generally stable, or are they fully instructed in the elements of Christianity previously to their admission into the church? May not almost the only condition that is required for their reception,—the firm persuasion that their sins have been forgiven,—be itself but a fruitful source of self-delusion? And are not many enlightened Protestants disgusted with all Religion by the exhibitions of a fearful fanaticism, so often witnessed in these revivals, especially at camp meetings?

8. Moreover, my Dear Brethren, how very meager are the only two sacraments,—Baptism and the Lord's Supper,—which are still retained amongst our dissenting brethren?* Are they viewed as channels of grace, as instruments of the divine presence and assistance, as having any intrinsic efficacy whatever, or as imparting any special grace to the recipient? Are they not, on the contrary, regarded as mere ceremonies and types? In what, then, do they particularly contribute to Holiness? In what do they differ from the exploded types and shadows of the old law? Do they really excel these in Sanctity, appropriateness of figure, or in efficacy? Are mere bread and wine, for instance, as striking symbols of the body and blood and of the death of Christ, as was the paschal lamb of the Jewish dispensation? Is the water of baptism a fitter emblem of purification than were the numerous ablutions enjoined by

---

* The Episcopalians retain also confirmation: but it is believed that they do not generally regard it as a sacrament, properly so called.

the Mosaic law? In what, I again ask, does the peculiar Sanctity of the Protestant sacraments consist? In their reference to Christ? But was not this also a distinctive feature of the Jewish sacraments? Has Protestantism, by thus throwing us back on the antiquated position of mere Jewish types and figures, really contributed to the increase of Sanctity?

9. Again, there is much talk among our separated brethren about the *Sabbath*. A particular manner of keeping this day holy has always been a main staple of Protestantism; and we often hear the bitter taunt uttered against those who do not keep it as holily as themselves! Is there not, to say the least, much exaggeration in all this? Is there not a manifest tendency to make this day one of mourning rather than of holy rejoicing, as it was always viewed by the Christian Church from the beginning? Was not the day changed from Saturday to Sunday, with a special view of making it commemorative of Christ's resurrection, the most joyous of all Christian mysteries? Were the Scribes and Pharisees the more holy on account of their exaggerated reverence for this day, or in consequence of their accusations against our blessed Saviour and His disciples for alleged violations of its sanctity?

And do not our Protestant friends, in their mistaken zeal on this subject, obviously imitate the Pharisees and Jews, more than they do Christ and His followers? Is not the very word *Sabbath* evidently more Jewish than Christian, the name of the Jewish *Sabbath* or Saturday, rather than of the Christian *Sunday* or Lord's day? And are not Protestant churches generally kept locked during the six days of the week, and opened for worship only on the *Sabbath*, and then only during the hours of service?* Is this any peculiar evidence of that Christian Sanctity which manifests itself at all times in daily and hourly prayer? How different is this practice from that of Catholic countries, in which all the principal churches are constantly kept

---

* They are, indeed, frequently opened for an hour or two once or twice during the week, at least in cities.

open from sunrise to sunset, and from that even in this
country, where the Catholic churches with a resident
pastor are thrown open every morning for divine service!

10. Moreover, what is there, My Brethren, in the distinctive and most prominent doctrines of Protestantism
which stimulates to any special piety or holiness? Is it
the boasted principle of private interpretation?—But does
not this foster a spirit of pride, by making the one who
adopts it think himself more wise in the things of God than
is all the world besides? Has it not always led, and does
it not necessarily lead to sects and divisions and bitter
dissensions, subversive of all Christian charity, the very
essence of the Religion of Christ?

Is it the doctrine of justification by faith alone without
works?—But is it not a necessary tendency of this principle, no matter how it may be explained and softened down,
to undervalue good works, if not to induce their neglect
altogether? Is it the principle of predestination, and its
cognate doctrine of the inamissibility of grace?—But does
not this tenet, if logically carried out, necessarily encourage sin in one who believes himself a child of election?
Will he not be saved at any rate, no matter how much he
may sin? What need has he, then, to put himself to any
great inconvenience to avoid sin? Is it the boasted reverence for the Bible as the only rule of faith?—But has not
this very boast led to all the evils of a frightful confusion
and sectarianism? And are these evils compatible with
real Sanctity? Does not St. Paul rank *sects* with murder
and drunkenness, and say of all of them, that they are a
bar to heaven?*

Or is this peculiar tendency to promote Holiness to be
found in the principle,—more or less generally received
among American Protestants,—that the minds of children
should not be influenced by their parents, but that they
should be permitted to grow up without any distinctive
religious principles, and be allowed to choose their religion

---

*Galatians, v: 20, 31.

for themselves after coming to the full use of reason?—But is not this principle dangerous in the extreme? Is not our nature corrupt from our very childhood, and, if not religiously trained up from earliest life, will its soil produce aught but thorns and weeds of vice and corruption? What would be thought of the husbandman who should apply this principle to agriculture, and should suffer his fields to be uncultivated and overrun with noxious weeds in the spring, under the pretence, that, when summer would come, it would be time enough to scatter the good seed? And is it not owing to this fatally current maxim, that so many of our youth grow up in vice and without religion, and afterwards swell the ever increasing ranks of infidelity?

11. Finally, What is there in Protestant doctrine, that is particularly painful to corrupt nature, or humbling to human pride? What is there, that is manifestly unearthly, and at open war with the secret passions of the human bosom? What is there, that keeps men in a state of continual watchfulness, prayer, and struggle with an evil nature? Is it to be found in the habitual sneering at confession to a sinful man, as degrading to the dignity of human nature; at celibacy, as impossible or impracticable; at seclusion from the world, as foolish and absurd; at fasting, mortification, and bodily macerations, as against human nature, and therefore unchristian; at humble obedience to the Church, as trammeling human freedom;—at every-thing, in a word, which our pious Christian forefathers looked upon as peculiarly holy or conducive to Holiness? Alas! my Dear Brethren, is it not now true, as St. Paul foretold when speaking of heretics in the latter days, that there are some, "having an *appearance*, indeed, of piety, but denying the *power* thereof?"*

Nearly akin to this scoffing spirit, is the disposition—alas too common among our Protestant brethren—to assail the mysteries of the Catholic faith with precisely the same weapons which infidels employ against Christianity. The

* II Timothy, iii: 5.

doctrine of the real presence of Christ in the Holy Eucharist, for instance, is opposed on the ground that it "is a hard saying," and difficult, if not impossible, of belief; just as the Unitarian and the deist attack the equally incomprehensible mysteries of the Incarnation and the Trinity. The sneering invectives which the impious Voltaire poured forth against the most mysterious and sacred institutions of the Catholic Church are identical with the *arguments* against the same holy doctrines now most current amongst Protestants, and they are probably those precisely which exercise the greatest influence over the uneducated masses. Whence this striking coincidence? Does it not indicate an ominous sympathy between Protestantism and infidelity? At any rate, every candid Christian must admit that Protestant controversialists often find themselves in very bad company, and that the alleged Sanctity of dissent must suffer greatly by "the evil communication which corrupteth good morals."*

12. But perhaps we shall be more fortunate in detecting among our dissenting brethren, the practical fruits of Holiness, than we have been in discovering principles leading thereto. Let us see. I would not willingly detract from the merits of our Protestant friends, much less would I, for a moment, question their sincerity. I will even grant, that they have produced as many fruits of Holiness as their very defective religious system would possibly allow; nay, that they have often overstepped their theory in their practice. I am not speaking of mere social or civic virtues, for which I cheerfully acknowledge that they have been always distinguished; but I am speaking of that high order of Christian virtue, which is usually called Sanctity or Holiness. I am discussing principles and their necessary logical development and tendency as evidenced by history, not men, in

---

* A highly intelligent Protestant gentleman from Virginia, who was familiar with the writings of Voltaire, and with those of modern assailants of Catholicity, lately made the remark to me, that he had been forcibly struck by the exact parallelism of the lines of argument pursued by both, the latter evidently copying from the former!

their moral character and religious sincerity, of which God only can judge, because He alone is fully acquainted with the heart and the motives of human action.

13. This distinction being carefully borne in mind, I may ask, where are the practical fruits of Christian Holiness which Protestantism has yielded during the three hundred years of its feverish existence? Where are the Christian saints which it has given to the world? Where are its holy men and its holy women, who have cheerfully "denied themselves, taken up their cross, and followed Christ"?* Where its holy virgins and celibataries, who trampling upon the world and conquering the flesh, according to the exhortation of Christ, "have made themselves eunuchs for the kingdom of heaven's sake"?† Where its lovers of holy poverty, who, despising riches and panting after higher perfection, have complied with the advice of the Saviour to the young man of the gospel: "If thou wilt be perfect, go, sell what thou hast, and give to the poor, and thou shalt have a treasure in heaven; and come, follow me."‡ Where its noble heroes, who, entering upon the service of Christ with all their hearts, have broken every earthly tie for His love, and have merited the reward promised by Him in the following remarkable words: "And every one that hath left house, or brethren, or sisters, or father, or mother, or wife, or children, or lands, for my name's sake, shall receive a hundred-fold and life everlasting."?§ Has Protestantism produced many such heroes; has it produced even one in the entire period of its history, who has given to the world an example of all these exalted virtues?

14. Where, in fact, shall we look for examples of extraordinary Sanctity among the various Protestant denominations? Shall we look for them, where we would naturally expect to find them, in the lives of the first reformers, the founders of Protestantism;—in Luther, Calvin, Zuingle, Henry VIII., Elizabeth, Cranmer, Gustavus Vasa? But no

---

* St. Matt. xvi: 24.   † St. Matt. xix: 12.
‡ St. Matt. xix: 21.   § St. Matt. xix: 29.

one will surely pretend at this day that these individuals
were gifted with any peculiar Holiness. Bold, talented,
courageous, they may have been; pious and holy they certainly were not.

Their writings and public acts bespeak ungovernable
pride and self-will, bitter and relentless zeal, great uncharitableness for those of their own brethren who differed
from them, and, in fact, most of the disgraceful passions
which have usually swayed bad men. Their own portrait-
ures of one another's characters place them all in any thing
but a favorable light before the world; while many of their
acts, both public and private, have affixed a dark stigma on
their memories. What, for example, was more utterly disgraceful than the written permission, signed by eight of the
principal reformers of Germany, with Luther at their head,
by which the Landgrave of Hesse was allowed to have two
wives at one and the same time!"* What more unprincipled than the truckling subserviency of Cranmer to the
brutal passions of Henry VIII. in the divorce and murder
of his numerous wives! And yet such men as these are
among the brightest lights of Protestantism; among the
fairest specimens of Sanctity which it has given to the
world!

15. Shall we look for examples of exemplary Sanctity in
the present or past moral condition of those countries which
have been most under the influence of Protestantism? If
we do, we shall be fearfully disappointed. The statistical
accounts published by a distinguished and recent Protestant
traveler, Samuel Laing, Esq., have fully established the startling fact that Protestant Sweden is the most immoral country in Europe, and that Protestant Stockholm is the most
immoral city in all Christendom; while Denmark, Norway,
and Prussia are but little behind Sweden! †

---

* This instrument is given in full by Bossuet in his Variations, Book
VI.; and there is no doubt whatever of its genuineness.

† See "Notes of a Traveler on the Social and Political State of France,
Prussia, Switzerland. Italy, and other parts of Europe, during the present

Shall we turn to Protestant England for an example? Here we are met by authentic and most fearful accounts published by order of Parliament, revealing the stupid ignorance and moral degradation of the laboring and poorer classes of the people, especially in the manufacturing districts, and presenting a state of morals of which, I venture to assert, the parallel cannot be found in any Catholic land under heaven! Do we turn our eyes to London, the giant metropolis of the Protestant world? Here, too, recent statistics tell a fearful tale of crime:—twelve thousand women who are public and notorious drunkards; nearly one hundred thousand females who have forgotten to be virtuous; hundreds of houses for gambling and for systematically training up youth to adroitness in theft; and full five hundred thousand who never go to any church, and are practically infidels!

Shall we, in fine, look to our own beloved republic for models of Protestant holiness? Alas! here too, facts which we all know, and which none can deny, proclaim, that with all the noise made about the Bible and the holy Sabbath, with all the religious agitation and excitement that have been gotten up, more than one-half of our adult population over twenty-one years of age, belong to no religious denomination whatever,* and that but too many of our youth are reared up without a suitable moral or religious training; and are, in consequence, deeply steeped in vice ere they have attained to man's estate! These may be unpalatable truths, but yet they are truths for all this.

16. What impartial man, then, with all these facts staring him in the face, will still venture to assert that Protestantism

century: by SAMUEL LAING, Esq." 1 vol. 8vo. Philadelphia: Carey & Hart, 1846. The Preface to the Second Edition furnishes abundant evidence for what is asserted above in the text. It contains an ample vindication of Laing against the attack of the Swedish Ambassador at the Court of St. James.

* A late number of the American Almanac, published at Boston, contains the statistics on which this fact is grounded. It has been already stated in a previous Lecture.

has produced any very extensive or remarkable fruits of
Holiness? And can any one who will weigh attentively the
nature and tendency of the distinctive doctrines of Protestantism, as above indicated, be surprised at this its remarkable dearth of men eminent for Sanctity? That it has produced great men in a worldly sense, I do not deny; that it
has been the mother of Christian heroes and saints, remains
yet to be proved. Therefore, it has not the essential and
distinctive mark of Sanctity which Christ impressed upon
his Church; and therefore it cannot possibly be the true
Church of Christ; and we must seek this Church elsewhere.

II. Turn we now to the reverse of the picture: and let
us glance, for a moment, at the signal Holiness of doctrine
and of life displayed in that venerable Church of all ages
and of all nations,—of my forefathers and of yours,—which
is, nevertheless, "every-where spoken against." The sketch
which I will be able here to present will necessarily be very
rapid; I must confine myself to the most prominent outlines
of the subject.

1. The distinctive doctrines of the Catholic Church, when
rightly understood and properly appreciated, have a remarkable tendency to promote holiness among her members. Here we have an altar, as Christians had in the days
of St. Paul;* a daily sacrifice; churches always open to
worshipers, and, in Catholic countries, constantly visited by
worshipers at almost every hour of the day; we have
churches decorated with all the ornaments of the fine arts,
and filled with beautiful and appropriate symbols that raise
the heart to heavenly things and to God; churches in which
Christ is really present in the Holy Eucharist, and is always
ready to receive the homage of His people, and to shower
His choicest blessings on their heads; churches in which
the Christian *feels* the presence of his God, and bends down
in lowly reverence and awe before Him; churches in which
the voice of silent prayer ever ascends, like incense, up to
heaven; churches, in a word, to which that respect is shown

---

* Hebrews, xiii: 10.

which is due to the house of God, in which He delights to dwell in the midst of His children.

2. Here, too, the standard of Holiness is very high. The Catholic is taught from earliest life to pray, not only at church, but also every morning and evening at home; he is taught to cultivate a spirit of prayer and of habitual union with God, kept alive by daily meditation on His holy law. He is taught to read spiritual books ;—and he has an abundance of them of every variety for his perusal;—to meditate on the lives and examples of the saints, in order to stimulate his fervor, and to excite him to the practice of every virtue; to examine his conscience daily, and thus to keep himself at all times in a state of watchfulness and preparation. He is also constantly told, that he must deny himself, mortify his carnal appetites, crucify his flesh with its vices and concupiscences, blend fasting with prayer, "chastise his body and bring it into subjection," as did St. Paul ;* that he must confess his sins to the minister of God, humble himself in all things, avoid all the occasions of sin, and keep himself undefiled by this world.

He is, moreover, taught that, if he feel a special grace and call of God, he may retire from the world, enter into holy solitude, embrace a life of poverty, chastity, and obedience; and devote himself, body and soul, to the more perfect service of God during his whole life. If he feel the grace and courage to embrace this manner of life, he has an abundance of examples to encourage him and to aid his weakness, besides a great variety of institutions among which to make his selection. In a word, he is told, that, whether he remain in the world or embrace the religious profession, he must live holily, go to church every Sunday and Holiday, and not expect to go to heaven but by the rugged way of the cross, and of daily and hourly mortification and penance.

3. He does not believe, that faith alone will either justify or save him, nor does he feel tempted to relax his exertions,

* I Corinthians, ix.

under the persuasion that his sins are already forgiven him,
and that he is one of the elect. He is, on the contrary,
taught " to work out his salvation with fear and trembling,"* and "to make sure his vocation and election by
good works,"† knowing full well that "faith without works
is dead."‡ He is taught, that God sincerely wills his salvation ; that Jesus Christ died on the cross to compass it;
and that sufficient grace is bestowed on every one to enable
him to attain to eternal happiness : but that his own co-
operation is withal necessary, and that, having free will,
he may neglect or reject the proffered grace, and thereby
run to his own eternal ruin. He is taught docility and
obedience to the voice of the Church as to that of Christ
Himself, whose official organ he considers the Church to be ;
and he is encouraged in this obedience by the obvious
and palpable fact, that the Church has always taught him
and his forefathers the self-same doctrines, without any
contradiction or variation in the long lapse of centuries.

4. He has, moreover, sacraments not merely weak and
empty figures, but life-giving institutions containing substantial graces for every emergency in life, and aids for every
human infirmity. In infancy, he is washed from original
sin in the sacred laver of baptism ; he is born again, and he
thus becomes the child of God. When he has come to the
age of discretion, he acquires additional strength by receiving the Holy Ghost in confirmation, which makes him
a soldier of Jesus Christ. Then he prepares himself to feast
on the divine bread which came down from heaven, none
other than the living flesh of Christ himself. If wounded
in battle, he finds a healing balm in the sacrament of penance. If he wish to enter the marriage life, or to become a
minister of God, a special grace is bestowed upon him for
either state. Finally, when on the point of death, he is
anointed with oil, while the prayer of faith is poured forth
in his behalf by God's minister, and he thus receives a
special grace to die well. After death he is again carried

* Philippians, ii: 12.   † II Peter, i: 10.   ‡ St. James, ii: 14.

to the church to receive the prayers of that tender mother
who had taken him to her bosom in early infancy, and now
prayerfully and tearfully consigns him to the grave, in the
blessed hope of his glorious resurrection!

5. Surely, my Dear Brethren, such doctrines as these are
as strongly conducive to Holiness, as they are manifestly
unearthly and supernatural in their character and origin.
Man could not have devised such a system as this; it is
plainly above his reach : it savors of heaven. This religion
abstracts man from the earth, makes him trample upon
riches, honors, and pleasures, makes him triumph over himself, makes him *feel* that he is but a pilgrim and stranger
here below, and that his true country is heaven. It bestows
upon him, moreover, a kind angel guardian, to take him
by the hand and conduct him in safety through the many
perils which beset this gloomy land of pilgrimage, even
unto the ever-blooming paradise of God. In health, it pro-
vides him with spiritual food; in sickness, with healing
remedies; in death, with a solace; and even after death, if
he should be still in need, it lends him the succor of fervent
prayers breathed in his behalf. This system binds all the
faithful into one society knit together by a thousand associations and ties; it reaches even to heaven itself, and establishes that blessed communion of saints, through which
we are encouraged by the example, consoled by the sympathy, and aided by the prayers of those who are already
reigning with Christ.

6. I may then ask you, what is there that is conducive to
Holiness, which the doctrines and worship of the Catholic
Church have not abundantly provided? What is there that
is requisite to the removal of sin or the bestowal of grace,
which her institutions do not contain? Has she ever sanctioned vice or proscribed virtue? If so, let us know when,
where, and under what circumstances? Has she not, in all
ages, given the brightest examples of heroic virtues, such
as the Protestant communions have never exhibited? Most
undoubtedly.

7. But you will say, she has also been at all times dis-
19

figured by grievous scandals; her clergy, her bishops, and
even her Popes, have sometimes been men of immoral lives;
and even at present, in such Catholic countries as Italy and
Spain, immorality prevails to a great extent among the
mass of the people.

Let us suppose, for a moment, my Dear Brethren, that all
this is true, and that the picture is not even too highly
colored; what does it prove against the position I am at
present maintaining? Christ himself foretold that scandals
should come, and there was a Judas among his apostles, as
well as a Nicholas among the seven first deacons chosen by
them. Among those who professed Christianity during the
first three centuries, an age to which we all look back with
reverence, there were many Christians, and even some clergymen and bishops, who led lives openly scandalous, as
appears from the writings of Tertullian, St. Cyprian, and
others. Was the Church the less holy for all this? Was
she then, or is she now, fairly responsible for scandals,
which she always endeavored to prevent, over which she
has constantly wept, and against which she has ever raised
the voice of warning?

I might answer those who insist so much upon this objection, as St. Augustine answered similar objectors more than
fourteen hundred years ago: "Now I earnestly admonish
you to give over abusing the Catholic Church, and to cease
vilifying her for the bad morals of men whom she herself
condemns, and whom she every day labors to correct as bad
children. But why are you, in the mean time, filled with
rage, and blinded with party spirit? Why are you still
implicated in the obstinate defence of so great an error?
Seek after fruits in the field, and wheat on the floor (of the
Church); these will readily appear, and will present themselves spontaneously to those who seek for them."*

8. But is it certain, My Brethren, that the charge of immorality against the members of the Catholic Church is
not, to say the least, very greatly exaggerated? Does it, at

---

* De Moribus Ecclesiæ; cc. 84, 85.

any rate, become our adversaries to make the accusation? should they not bear in mind the warning of our Saviour: "Let him that is without sin amongst you, first cast a stone?"* Are Catholic more immoral than Protestant countries? If there be any truth in statistics, as furnished even by Protestant writers themselves, the former are not even half so corrupt as the latter. The Catholic inhabitants may not, indeed, keep the Sunday with the same gloomy and death-like silence; but they all, or nearly all, go to Church on Sunday, and feel themselves bound to do so by an express law of their Religion; which is certainly not the case at least to the same extent in Protestant lands. They do not usually sport so long a face, nor make so much pretension to piety; but they may not, for all this, have less genuine or solid Holiness; for where there is least profession there is often the most practice, as where there is least smoke there is generally most fire. In some respects, they are immeasurably in advance of their neighbors in Protestant countries; there is generally found among them much less dishonesty in dealing, much less drunkenness, much less solicitude for this world and for growing suddenly rich, much greater cheerfulness and social benevolence, much more politeness, much more humility, much more charity, much less restlessness, and much more general contentment and happiness. These things are obvious to every traveler; they strike you at a glance as distinctive traits of character; they have been repeatedly witnessed and attested by many impartial writers of every shade of religious opinion.

9. Is it, moreover, true that the Popes, as a body, have been corrupt men? Upon how many of the two hundred and fifty-eight pontiffs, who have successively occupied the chair of St. Peter, have Protestant writers themselves succeeded in fixing the stigma of immorality? Upon only five or six at most; and even of these, some may be proved not to have been half so bad as they are represented, and others were thrust into the Holy See by violence, or in times of

---

* St. John, ch. viii.

trouble and revolution. Is it fair to estimate the whole line
of Roman pontiffs by such specimens? It is about as fair,
as it would be to appreciate the apostolic college by the
character of Judas!

History does not point to any body of men who were, in
the main, more conspicuous for learning, or more eminent
for virtue and Sanctity. Seventy-nine of them have been
enrolled on the catologue of saints, most of whom sealed
their faith with their blood; about a hundred more were
men of irreproachable morals, and patterns to the flock over
which they presided; while the rest were, in general, great
and good men, much in advance of the ages in which they
respectively flourished, and a few of them censurable, if at
all, only for a too worldly spirit or policy. Besides, the very
few bad Popes never broached any new system of doctrine,
nor attempted to reform Religion: their wickedness injured
only themselves; and it was rebuked by Catholics, with at
least as much candor and boldness, as it has since been by
Protestants themselves.

10. But, you will tell me, that the Protestant churches
excommunicate those of their members who are openly
immoral, whereas the Catholic Church retains such in her
communion, and therefore virtually encourages their immorality.

Is this a true statement? Do not Protestant writers constantly inveigh against the Catholic Church for her frequent
exercise of the right to excommunicate bad men? When
she had the boldness and courage, in times past, to cut off
from her communion wicked princes, kings, and emperors,
was not the cry of tyranny and usurpation raised by her
enemies? If she does not now fulminate her excommuni-
cations daily and for ordinary offences, thereby driving
sinners from her pale, and fixing a stigma on their character, it may be, that in this forbearance she has but caught
the merciful spirit, and imitated the all-pervading charity
of her divine Founder and Bridegroom. Did not He command that the cockle should remain together with the
good wheat even unto the day of the harvest?

Did He encourage vice when He ate and drank with
publicans and sinners, when He refused to condemn the
adulteress, when He showed mercy to Magdaleue? Did He
heed the clamors of the sanctimonious and hypocritical
Pharisees, who then cried out, as do the present enemies
of the Catholic Church, that He was the friend of publicans
and sinners? Was His Sanctity sullied by contact with a
corrupt world which He came to save? When did He ever
repel sinners? Does the Sanctity of the Church require
more sternness at her hands than did the Sanctity of
Christ? No, My Brethren, the mercy always exhibited by
the Church to sinners and to the poor, is one of the brightest
jewels in her crown; one of the most striking proofs that
she is the true Spouse of Christ, and that she is distinguished by the mark of Holiness; while the contrary conduct of
her adversaries evinces sanctimoniousness rather than any
real Sanctity.

11. But where, you will perhaps ask, are the examples of
heroic Sanctity presented by the Catholic Church? Where,—
I might rather ask you,—where is it that they are not
found? Go over the ages that have passed since the birth
of Christianity; traverse the countries in which Catholicity
has flourished for centuries; open the annals of history;
and lay your hand upon your heart, and tell me if you can,
when and where it is that examples of signal Catholic
Sanctity are not found? The Catholic Church is the fruitful mother of saints, of martyrs, of Christian heroes; her
children rise up in every age and country and call her
blessed; hers is the glory, hers are the treasures of all
ancient and modern Sanctity that is worthy the name.
Saints are her crown and her joy; saints have filled up the
measure of her glory.

Hers are the glorious martyrs of the first ages, "who
were stoned, were cut asunder, were put to death by the
sword; who wandered about in sheep-skins, in goat-skins,
being in want, distressed, afflicted; of whom the world was
not worthy; wandering in deserts, in mountains, and in

19*

dens, and in caves of the earth."* Hers are the fathers
and doctors of the olden time, whose writings are the bright
reflection of their own pure faith and heroic Holiness; hers
are the confessors, the virgins, the holy solitaries, the
hermits of the wilderness, the holy men and women who
trampled on the vanities of the earth and left the world for
Christ's sake. Hers are the apostles,—the Patricks, the
Palladiuses, the Augustines, the Remigiuses, the Bonifaces,
the Willibrords, the Stephens, the Galluses, the Columbans,
the St. Vincent Ferrers, the St. Francis of Sales, the St.
Francis Xaviers,—who successively evangelized the heathen
nations sitting in the region of the shadow of death, and
who shone before their eyes themselves the brilliant models
of the Holiness they taught.

All the riches of the past are hers by right; she claims
them as all her own; they are the exuberant fruits of her
own vineyard, fertilized by her cares, her tears, and her
blood. This vineyard is hers by long possession; she has
never renounced her title to it; she has never removed one
of its venerable landmarks; she is as much the legal pro-
prietor of it now as she was centuries ago. She never departed from the faith "once delivered to the saints;" she
never *protested* against any previous system; she never set
up new churches on the ruins of the old. She can, then,
rightly claim all the fruits of the vineyard yielded by it in
all past ages, in conformity with the expressed will and
intention of Christ in His address to His first body of
pastors: "I have appointed you, that you should go, and
BRING FORTH FRUIT, and YOUR FRUIT SHOULD REMAIN."†

12. This fruit has been most abundant, and it has remained even to the present day. Since the date of the reformation, the Church has numbered many glorious saints
among her children; holy men and women who rivaled
those of the olden time in holiness of lives, and whose
Sanctity has been attested by well authenticated miracles.

---

* Hebrews, xi: 37, 38.   † St. John, xv: 16.

I have already had occasion to speak of the virtues and miracles of St. Francis Xavier, the great apostle of the Indies.* Where, in the domain of Protestantism, will you meet with such a name as that of St. Charles Borromeo, Archbishop of Milan, who sold his ample patrimony and gave the proceeds to the poor, who led a hard and laborious life in the midst of his spiritual flock, who devoted himself for the love of his people, who denounced vice and reformed morals often at the risk of his life; whose whole life was one protracted martyrdom; who always loved the poor with a fatherly affection; who was the founder of Sunday Schools for their benefit, and who died in a visitation on foot of the poorer portions of his scattered flock far away in the mountains!

Where will you find among Protestants a parallel to St. Francis of Sales, who relinquished his large inheritance in favor of a younger brother, and labored for the salvation of souls during a long and painful life, beset by privations and dangers innumerable, and with a meekness and humility of heart that won over his most bitter enemies; who left all things and triumphed over himself for the pure love of God and of his neighbor; and whose meek, patient, and untiring zeal was rewarded by the conversion of more than seventy thousand fierce Calvinists to the Catholic Church! Where will you find a youth so pure and noble and heroic as was St. Aloysius Gonzaga, who also renounced all claims on the rank and honors attached to a noble lineage, voluntarily made vows of poverty, chastity, and obedience; and who died at an early age, unsullied by the contamination of the least breath of vice, as stainless as he was when first washed in the sacred laver of regeneration! Where will you find such men as St. Ignatius of Loyola, St. John Francis Regis, St. Francis de Hieronymo, St. Francis Borgia, St. Alfonso Liguori;—men who soared far above this world, into the purer atmosphere of God!

Where, in fine,—to omit many other brilliant names,—

* In the fifth Lecture.

will you find among Protestants a parallel to St. Vincent
of Paul, who labored during a long life for the good of his
neighbor and for the alleviation of every species of human
ills, both bodily and spiritual; and with a zeal and perseverance, surpassed only by the brilliant success which
every-where crowned his efforts; and who has left to the
world institutions of charity which have been its admira-
tion ever since!*

13. Again, has not the Catholic Church been, throughout all ages, the tender mother of the poor? Has she not
erected magnificent hospitals and asylums for their benefit
over the whole face of Europe? What other church has
done half so much for the alleviation of human misery!
What other has been half so lavish of wealth for this
benevolent purpose? There were no poor-houses, no poor-
laws imposing taxes, no legal provision made for the support of those whom misfortune had thrown on the charity
of the community, so long as she held sway over the minds
of men! Her abounding charity superseded the necessity
of any such compulsory means for assuaging human misery;
she gathered the poor under her wings, "even as the hen
gathereth her chickens;" they were always her dearest
and most warmly cherished children; she took care of
them, wiped away the tears from their eyes, and bade
them have courage and be cheerful! She would not allow
the poor to be stigmatized as "nuisances" to society; she
could not brook the idea of seeing them immured in
prisons called poor-houses, for the mere *crime* of poverty;
she continues to denounce a malediction on the rich, and to
utter a blessing on the poor, as her divine Spouse had
done before her. She knew and *felt* that there was, and
could be, no real Sanctity without charity for the poor
and afflicted members of Jesus Christ, and that He would

---

* Even Protestant writers have pronounced the eulogy of these men:
among others, see Palmer's "Compendious Ecclesiastical History." Had
St. Vincent founded no other order than that of the Sisters of Charity,
his name would still be immortal.

taken as done to Himself whatever was done to the least among them.

14. Long before Protestantism had come to distract the world with its endless sects and divisions, she had erected the hospital of the *Quatre Vingt*, for the blind in Paris, and those of *St. Michael* and of *Santo Spirito* for the afflicted and sick in Rome;—not to speak of hundreds of others of the same kind which she had already reared in great numbers all over Europe. As early as the thirteenth century, she already founded two religious orders for the redemption of Christian captives groaning in servitude among the Mohammedans and pagans, through the agency of her sainted children, St. Peter Nolasco and St. Raymond de Pennafort, St. John of Matha and St. Felix of Valois; and she approved of a standing vow imposed by St. Peter Nolasco on his disciples, by which they obligated themselves, if need was, to remain themselves in servitude for the liberation of their enslaved brethren! Can Protestantism, during its entire history, point to one example so heroic as this?

15. Again, will our dissenting brethren themselves venture to compare the zeal, disinterestedness, charity, labors, sufferings, and success of their missionaries among the heathens, with the similar traits of character which have always shone forth among those of the Catholic Church? Where are the Protestant missionaries who have left all things,—"father, mother, brothers, sisters, *wife*, *children*, and lands,"—in order to preach the gospel to pagans? Who have gone forth, as did the first apostles, and as do so many of our apostolic missionaries at this day, "without scrip or purse," putting all their reliance in God alone?

Take up, for example, Bancroft's history of the United States;[*] read the glowing accounts which he gives of the laborious lives and disinterested zeal of the Jesuit missionaries among the Indians of North America,—accounts which fall far short of the truth;—and then tell me can-

* Vol. iii. ch. xx.

P

didly, whether your churches have ever sent forth missionaries like these men? If they have not, then how can
they claim to have the spirit of Christ, or to be distinguished by that lofty Sanctity which He made a distinctive
attribute of His Church?

16. In fact, they seem to have abandoned almost entirely
the claim to Sanctity; they have no peculiar religious Holiness, and they frankly tell us so; they claim to have produced great men, and moral, edifying Christians—not *saints*
properly so called. Hence they call none of their great
men saints, and they show their candor by abstaining from
the appellation. But let them not attempt, under the plea
that they have no claims to any peculiar Holiness themselves, to wrest the crown of Sanctity from the brow of the
Catholic Church;—a crown so well earned, and which becomes her so well.

17. A silent, and, perhaps unwilling tribute to Catholic
Sanctity, is found in the fact, notorious to every observer,
that scandal given by a Catholic priest creates a much
greater sensation even among Protestants, than does a
similar or greater one given by a Protestant minister.
The Protestant public seems instinctively to expect more
Sanctity from the former than from the latter. The fall
of a preacher seems to create little or no surprise; that
of a priest is heralded forth from Maine to Texas, as something new, remarkable, and astonishing! There is no doubt
that enmity to the Catholic Church may be one cause of
this marked distinction; but it appears certain that the
reason I have just alleged is another and a very important
motive, lying at the basis of public feeling on this subject.

18. A more marked tribute to the utility and Sanctity
of Catholic institutions is found in the effort made in England, Prussia, and the United States,* some years ago, to
establish an order of Protestant "Sisters of Charity!" The
attempt, indeed, proved wholly abortive, notwithstanding

* See a number of the New York Observer—January, 1846—for an account of this attempt.

the anticipations of the brilliant success indulged in for a time by the friends of the enterprise.

The reason is obvious. Such an institution is above the strength and ability of Protestantism; it requires for its maintenance an abstraction from the world, and a love of voluntary poverty, chastity, and obedience, which Protestantism has never had, and which it never can have, so long as it will continue to look upon and to sneer at these abnegations as useless self-torture, and repugnant to the gospel. No religious order can subsist without vows of certain things connected with that higher perfection which is counseled in the gospel, though it is not of obligation on all; Protestantism discards all such vows as a delusion and a snare; therefore Protestantism can never have an order of Sisters of Charity. These ministering angels of mercy, who watch over the sick, who quail not before the most loathsome disease, who shelter the helpless orphan, who spend their whole lives in prayer to God and heroic devotedness to works of charity, are essentially and necessarily Catholic. In no other communion would they, or could they, have the grace necessary to carry out their sublime purpose. Facts have fully confirmed this conclusion, based itself on first principles; and Protestantism must change those facts, and must adopt those first principles, which it now discards, ere it can hope to have Sisters of Charity.

From what I have thus far said, My Dear Brethren, it is apparent that the Catholic Church alone is marked by the distinctive characteristic of Sanctity impressed by Christ on His Church; and therefore, by a necessary inference, that she alone can rightly claim to be the one, true, original Church of Christ.

THIS IS THE FIFTH EVIDENCE OF CATHOLICITY.

In my next Lecture, if you will favor me with your kind attention, I will endeavor to show you that the Catholic Church is also—and she alone—stamped with the attribute of apostolical antiquity; that she alone can trace back her lineage to the time when Christ first sent His apostles to preach the gospel; that she has not become decrepit with old age, but that she is as young and blooming, and virgin now, as she was when first washed from all stain and blemish by the blood of her divine Founder and Spouse; that there is no wrinkle on her brow, no trace of past sorrows on her countenance, nor any evidence of present decay.

May God, in His superabundant mercy and goodness, grant to all of us the grace to approach this momentous subject with a due sense of the eternal interests which are involved in its consideration; and may He vouchsafe to bestow upon us the light to know, and the strength to embrace and confess that truth, for which His well-beloved Son died on the Cross; through Jesus Christ, our Lord and only Redeemer. Amen.

LECTURE VIII.

APOSTOLICAL ANTIQUITY—THE SIXTH EVIDENCE OF CATHOLICITY.

Text from Jeremiah explained—Appropriateness of its warning to our own times—A divided Christianity—Its evils deplored—The remedy left by Christ—The mark of Apostolicity unfolded—And applied as a test of the true Church—The Greek and Oriental churches—The argument stated—A cavil—Antiquity of Protestantism—Theory of an invisible Church—Its manifold absurdities—Sleeping witnesses—Theory of a regular succession of dissenters from Rome examined—A heterogeneous ancestry—A striking coincidence—Theory founded on the assumption that Protestantism is the Religion of the Bible—The illustration from washing the face—The age of Protestantism fully settled—Apostolical antiquity of Catholicity established by historical facts—The line of Roman Pontiffs—The unbroken succession—Tertullian and St. Irenæus—Other ancient fathers—Objections answered—Macaulay's testimony—The allegation that the Catholic Church changed the original doctrine disproved—The *dark* ages—Specifications called for—Motto of the early Church—Mr. Hallam and the council of Trent—The origin of the Greek schism—Doctrines of the present Greek church—The promises of Christ—The conclusion—The sixth evidence of Catholicity.

"*Thus saith the Lord: Stand ye on the ways, and see, and ask for the* OLD PATHS, *which is the good way, and walk ye in it; and you shall find refreshment for your souls.*"—JEREMIAH, vi: 16.

ISRAEL had gone astray from the right path. The daughter of Sion, "like a beautiful and delicate woman," had listened to the soft accents of flattery and seduction, her heart had been puffed up with pride, and her conscience lulled into a fatal security by the false promises of those who should have warned her of her dangerous condition. "From the prophet even to the priest, all were guilty of deceit," * and false prophets cried out to her, "peace, peace, and there was no peace."† Distracted within, and menaced with utter destruction from without, she knew not, or heeded not the perils which encompassed her on all sides.

---

* Jerem. vi: 13.　　　　　† Ibid. verse 14.

20　　　　　　　　　　　　　(229)

She had left the Lord her God, had abandoned the old
paths which He had marked out, had entered upon new
ones of her own choosing, had listened in an evil hour to
the voice of seers falsely alleging a divine mission, who
ran, though God had not sent them: and she reflected not
meantime that she was fast hastening to her own ruin.

In this emergency, the plaintive prophet of God implored
her, with tears in his eyes, and burning eloquence on his
lips, to pause in her downward career; to bethink herself
while it was yet time, of the OLD PATHS, hallowed by the
footsteps of patriarchs and prophets and holy men of old;
and to re-enter upon them at once, that thus she might
find refreshment to her soul, which had been wearied out
with following the crooked paths of novelty. This impressive exhortation was introduced by the solemn, "Thus saith
the Lord," which came ringing into her ears and sending
a thrill to her very heart, like a voice from another world.

But yet, My Dear Brethren,—would you believe it,—
this voice did not arouse her from her fatal security, nor
break the spell of that false and dangerous vision of peace
with which she was then fascinated! She continued as
proud and wayward as ever, and she said: "I will not
walk" in those old paths;* "I will not hearken" to that
cry of warning uttered by the faithful watchman appointed
over me by God!† It was only when the rod of divine
chastisement was extended over her, and when her beautiful city was overspread with gloom and desolation, that
she finally bethought herself of her errors, and resolved to
return once more to the old paths of duty and obedience,
weeping bitterly that she should ever have abandoned
them for her own seductive fancies.

The lesson conveyed by this interesting passage of the
Old Testament is peculiarly appropriate to our own times.
Now, as then, the venerable "OLD PATHS," pressed by the
footsteps of our fathers in the faith, have been abandoned
in favor of new ones of men's own devising: now, as then,

---

* Jerem. vi: 16.   † Ibid. verse 17.

men "turn away their hearing from the truth, and are turned to fables; according to their own desires heaping to themselves teachers having itching ears :." * now, as then, we are fallen upon "dangerous times, when men are lovers of themselves, covetous, haughty, proud, blasphemers, disobedient to parents, ungrateful, wicked, without affection, without peace, slanderers, incontinent, unmerciful, without kindness, traitors, stubborn, puffed up, and lovers of pleasures more than of God; having an appearance, indeed, of piety, but denying the power thereof, ... always learning, and never attaining to the knowledge of the truth." † Now, as then, men have abandoned the OLD PATHS of unity, and are become "like children, tossed to and fro, and carried about with every wind of doctrine, in the wickedness of men, in craftiness by which they lie in wait to deceive."‡ Now, as then, there are false prophets, sent by themselves, and without any lawful mission from God, who cry out, "Peace, peace, when there is no peace," and who thus lull their unwary disciples into the sleep of a delusive and fatal security.

Under these saddening circumstances, when the one original Religion of Christ is rent into a hundred conflicting fragments; when Christian rises up against Christian in the name of Christ Himself; when, in the midst of contradictory systems, all claiming to be the genuine Religion of Christ, sincere inquirers are so often bewildered in their search after the one old truth; when Christianity,— alas, My Brethren, that it should be so,— has been made to become a complicated and most difficult problem, instead of a plain and matter-of-fact system, easily ascertainable by all; when the question,— Which is the true Church of Christ?— can be much more easily put than answered by many otherwise well disposed; when the Christian Religion, once so plain to even the dullest capacity, has become, in the view of some, like a labyrinth, amid the tortuous

---

* II. Timothy, iv: 3, 4. † Ibid. iii: 1, 2, 3, 4, 5, 7.
‡ Ephesians, iv: 14.

and complicated windings of which there appears to be
little hope of finding a clue by which to emerge into the
clear day of truth; — when such is the sad state of things,
what more natural than to ask, Is Christ the author of all
this uncertainty and Babel-like confusion? Is His holy
Religion, after all, nothing but a mere jumble of conflicting
elements and contradictory systems? Did He leave it in a
crude and informal state, and hand it over in this condition to the disputation of men? Was His purpose of teaching mankind the one truth with clearness and certainty
thus wholly frustrated; was His blood shed in vain upon
the cross for the salvation of men? Did He provide no
adequate means for enabling all sincere inquirers to ascertain what His Religion is, and where His one true Church
is to be found? Did he bequeath to the world no thread
of Ariadne by which men might easily escape from the
labyrinthine windings of doubt; and did He stamp upon
the countenance of His Church no distinctive features by
which it might easily be recognized, even by the most
simple and unlearned?

That he did, I trust I have already sufficiently shown.
That some of those distinctive characteristics,—such as
Unity, Catholicity, and Holiness,—are found in the Roman
Catholic Church and in no other, I hope I have also convinced you. It remains for me to establish the same in reference to the fourth distinctive mark,—that of Apostolical
Antiquity;—and to apply to the Christian Church the self-
same line of reasoning which the inspired prophet of God
formerly applied to the Jewish. If you will lend me your
patient and undivided attention, I hope, with the Divine
assistance, to persuade you that here also Catholicity stands
forth triumphantly vindicated, and shining forth in the
dazzling light of truth.

No one will deny, that the true Church of the present
day is the heir and successor of that established by Christ
Himself; that the former must derive her doctrines, her
sacraments, her orders, her mission, her whole essence,
from the latter; and that the two, in fact, are one and

identical. The very idea of the true Church necessarily implies all this. The logical inference from this principle is, that a Church which can clearly trace back its history to the days of Christ and His apostles; which can prove, by indubitable evidence, that its origin lies back in the very Apostolic era, and that it is as old as Christianity itself, presents to us a very strong and convincing proof that it is the true Church founded by Christ.

This proof becomes still more conclusive, if it should farther appear, that no other Christian denomination, claiming to be the true Church of Christ, can furnish evidence of such Antiquity : for no such denomination can certainly have any reasonable pretensions to be the true Church. It is, by the fact, deficient in a condition absolutely essential to the latter; it does not verify a distinctive trait in the character of the true Church as laid down by St. Paul, when he said, addressing the Ephesians : " You are the fellow citizens of the saints and the domestics of God, *built upon the foundation of the apostles and prophets*, Christ himself being the chief corner-stone ; in whom all the building framed together groweth into a holy temple in the Lord."* No church, then, that is not Apostolic in the sense above explained, is, or can be, the true Church of Christ ; while a Church which has this mark, and which is not, at the same time, deficient in the other essential characteristics already established in the two previous Lectures, must, of necessity, be that one true Church.

Before I enter into the development of the argument which naturally grows out of this principle, it may be well to say a few words concerning the Greek and Oriental churches, which claim to be the true Church, and base their claim chiefly on this very ground of Antiquity. Ancient those churches certainly are, if compared with the various Protestant denominations which are relatively but of yesterday ; yet there is no convincing evidence that they are strictly Apostolic ; and no Antiquity which does not reach

---

* Ephesians, ii : 19, 20, 21.

back to the Apostolic days themselves is of any real importance in the argument. We can point to the precise time when the Nestorian and Eutychian sects began; we can tell who were the men that respectively founded them, under what circumstances they abandoned the ancient faith in regard to the mystery of the Incarnation, and how the whole Church rose up against them, and cut them off from her communion. History tells us all this, and it clearly vouches for the fact, that they came into the .world more than four hundred years *too late* to lay any just claim to the attribute of Apostolicity.

We can also tell when the Greek church was torn by schism from the great body of the faithful; who were the ambitious men that began and consummated the schism;* what were the motives that guided them; and, in fact, all the circumstances of the unhappy division. We can also establish, by the plainest historical evidence, that Constantinople, the chief center of the self-styled orthodox Greek church, is not an Apostolical church, and that it was not even an important see until some time in the fourth century; while we can also prove, in the same way, that much the largest and most numerous division of that church,— the Russian,—does not date back further than the tenth century. Moreover, most of the principal and really Apostolical churches of the east,—as those of Alexandria, Antioch, and Jerusalem,—either exist only in name, or are separated from the communion of the Greek church.

Thus, it is simply impossible to make good the claim of the Greek church to be Apostolical in origin, in duration, or in doctrine. Besides, even if this claim could be sustained, the Greek Church would still be obviously deficient in the essential marks of Unity and Catholicity, as I hope I have already shown; and therefore, it cannot possibly be the true Church of Christ.

But the question does not lie, at present, between the Greek and the Roman Catholic Church, but between the

---

* Photius in the ninth, and Michael Cerularius in the eleventh century.

latter and the Protestant communions. The argument which I propose to develop in this Lecture is very plain and simple; the veriest child may understand it, and appreciate its force. It is this:

The true Church of Christ is more than eighteen hundred years old;

But the Roman Catholic Church is more than eighteen hundred years old, and no Protestant sect can claim this Antiquity;

Therefore, the Roman Catholic Church alone can justly claim to be the true Church of Christ.

The first or major proposition is self-evident, and no one will deny its truth. The second or minor proposition embraces two assertions, which must be proved separately: first, that no Protestant denomination is, or can claim to be eighteen hundred years old; and second, that the Roman Catholic Church can justly claim that age.

Before, however, entering upon the proofs, I must first answer an objection which is often put with an air of triumph, and which, if valid, would destroy the entire force of the argument. We are gravely told, that Antiquity is no certain criterion of truth; that there are old errors and new truths; and that paganism, for example, is none the truer for being older than Christianity.

I willingly admit that mere Antiquity is not an *absolute* evidence of truth; that is, that we are not to reason from the mere Antiquity of a thing to its truth; but I maintain that it may be, and is, a *relative* criterion of the most decisive character, in certain cases, and especially in regard to the settling of the question, which, among all denominations of Christians, is the true Church of Christ. The true Christian Church is historically more than eighteen hundred years old; therefore this amount of Antiquity is one of her essential and inseparable characteristics; and therefore, no church which has not this attribute of age, can possibly be that true Church. The question is not between Christianity and paganism, or any other system; but between different denominations of Christians.

The objection, then, is entirely beside the question, and it does not even remotely touch the merits of the real point at issue; it is the merest sophism, reasoning from an abstract and general principle to a particular case evidently not embraced under that principle.

These preliminaries being settled, I trust to your satisfaction, I proceed at once to the investigation of the matter of fact which lies at the basis of the argument above indicated, and upon which the solution of the whole question necessarily depends. I assert, then, distinctly, firstly, that none of the Protestant denominations is, or can wholly claim to be, eighteen hundred years old; and secondly, that the Roman Catholic Church not only claims this Antiquity, but can establish her claim to it by the most conclusive evidence.

I. NONE OF THE PROTESTANT DENOMINATIONS IS, OR CAN JUSTLY CLAIM TO BE, EIGHTEEN HUNDRED YEARS OLD.

If any of them can make good the claim to this amount of Antiquity, where were they to be found before the times of Luther and Calvin? Had they any existence or "local habitation" in the world before the dawn of the reformation, in the beginning ·of the sixteenth century? If so, where is the proof of the fact? Where is the line of their succession? Where are their ecclesiastical assemblies, their official acts and monuments, their books of worship and discipline, their confessions of faith? What did they do in the world during the first fifteen hundred years of the Christian era? Did they do any thing, or did they do nothing? If the former, what did they do, and where is the proof? If the latter, how can they be said to have had any real existence? Or were they buried in a profound sleep and in the lethargy of death, during all this period, and did they awake and begin to manifest symptoms of vitality and activity only after the lapse of fifteen centuries?

These questions can be put much more easily than they can be answered. The difficulty has been acknowledged by Protestants themselves; and the many different and often inconsistent solutions which have been attempted, prove how much even the most adroit advocates of the new doctrines were puzzled for an answer; whilst to the impartial reasoner all these pretended solutions must appear wholly unsatisfactory. I will briefly allude to the most prominent among them.

1: The first answer to the difficulty consists in a falling back on the singular theory of an invisible Church. The advocates of this opinion maintain, that the Christian Church is composed of all those, who, in different ages, believed in Christ, loved His Religion, and worshiped Him in spirit and in truth; that the number of these was known only to God; that they were invisible to the world, and were not necessarily connected with any visible Christian communion, but yet always existed, pure in faith and strong in charity, in the midst of the surrounding corruption. Such is the curious speculation which was first breached in the sixteenth century, and which has since become more or less popular among our dissenting brethren.

But it is manifestly a mere assumption without proof; it subverts the primary and essential notions of Christianity itself; it is fraught with endless contradictions and inconsistencies; and even if true, it does not meet the real difficulty. Where is the evidence that there was kept up in all ages of Christianity this constant succession of immaculate and *invisible* Christians? If they were *invisible*, how prove their existence? By history? But history bears evidence only to things that were visible and palpable. By reason? But reason has plainly nothing to do with the matter; and reason tells us that we should admit no historical fact without proof. By Scripture? But Scripture is wholly silent on the subject; besides that it cannot bear evidence to a fact, which, if it occurred at all, took place after it had been written. Moreover, Scripture, as we shall immediately see, lays down principles which plainly subvert the entire theory, and should put its advocates to the blush.

The attempt to prove the existence of an *invisible* Church which no one ever saw or ever could see, reminds one of the effort made by the Jews to disprove the resurrection of Christ. They bribed the Roman soldiers to say to Pilate, "His disciples came by night and stole Him away, *when we were asleep.*"* As St. Augustine well remarks upon this passage, if the soldiers were asleep, how could they bear evidence to the alleged fact that the disciples came and stole away the body by night? Could sleeping witnesses bear testimony to a fact which, according to their own account, took place, if at all, while they were buried in slumber, and were therefore wholly unconscious of external things? So also, I may ask, could men who were virtually asleep— because invisible to all the world besides—be competent witnesses of a public fact said to have occurred during the long night of Christian darkness, with which fact they themselves could not be supposed to be acquainted, and of which all the rest of mankind were necessarily ignorant? I say that they themselves could not be acquainted with the fact; for supposing even that each individual member of that invisible church could be conscious of his own peculiar sanctity—which is very doubtful—how could he be acquainted with that of the other members? Were they not all essentially *invisible* to him and known only to God?

But there is this remarkable difference between the two cases, that whereas the Jews brought forth their witnesses, though sleeping ones, to testify to the fact they wished to establish, our Protestant friends, though often challenged to do so, have never been able to produce theirs to prove the existence of the invisible church; and in the very nature of things, from what I have already said, they cannot produce them. And yet they would have sensible men believe their theory! And yet men of intelligence are still found among its warmest advocates!

An invisible Church! The very idea is a palpable absurdity. It subverts Christianity itself. All that we know of this divine system presupposes it to be essentially a visible body. All its sacraments, including those admitted

---

* St. Matthew, xxviii: 18.

by Protestants themselves, its public worship, its temples, its ministry, its Church government and discipline, all the elements which concur in its formation, are necessarily visible and palpable. How else could it be able to preach the gospel to all nations? How could it maintain its own organization? How could it be a bond of union for mankind? How could it gather them together into a body or society? How could it exist even for a day? Are men incorporeal and angels, that Christ should have established an invisible Church for their benefit? You might as well talk of an invisible man, as of an invisible Church! Man is invisible in his soul, and so is the Church; but man has necessarily a visible body acting through visible organs, and so has the Church. Both are essentially composed of body and soul; take away either of these essential elements, and you destroy their individuality. The soul of the Church is its internal life, consisting of Faith, Hope, and Charity; its body consists of its external acts and institutions: both are essential to its existence. It was established for *men*, and therefore it was made after their own image and likeness.

It is plain, from what I have said, that the theory of an invisible Church is fraught with endless inconsistencies and absurdities; it remains to be shown that it does not really meet the difficulty for solving which it was originally broached. Grant that this invisible Church really existed, how are Protestants to prove their connection with it? Will they assume this, too, without proof? Are they to take it for granted, that they now teach the self-same doctrines, have the self-same order of Church government, administer the self-same sacraments, which this pretended invisible Church taught, had, and administered? Where is the evidence for all this? And yet there must be conclusive proof on all these heads, before they can rightly claim to be the successors and heirs of the invisible Church.

Did this theoretical Church teach one and the same doctrine at all times and in all places, or did it teach various and discordant doctrines? If the former, how can

Protestants, who teach so many contradictory systems of
Religion, claim to agree with it in doctrine? If the latter,
how could it be the one true Church of Christ, which surely
taught but one system of belief; and farther, how can it be
made appear, in this case, that any or all of the present
denominations of Protestant Christians profess precisely
the same varying phases of belief as did the invisible
Church? Again, is it not a palpable absurdity to say that
the Protestants could derive their visible ministry, and
their visible mission to preach the Word and administer the
sacraments, from a Church avowedly *invisible?* The whole
theory, then, is as utterly useless to the Protestant, as it is
intrinsically inconsistent, untenable, and preposterous.

  2. Hence, I am not at all surprised that the theory has
been abandoned by many intelligent Protestant writers, in
favor of another, somewhat more plausible, indeed, but
really not less unsatisfactory and absurd. These apologists
of the reformation pretend to discover a regular and continuous line of dissenters from the Roman Catholic Church,
reaching back from the days of Luther and Calvin to those
of the Apostles, at least to the first three centuries of
Christianity; during which ages almost all of them agree
in acknowledging that the Church of Christ continued in
its original purity and integrity. They trace back this
line of their succession through the Hussites, the Bohemian
Brethren, and the Wicliffites, of the fifteenth and fourteenth
centuries; the Petrobrusians, Henricians, Albigenses, and
Waldenses, of the thirteenth and twelfth: the disciples of
Berengarius in the eleventh; the Paulicians in the ninth;
the Iconoclasts in the eighth; and the followers of Aerius,
Jovinian, Helvidius, and Vigilantius, in the fourth.

  A heterogeneous ancestry truly, and one of which they
may well be proud! I would be even disposed to be liberal,
and cheerfully give over to them, as their fathers in the
faith, all the dissenters, innovators, and heretics of the
olden time, from the disciples of Simon Magnus, of Ebion,
of Cerinthus, and of Nicholas, in the first century, to those
of Munzer and Stork in the sixteenth! They may have

the thousand and one sects,—all teaching contradictory, and many of them absurd and abominable systems,—that ever sprang into existence, from the time that St. Paul first uttered his warning against the heretics of the latter days, and St. Jude set the seal of divine reprobation upon those "who separate themselves,"* down to the memorable days of Miller and the Mormon prophet! They may have them all. The true Church has always discarded all such, as rebellious and unworthy children; they went out from her, but they were not of her, else they would have continued in her household;† they were withered and rotten branches cut off from the vine; our dissenting brethren may, if they will, gather them up reverently, and construct of them a shelter for their own tottering communions.

It is the glory of the true Church of Christ, that she has, in all ages, constantly and fearlessly combated error in all its Protean forms; that she has never "bent the knee to Baal," has never compromised the truth originally given her in deposit by her divine Founder and Spouse; and that she has set the stigma of her condemnation upon every innovation made by the fancy or wickedness of men against the one, old, unchanging truth. It is also a remarkable feature common to the innovators of all ages, that while perpetually disagreeing among themselves, they have all, nevertheless, been in the habit of burying their differences, and of "huddling up a peace,"—as Tertullian observed of those in the second century,—whenever it was question of attacking the Catholic Church. This is one of the strongest and most striking proofs that the Catholic is the true Church of Christ, and that dissenters from her communion in all ages, whether individually or collectively consider-ed, were, and are, nothing but innovators, errorists and sectarians.

But do all these heterogeneous sects of Antiquity, scat-tered over the various centuries of Church History, really constitute a chain of succession, of which the various

---

*St. Jude's Epistle, verse 19.   † St. John, I Epistle, ii: 19.

Protestant denominations have formed but additional
links? Had they any connection properly so called with
one another? Did they all teach the same, or even similar
doctrines? Did they agree even substantially in the administration of the same order of Church government?
Did they, in a word, form ONE Christian church, continued
on from age to age? All these things are necessary to a
succession, as the term is understood in our present discussion; and yet none of them are verified in the ancient
heretics, claimed by some of our dissenting brethren as
their religious ancestors. They broached very different
systems of doctrine, at different times, in different places,
under different circumstances, and generally without deriving their principles from one another, or claiming any
special relationship whatever.

Many of the ancient heresiarchs left very few or no
disciples after them—as Aerius, Jovinian, Helvidius, Vigilantius, and Berengarius; others founded sects, which, after
undergoing various changes, disappeared altogether, or
were merged in other and very different ones that succeeded them. This was the case with the Iconoclasts, the
Paulicians, the Petrobrussians, the Waldenses, the Albigenses, the Wicliffites, the Hussites, and the Bohemian
Brethren. The Hussites, indeed, derived many of their
distinctive doctrines from the Wicliffites; and the Protestants many of theirs from the Hussites, though these
had almost disappeared before the reformation. Beyond
the days of Wicliffe, the reformers could not boast of even
the shadow of a succession.

There were, besides, as many divisions among the sects
which preceded, as there have been among those which
followed the reformation. They had but few doctrines in
common, and no principle of assimilation or unity save
that of a common hatred to the old Church. Is it not
wholly preposterous to imagine a one continuous Church
of Christ to be made up of such inconsistent and heterogeneous materials? Is it not absurd to suppose a regular
succession constituted by sects which really did not succeed

each other at all, either in point of doctrine, or, continuously at least, in point of time?

Again, did the Protestants of the sixteenth century, do the Protestants of the present day, really agree in doctrine with the ancient sects from which they profess to have derived their succession? Is there now, on the face of the earth, a single Protestant sect which agrees *in all things* with any one ancient sect? If there be, let the two sects so agreeing be pointed out;—for no one has yet been able to discover them. If there be not, then with what plausibility can our dissenting brethren of the present day claim the ancient sectarians as their fathers in the faith? Modern Protestants reject many of the distinctive doctrines of the Wicliffites, Hussites, and Waldenses, and they protest against some Catholic doctrines which these sects constantly believed and maintained. The former are not, then,—they cannot be,—the successors of the latter in the faith; and they should at once candidly give up the claim as wholly untenable.

But suppose all these difficulties solved, and that our separated friends are able to trace back their succession to the days of the Arian priest Aerius, in the fourth century; —even so, their task is not yet half performed. For still how will they be able to continue the succession back from the fourth century to the apostolic days? Through the heretics of the first three centuries,—the Marcionites, the Encratites, the Gnostics, the disciples of Paul of Samosata, and many others of the same kind, teaching every variety of blasphemous and immoral doctrines? If so, then will I not envy them their religious forefathers. Will they attempt to do it through the great body of Christians, or the Catholic Church of that period? But this Church condemned Aerius, Jovinian, Helvidius, and Vigilantius; and it constantly taught one and the same doctrine, it was bound together in an indissoluble unity of government and worship, and it branded all separatists from its body as perverse heretics, while our Protestant brethren certainly do none of these things. Therefore these cannot

consistently claim the primitive Church, without abandoning their sectarianism altogether, giving up all their distinctive principles, and returning at once to the bosom of
Catholic unity.

It is a remarkable coincidence, full of significance, that
the very same arguments which we now employ against
Protestants, were used as conclusive by the ancient fathers
against the separatists of their day. Tertullian challenges
the heretics of the second century in these words: "Let
them show the origin of their churches, let them evolve
the order of their bishops in regular succession from the
beginning, so that the first bishop should have either one
of the Apostles, or one of the apostolic men who persevered
with the Apostles, for his predecessor."* St. Pacian, in
the fourth century, employs a similar argument against
the innovators of his time. He lays down this golden
principle for discriminating between truth and error;—
that the latter is new and various in its forms, whereas
the former is ancient, unchangeable, and equally held by
all persons, in all places, and at all times.†

I might easily multiply passages of the same kind; but
these will suffice to convince any impartial man that the
Catholic Church now occupies precisely the same position
upon which she stood while battling against the sectarians
of the earliest ages; and that Protestants cannot claim to
be the successors of the primitive Church without occupying themselves the same lofty ground.

Viewing the subject, then, in every possible light, the
difficulties in the way of the Protestant succession are insurmountable. Our dissenting brethren stand alone and
isolated from Christian Antiquity; they must overleap a
frightful chasm of fifteen centuries, before they can possibly
connect themselves with the apostolic days. To them, all
this period is an unexplored region, a void, a chaos; they

---

* Præscriptiones, c. 82.

† QUOD SEMPER, QUOD UBIQUE, QUOD AB OMNIBUS CREDITUR, ID DEMUM
CATHOLICUM EST. Epist. ad Sympron.

came into the world full fifteen hundred years too late to constitute, or even be connected with, the original and true Church of Christ! Neither learning, nor ingenuity, nor eloquence can extricate them from this difficulty. And I am not surprised that most Protestants now-a-days have given up this phantom of the succession altogether, and have fallen back on their old vantage ground, the Bible, and the Bible alone. In doing this they are at least consistent; but even so they do not succeed in proving that Protestantism is eighteen hundred years old, as I shall now proceed to show.

3. Their argument is this: Protestantism is the religion of the Bible; but the Bible is eighteen hundred years old; therefore Protestantism may boast the same Antiquity.

But this reasoning really contains no new argument whatever; it rests upon a mere assumption, a plain begging of the question. It assumes that Protestantism is the religion of the Bible, which is precisely the matter in controversy.—But Protestants can prove all their doctrines from the Bible.—We think very differently; and we are persuaded that they do not understand the Bible aright. The question is precisely about the meaning of the Bible, upon which this pretended argument throws no additional light. It makes no new issue; it leaves the controversy precisely where it found it; and therefore it is no argument at all. The ancient heretics, according to the testimony of St. Pacian, interlarded their books with Scriptural quotations;* but did they, for all this, prove their doctrines true? So also, as St. Pacian likewise remarks,† Satan himself quoted Scripture against our blessed Lord; but did he make good his point?

Again, if Protestantism be the Religion of the Bible, pray tell me which of all the discordant denominations comprised under the name is that Religion? Does the Bible contain a hundred contradictory Religions? Is it not, then, self-evident that Protestantism cannot be the religion of the Bible?

---

* Epist. ad Sympron. † Ibid.

21 *

How will the advocates of this opinion answer this simple
argument: the Bible has but one Religion; Protestantism
has a hundred; therefore Protestantism is *not* the Religion
of the Bible? They will not surely venture to deny either
of the premises; how, then, can they avoid admitting the
conclusion?

The foregoing are the principal theories that have been
broached by our dissenting brethren, in order to connect
themselves with the Apostolic days, and to prove that their
religion is eighteen hundred years old. And I leave it to
you, My Dear Brethren, to decide whether any of these
theories be at all defensible, or whether they prove the
Apostolic origin and Antiquity of the Protestant denominations.   I think you will all agree with me that Protestantism originated only in the sixteenth century; that it
stands isolated from all previous ages; that it can claim no
ancient Christian ancestry; that it is, in short, about three
hundred years old, and no more. We can tell you when it
began, who started it, and under what circumstances; we
can unfold to you all the facts and incidents in its early
history, all its official acts and early divisions; in a word,
we can tell you every-thing connected with its origin and
progress. If there be any truth in history, it had no existence in the world for the first fifteen centuries of the
Christian era; it is therefore much too young to be the
Religion of Christ.*

---

* Our separated brethren sometimes attempt to extricate themselves
from the difficulty by a witticism neither very new nor very conclusive.
To the question—Where was your religion before the days of Luther?—
they answer by another question—where was your face before it was
washed? If they merely *washed* the face of the old Church, they certainly did it in a great variety of ways, and pretty thoroughly. They
removed not only the accidental defilements, but also many of the distinctive features! Besides, this illustration of washing might be turned
against them. What would they say, if it should be granted that they had
really washed the face of the Church, by removing all the uncleanness from
it, and depositing it in the basin of the reformation! This is certainly the
usual process in washing. This latter answer, at least, contains as much
argument as the above Protestant rejoinder to the Catholic objection.

II. THE ROMAN CATHOLIC CHURCH IS MORE THAN EIGH-
TEEN HUNDRED YEARS OLD.

Can any one doubt this fact? All history proclaims it;
all writers on Church History testify to its truth. Even
Protestant Church historians virtually admit it, by the necessity under which they are of unfolding the public history
of Christianity, and tracing the succession of the Roman
Pontiffs, during the first fifteen centuries of Christianity.
Blot out the Catholic Church, and what becomes of Church
History during this long period? Where are its monuments, where its lines of bishops, where its public acts?
In this hypothesis, it were utterly impossible to write an
ecclesiastical history reaching beyond the sixteenth century;
all beyond this epoch would be a complete blank.

The Catholic Church was not certainly hidden under a
bushel, nor concealed in a corner of the earth, during all
these centuries. It stepped forth into the public arena of
the world, and acted out its part prominently and boldly.
It came into frequent and open conflict with the passions
of men, with the powers and principalities of the earth.
Every-where it left an impression upon society too deep not
to be felt, too vivid not to be remembered. The startling
events which, every-where and at all times, marked its
career, were of too stirring a character to be easily forgotten; and the light which it shed upon the world was too
brilliant to allow mankind to be heedless of its presence or
to deny its existence. You might as well deny that the
sun has shone in the heavens ever since the dawn of
Christianity, as to deny that the Church has constantly
existed during the same period. Both facts are equally
plain, palpable, and undeniable.

Even if there were no other evidence of this fact than
the continued and uninterrupted succession of the Roman
Pontiffs in the chair of St. Peter, this alone would suffice
to establish it beyond a doubt. That venerable line of
bishops extends back in unbroken unity through more than
two hundred and fifty incumbents of the Apostolical chair,
from Pius IX. to St. Peter himself. All church historians,

both ancient and modern, agree in bearing evidence to
this succession. Tertullian appeals to it as a conclusive
argument against the innovators of the second century.

"Come then," says he, "you who wish to exercise your
curiosity to more advantage in the affair of salvation; go
through the Apostolic churches, in which the very chairs
of the Apostles continue aloft in their places, in which their
very original letters are recited, sounding forth the voice,
and representing the countenance of each one. Is Achaia
near you? You have Corinth. If you are not far from
Macedon, you have Philippi, you have Thessalonica. If
you can go to Asia, you have Ephesus. If you are near
Italy, you have Rome, whence authority is at hand for us
likewise. How happy is this church to which the Apostles
poured forth their whole doctrine with their blood! Where
Peter is assimilated to the Lord in his martyrdom; where
Paul is crowned with a death like that of John (the
Baptist); where John the Apostle, after he had been
dipped in boiling oil without sustaining injury, is banished
to the island (Patmos); let us see what she learned, what
she taught, what she professed in her symbol in common
with the African churches."*

St. Irenæus, a Greek by birth, a disciple of St. Polycarp
who had been reared under the eye of St. John the Apostle,
and subsequently bishop of Lyons, is still more explicit
and forcible in unfolding this same argument against the
heretics of his day. His testimony is the more valuable, as
it may be said to reflect the joint faith of the Greek and
Latin Churches of the second century. He furnishes us
with a list of the Roman Pontiffs from St. Peter down to
St. Eleutherius, who was the occupant of the chair at the
time he was writing. He introduces this argument of the
succession for a purpose sufficiently indicated in the following splendid testimony, in which he is pleading against the
pretensions of the Gnostics:

"All who wish to see the truth, may see in all the Church

---

* Præscriptiones, c. 86.

the tradition of the Apostles, manifested throughout the
whole world; and we can enumerate the bishops who have
been ordained by the Apostles, and their successors down to
our time, who taught or knew no such doctrine as they
madly dream of. But since it would be very tedious to
enumerate in this work the succession of all the churches,
by pointing to the tradition of the greatest and most
ancient* Church, known to all, founded and established at
Rome by the most glorious Apostles Peter and Paul, and to
her faith announced to men, coming down to us by the
succession of bishops, we confound all those who in any
improper manner gather together, either through self-
complacency or vain glory, or through blindness and perverse disposition. For with this Church, on account of its
more powerful principality, it is necessary that every
Church,—that is, the faithful who are in every direction,—
should agree, in which the Apostolic tradition has been
always preserved by those who are in every direction." †

The very same reasoning is employed by many others
of the ancient fathers in their refutations of heresy. Eusebius, the father of Church History, in the eastern Church;
and St. Irenæus, St. Optatus of Milevi, and St. Augustine, in
the western, all furnish us with lists of the Roman Pontiffs
up to the second, fourth, and fifth centuries, in which they
respectively wrote their works. Whence this coincidence
in writers so remote from one another, unless the succession
of Roman bishops was deemed by them all as undoubted in
point of fact, as it was important in theological argument?
Why did not Eusebius insist upon the succession of the
bishops in his own see of Cæsarea; St. Irenæus, upon that
of Lyons; St. Optatus, upon that of Milevi; and St. Augustine, upon that of Hyppo? Obviously because these lines

---

* Or *authoritative*, as rendered by Archbishop Kenrick in his learned
and excellent work on the Primacy, (p. 85.) Those who wish to see all
the lights of Christian Antiquity concentrated on this subject, are referred
to this book.

† Adversus Hæreses, L. iii: c. 8.

were deemed of very little importance; at least of much
less than that of the great and central See of Rome.

As to the succession of the Roman Pontiffs after the
fifth century, it is so clear that no one will venture to
deny it, not even the most bitter enemies of the papacy.
Cavil they may at some minor difficulties which certainly
do not affect the substance of the question; deny the fact
of the succession they cannot. The occasional vacancy of
the Roman See for a few months; the intrusion into it of a
few unworthy individuals in times of trouble and civil war;
the conflicting claims of rival aspirants in times of schism;
could not break the succession, any more than similar con-
tingencies can interrupt that of a long line of monarchs.
Such things are evidently to be estimated by a moral, not
by a physical standard.

The most plausible objection is that presented by the
great schism of the west, when, during nearly forty years,
at the close of the fourteenth and the beginning of the
fifteenth century, there was kept up a warm contest for the
papal tiara by the two contending lines of Rome and Avig-
non; and, for the last six years of that unhappy period,
between these and a third line which claimed under the
election of the Pisan council, held in 1409. But one of
those lines was certainly the lawful one; and it obviously
matters not as to the substance of the succession which line
it was. Our ignorance of the subject, either from the want
of proper documents, or from the different statements of
facts by the contending parties, cannot be supposed to affect
its real merits. So far as our present argument is concerned, it is enough for us to know that the succession was
certainly kept up in one or the other of the different lines.

So also it does not matter, whether Clement or Cletus
was the first successor of St. Peter, or whether Cletus and
Anacletus were the same individual, or two different persons: in either case, the succession was certainly maintained
without any interruption whatever. Our not being able to
see the sun when it is clouded, does not blot it out from the
heavens; so our not being able altogether to dispel the

clouds which sometimes hang over the facts of history, does not obliterate or destroy them. The objections just alluded to are mere straws floating on the current of the succession; they do not interrupt it, much less do they turn back its waters.

The perpetual and unbroken succession of the Roman Pontiffs, from St. Peter, the founder of the See, to Pius IX., the present incumbent, is an undoubted historical fact, which cannot be denied without impugning the faith of all history.

"The proudest royal houses," says a brilliant Protestant writer of the day, "are but of yesterday, when compared with the line of Roman Pontiffs. This line we trace back IN AN UNBROKEN SERIES, from the Pope who crowned Napoleon in the nineteenth century, to the Pope who crowned Pepin in the eighth; and far beyond the time of Pepin, the august dynasty extends, until its origin is lost in the twilight of fable. The republic of Venice came next in antiquity. But the republic of Venice was modern when compared with the papacy; and the republic of Venice is gone and the papacy remains. The papacy remains, not in decay, nor a mere antique, but full of life and youthful vigor. The Catholic Church is still sending forth, to the farthest ends of the world, missionaries as zealous as those who landed in Kent with Augustine, and is still confronting hostile kings with the same spirit with which she confronted Attila. The number of her children is greater than in any former age. Her acquisitions in the new world have more than compensated her for what she has lost in the old."*

The Catholic Church is certainly as old as the papacy, with which it is as intimately and essentially connected, as is a monarchy with its line of kings, or our own republic with its line of presidents. The Catholic Church could not

---

* Thomas Babington Macaulay—Miscellanies—Review of "Ranke's History of the Popes." What does he mean by "the twilight of fable?" I am really at a loss to know, and I suppose he had himself no very distinct idea on the subject.

subsist without the papacy, nor the papacy without the Catholic Church. They are both blended together in indissoluble unity: they were espoused by Christ himself; and He has said, "What God hath united let no man put asunder." Therefore it is competent for us to argue the apostolical Antiquity of the Catholic Church from that of the papacy. But this, though one of the principal evidences, is not the only one furnished by history, of the fact that the Catholic Church is more than eighteen hundred years old. All her general and particular councils, all her widely extended missions, all her public acts and monuments, from the first dawn of Christianity to the present day, bear witness to this great leading fact. It is the plainest thing in all Church History; you cannot deny it, without denying every thing established by human testimony.

But the usual answer is, that the Church has changed; that she was not at the beginning of the sixteenth century, and is not now, what she originally was; that she corrupted the Word of God by adding to it human traditions;—in a word, that she apostatized, and that the reformers merely restored her to her primitive purity. In reply, I will submit to your consideration, My Beloved Brethren, a few plain remarks, by which, I trust, you may be able to estimate the truth and worth of this fashionable modern theory.

1. I maintain that, if the Catholic Church was once the true Church of Christ, she continued such during the whole of the first fifteen centuries, and she is such still. If she adulterated the Word of God, and thereby ceased to be the true Church, when did she do so? Who was the author of the bold innovation? Under what peculiar circumstances was he enabled to effect his nefarious purpose? Did he do it with, or without opposition? Silently, or amidst clamor, reclamation, and confusion? If the former, then what evidence can history afford for a revolution with which no one could be acquainted? If the latter, still I ask where is the evidence for the alleged change? I can believe nothing, at

least nothing of such vital importance, without sufficient evidence. Let us have no mere surmise, no crude theory, no idle opinion; let us have FACTS. We have been challenging the adversaries of Catholicity for three centuries to produce even one well authenticated fact in support of their assertion; and our challenge has been hitherto met by a most ominous silence, or by vague assertions without proof, worse, if possible, than silence itself. We have been long enough amused with the silly declamation, that "while men were asleep" in the night of the *dark* ages, this great religious revolution was silently accomplished, without any one becoming aware of the fact!! We have been gravely called on to credit the testimony of sleeping witnesses, who, however, seem to be still slumbering, for even they cannot be produced in open court!

Surely, if the change really took place, there should be sufficient historical proofs of a fact so very important. We should be informed as to THE TIME WHEN, THE PLACE WHERE, THE PERSONS BY WHOM, AND THE CIRCUMSTANCES UNDER WHICH, it occurred. We should be told of every thing connected with its origin, progress, consummation, and entire history. We are able to furnish all these details in regard to all the new systems of religion which have ever been broached, whether in ancient or in modern times. We can tell who started Arianism, Nestorianism, Eutychianism, Manicheism, Lutheranism, Calvinism, Church-of-Englandism, and every other *ism*, which was an innovation on the ancient doctrines of Christianity. If our adversaries are not able to do the same in regard to Catholicity, it amounts to an avowal that this Religion is, in all its parts, as old as Christianity itself.

Attempts have been, indeed, made to assign the time of the alleged change; but they have been vague, inconsistent, and wholly unsatisfactory. Some have asserted that the Church fell away from primitive purity in the fourth; others, in the fifth; others, in the sixth; others, in the seventh; others, in the eighth; others, in the ninth century; while others, with greater prudence, are content with

22

the more general assertion, alluded to above, that the falling off occurred gradually and imperceptibly, chiefly in what they are pleased to designate the dark ages! The vague assertions and conflicting opinions of our adversaries on the subject, prove conclusively that even they are not quite sure of their ground.' If you press them to be more explicit, and to enter into particular facts, details, and dates, they invariably refuse or neglect to do so. The reason is plain; they cannot be expected to produce facts which are nowhere to be found in Church History!

2. Besides, it was a fixed and cardinal principle of the Catholic Church in all ages, that nothing should be taught as of faith, which had not been handed down and believed from the beginning. The maxim announced by a Pope of the third century,—St. Stephen,—LET NOTHING BE INNOVATED ON WHAT HAS BEEN HANDED DOWN BY TRADITION,"*— was universally received and acted on by the Church at all times and in all places. This principle was constantly referred to and applied in all her general councils, from that of Nice, which condemned Arius in the fourth century, to that of Trent, which condemned Luther and Calvin in the sixteenth. It was not changed, nor even modified, in the long lapse of centuries. Neither time, nor revolution, nor storms, nor fire, nor flood, nor persecution, could erase this motto from the escutcheon of the Church! The great previous question in all the councils was,—what has been taught in all the Churches from the beginning? The heretics could quote Scripture as well as the assembled Catholic fathers; but they could not prove either the Antiquity or the universal acceptance of their peculiar opinions. Here they were completely foiled; upon this rock they all split, and were dashed into pieces.

A distinguished Protestant writer of the day, Henry Hallam, refutes as absurd and unfounded, "a strange notion that has been started of late years in England, that the Council of Trent made important innovations in the estab-

---

* NIHIL INNOVETUR NISI QUOD TRADITUM EST.   Inter Opp. S. Cypriani.

lished doctrines of the western Church; an hypothesis," he adds, "so paradoxical in respect to public opinion, and, it must be added, so prodigiously at variance with the known facts of ecclesiastical history, that we cannot but admire the facility with which it has been taken up." He continues: "But it may be said that they (the Tridentine fathers) had but one leading prejudice, that of determining theological faith according to the tradition of the Catholic Church, as handed down to their own age. This one point of authority conceded, I am not aware that they can be proved to have decided wrong, or, at least, against all reasonable evidence. Let those who have imbibed a different opinion ask themselves, whether they have read Sarpi through with any attention, especially as to those sessions of the Tridentine council which preceded the suspension in 1547."*

The Council of Trent, in thus rigidly adhering to ancient precedent, did but tread in the footsteps of all previous general councils in which doctrinal questions were under consideration. It is plain, that a Church which has always and invariably acted on this principle could not have changed the doctrines originally handed down. At least, the constant recognition and application of the principle furnishes a very strong presumption against any such change; a presumption so strong, that it cannot be destroyed but by the most explicit and cumulative evidence to the contrary. But no such evidence worthy the name has ever been even alleged, to prove the doctrinal change in question; therefore the presumption grows into a moral certainty.

3. Again, if the Roman Catholic Church really apostatized, I may ask from what Church did she apostatize? From the *true* Church? But where was the true Church? What does history say of it, if it was ever any thing different from the Roman Catholic Church? Where are its

* Introduction to the History of Literature, &c. Vol. I. p. 277, *Note.* American Edition.

public acts, its councils, its bishops, its monuments? Is
the Greek Church that true Church from which the Roman
Catholic fell away? But the Greek Church was united in
doctrine, in government, and in communion with the Latin
Church, and the two united formed the great Roman
Catholic Church, during the first eight centuries and a half
of the Christian era. Moreover, the first disunion, caused
by Photius, was soon healed, and the schism did not become final until the middle of the eleventh century, two
centuries later; and a temporary re-union of the two
churches was subsequently effected at two different times,
—in the general council of Lyons, in 1274, and in that
of Florence, in 1445. These are all plain and undeniable
historical facts. If then, the apostasy first occurred about
the middle of the ninth century,—the date of the first
Greek schism,—the Greek church received back the apos-
tate Church into her communion at three different times
thereafter; and this, too, without requiring from her any
retraction of her errors; for it is notorious that, in all
these re-unions, the Greek church drew back and retracted,
not the Latin. Besides, it is equally notorious, that the
Greek separated from the Latin Church, and not the Latin
from the Greek. The schism was begun and consummated
by the ambitious and reckless patriarchs of Constantinople,
with a view to attach to their see an importance and an
influence not warranted by Christian Antiquity.*

---

*I believe that no candid man, who will fully and fairly examine the
historical evidence bearing on the question of the Greek schism, can fail to
come to the conclusion, that it was brought about and consummated mainly
by the ambition of the Constantinopolitan bishops, as stated in the text.
The following brief summary of well authenticated facts is submitted on
this subject:—

1. The episcopal see of Constantinople was not one of those founded by
the apostles, or even, it would seem, by any one of their immediate disciples. During the first three centuries it had no pre-eminence of rank
whatever; its bishops were merely the suffragans of those of Heraclea, the
metropolis of Thrace.

2. The established discipline of the early Church recognized three great
patriarchates only, which held ecclesiastical pre-eminence in the following
order: that of Rome first, that of Alexandria second, and that of Antioch
third. This order of rank was observed in the first general council, held at

Again, this theory is wholly at war with that which is
the most current and popular among our adversaries;
namely, that the alleged apostasy took place in the fourth,
or, at latest, in the fifth century. At this period the Greek

Nice, in 325. Up to this date, the bishops of Constantinople are scarcely so
much as mentioned in ecclesiastical history. The patriarchate of Jerusalem
was established more than a hundred years later, at the Council of Chalcedon, held in 451.

3. After Constantine had removed the seat of his empire to the east, and
rebuilt Constantinople,—before called Byzantium,—as his imperial residence, in the year 330, the bishops of that city began to claim greater consideration for their see, which they from that epoch styled the new Rome.
From this period we are to date those successive encroachments by which
the prelates of that city sought gradually to extend their ecclesiastical influence; and the result of which was their total separation from Rome and
the great body of the Church, some centuries later. The eastern emperors
generally smiled upon their efforts for this purpose, and lent them the influence of their mighty name, considering this course well calculated to
advance their own political importance.

4. The first step of the kind seems to have been taken in the second
general council held at Constantinople in 381, composed entirely of Greek
bishops, and convened, with the approbation of Pope Damasus, for the condemnation of the Macedonian heresy. The third canon of this council enacted, that "the bishop of Constantinople should have the first place of
honor *after* the Roman bishop, because Constantinople is the new Rome."
It is almost needless to say, that this canon, which plainly subverted the
ancient ecclesiastical discipline, and impaired the time-honored rights of the
eastern patriarchs of Alexandria and Antioch, was never approved by Rome
or by the western Church.

5. The Greek bishops of the great council of Chalcedon, held in 451,
against the heresy of Eutyches, went one step farther. The famous 28th
canon of this council, clandestinely adopted after the assembly had closed its
regular sessions, and the Roman delegates had departed, gave to the Constantinopolitan prelates *equal* honor and jurisdiction with those of Rome,
and for the same reason as had been assigned at the council of Constantinople above mentioned. This canon was never approved by the Roman
Pontiffs nor the Catholic Church.

6. A similar spirit of ambition continued to be manifested, at intervals,
by the bishops of that city during the four following centuries; it was
always mildly but firmly rebuked by the Roman Pontiffs; but it did not
lead to an open rupture till the time of Photius, about the middle of the
ninth century.

7. This restless and ambitious man was intruded into the see of Constantinople by the influence of the imperial court, and while the sainted
Ignatius, the rightful incumbent, was still living! But the schism induced
by him was soon healed by the wisdom and firmness of the Roman Pontiff;
and the unity of the Church was thus secured for two more centuries.

8. Finally, about the middle of the eleventh century, Michael Cerularius,
another bishop of the imperial city, consummated the schism by his own
unauthorized act, and without any provocation whatever from Rome. We
are told as much by Dr. Palmer himself, surely an unexceptionable witness.
He says: "When Cerularius, bishop of Constantinople, wrote to the bishop

and Latin Churches were closely united in communion, as
every-body knows; therefore if the apostasy occurred at
all, it certainly had no connection whatsoever with the
Greek schism. So this point is settled.

The difficulty, then, returns in all its force ;—From what
church did the Roman Catholic apostatize when it fell away
from the truth? Are we to say that it apostatized from
itself? But this is a palpable absurdity. Will you say
that it simply ceased to be the true Church by changing
the ancient faith? Are you then prepared to admit, that,
for a thousand years and more, there was no true Church
of Christ on earth? That Christ died for the salvation of
men, and yet abandoned them, and left them without the
true Religion, and therefore without the means of salvation, for all this long period! That He built His Church on
a rock, cemented it with His blood, promised that "the
gates of hell should not prevail against it," and yet permitted it to go to ruin, to become corrupt to its very center,
to be infected with damnable superstition and idolatry,
for more than ten centuries? Had His one true Church,
His beloved Spouse "without spot or wrinkle," the organ
of His communication with the world, wholly disappeared
from among men, or become so spotted and wrinkled as to
be no longer His Church? Was His purpose thus wholly
frustrated? If so, what truth or certainty is there any
longer in Christianity itself? If Christ did not think
proper to preserve His own Church, how do we know that
he has thought proper to preserve any other, or Christianity itself?

But the reformation restored Christianity to its original
purity.—What assurance have we of this? Which of the

---

of Trani, in Italy, condemning several of the rites and ceremonies of the
Roman Church, *and shut up the Latin churches and monasteries in Constantinople*, the legate of the Roman see, Cardinal Humbert, insisted on his im-
plicit submission to the Pope; and, on his refusal, left an excommunication
on the altar of his patriarchial church of St. Sophia, at Constantinople."
(Compendious Ecclesiast. History, p. 106.) The restless ambition and
downright violence of Cerularius thus obviously led to the final schism
which had been so long threatened.

hundred contradictory systems of, Protestantism contains the genuine type of that restoration? Or does any one of them all fully realize the original Church of Christ? Must we take them all together, in order to have original Christianity in its purity and integrity? But this were absurd and impossible; for they mutually exclude one another, and the original Church of Christ was certainly not a chaos of discordant and irreconcilable elements. To think this, would be to blaspheme Jesus Christ himself.

But there was the Greek Church, which still remained, after the Latin or western had apostatized.—This is another signal delusion. As I have already shown, the Greek Church, even after its schism, continued to agree in belief with the Latin Church in all articles of faith, except in two; the procession of the Holy Ghost from the Son as well as from the Father, and the supremacy of the Pope; in regard to the former of which all evangelical Protestants of the present day differ from it and agree with the Roman Catholic Church. In all things else, in all those distinctive doctrines of Catholicity against which Protestants object as superstitious and idolatrous, the Greek Church of the present day, as well as the Oriental sects, still profess and retain precisely the same faith and practice as we do. Therefore, they are clearly with us, and against Protestants. And therefore, if the western Church erred in those things, the eastern erred also; and so the whole Church, both in the east and in the west, fell away together from the true doctrine. Then the true Church of Christ disappeared entirely from the face of the earth. Horrible inference! You can not believe it for an instant, My Dear Brethren, without losing all faith in Christianity itself, and turning deists at once, as perhaps more than half the Protestant world has accordingly already done!

4. But this pretended falling away of the Catholic Church is opposed to the very genius of Christianity; and it moreover openly falsifies the clearest, most explicit, and most solemn predictions and promises of Jesus Christ; nay, it subverts Christianity itself, and saps the foundation of all

faith. I have already had occasion to hint at some of these promises; but the subject is so very important, that I propose to devote the next Lecture to its consideration.

From what I have already said and endeavored to prove in the present Lecture, I hope you will agree with me in the belief that the two propositions upon which the present argument rests have been fully established:—that Protestantism is not, and cannot claim to be, eighteen hundred years old; and that Catholicity can clearly prove her claim to this amount of Antiquity. The conclusion is necessary and irresistible—that the Catholic Church alone is the one true Church of Jesus Christ.

AND THIS IS THE SIXTH EVIDENCE OF CATHOLICITY.

May Almighty God vouchsafe to grant to us all, My Dear Brethren, to be of one mind and of one heart in Christ Jesus; that there may no longer be any schisms amongst us; and that, by coming to a knowledge of the one ancient truth, and entering upon the OLD PATHS trodden by our ancestors, we may attain unto life everlasting. "For what doth it profit a man, if he gain the whole world and lose his own soul?" May God grant us His holy light and grace to enable us to see, understand, and walk in these things: through Jesus Christ, our Lord and Saviour! Amen.

LECTURE IX.

Text explained—Importance of the principle it involves—Doctrine of Infallibility—What it is not—What it is—Popular objections solved—The seat of Infallibility—The Pope and a general council—Councils of Constance and Basle—Can many fallibles make an infallible?—The charge of reasoning *in a vicious circle* answered—And retorted—The whole question depends upon a fact—Presumptive Evidence in proof of this fact—Four great principles applied to its elucidation—The Apostolic Age—Infallibility in possession at its close—Positive evidence—The promises of Christ addressed to St. Peter—And to the other Apostles—Testimony and reasoning of St. Paul—The spotless Bride of the Lamb—St. Cyprian—Recapitulation—The Seventh Evidence of Catholicity—St. Chrysostom and St. Augustine—Conclusion.

"*And I say to thee: that thou art Peter, and upon this rock I will build my Church,* AND THE GATES OF HELL SHALL NOT PREVAIL AGAINST IT."— ST. MATTHEW, xvi: 18.

SUCH, My Beloved Brethren, is the solemn declaration and promise in regard to the stability of His Church, made by our blessed Lord and Master more than eighteen hundred years ago. Prophet and God as He was, He could not be Himself deceived, nor could He deceive us; He could promise whatever He pleased, and redeem all that He promised. We are, then, to listen to His words with humility and reverence, and with the simplicity and docility of little children; and we are carefully to banish from our minds all prejudice and all disposition to cavil, if we would understand and profit by their sacred meaning.

These dispositions are the more important here, as it is question of a fundamental principle upon which the whole edifice of the Church securely rests, and by which it can show to the world that it is the self-same structure now

(261)

that it was eighteen centuries ago, when the great Man-God Himself built it upon a rock. For if we once establish that Christ is and always has been with His Church, teaching through it as His official organ, watching over its destinies, guarding it from error, averting from it all dangers both from within and from without: and that He pledged His eternal truth to preserve it in all its original purity and integrity to the very end of time;—if, in a word, we once admit that the Church is infallible in her public teaching, we have cut the Gordian knot of controversy, and have put an end to all religious disputes and sects: for we have established a competent and infallible judge of controversies, to whose decisions all are bound to submit, and upon the truth and certainty of whose judgments all may most implicitly rely.

Nay more, we are enabled, by means of this single principle, to thread with ease and safety all the intricate mazes of Church History, to discover the finger of God everywhere, and to connect the present Catholic with the primitive Christian Church. For, if the Church of Christ could not err in matters of faith and morals, she could not change, and therefore she is the self-same now as she was in the beginning. Therefore, if the Catholic was once the true Church, she is so yet. This, you will recollect, is the argument which I promised in my last Lecture to develop on this evening. Considering the vast importance of this tenet of Infallibility in the Christian system, and the great and eternal interests involved in the belief or rejection of it, may I solicit your patient and undivided attention?

"The Infallibility of the Church!"—I fancy I hear some of you exclaim, with a smile or a lurking sneer—"Surely you are not going to attempt proving this absurdity to an intelligent audience in the nineteenth century! It is too late in the day to attempt persuading men of sense that your popes, bishops, or priests are infallible; as if they were not all as fallible men as any other; as if they were not as much liable to sin and frailty as the rest of mankind; as if history did not represent many of them to be very corrupt, and a disgrace to the Church and to humanity itself!"

Have a little patience, My Dear Brethren, and I hope to show you that this popular objection, upon which declaimers have rung so many changes during the last three centuries, is based upon a series of strange misconceptions, and that it does not really touch the matter at issue between Protestants and the Catholic Church, on this subject of Church Infallibility. For what do we mean when we assert that the Church is infallible? Do we mean to say that any priest or bishop, or any particular body of priests or bishops, not representing the whole Church, is necessarily impeccable or infallible? Not at all; we hold no such doctrinal tenet; our adversaries may impute it to us for their own purposes; we maintain it not.

Do we mean to say that even the Pope is impeccable or infallible in his private and individual capacity? No Catholic divine ever so much as dreamed of saying or even thinking so. Do we mean to say that the Pope, viewed in his public and official capacity, when he speaks out as the organ and visible head of the Church, is gifted with Infallibility? No Catholic divine ever defended his Infallibility, even under such circumstances, unless when the matters on which he uttered his definition were intimately connected with the doctrines of faith and morals, and when, if he should be permitted by God to fall into error, there would be danger of the whole Church being also led astray. Those numerous and learned Catholic theologians who maintain the Infallibility of the Roman Pontiff in this particular case, consider it as a matter of *opinion* more or less certain, not as one of Catholic *faith* defined by the Church and obligatory on all. Though not an article of Catholic faith, it is, however, the general belief among Catholics; and I myself am inclined strongly to advocate its soundness, chiefly on account of the intimate connection between the Pontiff and the Church, as will be shown in a subsequent Lecture. Still it is an opinion, for all this, and no Catholic would venture to charge the great Bossuet, for

example, with being wanting in orthodoxy for denying it,
while he so powerfully and so eloquently established the
Infallibility of the Church.

In regard to papal decrees or bulls having reference to
particular cases of Church discipline and government, to
matters of fact dependent on human testimony, to affairs
of a political or temporal nature, and to all other things
not necessarily connected with faith or morals, all our divines unanimously agree in maintaining that, how great
soever may be the respect which is due them, they are not
to be considered as infallible. And that you may understand within what narrow limits the papal Infallibility is
restricted even by the warmest advocates of this opinion, I
must farther observe, that a number of circumstances and
conditions are required to prove the fact that the Pope
meant to speak *ex cathedra*, or as the official visible head
and organ of the Church; and that cases of the kind are
of very rare occurrence, not averaging more than one or
two to a century, at least for the last three hundred years.
I mention all these undoubted facts, to show you that most,
if not all, of the arguments usually alleged by our adversaries from papal acts and bulls of ages past to disprove
the Infallibility of the Church, are entirely beside the real
question; and that they do not even refute the mere opinion
in favor of the papal Infallibility.

What, then, is our real doctrine in regard to the Infallibility of the Church? It is simply and plainly this, and
this alone: that, in virtue of the solemnly promised presence and assistance of Christ, the Church, as a Church, in
its public official capacity, never can err in matters of faith
and morals; or never can teach as truth what is error.
Christ divided His Church into two great departments or
provinces: that of the teachers, and that of the taught;
that of the spiritual governors, and that of the spiritually
governed; that of the ministry, and that of the people.
The former were to teach, rule, and administer the sacraments. The latter were to be taught, to obey, and to
receive the sacraments. These two things went together,

and were inseparable. The duties of the people were co-relative with those of their pastors; and the former necessarily grew out of the latter. Now, we hold that the great body of the pastors, and especially the great body of the bishops, whom we view as successors of the Apostles, and therefore as chief pastors in the Church, cannot go astray from the true faith, or teach erroneous doctrines; else the whole body of the people would necessarily, and, in consequence of an essential feature in the organization of the Church as settled by Christ himself, be drawn into error, and thus the whole Church would fall into heresy, and would cease, by the very fact, to be the Church of Christ; for a false and heretical Church is certainly no Church of Christ at all.

The body of bishops may be viewed in a twofold light, either in their natural condition of dispersion throughout the world, or as assembled by their representatives in a general council; and in either case, when their judgment concurs with that of the Roman Pontiff, or chief bishop, we hold it to be authoritative and infallible in matters of faith and morals. Without the concurrence of the Pope, the whole body of bishops would not be adequately represented; and therefore, the doctrinal decision of any body of bishops, no matter how numerous or respectable, without the Pope's sanction and assent, either express or clearly implied, would not be necessarily infallible. The same may be said of a doctrinal decision of the Pope without the concurrence of the bishops.*

In short, we hold that the CHURCH TEACHING, in its official capacity, is infallible in doctrinal matters, and that whenever a decision on points of Christian faith and morals emanates from this body, whether in a state of dispersion, or represented in a general council, it is to be received as the decision of Christ himself, the great invisible Head of the Church. This is all that the Catholic is bound to

---

* In both these cases, I merely make an hypothesis, and I do not thereby mean to admit the possibility of the doctrinal decision of the Pope being ever different from that of the body of bishops.

believe on the subject. This is all that is strictly of Catholic faith on the question of Church Infallibility, and consequently all that the subject of the present Lecture requires me to defend.

This explanation naturally leads us to the solution of another difficulty which has been often raised with an air of triumph, but which certainly has more apparent plausibility than real force. We are told that Catholics differ as to the seat of the Infallibility, some placing it in the Pope, others in the general council, and others again in the body of bishops dispersed over the world; and that, therefore, there is no certainty about the entire doctrine, or at least about its practical operation and application to particular controversies. But this statement is manifestly defective, and it places the whole matter in a false light. In common candor, the objectors should have stated—what is clearly the fact—that ALL Catholics unanimously agree in maintaining that the body of the bishops, in conjunction with the Pope, is infallible. This is all that a Catholic is bound to hold; and upon this there is, there can be, no difference of belief among Catholics. The other matters of individual opinion are of very little, or rather of no practical importance whatever. They are mere speculations on abstract principles, or on cases which, if possible at all, are of very rare occurrence, under the most anomalous and extraordinary circumstances of the Church. If this be not so, let our adversaries, if they can, point to one single case during the last four centuries, in which any considerable number of bishops dissented from the Pope in doctrinal matters. The fact is, they can not do it; for no such case exists.

Nay farther, let them turn over all the annals of Church History for eighteen centuries, and produce one single instance of the kind, in which the body of bishops, or a council held by Catholics to be general, ever taught doctrines opposed to those taught by an *undoubted* Pope. Here, too, history fails them, or its facts will not serve their purpose. If they refer to the stereotype objection founded on the early sessions of the council of Constance, and the later sessions of that of Basle, I answer,—as has been already answered a thousand times,—that the alleged decrees of the former council contemplated only a state of schism, in which it was not apparent who among three different claimants of the papacy was the real Pope; that they were enacted at a time when the maxim was universally current,—"A doubtful Pope is virtually no Pope at all;"*—and that the council of Basle, at the time the decrees objected were passed, was very thinly attended, was almost universally viewed as a schismatical conventicle rather than as a legitimate council, was finally abandoned by the few bishops who had still lingered therein after its dissolution or prorogation by the Pope Eugenius IV.; that its decisions were condemned by the council of Florence, in which it was finally merged; and that this latter council was at the time, and is still generally admitted to be, a general one, fairly representing the whole body of bishops in union with the Pope, while that of Basle, at least in its later sessions, is as universally rejected. The only case, then, which can be objected with any degree of plausibility, to prove that the body of bishops may dissent from the Pope, proves precisely the contrary; for so soon as the synod of Basle attempted to dissever the union, it was rejected with indignation by all except a few hot and misguided partisans, and the vast majority of the bishops immediately rallied around the Pope at Florence.

The truth is, My Dear Brethren, the whole controversy which was carried on, chiefly in the fifteenth century, as to whether the council was superior to the Pope, or the Pope to the council, originated in the anomalous state of schism, and was referable to it alone. Besides, it was really rather a dispute about words than about things; at least after it had been taken out of its legitimate connection, and generalized by the Gallican prelates of the seventeenth century, with Bossuet at their head. All Catholics were agreed, that there could be no general council without the inter-

---

* Papa dubius est papa nullus.

vention or approval of the Pope.* So that, in ultimate
analysis, the question was resolved into this: Is the Pope,
together with the council, superior or inferior to the Pope
alone?—which was plainly no question at all.

From what I have said, it is clear that the objections just
answered do not touch the real merits of the question, but
tend only to distract the mind from its calm consideration,
by making a number of collateral issues, of no real importance, and wholly beside the matter in controversy.

The same remark may be extended to another very trite,
and very silly objection. We are gravely told that the
doctrine of Infallibility is absurd, because many fallibles
cannot make an infallible! As if we founded the doctrine
on the mere natural fallibility or infallibility of men, and
taught that a large body of men might naturally possess
an attribute which could not be predicated of each of its
component parts! We teach no such absurdity. We take
much higher ground. We base the Infallibility of the
Church on the solemn declarations and promises of Christ
—who was surely infallible—and upon those no less explicit
of His inspired Apostles. We hold that the Church is
infallible, because Christ is with it, and promised to guard
it from error, notwithstanding the passions and natural
fallibility of men. He did not promise Infallibility to individuals, but to the Church, as a Church, as His Church,
appointed by Himself to be the organ of His communication with the world, and therefore speaking His language
and expounding His doctrines with infallible certainty.
This is our real position; and it cannot surely be shaken
by the shallow objection just noticed.

But how do we prove that Christ promised to make
the Church infallible, and that His inspired Apostles bear
evidence to that promise? Is it not from the Holy Scriptures? And how do we know that the Scriptures are the
inspired Word of God? Is it not by the authority of the

---

* At least in all cases in which the Church is not distracted by a papal
schism; an event, thank God, of very rare occurrence.

infallible Church? Do we not thus reason in what is called
a *vicious circle*, proving the divine authority of the Scriptures by the infallible Church, and again, the Infallibility
of the Church by the divine authority of the Scriptures?
How do we get out of this difficulty?

We get out of the circle with the greatest facility im-
aginable. The fact is, My Dear Brethren, it is no circle
at all; it exists only in the fertile brain of our adversaries, who vainly imagine that they have inclosed us in a
net of logic from which there is no escape, when really
the objection presents no logical difficulty whatsoever. I
am even tempted to smile at the simplicity that continues
to urge, as a serious objection, a very shallow sophism,
which, like every thing else alleged against Catholicity,
has been already put and answered a thousand times!
The difficulty is really not on our side, but on that of our
adversaries; as the following very plain considerations will,
I hope, serve to convince you.

1. In arguing with Protestants, who already admit the
divine authority of the Scriptures, but deny that of the
Church, it is surely competent for us to prove the latter
by the former. Where is the vicious circle in proving a
thing denied from a thing already admitted? Is it either
logical or necessary to attempt proving what is not denied
by your adversary? Now, as this is precisely the course of
reasoning adopted by Catholics, and as our controversy in
regard to the Infallibility of the Church lies with Protestants only, and not with Jews or infidels, it is plain to the
dullest capacity that we move in no *vicious circle* whatever.

2. We can prove the inspiration of the Holy Scriptures
without the authority of the Church, at least as well as
can our adversaries; and therefore, in this respect, we
stand on as good ground at least as they.

3. The sophism called reasoning in a circle, consists in
mutually proving two different things by each other, in such
sort that the *only* evidence upon which each one rests is
that derived from the other. If either proposition be sus-
ceptible of proof from other sources, the circle ceases to

28 *

be *vicious*, or as logicians say technically, it is *opened*. . The mere fact, then, that a reasoning is *circular*, does not always vitiate its force. Two persons may mutually bear testimony to each other, and yet the evidence of each be valid and worthy of acceptance. Thus St. John, the Baptist, bore testimony to Christ, and Christ bore testimony to St. John, the Baptist; yet the testimony of both was viewed as authoritative and conclusive. Those who believed in the divine mission of John, naturally received his testimony in favor of Christ; and those, on the contrary, who believed in the divine mission of Christ, as naturally accepted His testimony in favor of John. Was there any vicious circle in this obviously *circular* reasoning. Thus again, a man of respectable appearance takes a check to the bank purporting that a certain amount is to be paid to the bearer, and the check is immediately honored, though the check bears testimony to the identity of the man and he to the genuineness of the check. Thus also, an ambassador presents his credentials at a foreign court, and he is received and duly accredited, though the credentials bear evidence to him, and he to the credentials. Such things happen continually in every-day life, and yet there is certainly no defective reasoning involved in them; else we must suppose that human affairs and reasonings move frequently in a vicious circle.

4. Let us take another example, which will lead us still nearer to the matter in question. We prove the genius, character, and principles of our own government* from our written constitution; and yet we also prove the genuineness and authority of our constitution by the authority of our government which originally framed and adopted this instrument. The government was fully established, and its independence and authority recognized both at home and abroad, for years before the constitution was written: and if no written constitution had ever been adopted, the

* By the *government* I mean here, not merely the executive department of it, but all its essential parts, including the legislative and judiciary.

authority of the government would still have remained unimpaired. Once the constitution had been written and adopted, its principles become authoritative in regard to the general structure and powers of the government; still the latter had the guardianship of the instrument, and was the only legitimate expounder of its meaning in cases of doubt and controversy. Thus the government is older than the constitution; the former might have subsisted though the latter had never been written; and it was the natural expounder, and the only legitimate one in ultimate resort, of that document; and yet the two bear mutual testimony to each other. Is our whole theory of government based upon a vicious circle?

5. Let us now apply the facts and principles of this last example to the mutual testimony borne to each other by the Church and the Scriptures,—especially by those of the New Testament, of which alone, in the present case, there can be question. In the comparison, the Church corresponds to our government, and the New Testament, in a certain qualified sense, to our written constitution. Bearing this in mind, you will instantly perceive that, in the mutual relations of the Church and the New Testament, precisely the same facts and principles are developed as in those of our government and its written constitution. The Church is older than the New Testament; for the last book of the latter was written about the close of the first century, after the Church had been already established for about sixty-five years: the Church might have continued to exist in unimpaired authority, though the New Testament had never been written, as it did really so subsist without it for more than half a century; the Church was the only natural and legitimate expounder of the New Testament, as well as the main witness of its authenticity, canon, and inspiration: and finally, the Church and the New Testament bear mutual testimony to the authority of each other. Is not the parallelism almost complete in every detail? And if no vicious circle is involved in the former process of

reasoning, with what semblance of truth can it be said to
be involved in the latter?

6. Again; how was a Christian of the first centuries to be
certain of, and to be able to prove, the canon and inspiration of the New Testament? By mere intrinsic evidences?
But these, however strong they might seem to one who
was already a believer, were still, considered in themselves
alone, not wholly conclusive even to him; while to the
unbeliever they were almost entirely powerless for conviction. Besides the genuine and inspired books of the New
Testament, there were also many others then in circulation,
either wholly spurious, or intrinsically good and genuine,
but written by uninspired men.* The intrinsic evidences of
many among the latter books seemed so strong during that
period, that not a few sincere and well-disposed Christians
received them, and even placed them on a level with those
which we now hold as divine. This proves that the mere
intrinsic marks were not sufficient. How was this matter
finally and definitively settled? Simply and only by the
living and speaking authority of the early Church. And
how was the authority of the Church herself established?
By her public acts, and by the divine and bright seals of
her heavenly mission, every-where and at all times stamped
by God himself upon her public teaching and ministration :
by her rapid and wonderful propagation throughout the
world through means naturally the most inadequate, and in
the face of a fierce and relentless opposition, which would
have crushed any merely human institution ;—and all this
though her doctrines were at open war with the passions
of men, and necessarily tended to break down and crush
all the most dearly cherished institutions then universally
received by mankind, and interwoven with all forms of
human society and government; by the astonishing beneficial effects on public morals which every-where followed
her progress; by the holy lives of her ministers and people,
and the blood of her countless martyrs, poured out like

---

* See the third Lecture, *supra.*

water to attest her divine origin and truth : finally, by the many and brilliant miracles by which God set the seal of His approbation on her divine mission to the world. In short, her divine authority was proved by such motives of credibility as no reasonable man could resist, and as actually did convince the world, in spite of itself, that she was the handmaid of heaven ;—by the self-same arguments as established the divinity of Christianity itself.

All these brilliant and overwhelming evidences were plainly independent of the New Testament; and yet were they deemed adequate and conclusive by the mass of the early Christians, and by the most gigantic intellects and acute reasoners of the early ages. They were not only for Christians, but for heathens and unbelievers. They convinced and converted such men as St. Justin and St. Augustine. The latter assigns most of these very motives for his firm and unwavering belief in the divinity of the Catholic Church, as I intend to show more fully hereafter in the proper place.* What reason moved this great man and deep Christian philosopher to believe in the New Testament? He says: "But I would not believe the gospel, if the authority of the Catholic Church did not move me to do so." †

7. Thus the Church was not only older than the New Testament in point of fact, but her authority might be admitted and proved, by both the learned and the unlearned among the early Christians, independently of the New Testament. It is an undoubted historical fact,—little attended to now-a-days, when we hear almost nothing but the constant cry of the Bible, the Bible,—that, as we have already shown,‡ for more than three centuries the various books of the New Testament were not collected together into one volume ; and that, therefore, it was utterly impossible for

---

* In the concluding Lecture of this course.

† Ego vero evangelio non crederem, nisi ecclesiæ Catholicæ auctoritas me commoveret. Contra Epist. Fundamenti, c. 4.

‡ In the third Lecture of this course.

the great body of Christians during that long period to learn Christianity, or to prove the Church from the New Testament alone. It is another fact equally certain, that for more than a thousand years afterwards,—until the invention of printing,—it was utterly impossible that one in ten thousand could have access to the New Testament. How were Christians, during all this time, to know which was the true Church, or to prove its divine authority? Obviously by the very means and by the very process of reasoning just indicated. If not, what other means of proof or motives of belief had they?

8. The authority of the Church once established by the motives of credibility just alluded to, she was naturally received as a competent witness of the whole Christian revelation, and, among other parts of it, of the canon and inspiration of the New Testament itself. The Church, thus universally acknowledged as the organ of God, put this book into the hands of her children, told them that it was the word of God, and commanded them to receive it as such, according to her own exposition of its meaning. They opened the book, and found that it contained the strongest and most explicit declarations of Christ and His inspired Apostles in regard to the authority of the Church herself, and her Infallibility in her public teaching. Their faith in the Church, already strong, grew stronger by this striking confirmation; and this additional argument was wielded with great strength against heretics, who admitted the inspired book, but denied the authority of the Church. Where was the vicious circle in all this? If our sainted forefathers reasoned logically, are we to be called sophists for reasoning precisely in the same way?

9. But I will go a step farther, and retort the objection against those who raise it, in order to show who it is that really reasons in a vicious circle. I will ask the Protestant objector: How do *you* prove the canon and inspiration of the New Testament? He will answer,—he is bound according to his principles to answer,—by the New Testament itself, by its intrinsic marks and evidences. What? You

prove the New Testament from itself? You first receive the book as divine, and then prove its divinity by the book itself? Is not this a vicious circle of the most palpable kind? If it be not, please show me an instance that is. Jesus Christ himself said : "If I bear witness of myself, my witness is not true ; '* and yet, these men but of yesterday, who take it upon themselves to catechize us in logic, make the New Testament bear witness to itself, thereby plainly reversing the maxim of our Lord ; and then they cry out about our reasoning in a vicious circle !

10. In short, to sum up all that I have said in two words : if I am arguing with a brother Christian who admits the authority of the New Testament, and denies the authority of the Church, I may logically reason from the former to the latter : if arguing with an infidel who denies the New Testament, I adopt another course altogether ; I first prove to him the divine authority of the Church by the self-same arguments by which a Protestant would attempt to prove to him the divine origin and character of Christianity ; and then, and not till then, will I attempt to convince him of the divine authority of the New Testament.† In neither case is there even the shadow of a vicious circle.

After this exposition, I leave it to you, My Dear Brethren, to decide whether the vicious circle does not exist in the brain of our adversaries, and in their line of reasoning, much more than in our own argument. And after having thus endeavored to clear away some of the rubbish which our opponents have been for three centuries accumulating around the venerable edifice of Catholic truth, I may proceed at once to point out to you, along with its fair proportions and prominent outlines, the great fundamental principle of Infallibility, which gives strength and unity and durabilty to this rock-built House of the living God.

---

* St. John, v : 81.

† In the argument with the infidel, I may also logically use the New Testament, not as an inspired record, but as an *historical* book of undoubted genuineness and great weight of authority.

The whole question, stripped of all disguise, of misrepresentation, and of all collateral issues, is narrowed down to an inquiry into a very plain matter of fact, to be examined, like all other facts, by the weight of testimony :— Did Christ promise Infallibility to His *Church Teaching*,* in her public and official capacity? If He did, then was He surely able to redeem His promise, in spite of the natural errors and passions of men; and, in this case, to assert that He has not redeemed it, under the pretext that the Church has actually fallen into error, would fall little short of blasphemy :—for it amounts to a virtual denial either of the wisdom, or of the power, or of the goodness of Christ, or of all these together. If Christ did establish an Infallible authority, and vest it in His Church, then all that we have to do is, to learn and to bow down reverently before the decision of this divinely established tribunal; and thus all controversy will cease at once and for ever. This point once settled and admitted, all others necessarily follow.

But, before entering into "the law and the testimony" for establishing this fact,—that Christ did solemnly promise Infallibility to His Church,—it may be well to pause for a moment, and examine whether, from the very nature, genius, and objects of the Christian Religion, we would not naturally be led to expect some such attribute in the Church founded by Christ as the guardian of His Religion.

As I trust I have already shown,† the Religion of Christ was marked by four essential qualities, which were to be inseparable from it in all ages and in all places : 1st, Christ established but *one* Religion, and this Religion was marked by a complete harmony and oneness in all its parts; 2nd, He Himself defined it, and left nothing vague or indeterminate about its constitution; 3d, He required all mankind to embrace it, if they would be saved; and 4th, He provided means by which all mankind might easily ascertain

---

* *Ecclesia Docens*—the technical phrase employed by our theologians.
† In the second Lecture.

its existence, and distinguish it from all other systems. Now, I maintain that none of these primary qualities or conditions of original Christianity could possibly be realized without Infallibility in the Church.

1. Without this attribute in the Church Teaching, it is manifest that the Christian Religion could not have been preserved in its original and essential *oneness*; its doctrines and principles would have varied with the variations of its fallible expounder; its body would have been torn up into a thousand discordant fragments; and all unity would have disappeared for ever. This is precisely the present lamentable condition of all those Christian denominations which have rejected this principle; it is so at the present day, it was so with separatists and heretics from the very beginning of Christianity. Without this Infallible guiding principle, the Church would have been left, like a ship without rudder or compass or pilot, to the mercy of the storms and the waves of human passion, and it would have been necessarily "carried to and fro by every wind of doctrine." Thus the intentions of Christ would have been entirely frustrated, and the unity and harmony of His master-work would have been marred for ever.

2. Not only this, but there would have remained little or nothing definite or determinate in the Christian Religion; all its principles would have become unsettled, vague, and uncertain; men would not have known any longer, with any degree of certainty, what was truth and what was error; and they could not have made an act of divine faith, without which, however, "it is impossible to please God."* For faith excludes all doubt and uncertainty whatever; it is unhesitating and unwavering in its very nature; else it may be human opinion; it cannot be divine faith.† Without an infallible guide to tell men with unerring truth what is revealed and what is not, how could there be any certainty as to the objects of faith, especially in cases of controversy? It is plain that there could be none, and that

---

* Hebrews, xi: 6. † See more on this subject in Lecture iii. *supra*.
24

doubt would overshadow every thing in Christianity. Men would be "always learning and never attaining to the knowledge of the truth."* In fine, they would be precisely in the distracted, feverish, ever varying, and utterly forlorn condition of modern Protestants. Some might, indeed, cling to one or another human system of Religion with greater or less tenacity; but others would reject all Religion as uncertain, if not false, and would precipitate themselves, with the majority of the Protestant world at the present day, into the yawning gulf of infidelity!

3. Had Christ left his Religion in this frightful condition of distraction and uncertainty, how could He have required all men to embrace it, under the penalty of eternal damnation? How could He have commanded men to hear the voice of a Church which spoke no certain language, was itself fallible, and might easily mislead them into fatal error?

4. Moreover, how could He have made faith an essential condition of salvation for all mankind; when, in the supposition above indicated, He would certainly not have provided the means absolutely necessary for any one man to elicit an act of divine faith? Did He mean merely to tantalize men with the hope of an imaginary but impossible salvation? Did He, by constituting a fallible and erring Church as our guide, place "the blind to lead the blind," and then condemn men to eternal perdition for "falling into the ditch?" Had He left no better provision than this to enable us to attain to a knowledge of the truth, and thereby to save our immortal souls, His Religion would have been wholly powerless, and totally unworthy its divine origin. It would have promised unity, and certainty, and truth; but at the same time it would have sown the seeds of division, of uncertainty, and of error among mankind.

Thus you see, My Dear Brethren, that the Christian Religion could not have subsisted for even a century, in its original nature and essential qualities, without this attri-

---

* II Timothy, iii: 7.

bute of Infallibility in the body of its public authorized teachers. The inference is plain :—that Christ, who was a Prophet and God, would not, and could not, have left it without a quality so essential to its durability and very existence.

But there is yet another very strong presumptive argument in favor of the intention of Christ to confer this attribute of Infallibility on His Church Teaching. It is admitted on all hands, that the body of Christian pastors was infallible in their official oral teaching during the Apostolic age; that is, till the close of the first century. The New Testament was not yet completed, and of course there was on earth no infallible guide, save that of the public authorized teaching of the ministry. Thus, after the death of the last Apostle,* or at the beginning of the second century, the body of Christian Pastors was in undoubted and unchallenged *possession* of Infallibility, and it had been so for sixty-six years—ever since the day of Pentecost. Now, what evidence is there, whether in Scripture, in history, or in natural reason, to prove that the Church should then be stripped of a quality which she had so long possessed, and which she had received from Christ Himself through the presence of the Holy Ghost whom He promised to send? Was there less necessity for an infallible guide in the second century than there had been in the first? Were the passions of men less strong, and their pride of opinion less headlong? Or had Christ's love for mankind suddenly cooled down, after having burned brightly for but little more than half a century? Where, I ask, is the evidence that Christ meant, at this precise epoch, to change an avowedly essential feature in the earlier constitution of the Church?

Is it, because the New Testament was then completed and put into the hands of Christians as the only infallible guide after the death of the Apostles? But how do you prove this? Does the New Testament itself say so? And

* St. John, who died at Ephesus, about the year 100, or 66 years after our Lord's ascension.

if it does not, what right have you, who profess to take all your faith from the New Testament, to make the assertion? Does not history clearly falsify your assumption, by declaring that the whole New Testament was not even gathered into one volume,—much less put into the hands of the people as an infallible guide,—for more than two centuries afterwards?

Is it, because Infallibility was meant by Christ to be confined to the Apostles, and to cease after their death? Again, I ask, Where is the proof of this? Does Christ say so? Do His Apostles say so? If neither says so,—and neither does say so,—what right have you to take it for granted? What right have you to base your whole system upon a mere assumption, when you are continually calling on us for proofs?

But had the Apostles no personal qualities which were not transmitted to their successors in the ministry? Certainly they had; they were inspired men, and individually infallible in matters of faith. This privilege was necessary for the first founders of the Church in different parts of the world; it was not so necessary after the Church had been once firmly established. But they were also infallible as a body, as, for instance, when they met in council at Jerusalem; and this collective Infallibility was necessary for the preservation of the Church in the purity and integrity of her doctrines, just as much as was the power to preach, to baptize, to administer the sacraments, and to govern the Church; therefore, it is fair to infer that it was to be transmitted, along with those ordinary ministerial powers, to the body of their successors in office to the very end of time. At least, there exists the strongest presumptive evidence 'that this privilege was to be so transmitted; and this presumption can be destroyed only by the strongest reasons to the contrary.

But does any such evidence exist? Does Christ, do His inspired Apostles, breathe one word from which we might infer that this privilege was to cease with the Apostolic age? Let us see.

1. Christ addresses St. Peter, in presence of the other Apostles, in the language of my text: "Thou art Peter, and upon this rock I will build my Church, AND THE GATES OF HELL SHALL NOT PREVAIL AGAINST IT." This is, surely, a clear, emphatic, and most explicit promise; it is limited to no time and to no place; it was to be fulfilled after, as well as before, the death of the Apostles. It clearly imported that the Church was to be built upon a firm and immovable rock; that it was to be an unshaken and im-pregnable fortress throughout all ages; that it was to be, indeed, fiercely assailed by the powers of darkness, sym-bolized by the "gates of hell;"* but that, strong in the power and assistance of Christ, its divine Architect, it was to defy all assaults, and to remain unconquered† by all the combined power and opposition of wicked men and of demons.

Christ himself elsewhere more fully explains what He meant by the figure of building a house upon a rock. He says: "Whosoever heareth these my words and doeth them, shall be likened to a WISE MAN who built HIS HOUSE UPON A ROCK; and the rain fell, and the flood came, and the winds blew, and they beat upon that house, and it fell not, for IT WAS FOUNDED UPON A ROCK. And every one who heareth these my words and doeth them not, shall be like a foolish man, who built his house upon the sand; and the rain fell, and the floods came, and the winds blew,

* In the Greek Πυλαι Αδου,—*the gates of Hades,* or of the lower regions of darkness, death, or more properly *hell.* It was usual to hold courts of judicatory in the spacious gateways of the eastern cities; and from Dr. Durbin's recent "Observations in the East," it appears that the same custom is still retained there: hence, by a natural figure of speech, the *powers* of a city were meant by its *gates.*

† The Greek Κατισχυσωσι, is rendered in Hederici's Lexicon: viribus valeo adversus aliquem, obruo, deprimo, dejicio præpollentia virium,—to prevail against a person by main strength, to overwhelm, to break down, to overthrow by excess of strength. I give these primary meanings to answer the silly cavil founded on the English word *prevail,* as if it only meant to exclude a final and permanent overthrow of the Church. Men sometimes catch at straws.

24*

and they beat upon that house, and it fell, and great was the fall thereof."* Shall we say, My Brethren, that Christ was himself like the foolish man, and built His Church upon a sand-bank, from which it was soon to be thrown down by the sweeping winds and undermining rains? If so, He was not God, nor was He even a Prophet. Or shall we say, that, like the wise man, He built his Church firmly and solidly upon a rock, from which all the fiercest storms and most deluging rains could not dislodge it, or effect its overthrow? Most certainly. And yet He would not have been this wise Builder, had he founded His Church on so unstable a foundation, that it was destined to be overthrown by the least breath of opposition.

Our dissenting friends tell us, that the Church is not Infallible; that it corrupted the truth of God, that it fell away from its divine Founder, that it was overthrown and PREVAILED AGAINST for more than ten centuries by abominable errors and superstitions, and the. most fatal and soul-killing idolatry; in a word, that it ceased to be the true Church, and that it was overcome by the powers of darkness. Christ said,—and He was God who uttered the promise,—THE GATES OF HELL SHALL NOT PREVAIL AGAINST MY CHURCH BUILT UPON A ROCK! Which are we to believe? Luther and his followers, or Jesus Christ? Both cannot be right. Which will *you* believe?

2. Again, Christ commanded His first body of ministers to preach the gospel and to establish His Church; He clothed them with full plenipotentiary powers for carrying out this purpose,—"As the Father hath sent me, so also I send you;† He promised to ratify their official acts,— "Amen I say to you, whatsoever you shall bind upon earth, it shall be bound in heaven, and whatsoever you shall loose on earth, it shall be loosed in heaven;"‡ He told them, "He that receiveth you, receiveth me,"§ and, "He that heareth you, heareth me, and he that despiseth you,

---

* St. Matthew, vii: 24, 25, 26, 27.   † St. John, xx: 21.
‡ St. Matthew, xviii: 18.   § St. Matthew, x: 40.

despiseth me;"* finally, He commanded all men to hear and obey this Church teaching in His name and with His authority, under the awful penalty of being ranked with heathens and publicans, the off-casts of Jewish society: "And if he will not hear the Church, let him be to you as a heathen and a publican."†

There is obviously no limitation whatever as to time, place, or persons in all these solemn declarations; they are as general as they are explicit and emphatic; they develop a cardinal principle of the Christian Church,—its authoritative, divine, and INFALLIBLE teaching, until the end of time. If the Church could lead men astray by teaching them error instead of truth, how could Jesus Christ have commanded all mankind to hear and obey that teaching? Could He command them to hear what might be, and what according to our adversaries was, damnable error and idolatry? Here again, My Dear Brethren, we have Luther in direct opposition with Christ. The latter says, "Hear the Church;" the former, "Do not hear the Church, but *protest* against it with all your might, for it teaches fatal error, and 'the gates of hell have prevailed against it' for more than a thousand years!" I ask you again, which of the two are we to believe and follow?

3. Our divine Redeemer, moreover, promised to the first incumbents of the ministerial office, in the most explicit language, and under the most solemn circumstances, the continual presence and assistance of the Holy Ghost; and to show that He did not mean to confine the fulfillment of the promise to them personally, He added that the kind offices of this divine Paraclete were to continue,—of course in the body of the ministry, their lawful successors in office,—FOREVER. The meaning of His words cannot be mistaken but by the wilfully blind and perverse. "And I will ask the Father, and He will give you another Paraclete, THAT HE MAY ABIDE WITH YOU FOREVER, the Spirit of Truth whom the world cannot receive."‡ "And when He,

---

* St. Luke, x: 16.   † St. Matthew, xviii: 17.   ‡ St. John, xiv: 16, 17.

the Spirit of Truth, shall come, HE WILL TEACH YOU ALL
TRUTH."* Surely, if these consoling and splendid promises
mean any thing, they mean precisely what we contend
for;—that the great body of Christ's ministers, even until
the end of time, were to be taught all truth, by the Holy
Spirit of Truth Himself, who was to abide with them for
ever for this very purpose; and that they were consequently
to be preserved from all doctrinal error: in short, that they
were to be *infallible* in matters of faith and morals.

4. But there is still another solemn promise of Christ to
the same effect, equally striking, equally emphatic, and
equally conclusive. It would seem, indeed, that our blessed
Lord, knowing the vital importance of this great principle,
wished to announce it in every form of language, and
under all the more solemn circumstances of his life, so that
there might be no possibility of mistake on the subject. The
promises to which I last alluded were made on that sad occasion, when He announced to His grief-stricken Apostles,
in words of the most tender and divine eloquence, His
speedy departure from them. The promise, to which I shall
now invite your attention, was made in His farewell address
to them, on the eve of His ascension into heaven: "All
power is given to me in heaven and in earth: go ye, therefore, and teach all nations; baptizing them in the name of
the Father, and of the Son, and of the Holy Ghost; teaching them to observe all things whatsoever I have commanded you; AND BEHOLD I AM WITH YOU ALL DAYS, EVEN
TO THE CONSUMMATION OF THE WORLD."†

What, My Dear Brethren, is the meaning of these solemn

---

* St. John, xvi: 13.

† In the Greek this clause is: Και ίδου, εγω μεθ' υμων ειμι πασας τας ημερας
εως της συντελειας του αιωνος;—literally; "And behold, I am with you *all the
days* even unto the consummation of the world." The Protestant version
always is not so explicit or emphatic; while that of Campbell utterly and
most glaringly perverts the sense of the whole passage, translating the
latter half of it—"*unto the end of the present state!!*" How impious thus
to lay violent hands on the word of God! This instance alone may serve
to show the fallacy of private judgment, and the necessity of an infallible
guide in matters of Religion.

words? What, in particular, is the signification of that last expressive clause to which such especial attention is invited by the emphatic *behold?* It is manifestly this: Christ sends His Apostles to preach, to teach, to baptize, to perform all the duties of their ministerial office, and to encourage and strengthen them in the arduous undertaking, He promises them his ever-abiding presence and assistance in the discharge of all these official duties—so that they might be preserved from error, and might thus teach mankind, with unerring certainty, "all the things" which He had given them in charge. He had taught them the principles of His holy Religion; He had concealed from them none of the mysteries of His heavenly kingdom; He had promised them the Holy Spirit of Truth to bring back all His teachings to their remembrance; He had died on the cross to seal the truths of His Religion with His precious blood: and now, about to take His final leave of His dear Apostles, He solemnly charges them to teach all those holy truths, and He pledges His own unerring veracity to them, that He will be with them and assist them in doing so, in order that they may discharge this essential duty without falling into error. They were naturally weak, erring men; but He was the God who had already triumphed over death, and who was going to enter triumphantly into heaven; and He here pledges Himself to throw around their natural weakness and frailty the impenetrable panoply of His own immortal power and truth.

Had He not meant thus to secure the body of His ministry from error in teaching and baptizing the nations, all the fruits of His labors and blood would have been scattered to the winds. Error would have been taught instead of truth; human inventions would have been substituted for His own divine sacraments; His one Church would have been split up into a thousand fragments; in a word, this Church, the object of His greatest solicitude, would have become thoroughly distracted and corrupt from its very birth, and therefore wholly unsuited to the purpose of conducting men to a knowledge of the truth. Who does not

perceive all this at a single glance? Christ surely foresaw all the grievous evils which would be consequent
upon His Religion being left to the weak, fallible, and
unaided judgment of His pastors; and He could have
guarded against those evils in no other way than by securing them from error, by His constant presence and
assistance, in their public and official ministerial acts.

But this promise was meant to be confined to the Apostles, and was not intended to be transmitted to their successors.—Pray, who told you so? Does Christ say or intimate any thing of the kind? No, certainly; but He clearly
implies the contrary. His promise plainly extends to all
ages, "even unto the consummation of the world." Were
the Apostles to live till the end of the world? Did Christ
care only for the Apostolic age, and did He make adequate
provision for securing it only from error? Did He not
foresee that this provision would be even much more
needed after, than before the death of His Apostles? Did
He die for the men of the Apostolic age alone, or for those
of all ages? And ought you not also, according to this
strange canon of interpretation, to limit the power to
preach and to baptize to the Apostles themselves? Why
admit the perpetuity and transmission of these ministerial
offices, and deny the same of the promised assistance
annexed to them? Is it fair or reasonable to interpret consecutive and connected clauses of the same passage by different rules, without any thing in the context to warrant
the difference? What are we to think of a cause which
feels compelled to resort to such expedients as this? In
fine, My Dear Friends, if words have any definite meaning
at all, it is plain that Christ meant, by this promise, to
secure from error the body of His ministers to the very
end of time, by His uninterrupted and *daily* presence and
assistance.

5. Surely, St. Paul, the great Apostle of the Gentiles, and
that chosen vessel of election who had been rapt to the
third heaven, knew full well the genius of Christianity,
and the purpose of Christ in the organization of His

Church. Yet, St. Paul, writing to Timothy, a bishop, and an immediate successor of the Apostles, uses this emphatic language concerning the Church: "These things I write to thee, hoping that I shall come to thee shortly; but if I tarry, that thou mayest know how thou oughtest to behave thyself in the house of God, which IS THE CHURCH OF THE LIVING GOD, THE PILLAR* AND GROUND† OF THE TRUTH."‡

Think you, My Dear Brethren, that God either will not, or cannot, preserve his own *house* from being contaminated by the abominable defilements of error, superstition, and idolatry? Think you, that the *living* God cannot, or will not, watch over His own cherished Church, and guard it from error? Think you, that this firm and unshaken *pillar*, which supports the holy edifice of truth, can become itself the main stay of falsehood; or that the very *groundwork* and solid foundation of the truth can become itself the basis of error? You may think so, if you choose to listen to false teachers; but St. Paul thought very differently, and we prefer to think with him.

Does not this same great Apostle evidently suppose the Infallibility of the Church, when, writing to the Galatians, who had been seduced by false teachers, he uses this strong language: "But though we, or an angel from heaven, preach a gospel to you besides that which we have preached to you, let him be anathema."‡ Does he not manifestly suppose it likewise, when he so strongly inveighs against all sects and divisions in Religion in many passages of his epistles? For, where would be the reason or motive for this denunciation, if, according to the original genius of Christianity, every one was to read and judge

---

* In Greek, Στυλος,—columna, fulcrum—column, fulcrum.

† In Greek, Εδραιωμα,—stabilimentum, firmamentum, columen—a stable support, a firm and solid foundation, a column of strength—from Εδραιω to establish, to strengthen. See Hederici Lexicon. The attempt to connect these epithets with the following verse, by a change of punctuation, is wholly unwarrantable, and manifestly contrary to the construction of the Greek text.

‡ I Timothy, iii: 14, 15.   § Galatians, i: 8.

for himself, untrammeled by any infallible guide? If the Church was not Infallible, how could dissenters from it be deemed so very censurable as to be wholly excluded from the kingdom of heaven?*

6. Finally, such a thing as a fallible Church, or one that may be separated from Christ by error, is an utter absurdity, and a glaring solecism in language, according to all the notions which the Scriptures themselves furnish us of the Church. Is not the Church often represented in the New Testament as the kingdom of Christ, of which He is King,—as the one sheepfold of which He is the one Shepherd,—as the household of which He is the Father,—as the body of which He is the Head? Will you separate the kingdom from the King, the sheepfold from the Shepherd, the household from the Father of the family, the body from the Head? Is not the separation unnatural, impossible? Could a kingdom subsist at all without a king, or a sheepfold without a shepherd, or a household without a head of the family, or a body without a head? By the very fact of the separation, they would all be destroyed or scattered to the winds. And yet you would suppose it possible that the Church,—"the body of Christ, and the fullness of Him who is filled all in all,"—can be severed, by false teaching, from Christ, its great invisible Head, from whom it derives all its strength, and health, and life, as truly as does the natural body from the natural head!

Moreover, the Church is indissolubly united to Christ by a yet more intimate and a more tender bond,—that of holy espousals, prompted by a love as strong and generous as it was disinterested and enduring, and sealed by His own most sacred blood freely poured out. The Church is the Bride of the Lamb;—more pure and stainless than the dew-drop; always fresh, and blooming, and virginal. She shines forth with the mild beauty of the moon during the night of this world, after the departure of the great SUN of day;—"pulchra ut luna—beautiful as the moon."† St. Paul

---

* See Galatians, v : 20, 21.

† See Canticle of Canticles.—or Song of Solomon.

tells us as much in the following exquisite passage: "Therefore, AS THE CHURCH IS SUBJECT TO CHRIST, so also let the
wives be to their husbands, IN ALL THINGS. Husbands, love
your wives, as Christ also loved the Church, and delivered
himself up for it, that He might sanctify it, cleansing it
by the laver of water in the Word of Life; that He might
present it to himself AS A GLORIOUS CHURCH, NOT HAVING
SPOT OR WRINKLE, NOR ANY SUCH THING; BUT THAT IT SHOULD
BE HOLY AND WITHOUT BLEMISH."*

Who will dare slander the spotless Spouse of Jesus
Christ? Who will dare say, that she is not subject to Him
in all things, when St. Paul says precisely the contrary?
Who will dare say that she is not glorious, is not without
spot or wrinkle, is not holy and without blemish; but that
she is, on the contrary, all stained and spotted, because
sullied with error and vice? Who will dare say this of the
chaste and virgin Bride of Christ? Is he not afraid that
some thunderbolt, swifter and more terrible than any yet
aimed at human wickedness, will overtake him in the midst
of his horrid blasphemy? For what else is it but the most
atrocious blasphemy against the divine and omnipotent
Bridegroom to libel and slander His ever glorious and radiant Spouse? Not only is she His Spouse, but she is the
fruitful mother of all His children; for, according to the
beautiful thought of St. Cyprian, "No one can have God for
a Father, who has not the Church for a Mother." "The
Church," says the same ancient father, "is the Spouse of
Christ, which cannot be contaminated; for she is always
chaste and incorrupt."†

On the whole, then, My Beloved Brethren, I sum up and
conclude as follows: 1st, that Christ was Himself Infallible;
2dly, that He could, if He would, impart this Infallibility
to the body of His pastors to the end of time, in order to
secure them from teaching, and the whole mass of His
people from being thereby led to believe, dangerous and
fatal error; 3dly, that there are the strongest presumptive

* Ephesians, v: 24, seqq.   † De Unitate Ecclesiæ, c. 5.
25   T

reasons for supposing that He did impart this privilege in
the manner indicated, even if there existed no positive testimony to prove the fact; and 4thly, that He did certainly
impart it, unless we contradict and gainsay His plainest and
most solemn declarations, as well as those of His inspired
Apostles; and thus subvert all the notions of the Church
contained in the Bible.

Thus, it is proved that the true Church of Christ is Infallible; but no other Church besides the Roman Catholic
has ever even so much as claimed this attribute; therefore
the Roman Catholic Church alone is the true Church of
Christ.

THIS IS THE SEVENTH EVIDENCE OF CATHOLICITY.

Yes, the gates of hell may rage against the Church: the
powers of the earth may rise up in opposition to her;
rhetoric, philosophy, human cunning, malice, and slander,
may all be directed against her; all the jarring sects that
have ever existed may conspire for her destruction; the
combined powers of earth and hell may attempt her ruin;
but she is built upon a rock, and the God who dwelleth
in heaven, and whose words will not pass away, though
heaven and earth may pass away, hath said: "THE GATES
OF HELL SHALL NOT PREVAIL AGAINST HER." She
may be daily "doomed to death," but she is "fated not to
die." Immortality is written on her brow. She is as
imperishable as is her divine Head and Bridegroom; for
when her earthly pilgrimage shall be over, she will reign
eternally with Him in heaven.

"Nothing," says the eloquent St. John Chrysostom, "is
stronger than the Church of Christ; if any one should
propose to attack her, he must needs waste his strength,
as though he waged war against heaven itself. No power
can conquer the Church; GOD IS IN THE CHURCH, WHO IS
STRONGER THAN ALL."*

"This is the holy Church," exclaims St. Augustine, "the
one Church, the true Church, the Catholic Church, which

* Sermo de expulsione sua.

wars against all heresies. She may battle against them, SHE CANNOT BE OVERCOME. All heresies went out from her, like useless branches cut off from the vine. But she remains in her root, in her vine, in her charity. THE GATES OF HELL SHALL NOT CONQUER HER."*

May God grant, My Dear Brethren, that we may view this venerable Church of all nations and of all ages in the same light in which these two illustrious luminaries of the ancient Greek and Latin Churches viewed her; and that, like them, we may renounce every thing opposed to her teaching, recognize and bow down to the Infallible authority conferred on her by the solemn promises of Christ, hear her voice, obey her commands, humbly kneel at her altars, and become her dutiful children; that we may be also acknowledged as the children of her divine Founder and Bridegroom, Jesus Christ! Amen.

---

* De Symbolo ad catechumenos —Sermo 1: c. 6.

LECTURE X.

TRIALS AND TRIUMPHS OF THE CHURCH—THE EIGHTH EVIDENCE OF CATHOLICITY.

Two Scriptural texts applied to the Church—Her early trials—The persecutions—Ancient slanders and mobs—The cross of Constantine—The triumph of the Church—Her conflict with ancient heresy—The heretics of the first three centuries—Historical sketch of Arianism—The northern invasions—Condition of the Church during and after them—Pagan and Christian Rome—The Crescent and the Cross—Alleged darkness and corruption of the middle ages—Scandals—The great schism of the west—The reformation—Its violent action and sudden reaction—Macaulay—A parallel between the history of Arianism and that of Protestantism—The French revolution—The test of Gamaliel applied—The indestructible Church—Eighth Evidence of Catholicity.

" And the rain fell, and the floods came, and the winds blew, and they beat upon that house, and it fell not; for it was founded upon a rock."— ST. MATTHEW, vii : 25.

" And Jesus saith to them : why are you fearful, O ye of little faith ? Then rising up, he commanded the winds and the sea, and there came a great calm."—ST. MATTHEW, viii : 26.

THESE two passages from the New Testament, My Dear Brethren, present, under two different figures, a forcible illustration of what has often happened to the Church at various epochs of her long and eventful history. A house, strongly and securely built upon a firm foundation by an all-wise and all-powerful Architect, she has been at all times the object of the fiercest and most obstinate attacks. The armies of the world, those of all innovators and heretics, and the hosts of Satan himself, have been successively marshaled against her in formidable array ; dark and threatening storms have often broken over her ; the elements, men, and demons, have, over and again, conspired her destruction : still " she fell not, for she was founded upon a rock."

(292)

Launched,—according to the expressive figure of the other text,—like a bark on the boisterous sea of this world, she has been, at all times, assailed by the most terrible tempests; the winds have howled fiercely around her; the waves, lashed into fury, have threatened to swallow her up; with every thing portending a speedy and fatal ship-wreck, her stoutest-hearted mariners have quailed and trembled with fear: still the goodly old ship has braved all storms and outlived all dangers! She could not suffer ship-wreck; for she was freighted with the riches of redemption and the hopes of mankind, and JESUS was constantly on board of her, watching over her destiny and guarding her from every impending danger. Sometimes, indeed, He seemed to slumber; but even then His divine heart was wakeful; and, in the hour of the greatest gloom, and of the most imminent peril to His trembling disciples, He listened favorably to their earnest supplication,—"Lord, save us, we perish;" He rebuked their want of faith,—"Why are you fearful, O ye of little faith?"—and "rising up, He commanded the winds and the sea, and there came a great calm!"

It has ever been so in the history of the Church. In the midst of her greatest TRIALS, her TRIUMPHS have always been the most signal and brilliant. When her prospects have been most gloomy; when darkness has hung around her, unillumined by one single ray of human hope and comfort; when her future has appeared most sad and low-ering: then precisely has it always happened, that some unforeseen event dazzled the world by its suddenness and brilliancy, changed the entire face of things, dissipated all the clouds that hung heavily over her, struck her enemies with dismay, and left her fortunes completely in the ascen-dant. It would, indeed, appear that, in such emergencies, some invisible but omnipotent Hand was ever stretched forth for her relief and protection; and in such a manner and under such circumstances, that all the glory of her triumphs should be necessarily referred, not to men, but to God alone.

25 *

She has come victorious out of every conflict; sometimes, indeed, "bearing on her body the marks of cruel wounds, but always with the principle of life as strong" in her as ever.* She has survived revolutions which have swept away the most mighty states and empires; she has weathered storms in which the stoutest barks have suffered shipwreck; she has come unscathed out of fiery ordeals which have consumed all other institutions which were the mere creations of human wisdom and power. Empires have fallen around her, dynasties have disappeared, thrones have tottered and crumbled to dust, scepters have been broken in pieces, laurels which decked the brows of conquerors have faded, and regal crowns have dropped to the earth; yet *she* has survived every change and revolution, and has stood forth, a pillar of strength, solitary and alone in her wonderful stability, amidst the ruins every-where strewn in her pathway. And now, after all her conflicts, she is still as vigorous, as full of health and life, as buoyant with hope, as when she first entered the great battle-field of this world eighteen hundred years ago!

Who will say that the finger of God has not been in all this? Who can explain the singular phenomenon of her preservation under such circumstances, without supposing a divine intervention in her behalf? Who does not see, that a Church, upon whose banner victory has never failed to perch, and which alone has always triumphed and remained firm, unshaken, and permanent in the midst of universal changes, must have been favored by a special protection of heaven? Who does not perceive, in the bold and prominent outlines of her eventful history, a notable commentary on the divine promises recorded in the previous Lectures, a commentary written by the finger of God Himself, and in characters so distinct that "he who runneth may read"?

That the Catholic Church is more than eighteen hundred years old, while her rivals cannot prove for themselves an

* Macaulay—*infra cit.*

antiquity of more than three hundred, is a glorious feature in her history; but that she has been able to attain to this venerable age in spite of all the difficulties and conflicts through which she has had to pass, is a most striking and conclusive evidence of her divine origin. That she alone claims to be, and is, the heir to the splendid promises of Christ set forth in the last Lecture, is a consoling truth; but that she alone can show the complete fulfillment of those divine promises in the most prominent and striking facts of her history, and in the manifold Trials and Triumphs by which this history has been marked; this is an additional evidence, plain and palpable to every one, that she is really what she purports to be, the true Church of Christ, the Bride of the Lamb, the cherished object of His love and solicitude, and His unfailing and INFALLIBLE organ of communication with the world.

This is, My Dear Brethren, no idle declamation; it is sober history. I hope to convince you of this, if you will have the kindness and patience to follow me this evening, in the rapid sketches I mean to present of some leading epochs of Church history, in special reference to the Trials and Triumphs of the Church. The subject opens to our view a vast and expansive field, full of the most interesting and instructive historical monuments.

1. When Jesus Christ, in His farewell address, sent forth His apostles to teach all nations, and to establish everywhere that Church for which He had died, on the ruins of a time-honored, wide-spread, and universally cherished idolatry; when He bade them fear nothing, for that "He would be with them all days, even to the consummation of the world;" who, reasoning upon merely human principles, would have believed that they could have succeeded in their arduous and seemingly impossible mission! Who could have even dreamed, that not only would their labors be crowned with the most complete and brilliant success, but that their work would survive the tempests and changes of eighteen long centuries; and, even at the end of this period, would exhibit no indications of decay, but would

be as strong and firmly established as ever! When, for example, the blessed Apostles Peter and Paul came to Rome, from a remote and despised foreign province of a vast empire, and first entered its marble palaces and halls, the former a poor pilgrim, well stricken in years and leaning upon his staff, the latter a prisoner in chains, on his trial for alleged crimes against the state, who would have imagined that these two men were destined to become the second founders and fathers of the great city of the Cæsars, that the despised cross which they bore as their standard would, in less than three centuries, surmount the loftiest pinnacles of that imperial queen of the world, and that the Religion of which it was the banner would change the destinies of the empire and of the earth!

A mere handful of poor unlettered peasants, without any remarkable natural talents or eloquence, without any worldly influence whatever, and coming from a land held in contempt among the most highly civilized and powerful nations of the earth; teaching a doctrine incomprehensible to human reason, humiliating to human pride, and at utter war with the passions; preaching the cross, an object of bitter taunt to the polished Greek, and of horror and loathing to the proud and haughty Roman; every-where encountering the most deadly hatred and inveterate opposition in their mission; threatened with tortures and death at every step of their progress;—and yet succeeding against all odds, and triumphing over all opposition! Who especially would have believed in the successful establishment and glorious triumph of the Church which they founded under circumstances so unpropitious, had he but foreseen the awful conflicts and fiery trials this Church was to sustain during the first two hundred and fifty years of its existence?

The following brief summary of those trials will suffice for our present purpose.

The infant Church had to encounter the dreadful and long sustained and concentrated opposition of iron-hearted Rome, the mistress of the world; her martyrs were reckoned by thousands and tens of thousands, and her progress was every-where sealed with the blood of her own children poured out as water. No less than ten Roman emperors, wielding the destinies of the world, successively unsheathed the sword of persecution against her, and published edicts for the utter extermination of the Christian name; and this relentless policy was steadily persisted in for two centuries and a half:—from the time that the bloody monster, Nero, apprehended an "immense multitude"* of Christians at Rome—about the year 64—and clothing them in the skins of wild beasts, caused them to be worried and torn to pieces by dogs; or covering their bodies with pitch, made bonfires of them for the *amusement* of the Roman populace;† down to the time—the year 313—when Diocletian caused their sacred books to be destroyed, their churches to be demolished, and themselves to be burned or butchered by thousands.

During nearly all this period, legal prosecution, urged on by cruel, subservient, and avaricious pro-consuls and magistrates, was rendered still more terrible by popular violence, to the blind fury of which tens of thousands of Christians were doomed to fall victims. From theater and circus, from basilica and forum, from city and country, the demoniac shout went forth,—"The Christians to the lions! Death and extermination to the Christians!!"‡ The infuriate mobs followed the Christians even to the catacombs far under ground, whither they had fled for safety; and they caused to ring through those deep dark caverns the fiendish exclamation,—"Let the catacombs be destroyed!"§

To the persecution of bloodshed was added that of the foulest slander. Christians were every-where represented as *foreigners*, as secret enemies of the empire, as the cause of all its calamities, as atheists, as magicians addicted to secret and atrocious orgies, and to Thiestean banquets on the flesh of an infant newly slain; as "enemies of the

---

* Ingens multitudo. Tacitus. ‡ Christiani ad Leones! Christiani non sint?
† Tacitus, Lib. xiv: c. 44. § Areæ non sint!

human race;"—as every thing, in a word, that was wicked
and hateful. Add to this, that the combined influence
and malice of a powerful and interested pagan priesthood,
and all the fascinations of a cherished idolatry closely
intertwined with the iron framework of the Roman juris-
prudence itself, were constantly invoked against them; and
that their bishops and priests were hunted down like wild
beasts, were massacred by blood-thirsty mobs, or were
driven into exile; while their sanctuaries and altars were
every-where overthrown.*

And yet all this is not half of what the Church really
suffered during the first three centuries of her existence.
Through so terrible and fiery an ordeal as this had she to
pass while she was yet in her infancy, and before she had
attained a sure foothold, or could walk forth with safety
in the world. And yet she triumphed; Christ was with
her, as He had solemnly promised to be; the gates of hell
could not prevail against her, because He had promised
that they should not prevail.

Nay more, My Dear Brethren, it is remarkable, that the
appalling Trials she endured during this whole period of
the persecutions, were those precisely which ushered in her
more glorious and permanent Triumph! While Diocletian
and his three colleagues, as Lactantius says, were raging
against her from one end of the world to the other, like
four terrible wild beasts; while her churches, along with
her cities and villages, were reduced to heaps of smoking
ruins:—when her complete destruction and death seemed
to have been fully accomplished; and her sepulchral monument had been already reared, bearing the proudly boasting
inscription,—THE CHRISTIAN NAME ABOLISHED:†—then it was
precisely that her final Triumph was at hand. Her haughty
persecutors were laid low in the tomb, stricken by the
visible hand of God, as had been Antiochus of old;‡ while

* For a graphic picture of the early persecutions, see "Rome under
Paganism and under the Popes;" in 2 vols. 8vo., by the Rev. Dr. Miley.
† Nomine Christianorum deleto.
‡ See Lactantius—de Morte Persecutorum.

she came forth from the catacombs and the wilderness, re-constructed her fallen temples, took off her weeds of mourning, and put on the garments of joy; performed her public worship in security, in splendor, and in the open light of day; and stood forth the acknowledged spiritual queen and mistress of the world. She had made but one campaign; and she returned from it, with her garments indeed dripping with the blood of her own children who had fallen in battle, but with her face all radiant with joy, and her brow decked with the laurels of victory! The bright vision of her own Constantine was now fully realized. The motto inscribed upon that heavenly cross, which had appeared to him at mid-day while on his march against the tyrant Maxentius,—IN THIS SIGN SHALT THOU CONQUER,*— became now her watchword as well as the auspicious omen of her future victories. She had conquered, because Christ had foretold that she should conquer. Who does not see the finger of God in all this?

2. But the Trials of the first three centuries, though perhaps the most striking, were far from being the most dangerous which the Church was destined to encounter during her protracted and eventful pilgrimage on earth. She had met and conquered external foes in their most terrible array; she was now destined to encounter the gathering hosts of her own rebellious children, whom she had reared with her own hands and fed at her own maternal breasts. The hideous monster, heresy, more dreadful than the sword of the persecutor, now threatened to tear her bosom, to rend her unity, and to scatter all her hard-earned glories to the winds. She had triumphed over open enemies; could she hope to conquer secret foes wearing the mask of friendship—traitors lurking in her own camp—serpents, who had crawled into her own beautiful paradise, and were blighting its flowers and fruits, and tainting its very atmosphere with their pestilential breath? Could she hope to conquer Arianism as she had conquered paganism?

True, she had already encountered heresy in all its Pro-

---

* Ἐν τούτῳ νίκα.—Eusebius, in vita Constantini.

tean forms, even while the sword of persecution was suspended over her head. During the first three centuries
many had departed from the faith, and had been seduced
into the crooked ways of error. Heresies and sects had,
even at that early period, sprung up around her, in almost
as great number and diversity as at a subsequent period.
St. Epiphanius numbers no less than eighty of these sects,
the large majority of which originated in the time of the
persecutions. But most of these new religions had already
disappeared with their authors. The secret, abominable,
and wide-spread ramifications of the Gnostics, the stern and
pharisaical Novatians, the sanctimonious Encratites, the
impious Marcionites, the impure Adamites, and the vision-
ary Montanists, had all vanished from the face of the earth,
after a career as brief as it had been mischievous. But,
while the Church was indulging in the first moments of
repose which had been vouchsafed to her since her establishment on earth, another heresy suddenly sprang into
being, much more formidable than any of its predecessors,
and one which was destined to disturb her peace and endan-
ger her very existence for nearly a century. I allude to the
stormy days of Arianism; to its first apparent triumph, and
its final and overwhelming defeat.

Early in the fourth century, Arius, an Egyptian priest,
raised the standard of revolt against her authority, by
denying the divinity of Jesus Christ. Though his blasphemous system was promptly condemned by his immediate
ecclesiastical superior, the sainted patriarch of Alexandria,
yet it gained followers apace, its cunning author seducing
many by his arts and chicanery. The little speck which
thus gathered on the horizon in a corner of Africa, soon
grew into a dark and angry cloud, which overcast the
heavens, darkened the atmosphere, and portended a storm
that was to shake the battlements of the Church to their
very foundations.

True, the monster of Arianism was cast out of the Church
at Nice, in 325, when three hundred and eighteen bishops,
representing all the principal churches of Christendom,

unanimously agreed in stamping upon its brow the brand
of condemnation and excommunication. But, though cast
out, it was not dead. Like a ravenous wolf, it soon re-
entered the fold, to tear and devour the flock. It extended
its seductions, reckoned its followers by hundreds of thousands, counted even a considerable number of bishops and
priests among its open or secret friends, basked in imperial
favor, was publicly enthroned at Constantinople, at Milan,
at Nicomedia, and in many other principal cities, and was
making rapid strides towards the subjugation of all Christendom. Sustained by emperors and empresses, it put
forth its ruthless hands against the holiest things and the
holiest persons; it drove out the Catholic bishops from
their sees, and placed in them its own partisans; it sent the
intrepid champion of orthodoxy, St. Athanasius, at five
different times, an exile and a wanderer over the earth; it
drove St. Hilary from France; it dragged the aged Pontiff
Liberius from his see of Rome, and consigned him to a
prison for two years; it enacted appalling scenes of violence
and sacrilege wherever it made its appearance; it packed
ecclesiastical conventions at Constantinople, at Seleucia, at
Milan, at Sirmium; and it practised a most wicked decep-
tion on the Catholic bishops assembled at Rimini:—in a
word, it violently seized on the Christian world, and claimed
it as all its own. The Nicene faith was put down, condemned, proscribed for ever; the Catholic bishops were
exiled, silenced, or in prison; the Catholic Church, which
had triumphed over persecution, had seemingly fallen under
the stout blows of Arianism! The Church was no more;
she was dead and buried, totally annihilated, and Arian
zealots united with Goth and Vandal in singing canticles
of triumph over her fall!*

Vain and foolish boast! Short-lived victory! In less
than fifty years afterwards,—at the accession of Theodosius
the Great,—Arianism was no more, or had to hide its

---

*It is almost needless to say, that this is meant to convey the proud
boasts of Arianism, not the real facts of history. It is in the satirical
strain of St. Jerome, already quoted in a previous Lecture.

hideous head among a few tribes of the Goths in Germany, and of the Vandals in Africa; and Catholicity, which had always retained the vast numerical majority in Christendom, came forth once more in all its former strength and glory, and became again the avowed queen of the world, and the mistress of Christendom. When Arianism was chanting its songs of triumph, and the Catholic Church was apparently stricken down to the very dust, at that very moment, Christ rose up from His seeming slumber, stretched forth His omnipotent hand, rebuked the angry winds and waves, and suddenly "there was a great calm." God "rose up and judged His own cause," and even His enemies "justified Him in His words." The Church conquered Arianism, as she had conquered the more ancient heresies, and as she was destined soon to conquer Nestorianism, Macedonianism, Eutychianism, Monotholetism, Iconoclasm, and every other heresy in all subsequent ages. She was always sure of victory; because "God was in her," as St. Chrysostom says, and nothing could, therefore, be stronger than she was.

3. Having achieved so glorious a victory over Arianism and other heresies, which had menaced her with destruction from within, the Church was now destined to experience another long continued and most furious assault from external enemies; an onslaught much more formidable and dangerous than even that which had been made against her by the embattled hosts of the ancient Roman paganism. It would, indeed, seem that her divine Founder and Head wished to make a trial of her strength, and to prove to the world, by the most striking and brilliant evidences, that she was wholly indestructible, because He had pledged himself for her safety.

During more than two centuries after the year 400 of the Christian era, successive hordes of fierce barbarians from the fastnesses of the north,—of Goths, Vandals, Huns, Alans, Heruli, Visigoths, Ostrogoths, and Lombards,— spread the angry tide of invasion over all the provinces of the Roman empire in the west. Desolation and ruin marked their pathway. Pillaged cities, dismantled castles, ruined churches, overthrown altars and sanctuaries, were every-where left behind them. The grass was withered and the soil doomed to barrenness wherever the tramp of their chargers was heard. The people butchered without distinction of age or sex, whole masses of population cut off by the sword, whole districts laid desolate, widows in tears, and orphans begging for bread which no one gave them:—these were some amongst the bloody trophies of their victorious career! In hundreds of thousands they came thundering at the gates of imperial Rome herself; the mistress of the world was at their feet, a degraded captive; they reveled amidst her marble palaces, and scattered her wealth and her glory to the winds. All society was upturned from its very foundations; the old order of things disappeared, and a new one rose up on its ruins. Every thing was darkness, chaos. Centuries elapsed before order was again restored. Pagan Rome had fallen to rise no more!

Where was the Church during all these commotions, and in the midst of all this wide-spread ruin? Did she share the fate of the Roman empire, the strongest institution ever reared by the hands of man? Were the causes which had effected its downfall able to compass hers? If so, then you might suspect, that, like the Roman empire, she was a merely human institution. If not, you must acknowledge that she was divine, and therefore indestructible.

Now what are the facts? Did she suffer death; or did she rather give out of the superabundance of her own innate life even to those who had conquered imperial Rome? Was she conquered by the latter; or did she conquer them? Open the annals of her history, and you will find that she at first indeed bent somewhat to the storm, but that speedily she rose again stronger than ever, to conquer the conquerors themselves! She exhibited her traits of divine beauty to the fierce Northmen; and these, charmed by her loveliness, or awed by her majesty, dropped their arms, fell down in the very dust, and humbly worshiped her! One and all, whether Arians or pagans, they were, sooner or later, converted to her faith, and were changed from fierce and devouring wolves into quiet and gentle lambs of her own fold! Her missionaries, in the following centuries, rolled back the tide of invasion into the farthest north, and reared the standard of her cross in the center of nations where the old Roman eagles had never floated!* Who can explain this wonderful phenomenon, without supposing a divine intervention in favor of the Church at this great crisis of her existence?

Pagan Rome,—with all her pride, pomp, and magnificence,—fallen, crumbled into dust, swept from the face of the earth; Christian Rome, rising in mild splendor amidst its ruins, and defying, for long centuries, the combined power of the world to crush her; what a contrast! The fall of the former may teach us the necessary fate of all merely human things; the rise and durability of the latter will impress us with a deep sense of a divine protection extended to God's own chosen work. While of the former, existing in its melancholy ruins, we may say with the poet:

"The Niobe of nations, there she stands,
    Childless and crownless in her voiceless woe;"—

we must say of the latter, that, instead of being childless and crownless, she reckons now, after centuries of struggle with all the powers of the earth and of hell, a far greater number of children than the former ever did in its palmiest days; and that her crown, too, is much more brilliant, and her empire much more extended.

4. Let us now, My Dear Friends, glance rapidly at another very remarkable group of facts connected with the great struggle of a thousand years' duration between the Cross and the Crescent, between the Church and the Mohammedan imposture. The false prophet of Mecca had not been laid in the tomb more than a hundred years, when his enthusiastic and warlike followers, bearing the scimitar in one hand and the Koran in the other, were already masters

---

* See Lecture IV. for details on this subject.

of nearly half the world. They had extended their empire to the center of Asia, and were fast penetrating to the most remote India; they had swept around the Mediterranean coast from Syria and Palestine, through Egypt and all northern Africa, to the straits of Gibraltar, and had obtained a foothold in Spain. Already was nearly one-third of Christendom bowed down under their heavy and ignominious yoke; and the other two-thirds stood trembling with fear. What power was to stem the rushing tide of their conquest? What was to stop the career of their all-conquering armies, which had never yet known defeat? What was to prevent the Church from being swallowed up, wholly annihilated?

True, a strong temporary check to their progress was given in the famous victory gained over them at the battle fought near Tours, in 732, where Charles Martel, with the chivalry of France, gave them an overwhelming defeat, and drove them back across the Pyrenees into Spain. But they were not discouraged by this first disaster; they marshaled their hosts again, brought new armies into the field, covered the bosom of the Mediterranean with their fleets, planted a colony in Sicily, marched to the very gates of Rome, menaced the whole southern coast of Europe, threatened Constantinople, and aimed at nothing less than the subjugation of all Christendom! Meantime, Europe was distracted and rent into a hundred fragments by the feudal system. The warlike descendants of the Northmen were wasting their energies in petty border warfare, and Christian was shedding the blood of his brother Christian, apparently heedless of the formidable attitude and terrible array of the common enemy, who was meantime marching, with giant strides, to the conquest of the world.

In this emergency, when every thing boded ruin to Europe and to Christianity, what saved both from utter destruction? What healed the divisions of European society, united its people for the first time in a common cause against the common adversary, and thereby adopted the only effectual means for warding off the impending danger?

What but the visible protection of God, exhibited in the divinely re-active energies of the Church, and in the eloquent voice of the Roman Pontiffs, which re-echoed from one end of Europe to the other, calling upon all Christians, as they loved Jesus Christ, to bury their private feuds, to cease their disgraceful warfare with one another, and to unite in a holy brotherhood for the defence of their common country and their common Religion? Who but the Roman Pontiffs originated the crusades;—those master-strokes of Christian policy, which, by carrying the war into the enemy's territory, made Palestine for two centuries the battle-ground of the world, taught the Mohammedans the potency of Christian valor, retarded the fall of Constantinople for ages, and gave Europe time to breathe, to collect her energies, and to prepare for the fiercer conflict that was yet to come? Had it not been for the crusades, had the Mussulmans taken Constantinople in the twelfth instead of the fifteenth century, and then marched their armies into Europe—as they actually did three centuries later under Mohammed II., no human power could have prevented all Europe from sharing the terrible fate which had already befallen western Asia and Northern Africa.

Even as it was, the struggle was for a long time as doubtful in its result, as it was fearful in its character. For more than a hundred years after the fall of Constantinople, in 1453, vast and powerful Turkish armies and fleets threatened European independence on all sides; and even more than a century after the Turkish fleet had been completely annihilated in the decisive naval engagement of Lepanto, in 1571,* a Turkish army was thundering at the gates of Vienna; which was saved only by the timely appearance of Sobieski with his thirty thousand valiant Poles, who chivalrously rushed to the rescue.

Who that reads history aright, and believes in an all-ruling Providence watching over human affairs, can fail

---

* The credit of this signal victory is due mainly to the energetic exertions and the fervent prayers of the sainted Pontiff, Pius V.

to perceive, in all the eventful vicissitudes of this mighty
struggle, the hand of God visibly stretched forth for
the defense of that Church which His Son had died to
establish, and of which He had promised, that "the gates
of hell should not prevail against it"? How else are we
to explain the remarkable fact, that while the Oriental
-churches, torn from the bosom of Catholic unity, have been
crushed for centuries under an iron Mohammedan despotism, those portions of Christendom which remained
faithful to the Church were preserved from a similar fate?
Singular chastisement of an inveterate schism; singular
providence of God in favor of His Church!

5. Look, now, for a moment, My Dear Brethren, at the
lights and shades of another very striking historical picture. The gross ignorance, the grievous abuses, the manifold scandals, the moral corruption of the middle ages,
have formed for three centuries one among the most fertile
themes of declamation against the Catholic Church. I
think every candid man, well versed in history, will
admit that there exists great ignorance and much exaggeration on this subject. But allow the evils complained
of to have been even a hundred-fold worse than they are
represented; add to them the appaling scandal of the great
papal schism of the west at the close of the fourteenth and
the beginning of the fifteenth centuries; make the shades
of the picture as dark as you will;—and I will then ask
you, what was it that preserved the Church from utter
destruction amid this frightful deluge of moral pollution?

How, especially, was she able to survive all those alarming evils which necessarily grew out of the unsettled state
of society consequent on the invasions of the Northmen?
Was she swept away by the rushing torrent, or did she
stem it by the divine energy that was in her? Did she
sanction the evils of the times, or did she protest against
them with all her might, and with a voice which made
itself be heard and *obeyed* even amidst the din of arms and
the chaos of society? Did she flatter the passions of powerful kings and emperors, or did she openly and fearlessly

withstand them to the face, with as much courage as that with which her St. Leo the Great had confronted Attila? Did she quail beneath the frown of omnipotent tyranny, or did that frown prevent her from lifting her voice against oppression in high places, and invoking protection for the weak and the poor down-trodden victims of brute force? Did she allow emperors or kings to mistreat or to divorce their wives at will, or did she nobly step forth to the rescue, and throw her powerful panoply around weak and helpless woman? In a word, did she sink down, powerless and lifeless, amidst all those accumulated Trials, or did she come out of them stronger than she had gone into them? If she was a merely human institution, she must have succumbed and fallen at once; if she was divine, she might come unscathed out of this ordeal, as she had already come out of so many others equally terrible. This is the test by which we are willing to abide.

Now, what are the facts? Open the chronicles of the middle ages, and they will tell you, that she was never stronger, never more powerful, never more full of life and energy, never exhibited brighter specimens of faith, of sanctity, and of heroic virtue, than during that precise period. They will tell you, that, unappalled by scandals at which she was not surprised,—for her divine Founder had predicted them,—she labored incessantly for their extirpation; that, instead of being soiled by the muddy and bitter waters of barbarism, she rolled them back from her spiritual territory, or purified them and rendered them wholesome and sweet, by casting into them the salt of her own wisdom, as had been done by the prophet of old with the waters of Jericho;* that she softened down the manners, improved the morals, elevated the legislation, and humanized the feelings of those descendants of the Northmen who laid the foundations of modern European society: and, that to her we are consequently indebted for the rise, development, and progress of all modern civilization.

They will tell you, that so strong was the power of God

_____
* IV Kings, ii: 21, 22. In Prot. version, II Kings.

within her, that a protracted papal schism of nearly forty years' duration, could not, in the long run, weaken her strength, much less destroy her unity or mar her organization; and that she even came out of this fearful trial with renewed vigor and energy. They will tell you, in a word, that trials and difficulties which would have crushed any merely human system, were wholly powerless against *her*; nay more, that the difficulties she encountered, instead of arresting her triumphant progress, rather aided it the more; that they buoyed her up, even as the conflicting waves do the vessel at sea :—that, in one word, she bore a charmed life, and was plainly indestructible.

6. Come we now, My Beloved Brethren, to another memorable epoch nearer our own times, upon which I must, however, touch as lightly and gently as may be; both because its facts are familiar to us all, and because I would not willingly say any thing to shock the prejudices, much less to wound the feelings of any one of those whom I have the pleasure to address. The reformation, so called, came at length, with all its fierce excitement and startling events. At the voice of a bold monk, who, with stentorian lungs and withering invective, denounced the alleged abuses and corruptions of the age, all northern Europe, and half of Germany, arrayed themselves in deadly opposition to the Church. The number of those who joined the standard of revolt daily increased. Switzerland was half won over to the 'new cause; Austria and Bavaria trembled in the balance; England pronounced in its favor; France also threatened for a time to follow the contagious example; and even Italy was invaded by its enthusiastic emissaries, who promised to carry their victorious banner to the very gates of the eternal city, and to plant it in triumph in the halls of the Vatican. Kings and princes declared in favor of the new *religions* which had suddenly sprung up; new thrones were erected and new dynasties sprang up under their auspices; all European society was thrown into a ferment; long and bloody and general wars ensued; a new order of things, based upon new principles, and promising new and more

glorious results, was seen fast rising upon the ruins of the
old; and no one, reasoning upon mere human principles,
could tell at what point the revolution would stop, or
whether it would stop at all, until it would change the
entire face of Christendom.

Was the principle of authority to be entirely annihilated,
and that of unchecked private judgment to gain the full
mastery in the religious world? Was the deeply rooted
reverence for the ancient order of things to be wholly extin-
guished from the bosoms of men, in the growing enthusiasm
for novelty? Was the old Church, with all its glorious
Triumphs and hallowed reminiscences, with all the benefits
it had conferred upon civilization and humanity, and with
all its time-honored and cherished institutions, to be blotted
out from existence, and the new Churches, or sects, to be
built upon her ruins? Was Christ now to abandon His
Church, after having in ages past brought her out victorious
from so many equally terrible conflicts? Was His presence
and assistance, which had been promised her "ALL DAYS
even to the consummation of the world," now suddenly to
cease; and were "the gates of hell to prevail over her?"
The timid and wavering—those who were "of little faith,"
—might have thought so; the firm believer in the infallible
promises of Christ could not have entertained such a mis-
trust, even for one moment.

In less than fifty years after the rise of the reformation,
the problem was completely solved, and all hesitancy and
doubts ceased for ever. After the first burst of enthusiasm
and passion had subsided, the reaction came; and the victory declared,—as it had ever declared before,—for the old
Church. The reformation suddenly recoiled, and ceased to
make proselytes; nay, it lost ground every day. Austria,
Bavaria, and many of the smaller states of the Germanic
confederacy, were soon, in a great measure, won back to
the Church; the reformers were expelled from Italy by an
indignant public opinion; about one half of Switzerland
remained faithful to the ancient faith which was there daily
gaining ground; while in France, the contest was decided

triumphantly in favor of Catholicity. The Catholics rallied around the decisions of the council of Trent as one man; their faith was confirmed, their hopes began to brighten, and their confidence in the venerable Church of their forefathers was greater, if possible, than it had ever been before.

Nay more, at the very time that her enemies were exulting over her fancied destruction, and were busily engaged in erecting her sepulchral monument, the Church, not dead nor even slumbering, arose in her giant strength; and with a supernatural energy, pushed her spiritual conquests into the center of new worlds which had been just discovered by her children!

"Her acquisitions in the new world," says the brilliant Protestant writer whom I have already quoted, "more than compensated her for what she had lost in the old. Her spiritual ascendancy extends over the vast countries which lie between the plains of the Missouri and Cape Horn, countries which, a century hence, may not improbably contain a population as large as that which now inhabits Europe. . . . . . The number of her children is greater than in any former age."* He adds: "Yet we see that, during these two hundred and fifty years, Protestantism has made no conquests worth speaking of. Nay, we believe, that as far as there has been a change, that change has been in favor of the Church of Rome. We cannot therefore feel confident that the progress of knowledge will necessarily be fatal to a system which has, to say the least, stood its ground in spite of the immense progress which knowledge has made since the days of Queen Elizabeth."†

In all this, Macaulay does but re-echo the opinions of two other distinguished living Protestant writers, Henry Hallam‡ and Leopold Ranke.§

Who, My Dear Brethren, is so blind as not to see in all this the visible protection of God extended to His Church

---

* Thomas Babington Macaulay. Review of Ranke's Hist. of the Popes, &c.
† Ibid.
‡ Introduction to History of Literature, I. 272, seqq. American Edition.
§ Work, sup. cit.

in the hour of her greatest need ? Who does not observe a striking parallelism between the rise, progress, evanescent triumph, and final decline of Protestantism in the sixteenth century, and the corresponding phases of Arianism in the fourth ? In both cases, the progress of the new systems was immediate and rapid; in both cases, the advocates of the new doctrines sought and obtained the protection of powerful princes; in both cases, the world was for a time thrown into a fever of excitement and agitation; in both cases, prodigious and almost superhuman efforts were made to put down the Church which stood up the dauntless champion of the old faith; in both cases the innovators were divided into various and conflicting sects, while the Church presented a united and unbroken front; in both cases, the storm had spent its fury in less than fifty years ; and in both cases, the Church achieved a complete and glorious victory. Arianism changed, dwindled away, was merged in other sects, or returned to the Catholic Church. Protestantism has undergone precisely similar vicissitudes. It has changed from what it was in the beginning, has split up into a hundred conflicting sects, which waste their energies in mutual strife; and in Germany, its birth-place, it has, in a great measure, dwindled down into an infidel rationalism or a sickly pietism !

In the midst of all these changes, constantly going on around her, the Church yet stands, built upon her ROCK; united, immovable, unchangeable, as is the truth she advocates, and the God of truth who is in her,—an impregnable fortress of strength.

7. I must present to you still one more striking picture, portraying the most terrible ordeal, perhaps, through which the Church has ever passed in her protracted history. The principle of religious individualism and of revolt against constituted spiritual authority, had grown into one of absolute rebellion against all authority, and of an open and rabid infidelity. Voltaire, Rousseau, Diderot, and the whole gang of French infidels, prated fully as much about spiritual liberty and the emancipation of the human mind,

as Luther, Calvin, Zuingle, and the other reformers, had done two and a half centuries before. The results of their preaching were as immediate and tremendous, as had been those which followed the preaching of the reformers; while they were much more startling and terrific. The French Revolution broke upon the world like an awful and desolating hurricane; and wherever its influence was felt, it left nothing but ruins in its course. It was born in blood, it grew and flourished in blood, it rioted in blood, and it expired in blood. Kings and queens were led to the block; vast multitudes of the good, the virtuous, and the wealthy, expiated these *offenses* against the modern philosophy under the guillotine; bishops, priests, and helpless religious women were hunted down like wild beasts; the churches were demolished or desecrated with obscene and horrible orgies, the bare memory of which is enough to freeze the soul with horror. The Church was violently crushed in France; its ministers were butchered or banished, its worship was prohibited, and the Sunday itself was abolished.

The French infidels even dreamed that they would succeed in annihilating the Church altogether, and in making men forget that it had ever existed! Their victorious armies invaded Italy, marched to the gates of Rome, and dragged the venerable Pontiff Pius VI. into exile. Then was the final destruction of the Church, and the utter annihilation of the papacy, publicly and exultingly proclaimed at Paris, at London, at Berlin, at St. Petersburgh, at Rome itself! No other Pontiff should sit on the chair of Peter; the venerable line of Popes was broken and destroyed for ever; Pius VI. could not long survive the hard usage he had endured, and the French armies would see that no election should take place to fill the vacancy which would be caused by his death!

Vain and idle boasting of weak, sinful and mortal man! "Why have the nations raged, and the people devised vain things: . . . but HE who dwelleth in heaven laughed at them, and the Lord derided them!"*

---

* Psalms, ii : 1—4.

Pius VI. died of old age and hardships; the French armies were driven by the Austrians from the greater portion of northern Italy, and before they could recover from the blow, and re-establish their power in that country, the cardinal electors had already assembled at Venice, and had quietly and calmly elected his successor, Pius VII.! The battle of Marengo* again obtained for the French Directory a strong foothold in the land of the Popes:—but it was too late; the crisis had passed; the succession in the chair of St. Peter had been already secured, and Christendom had yet a head, and one, as the event proved, worthy in every respect of the terrible times in which his lot was cast.

Calm, mild, collected, dignified, and strong in faith and in hope, Pius VII. was not appalled by the dreadful storm that was raging around the vessel of the Church, of which he held the helm; he knew and felt, that the tempest would soon subside, and that the bark of Peter would soon again pursue its prosperous course over the placid waters. What though he was dragged into exile by the imperial despot who now rode the storm of the French revolution, and controlled its destinies; what though the enemies of the Church again chanted their songs of victory;—did he quail? Did his purpose falter? Did he lose faith or hope? Did he fear the result? And was his hope groundless?

The world is not doomed to be left long in suspense. Soon the scene shifts; the long persecuted Pontiff is borne back in triumph to his see; all Italy rings with acclamations as he passes; his victory and that of the Church is glorious and complete: while the great all-conquering emperor, who had put forth his hands against the Lord's anointed; who had tauntingly boasted when the Pope excommunicated him, that this should not cause the arms to fall from the hands of his brave soldiers; who had flattered himself with the vision of an universal empire over

---

* The battle of Marengo was fought on the 14th of June, 1800; the election of Pius VII. had taken place on the 14th of March of the same year. See Allisons's History of Europe, &c.

Europe, of which Paris and Rome should be the two great centers;—what was the fate of this towering genius and proudly boasting conqueror of Europe? Every one knows what it was. Bound to a barren rock of the ocean, he languished out the last years of his feverish existence; with full leisure to reflect on the evils he had done to the people of God, and on the blind ambition and sacrilegious invasion of the Church which had marred his destiny; and with time enough, too, to repent of his misdeeds, to lament his false steps, and to return to a more sober and more Christian frame of mind. Forgetful of all past injuries, the noble Pontiff exerted his influence with the European powers and the British government, and succeeded in obtaining permission to send him the spiritual guides for whom he had earnestly asked.

One of the most remarkable incidents, perhaps, in this whole group of facts, is found in the circumstance, that Napoleon was overthrown, the Pontiff restored to his see, and the Church to her rights, chiefly by the agency of three great powers,—England, Russia, and Prussia,—all distinguished for their firm, constant, and relentless opposition to the Church and to the Papacy! Who, My Dear Brethren, does not see the finger of God in all this? Who will not conclude, that both the Church and the Papacy bear a charmed life; that God himself stands pledged for their defense and protection; and that man cannot therefore destroy them!

Who, that has calmly and dispassionately surveyed with us all the terrible Trials and signal Triumphs of the Church, as plainly set forth in the great epochs of her history already glanced at, will not be disposed to think of the test proposed by the wise Gamaliel, when Christianity was yet in its infancy! "And now, therefore, I say to you, refrain from these men, and let them alone; for if this design or work be of men, it will fall to nothing; BUT IF IT BE OF GOD, YOU ARE NOT ABLE TO DESTROY IT; lest perhaps you be found to oppose God."* Eighteen centuries

* Acts, v: 88, 89.

have elapsed since this simple test was first proposed as a
criterion of truth; and now we are willing to abide the
result of its application to all the eventful struggles of the
Church, during her long pilgrimage on earth. Had she
been a merely human work, she would have been long
since destroyed along with the other works of men. Her
not having been so destroyed; her having, on the contrary,
come gloriously and triumphantly out of every alarming
trial and difficulty that ever threatened her safety, is a
striking and conclusive proof that she is the work of God,
and that men are therefore not able to destroy her.

Like the sturdy oak shaken by the storm, she has taken
deeper root, and become more firmly established in the soil
of the earth, by each successive tempest that has swept by
her, in the long lapse of ages. Persecution has not only
not impaired, but it has rather served to extend her empire;
—even as the wind scatters the seed of the plant, and sows
it broadcast upon the earth. She cannot be destroyed, she
cannot perish, because God is her light and her strength;
Jesus Christ is her Head; and the Holy Ghost is her
Teacher and Comforter. She cannot fall, unless the Saviour
God fail in His word; and He has said: "Heaven and earth
may pass away; but MY WORD shall not pass away."*

"Strong as the rock of the ocean that stems
A thousand wild waves on the shore,"

she has survived every tempest, and withstood every
assault. Her Triumphs are strewn over the history of
the past; other Triumphs await her in the future. As
Macaulay beautifully says:

"Nor do we see any sign which indicates that the term
of her long dominion is approaching. She saw the commencement of all the governments, and of all the ecclesiastical establishments that now exist in the world; and we
feel no assurance that she is not destined to see the end of

* Some of these epochs in Church history have been already glanced at
near the close of the fourth Lecture, but in a different connection and for
a different purpose.

them all. She was great and respected before the Saxon set foot on Britain,—before the Frank had passed the Rhine,—when Grecian eloquence still flourished at Antioch —when idols were still worshiped in the temple of Mecca. And she may still exist in undiminished vigor, when some traveler from New Zealand shall, in the midst of a vast solitude, take his stand on a broken arch of London bridge to sketch the ruins of St. Paul's. . . . . Four times since the authority of the Church of Rome was established in western Christendom, has the human intellect risen up against her. Twice she remained completely victorious. Twice she came forth from the conflict bearing the marks of cruel wounds, but with the principle of life still strong within her. WHEN WE REFLECT ON THE TREMENDOUS AS- SAULTS WHICH SHE HAS SURVIVED, WE FIND IT DIFFICULT TO CONCEIVE IN WHAT WAY SHE IS TO PERISH."*

It was fitting, My Dear Brethren, that the Church, which is the pure and immaculate Spouse of Jesus Christ, should be in all things assimilated to Him; should. share in His sorrows, and in His joys, in His Trials, and in His Triumphs. The disciple was not above the Master; the earthly Bride was not above the heavenly Bridegroom. Like Him, she was to be scourged through the world' in her earthly pilgrimage, to be hated of all men, to be calum- niated, to be nailed to the cross; but like Him, too, she was, after the momentary Triumph of her enemies in her seem- ing death, to arise from the tomb, all radiant and glorious, and more full of life and of divine activity than ever!

Who will not admire, if he will not even love, this glorious Spouse of Christ,—"pure as a virgin, and as a virgin weak,"—this heroine of a thousand Triumphs, this imperishable Mother of Christians! Who will not be proud " to rise up" among her millions of children, and " to call her blessed!"

God grant, My Dear Brethren, that none may be ashamed of this venerated Mother of all our Christian ancestors;

---

* In the Review above quoted.

27 *

that all may recognize her by the traits of divinity stamped upon her brow by Almighty God himself; and especially by that of her signal Triumphs over Trials which would have crushed any merely human institution; and that thus finding her out by the aid of this EIGHTH EVIDENCE of her divine origin, we may all cheerfully enlist under her all-conquering banner; and thus march on to the eternal victory of the saints; through Jesus Christ our Lord and Saviour! Amen.

LECTURE XI.

CHURCH GOVERNMENT — THE PRIMACY — THE NINTH EVIDENCE OF CATHOLICITY.

Recapitulation of previous Lectures—The power of the Christian ministry threefold—the governing power in the Church also threefold—The latter established by presumptive evidence—An objection answered—Origin of this power divine—Its fountain not the people—Scriptural proofs—Not personal to the apostles—Organization of Church government settled by Christ—Bishops, priests, and deacons — Scriptural testimonies—Those of some early fathers—The argument stated—And developed—The Primacy—Three propositions laid down—The first of these established—Primacy of St. Peter—Objections met—The precedent set under the old law—Reasoning from analogy—And from the nature and objects of the Church—Positive proofs from the new testament—Minor circumstances and incidents—The promise of the Primacy—The rock and the keys—Confirming the brethren—The promise redeemed by Christ—Feeding the lambs and the sheep—Recapitulation—The argument resumed—And continued to the next Lecture.

"And some indeed He gave to be apostles, and some prophets, and others evangelists, and others pastors and teachers; for the perfection of the saints, for the work of the ministry, unto the edification of the body of Christ; till we all meet in the unity of faith, and of the knowledge of the Son of God."—EPHESIANS, iv: 11, 18.

THOSE of you, My Beloved Brethren, who have favored me with your patient attention during the previous Lectures, will, I trust, agree with me in admitting the following propositions as already established: 1st, that a Church was instituted by Jesus Christ to be the guardian of His Religion, to transmit it unchanged to after generations even until the end of time; 2d, that this Church is a visible and thoroughly organized society or body, acting in a visible manner and through visible organs; and 3d, that a main feature in its organization is found in the distribution, by Christ Himself, of this society or body into two great de-

(319)

partments, each with appropriate and distinctive duties;—
that of the ministry or Church officers, and that of the
people, or the bulk of individuals composing the society.

No one can call in question or deny any one of these
propositions, which are all clearly laid down in the New
Testament, and are, in fact, practically admitted by every
denomination claiming to be Christian. No matter how
much the various Christian sects of the present day may
differ among themselves about the doctrines of Christ, the
powers of the ministry, and the order of discipline and
church government, they all agree in holding that Christ
established a visible and organized Church for the guardianship of His Religion, and that there is, and must be,
some distinction between the ministry and the people in
this Church.

It is equally plain from the New Testament, that Christ
imparted to His ministry a threefold power in reference to
the Church: 1st, the power of preaching and teaching in
His name and under the sanction of His high authority;
2d, the power of administering the sacraments, and of
regulating public worship; and 3d, the power of governing
the Church,—of making all laws and regulations necessary
for this purpose, of judging in all controversies that might
arise, and of enforcing the decision with spiritual pains and
penalties. Of the two first I have already treated, to a
certain extent, in the previous Lectures; and in regard to
them there can be little controversy between us and our
Protestant brethren. These all agree in substantially admitting those two ministerial powers as belonging to their
own respective bodies of ministers, how much soever they
may differ from us or among themselves in reference to
their origin and extent. It is not necessary, then, to dwell
any farther upon this branch of the subject; and I shall
accordingly pass at once to the examination of the third
power of the ministry, that of governing the Church of
Christ. This, as I have already intimated, is likewise
threefold in its nature and objects: legislative, judiciary,
and executive. That the Church was invested by Jesus

Christ with this triple governing power, and that He meant
it to be permanently lodged in the hands of Church officers
or ministers duly appointed, and to be kept up in regular
succession till the end of time, will appear from the following very plain considerations.

1. From the very nature of the Church and the objects
for which it was instituted, we would be naturally led to
expect, that its Divine Founder bestowed upon it some
such governing authority. The Church is a visible society,
divinely organized for the securing of certain special ends
contemplated by no other. These ends are: the drawing
and keeping of men together in the profession of the same
faith, in the practice of the same worship, and in the observances of the same Religion; their sanctification by the
application of the atonement to their souls through certain
external channels of grace; and the final leading of them,
by these means, to eternal happiness in heaven. They thus
regard objects of the very highest importance, both in time
and in eternity.

Now, how could these ends be secured, without a governing authority in the Church? Without it, how could men
be kept together in society for the joint pursuit of the high
objects indicated? A merely civil society, which has only
temporal ends in view and looks only to worldly interests,
could not exist for one year without some form of government to bind its members together. Men are differently
constituted; they move in different ways; they are actuated
by different feelings and opinions; and they are agitated by
conflicting passions and interests. They cannot be kept
together in society without a restraining influence and authority to which all must bow, and before the decisions of
which all private interests and passions must give away.
Hence, no human society has ever existed, or ever can exist
in the very nature of things, without an external government of some kind. Are we to say that Christ in the establishment of His Church was less wise than the founders
of merely human organizations? That he did not make in
its behalf, a provision without which human wisdom and

V

the experience of mankind have proved that no society whatever can subsist?

2. Nor is it a valid objection, that the Church is a *spiritual* society, and therefore does not need a visible government to control its members, and to bind them together in the lofty pursuits to which it points their attention. The Church is, indeed, a spiritual society in its ends, and in the means most proper and necessary for securing them; but it is nevertheless external and visible, and is composed of men, not of incorporeal spirits. Like every other society, it has to do with men, to act on them, to control them, to unite them in striving for the same ends; and like every other society, it must necessarily have an external and visible governing authority, to be enabled to accomplish these purposes. This authority, to be adapted to the nature and objects of the society, must be spiritual in its origin, spiritual in its general principles and character, and mainly spiritual in the means which it employs; but still, for the very same reason, it must be also visible and external. If men were angels without bodies, there would be no need of a visible government to control them in Religion; but as men have bodies, the government necessary for them must also have a body, or a form external and palpable.

This principle is practically admitted to be a sound one even by the sects separated from the mother Church; for these have all of them, an external form of government of some kind for their respective members. It matters not whether the governing authority be vested in an association, a general conference, a general assembly, or a general convention of bishops; the principle in all of these cases is the self-same,—that an external and visible government of one form or another is indispensable to the welfare and to the very existence of the Church. Upon this all are agreed: and without its adoption no denomination could subsist.

3. The same universal consent of all the Christian denominations of the present day exists, in regard to the substantial extent and privileges of the governing authority.

They all practically hold, that the Church government,
like every form of civil government on the face of the
earth, must embrace three essential elements; a legislature,
a judiciary, and an executive: a legislative power to make
such laws and regulations as the exigencies of the times
may seem to require; a judiciary, to decide on all difficult
matters involving the interests of the society; and an executive to enforce the decisions, and to establish uniformity,
by cutting off from the society, if need be, all refractory
members. Every one who is at all acquainted with the history and discipline of the various modern sects, will at once
admit the truth of this assertion. The only, or at least the
chief difference between them and the Catholic Church
upon this subject, seems to be, that, whereas the former in
general hold that the legislative enactments and judicial
decisions of their respective church governments are not
infallible nor obligatory on conscience; the latter, on the
contrary, views the official acts of the Church as the acts of
Christ Himself, who commanded all his followers to hear
the Church, under the awful penalty of being considered as
heathens and publicans. The sects have the shadow, the
Church has the reality: the former are necessarily driven
into endless variations and inconsistencies, the latter is
straightforward, united, and consistent throughout.

4. This leads us at once to the great question as to the
origin of this governing power in the Church. Does it
come directly from God, or does it come directly from men?
Did Christ bestow it directly on a certain body of men, who
were to succeed each other in the ministerial office till the
end of time; or did He impart it to the body of His followers, to the *people*, who would embrace His Religion, to be
by them vested in a certain ministry to be chosen by themselves? This is plainly a question of fact, to be settled, not
by mere speculations or reasoning on preconceived theories
of government, but by the positive testimony of Christ
Himself and by that of His inspired apostles. The whole
doctrine and practice of Church government is precisely
such as Christ and His apostles settled it, eighteen hundred

years ago; neither more nor less. With the exception, perhaps, of the Anglican church, * most Protestant denominations in this country hold, that all spiritual power is lodged primarily in the hands of the people; while the Catholic Church has ever maintained, that it comes directly from Christ through regular channels appointed by Himself. Which of these two contradictory views is correct? Which will abide the test of scriptural evidence? Which is sanctioned by the positive testimony of Christ and His apostles? —To the law and to the testimony!

5. Surely, My Dear Brethren, if Christ had intended to make the people the fountain of all spiritual power in His Church, He would have somewhere told us so. He would have somewhere addressed to them, and not to certain men specially appointed by Himself, the words conferring this power; and He would have told them to elect from their own number certain individuals, to whom it should be delegated only to an extent warranted by their own will. But did He do this? Is there one word in the whole New Testament, which would warrant the belief that such was the theory of government devised by Him! On the contrary, did He nòt Himself immediately select and call from the midst of the multitude, the twelve apostles, His first body of ministers; and subsequently, the seventy-two disciples?† Did He not address to them only, and not to the people, the language which bestowed ample spiritual powers? Every one knows that He did; no one can contest this fact.

· Does not St. Paul, speaking of the call to the priesthood, say in the most explicit language: "Neither doth any man take the honor to himself, but he who is called by God, as Aaron was?"‡ Does he not say in the text which I have selected for this Lecture,§ that it was Christ Himself, and

---

* Even the Anglican church government, at least as it exists in this country, has some features which appear to recognise the principle, that the body of the church members have an important share in the government. In England, the civil government is paramount.

† St. Luke, x: 1.   ‡ Hebrews, v: 4.   § Ephesians, iv: 11.

not the people who appointed the different orders of the Christian ministry? And after having said, in another place, "God hath set some in the Church, first apostles," &c., does he not ask emphatically : "Are all apostles? Are all prophets? Are all teachers?"* Does he not emphatically inquire again—as if the matter were well known as beyond all doubt or controversy, "How can they preach unless they be sent?"† And after these solemn declarations of inspiration, and many more of the same kind which might be alleged, will it still be said, that the people were constituted by Christ the sole depository of all spiritual power? I repeat it, this modern theory of Church government is a mere assumption, not only unwarranted by scriptural authority, but directly opposed to all its facts and principles.

6. The Apostles received directly from the lips of Jesus Christ Himself the fullest and most ample spiritual powers; and to them only were addressed those remarkable words which constituted them His ministers plenipotentiary to the world: "As the Father hath sent me, so also I send you."‡ They alone originally received the power of preaching, of baptizing, of binding and loosing; and to them did Christ vouchsafe to explain all the hidden mysteries of the kingdom of heaven, while He spoke to the multitudes in parables.§ To them only was committed the task of establishing the Church, of regulating all its concerns, of settling its discipline, of establishing the details of its external polity. In conformity with the instructions and will of Christ, they associated with themselves other men in the great work of the ministry;|| but these were to be subordinate to themselves, to act according to their directions, and to look up to them as the original and chief depositories of all spiritual power in the Church. Without this subordination, there would have been clearly no order in church government. In a word, to them, and to them alone, was given the fullest legislative, judiciary, and

---

* I Corinthians, xii: 28, 29.   † Romans, x: 15.
‡ St. John. xx: 21.   § St. Matthew, xiii.
|| As the seventy-two disciples, and subsequently the seven deacons.
28

executive power; and men were commanded to look up
to their decisions, as to those of Christ Himself. This is
clearly what the New Testament tells us on the subject.

The Apostles so understood the origin, nature, and extent
of the powers bestowed on them. We find them in the
council of Jerusalem passing legislative enactments, deciding with authority on a difficult question referred to
them from Antioch, and declaring their decision to have
emanated from the Holy Ghost himself: "IT HATH SEEMED
GOOD TO THE HOLY GHOST AND TO US."* We find St. Paul
traversing Syria and Cilicia, "confirming the churches,
commanding them to keep *the precepts* of the Apostles and
ancients."† We find St. Paul, who had been called in a
wonderful manner by Christ to be His chosen apostle to
the gentiles, boldly declaring, that he holds in his hands
spiritual weapons by which he is "in readiness to revenge
all disobedience;"‡ and threatening the Corinthians with
the spiritual rod: "What will you? That I come to you
with a rod, or in charity, and in the spirit of meekness?"§
We find him using the executive power divinely vested in
him, by cutting off from the communion of the Church the
incestuous Corinthian, and delivering him up "to Satan for
the destruction of the flesh, that the spirit may be saved in
the day of our Lord Jesus;" and doing this, too, "in the
name of our Lord Jesus Christ."‖

7. Nor were these powers personal to the Apostles, or
meant by Christ to be confined to them. They were clearly
to be transmitted to their successors in the ministerial
office. Christ did not die for the apostolic day only; and
His Church, with all its ample spiritual privileges and
powers, was to be for all ages, as well as for all nations.
We find the apostles every-where choosing bishops, "to
rule the Church of God, which He had purchased with
His own blood."¶ Thus, we find St. Paul appointing
Timothy and Titus bishops at Ephesus and in Crete; and

* Acts, xv : 28.   † Acts, xv : 41.   ‡ II Corinthians, x : 6.
§ I Corinthians, iv : 21. ‖ I Corinthians, v : 4, 5. ¶ Acts, xx : 28.

bidding them appoint others to aid, and others again to succeed them in fulfilling the onerous duties of the episcopal office. "For this cause," he writes to Titus, "I left thee in Crete, that thou shouldst set in order the things that are wanting, and shouldst ordain priests in every city, as I also appointed thee."* He lays down for his two cherished disciples the qualities which should distinguish the different orders of ministers who should present themselves to them for ordination; he prescribes to them the form of trial for offenders and heretics; he gives them various instructions in the details of church government; he tells them, that "they should stir up the grace of God which was in them by the imposition of his hands;"† and he exhorts Titus "to let no one despise him," but "to rebuke with all authority."‡

What do all these things indicate, but a transmission to faithful successors in the ministerial office, of all the substantial powers for church government which were originally bestowed by Christ upon His apostles? Do they contain any intimation, from which we would be led to infer the strange modern theory broached by our adversaries, concerning the derivation of all spiritual authority from the body of the people? Did even St. Paul, though called in so miraculous a manner, venture to enter on the exercise of the ministry, until he had been regularly ordained in the church of Antioch for this purpose? "And as they were ministering to the Lord, the Holy Ghost said to them: separate me Saul and Barnabas, for the work to which I have taken them: then they, fasting and praying, and imposing their hands upon them, sent them away."§

8. From all these scriptural evidences we are bound to infer: 1st, that Christ Himself is the sole Fountain of all ministerial power, not only for preaching the gospel and administering the sacraments, but also for governing the Church. 2dly, That He imparted this power, in all its fullness, to the Apostles, to be by them, in conformity with

---

* Titus, 1, 5.   † II Timothy, 1, 6.   ‡ Titus, ii: 15.   § Acts, xiii: 2, 3.

His will or special instructions, communicated to others
acting with and under them, according to the various
exigencies of times and circumstances; 3rdly, that this
governing power was to be perpetuated in His Church to
the end of time; and 4thly, that it was to be transmitted in
regular channels, and that each successive ordination was to
be made through the imposition of hands by the principal
ministers of the Church, the successors of the Apostles,
already called by God and regularly appointed themselves
in the same way. If the Scriptures of the New Testament
do not prove all this, they prove nothing whatever on the
subject.

9. God is the God of order and not of confusion; and
we would naturally be led to expect in the organization of
the Church, which is the most perfect work of His hands,
the most complete harmony and subordination of parts
in the various elements of its government. There were,
indeed, to be different orders of ministers, or spiritual
officers; but their different powers and spheres of action
would be assigned and so clearly marked, that there would
be no confusion, no clashing of jurisdiction, no contest
about prerogative. Accordingly, we find two other orders
of ministers divinely established, who were invested with
a certain portion, more or less large, of that plenitude of
power bestowed originally on the apostolic college. Thus
Christ named the seventy-two disciples, and sent them to
preach the gospel, two and two together, through the
various parts of Judea.* Thus again, the Apostles appointed the seven deacons, not only to relieve themselves
of temporal solicitude, but also to assist in preaching and
baptizing:—for we find these latter offices discharged by
at least two among them, Stephen and Philip.†

10. From all these facts, we are necessarily led to infer,
that there are in the Church, of divine appointment,
three distinct but mutually subordinate orders of ministry,
corresponding respectively with the apostles, the seventy-
two disciples, and the seven deacons; and that these three

---

*St. Luke, x: 1.   †Acts, vi.

orders were to be perpetuated in the Church, in all their substantial powers, to the very end of time. For otherwise, where would have been the necessity of their original institution? If they were deemed necessary by Christ and His Apostles at the very commencement of the Church, when the number of Christians was comparatively small and easily governed, by what process of reasoning can it be made out, that they were not at least equally necessary when the number of Christians had greatly increased, when the Church had been established throughout the whole world, and when the task of Church Government had consequently become much more difficult and complicated? Are we to suppose that Christ and His Apostles established a system of Church Government adapted to the wants of their own times only, and which was to be abrogated or changed immediately afterwards? If we so think, we practically deny the wisdom and divinity of Jesus Christ, and sink His holy Church to the level—if even not below the level—of merely human institutions!

11. Accordingly, from the very beginning of the Church, the three orders of bishops, priests, and deacons, corresponding respectively with those just named, have always existed and been held as of divine origin and appointment. A volume might be filled with testimonies to this effect; but I must content myself with one or two selected from the first and second centuries of the Church.

St. Ignatius, martyr, a disciple of St. John the Apostle, writing to the Christians of Smyrna, says: "All of you must follow the bishop, as Jesus Christ followed the Father, the priests as the Apostles, and reverence the deacons, as the command of God: without the bishop let no one do any of those things which belong to the Church; it is not lawful without the bishop to baptize, nor to celebrate the *agape*."* "The high priest, who is the bishop," says Tertullian, "has the right of giving baptism; hence, the priests and the deacons, not, however, without the authority of the

* Eucharist, or love-feast.

28*

bishop."* St. Irenæus,† Tertullian,‡ and all the ancient
fathers who had occasion to allude to the subject, are
unanimous in representing the bishops as the successors of
the Apostles, and as holding in consequence the chief place
in Church Government.

12. All the ancient councils, whether particular or general, were predicated on this principle. In all of them, the
bishops alone were recognized as having a definitive vote in
the various matters which came under consideration. We
must either admit this fact, or discard all authority, reject
Church history, and say at once that the Church of Christ
went astray in this particular from the very beginning.
Who is prepared to say this? Who will say that the early
Church, taught by the Apostles and their immediate successors, was not much more likely to understand aright the
original and divinely-appointed order of Church Government than we can be at this remote day? Can we be
supposed to understand the true and original meaning of
certain words in the New Testament designating the different ministerial offices, as well as those holy men who
lived when those words were in the vernacular tongue of
Christendom, and were, moreover, fully explained by the
institutions which they indicated? Surely not.

The argument in favor of the Roman Catholic Church,
based upon the principles and facts hitherto developed or
established, is this:

That is the true Church of Jesus Christ, which alone has
and retains the original form of government established by
Him, and meant to be perpetuated in His Church to the end
of time;

But the Roman Catholic Church alone has this form of
government; at least no one of the Protestant denominations has it;

Therefore, the Roman Catholic Church alone is the true
Church of Jesus Christ.

The major, or first proposition, is self-evident; for mani-

* De Baptismo.   † De Hæresibus, Lib. iii, c. 3.
‡ De Præscriptionibus, c. 32. et *passim.*

festly no church can claim to be the Church of Christ, which has not all the essential elements of Church Government which He established in His Church. It may, indeed, be more or less conformable to that Church, accordingly as it approximates to its original type; without a complete conformity in every part, it cannot certainly be that identical Church.

The minor, or second proposition, might seem at first sight to suffer more difficulty; but, in reality, it is as incontrovertible as the major. That the Roman Catholic Church has the three orders composing the original hierarchy established by Jesus Christ and His Apostles, no one will or can deny; that none of the Protestant denominations has it, or, with the exception of the Anglican, even claims to have it, is equally evident. The Anglican church, indeed, claims this hierarchy, with the apostolical succession; but has it made good the claim? Much learning and ingenuity have been expended on this subject; but do not dark clouds of doubt still hang over it? It would lead me much too far to enter, at present, upon a discussion to which whole volumes have been devoted; and it is enough for my present purpose that the claim is certainly doubtful, as every candid man at all versed in the controversy must admit. * The claim of the Greek church is much more plausible and defensible; but our controversy is not, at present, with the Greek church, but with our separated brethren nearer home. I cannot consent to weaken the force of the argument against the latter, by making any collateral issues. †

---

* For more on this subject, see, among other works, the learned publication on "Anglican ordinations," by Archbishop Kenrick of St. Louis; and a chapter in Fletcher's "Comparative View."

† What the Greek church wants, is not the three Divinely appointed orders of the hierarchy, which it has, but a visible head and conservative center of Church Government, which it has not. Hence, as has been previously remarked, it has not the distinctive marks of Unity and Catholicity, and cannot therefore claim to be the Church of Christ. These remarks apply, with much more force, to the Anglican Church, which has but the shadow of a hierarchy, is distracted by doctrinal differences, and has clearly no Unity much less Catholicity.

But there is, My Dear Brethren, another essential feature in the original form of Church Government as established by Jesus Christ, to which neither the Greek nor the Anglican, nor any other church except the Roman Catholic, can possibly lay any claim whatever; and to the examination of which I mean to devote the remainder of this, and the whole of the next Lecture. If it can be clearly made out that Christ established a PRIMACY of power and jurisdiction in His Church, that He wished it to be perpetuated to the end of the world; and that the Roman Catholic Church alone has it, or even claims to have it, then is the argument above stated entirely and overwhelmingly conclusive in favor of our Church, and against all other Christian denominations on the face of the earth. Hence, all that I have to do is to establish these three facts, which I again state, in order that they may be clearly understood by all.

I. CHRIST ESTABLISHED A PRIMACY OF POWER AND JURISDICTION IN HIS CHURCH.

II. CHRIST WILLED THAT THIS PRIMACY SHOULD BE PERPETUATED IN HIS CHURCH TO THE END OF THE WORLD.

III. THE ROMAN CATHOLIC CHURCH ALONE HAS THIS PRIMACY.

I proceed at once to the proofs of these propositions, or facts, in the order in which they are stated.

I. CHRIST ESTABLISHED A PRIMACY OF POWER AND JURISDICTION IN HIS CHURCH.

We are met, on the very threshold of this investigation, by several objections, which are deemed more or less plausible by those who make them. We are told that the establishment of a Primacy by Christ would have been wholly repugnant to the genius of His Religion, and particularly to the humility and meekness which it enjoins; and that when " there was a strife amongst them (the Apostles) which of them should seem to be greater," Christ immediately rebuked their pride and ambition in the following memorable words: " The kings of the gentiles lord it over them; and they that have power over them are called beneficent: but you not so; but he who is the greatest among you, let him be as the least, and he that is the leader, as he that serveth." *

But this admonition of our blessed Lord was evidently intended only to chide undue pride and worldly ambition, and to warn His apostles against the haughty and domineering spirit of the gentile rulers. It was certainly not meant to exclude all idea of a leadership or Primacy among them, but only to enjoin upon their "leader" or Primate, to bear his honors meekly and not to "lord it" over his brethren. This is plainly the import of the passage, which consequently is very far from being incompatible with the idea of a Primacy. Nay, it rather supposes than excludes this feature of government. Does not Christ speak of some one among the Apostles who was to be "the greatest" and "a leader!" In any other supposition, where would have been the appropriateness or necessity of the admonition? The words of Christ might, perhaps, be alleged with some force against a Primacy of mere honor and precedence combined with worldly pomp, parade, and a haughty bearing; they prove nothing against, but rather something for, the Primacy of power and jurisdiction for which I am now contending.

But did not the other Apostles receive from the lips of Christ the same powers of binding and loosing, of forgiving and retaining sins, and of preaching and baptizing, as did St. Peter himself, whom we believe to have been the first divinely appointed Primate?

I answer: they did receive the same powers *substantially*, but not to the same *extent*. In other words, St. Peter was with them, and received along with them, all the powers alluded to; but besides these, he received other *special* powers and prerogatives, which were peculiar to himself, and which were not imparted to the other Apostles. This I hope to establish by incontestable evidence, a little further on; and if this can be once proved, the objection evidently falls to the ground of itself.

* St. Luke, xxii: 25, 26.

But is not Christ Himself the great Head of the Church? and if so, what need is there of any other head or Primate?

In answer, I beg you to tell me what you would think of this similar objection:—is not God the great Head of our own republic; and if so, what need have we of a president? How would you answer this argument,—if argument it can be called? You would probably say, that God is, indeed, the great Head of our republic, but that He is *invisible*, and that the republic consists of visible men, who stand in need of a *visible* and palpable government with a visible head. If the objector should still insist, that our president usurps the place of God, the only rightful Head of the government, you would deny that he does, and make good your denial, by showing that he acts not independently of God, but in due subordination to Him; and, in fact, in strict conformity with His known will and the usual order of His providence, which not only permits, but requires such visible rulers in all human governments.

I answer in precisely the same way, in order to show the appropriateness, if not the absolute necessity, of a *visible* head of the Church. Christ is its great Head and Ruler; but He is invisible; and He chooses to act through *visible* agents or ministers. If it be not repugnant to His Headship to say that He has delegated a portion of His powers to men, who act as His ministers and in His name, while discharging certain functions of the ministry common to all Christian denominations, how should it be deemed incompatible with it, that one of His agents should have received more power and more ample jurisdiction than the rest? Was the office of high-priest under the old law derogatory from God's prerogative as Head of the Jewish Church? Certainly not. Neither, then, does a Primacy of power and jurisdiction in the Christian Church derogate from Christ's prerogative as its great invisible Head.

On the contrary, from the precedent set by God Himself in the Jewish Church, of which He was, in a peculiar manner, the Head and Governor, as well as from the analogy of all other governments among men, we would be naturally led to expect this element in the government of the Christian Church. Under the old law, there was not only a high-priest, but one who was effectually the visible head of the Jewish Church, and who was, together with his council, the supreme judge of all controversies concerning Religion. This is clear from the following remarkable passage of Deuteronomy.

"If thou perceive that there be among you a hard and difficult (matter) in judgment, ... and thou see that the words of the judges within thy gates do vary; arise and go up to the place which the Lord thy God shall choose. And thou shalt come to the priests of the Levitical race, and to the judge that shall be at that time; and thou shalt ask of them, and they shall show thee the truth of the judgment. And thou shalt do whatsoever they shall say that preside in the place, which the Lord shall choose, and what they shall teach thee according to His law; and thou shalt follow their sentence, neither shalt thou decline to the right hand nor to the left hand. But he that will be proud, and refuse to obey the commandment OF THE PRIEST WHO MINISTERETH AT THAT TIME TO THE LORD THY GOD, and the decree of the judge, that man shall die, and thou shall take away the evil from Israel."*

Are we to say, that God meant to impart less ample power to His ministers under the new law, than he had bestowed on those under the old? Or that there should be a less thorough ministerial organization in the Christian, than there had been in the Jewish Church? Was the law of grace to be inferior to the law of fear; that of the living and abiding realities less perfect than that of the passing types and shadows? If, as St. Paul clearly intimates,† all things happened to the Jewish Church in figures foreshadowing what was to take place in the Christian, then where, I ask, are we to find the counterpart or anti-type of the office of high-priest under the old dispensation? In Jesus

* Deuteronomy, xviii: 8, 12.
† See I Corinthians, x: 7 and 12. Also, Hebrews, x: 1 and *passim*.

Christ?—He is, indeed, the great High-Priest, " ever living
to make intercession for us," but He is no longer visibly
present upon earth ; and a visible type requires a visible
anti-type, else it is not fulfilled. The other elements of
government in the Jewish Church, — the priests of Aaron's
family, and the Levitical race,—have their counterparts in
corresponding orders of the Christian ministry,—those of
priests and deacons; where, then, I again ask, is the Christian anti-type of the Jewish high-priesthood? It can be
found nowhere but in a visible Primacy or high-priesthood
in the Christian dispensation ; and if we are not prepared
to admit this, we leave an essential and distinctive element
in the government of the Jewish Church without its fulfillment and counterpart in the Christian ; and we virtually
falsify the admitted principle, that the former Church fore-
shadowed the latter in all its principal characteristics.

Again, no civil government on earth has ever existed, or
could ever exist for any time, without a visible head, or
chief executive. Without this element, there could be no
unity, and the different parts of the government would fall
to pieces of themselves. Now, the Church of Christ is a
visible society, and it has a visible government, as we have
already seen. Therefore, it must necessarily have a visible
head ; else it could not subsist or be kept together. Are
we still to be virtually told that Christ was less wise than
even the least enlightened of human legislators? That He
was so ignorant of human nature and of the exigencies of
all human society, as to have neglected the establishment of
a principle proved by the experience of mankind to be of
vital importance and of absolute necessity in every condition
of organized society that ever existed on earth.

This truth is so striking and so self-evident, that our
separated brethren, though they reject the idea of a universal Primate, yet virtually admit the principle itself in the
practical government of their own particular denominations.
They all have a visible head of some kind or other ; they
all recognize a supreme power, central to the church organization, and without which it could not be kept up. All

that they have done has been to multiply these centers of union, and thereby to perpetuate discord and division among Christians. Instead of the one great center of Unity towards which all the portions of the Christian society once gravitated, and in which they were all united as one body, they have a hundred centers drawing Christians in different directions, and thereby distracting, instead of uniting them.

Did Christ wish his Church to be ONE; united in the same faith, in the same worship, in the same government? If so, He must have established but one center of Unity, but one Primate and visible head for the whole Church. The experience of Protestantism during the last three centuries has abundantly proved, that disunion and an almost endless multiplication of conflicting sects are the result which necessarily flow from a rejection of this principle. And if there were no other argument than this to prove the necessity of the Primacy, we might, from this alone, infer the fact that Christ really established it. His Church could have been preserved in its essential Unity and integrity in no other way.

But is this presumptive reasoning *à priori* fully justified by the facts of the case? Did Christ really establish that Primacy which so many strong reasons already inclined us to look for in His Church? Was St. Peter singled out from the rest of the Apostles and appointed by Christ the first visible head of His Church? If such was the fact, then should we at once and unhesitatingly admit the Primacy, and bow to that Church which alone has, or even claims to have, this element of government. And that such is clearly the fact, the following considerations must convince every unprejudiced Christian mind.

I. In the first place, there are many minor circumstances and incidents related in the New Testament, from which it is natural to infer that Peter had a precedency, not only of honor, but also of power and jurisdiction over the other Apostles.

1. In the catalogues of the Apostles furnished by the evangelists, he is invariably placed first, as Judas invariably

occupies the last place. St. Matthew begins his catalogue thus: "THE FIRST, Simon who is called Peter, and Andrew his brother, &c."* That he did not mean to indicate that Peter was merely the first in order, is apparent from the fact that he does not continue the ordinal numbers in reference to the others. That he was not styled the *first*, merely because he was the first called to the apostleship, is equally certain; for St. John tells us that. his brother Andrew was called before him. † Therefore, it is fair to infer that he was put down as *the first* because he really occupied the first rank in power and jurisdiction among the Apostles.

Again, it is apparent to the most casual reader of the gospels, that Peter every-where stands forth as the leader, and spokesman of the apostolic college. He is every-where *first*, both in word and in action. Does Christ ask the sentiments of the Apostles on a particular point? Peter speaks out in the name of all. ‡ You frequently meet with such phrases as these: "Peter with the eleven;" "Peter and they who were with him;" "Go, tell the Apostles and Peter," &c. Peter is the object of the special care of Jesus Christ; He is the head of Christ's little household of disciples. "From his bark," says a learned living writer, "He (Christ) teaches the multitude; to him He gives the command to let down the net, and He rewards his obedience by a miraculous draught of fishes; to him He promises that he shall henceforth catch men. He commands him to walk to him on the waters, and stretches forth His hand to support him when the weakness of his faith causes him to begin to sink. He pays tribute for Him as well as for himself. All these facts are not without solemn import, and have forced themselves on the attention of the declared enemies of the Primacy." ‡

---

* St. Math. x: 2. In the Greek text, O Πρτς.
† St. John, ch. 1.   ‡ St. Math. xvi. and *passim*.
‡ "Primacy of the Apostolic See Vindicated," by Archbishop Kenrick; p. 28. We commend this ample and learned work to the attention of all sincere inquirers after the truth.

2. Moreover, Peter is the only one of the Apostles whose
name Christ changed; and it is not a little remarkable, that
the change was announced so soon as Christ first laid His
eyes upon him, and also that the new name signified a
ROCK: "And Jesus, looking upon him, said, thou art Simon
the son of Jona; thou shalt be called Cephas, which is interpreted Peter (a rock)."* What was the particular object
of our Lord in making the change, we shall soon see more
fully; but the circumstance itself is very significant.

Again, amidst the doubts and anxiety of the Apostles on
the morning of the resurrection of Christ, the circumstance
that He had appeared to Peter was deemed by them conclusive evidence of the fact. They exclaimed: "The Lord
is risen indeed, and hath appeared to Simon!" †

3. After the ascension of Christ, Peter enters at once upon
the active exercise of the Primacy. He is ever THE FIRST
and the efficient leader of the apostolic band. Is a new
apostle to be chosen to fill the place of the traitor Judas?
Peter rises up in the midst of his brethren, decides that it
must be done, and sets forth the qualities which should mark
the new apostle.‡ Are the Jews to have the gospel announced
to them? Peter is the first to do it, and God pours an
abundant blessing on his first sermon.§ Are unbelievers to
be convinced by miracles? Peter works the first miracle.‖
Are the gentiles to be called to the fold of Christ? Peter
is the first to undertake their conversion, admonished to
that effect by a special heavenly vision.¶ Is Peter cast in
prison? The whole Church is thrown into mourning, as
deprived of its visible head, prayers are poured out in his
behalf, and an angel is sent from heaven to effect his re-
lease.** Is a difficult controversy to be settled in a council
of the Apostles at Jerusalem? After "much disputing,"
Peter rises up, speaks with authority, decides the matter; "all the multitude held their peace;" and the whole

* St. John, i. 42.   † St. Luke, xxiv: 34.   ‡ Acts, i.
§ Acts, ii.   ‖ Acts, iii.   ¶ Acts, x.
** Acts, xii.

council reverently acquiesces in his decision sustained by St. James.*

4. St. Paul is called, in a miraculous manner, to be the special apostle of the gentiles; yet St. Paul "goes up to Jerusalem *to see Peter*, and stays with him fifteen days;"† and the object of his visit may be farther gathered from the remarkable reason he assigns for another subsequent journey to Jerusalem: "Lest perhaps I should run in vain."‡

5. Finally, in his Epistles, Peter takes the elevated and dignified tone of a Primate; he addresses all grades of the hierarchy in language which might be adopted by a modern Roman Pontiff: "Feed the flock of Christ which is among you; taking care (thereof) not by constraint, but willingly according to God; neither for the sake of filthy lucre, but voluntarily, neither as domineering over the clergy, but being made a pattern of the flock from the heart."§ St. Paul also indeed adopts a tone of boldness and authority in addressing bishops and priests; but it is chiefly in regard to Timothy, Titus, and others whom he had himself ordained; St. Peter addresses all without exception, as universal Primate of the Church.

Whatever may be thought in regard to the weight of each of these facts or circumstances taken singly, it can not be denied, that, when taken together, they present a cumulative evidence in favor of St. Peter's Primacy, of the strongest, if not of the most conclusive character. Nothing similar can be alleged of any one of the other Apostles, nor of St. Paul himself. The fact that the latter thought proper to reprove St. Peter for his conduct in reference to eating with the gentiles, has been frequently objected as an argument against St. Peter's Primacy. But surely our adversaries must be badly off for an objection when they insist on this. It is certainly lawful for an inferior to reprove a superior under certain circumstances, provided he do it, like St. Paul, with becoming respect. St. Bernard told a great many very plain truths to Pope Eugenius III.;‖

---

* Acts, xv.   † Gallatians, i: 18.   ‡ Ibid. ii: 2.   § I Peter, v: 2, 3.
‖ See his book "De Consideratione," addressed to that Pontiff.

and yet St. Bernard never dreamed of denying his Primacy. I may surely disapprove of the acts of our president, and yet not thereby impugn his authority.

II. But there are much stronger and more conclusive proofs of the Primacy of St. Peter than any of the minor evidences hitherto alleged. On two different occasions, Christ solemnly promised to bestow this high office upon him; and on a third, after His resurrection, He fully redeemed the promise. All that I ask, My Beloved Brethren, is that you would dismiss for a moment all preconceived opinions on the subject, in order that you may be able to approach it with the calmness and impartiality indispensable for coming to a sound conclusion: and that you would, moreover, humbly pray to God for His light and guidance, without which all our efforts to ascertain the truth would prove unavailing.

I have already said, that St. Peter was the only one among the Apostles whose name Christ himself changed.* What was the important object our blessed Saviour had in view in making the change, we gather from the following very significant passage of the New Testament. Christ had asked His disciples, what opinion was entertained of Him by the world; and they had informed Him of the different speculations of various classes of men on the subject. Then he asked: "But whom do *you* say that I am?" Peter answers, as usual, in the name and as the organ of the whole apostolic college: "Thou art Christ, the Son of the living God." Then "Jesus, answering, said to him: blessed art thou, Simon Bar-Jona (son of John); because flesh and blood hath not revealed it to thee, but my Father who is in heaven. And I say to thee, that THOU ART PETER (a rock), AND UPON THIS ROCK I WILL BUILD MY CHURCH, and the gates of hell shall not prevail against it; and TO THEE I will give the keys of the kingdom of heaven; and whatsoever thou

* The title *Boanerges* given to the two sons of Zebedee, was not properly a name. It designated the quality of ardent zeal which marked these two apostles, not the individuals themselves. And accordingly we find that neither of them ever bore this appellation.

29 *

shalt bind upon earth, it shall be bound in heaven; and
whatsoever thou shalt loose upon earth, it shall be loosed
in heaven."*

These words are very clear, and they need little comment.
If they mean any thing, they certainly imply all that I am
at present contending for:—that Christ intended to bestow
upon Peter more ample power and authority in his Church
than upon any of the other apostles. The following rapid
analysis of the text will show this.

1. The words are addressed to Peter alone in his individual capacity. The other apostles are present, but he is
singled out from their number; he is called by his old name,
Simon; the name of his father is also introduced, that there
may be no misapprehension as to his individuality; and
finally, he is designated by the new name which Christ himself had already promised to bestow upon him. Every
circumstance goes to show that the words refer to the person
of Peter alone, as contra-distinguished from the other apostles who were present.

2. The language clearly promises to him a special reward,
some high privilege, for the boldness and truth of his confession of faith in the heavenly mission and divinity of
Christ. A blessing is pronounced over his head in his old
character of Simon Bar-Jona; and a new benediction of a
still more ample nature is promised him in his new capacity,
as Peter, or A ROCK. If Christ meant really to confer on
Peter nothing but what had been already bestowed upon
the other apostles, where was the promised reward of his
faith; where the special blessedness invoked on him? In
such an hypothesis, the language of Christ is wholly without meaning, or rather it implies an inconsistency, if not a
glaring absurdity. A captain conducts himself with signal
bravery in battle; his general sees him afterwards, and ap-
plauds his conduct in presence of his brother officers; he
talks about certain great honors which are to be showered
upon his head as a reward for his services;—yet he leaves
him where he was, and takes no thought whatever for his

---

*St. Mathew, xvi: 16, 19.

promotion! He deludes and tantalizes him with mere un-
meaning words! Are we to say that Christ meant to pursue
the same course in regard to Peter?

3. But our blessed Saviour says expressly: "Thou art
Peter, and upon *this Rock* I will build my Church:" that
is, "Thou art a *Rock*, and upon this *Rock* I will build my
Church." In the language which he actually used,—the
Syro-Chaldaic,—these were the precise words he employed;
for, in that language, the same word stood for *Peter* as for
the *Rock*. So it is also in the Syriac version,* thought to
be as old as the apostolic times, and the one nearest in
structure and genius to the language used by Christ; so it
is likewise in the Arabic version,† of almost equal antiquity,
and likewise in a cognate dialect. The genius of the Greek
and Latin languages requires a slight change in the termination, on account of diversity of gender; and the same
may be said of the Italian, Spanish and Portuguese versions
of the passage.‡ Still, in all of them, the allusion is clearly
marked and is unmistakable; and the argument which
some have attempted to build up on this difference of termination and gender, in order to show that *Peter* and the
Rock are not identical, is puerile in the extreme. It only
shows the desperate extremities to which the adversaries of
the Primacy are driven, in their attempt to wrest the passage from its natural and obvious meaning. Did Christ
speak those words in the Greek or Latin, or in any other
language but the Syro-Chaldaic? And is it not admitted
by all, that, in this language, and in most of the kindred
dialects, the word is unchanged and precisely the same,
even in termination?

4. Still more puerile is the attempt to refer the clause,
"and upon this Rock," to Christ himself, as if He pointed
to His own person while using those words! Where is the

---

* In this version, the passage reads, in our characters: Anath CHIPHA,
vehall hada CHIPHA. See Archbishop Kenrick on the Primacy; p. 18, 19,
note.

† In Arabic: Anath ALSACHRA, wahal hada ALSACHRA. Ibid.

‡ In the French language, the same word—*Pierre*—denotes both *Peter*
and the *Rock*; as in the Syro Chaldaic, and other kindred tongues.

evidence for this in the text? Is it not plainly an arbitrary interpretation, opposed to the whole context and drift of the passage? Does it not clearly break the connection, disjoint the language, and stultify the meaning of the Saviour? Is not the whole passage evidently addressed to Peter? "Thou art Peter, and upon this Rock . . . . . and to thee, &c.;"—what can be plainer?

But Christ is the foundation of the Church, besides which no other can be placed, as St. Paul positively states;[*] therefore, Christ, and not Peter, is the rock upon which the Church is built. This is a mere sophism, which a very child might refute. Christ is, indeed, the great *primary* foundation, upon which the whole Church edifice firmly rests, and without which it would totter and fall; but this does not exclude secondary foundations, built up upon this primary one, and deriving their strength and solidity therefrom. Does not St. Paul himself say as much, when he asserts that the Church "is built upon the foundation of the Apostles and Prophets, Jesus Christ himself being the chief corner-stone, in whom all the building framed together groweth into a holy temple in the Lord?"[†] Christ is thus the principal foundation and the chief corner-stone; but in the superstructure reared upon this foundation, Peter is the great fundamental Rock, which sustains its weight, holds it together, and keeps it from toppling down; whilst the other Apostles also aid in supporting it, but in a different, and evidently a subordinate degree. Thus, parallel passages of the New Testament throw additional light upon the clear and obvious meaning of the text under consideration, instead of obscuring or impairing its force.

5. But the concluding portion of the passage clearly indicates the superior powers which were to be vested in Peter: "And to thee I will give the keys of the kingdom of heaven; and whatsoever thou shalt bind upon earth, shall be bound in heaven; and whatsoever thou shalt loose upon earth, shall be loosed in heaven." What power could

---

* I Corinthians, iii.   † Ephesians, ii: 20, 21.

be more ample than this? There is no reservation, no limitation; Christ pledges himself to ratify all the official acts of his earthly minister-plenipotentiary and vicegerent. He imparts to Peter the power of opening and shutting the kingdom of heaven, according to his discretion and judgment, and He promises that He will sanction and confirm his decisions in the premises. He that has the *keys* of a house, is master of the house; and he may open and shut it at will. Therefore, whether we understand by *the kingdom of heaven*, the Church on earth or the Church triumphant in heaven, it is manifest that, in either interpretation, Peter received the fullness of spiritual power. This is still more apparent from the fact, that two inspired writers, the one a prophet under the old, and the other an evangelist and prophet under the new dispensation, employ this very figure of the keys, to denote the ample and unbounded power of Jesus Christ himself,—"Who hath the key of David; He that openeth, and no man shutteth; shutteth, and no man openeth." *

Is it not manifest, then, My Dear Brethren, from all these obvious considerations, that Christ really meant to impart to Peter a Primacy of power and jurisdiction of the most ample kind? Can you come to any other conclusion, without wresting His words from their plain and obvious meaning, and violating all the canons of sound interpretation? Many Protestant writers of the greatest learning and eminence, have accordingly rejected the interpretations of some hotter partisans of less note; and they substantially agree with us as to the construction of the passage. †

But there was still another occasion on which Christ also clearly promised the Primacy to Peter. It was on the eve of his passion, when the storm of persecution, which was soon to break upon the divine Shepherd and to disperse the flock, was already gathering. With a sorrowing heart, and with a feeling of paternal affection, Christ, on that solemn

---

* Apocalypse, iii: 7. See also Isaiah, xxii: 22.

† Such as Bloomfield, Bishop Marsh, Rosenmuller, Thompson, and others, quoted by Archbishop Kenrick, work above cited, p. 18, seqq.

occasion addressed his anxious Apostles in the following significant language:

"But you are they who have continued with me in my temptations: and I appoint to you, as my Father hath appointed to me, a kingdom; that you may eat and drink with me in my kingdom, and may sit upon thrones judging the twelve tribes of Israel." The sacred text then immediately adds: "And the Lord said: Simon, Simon, behold, Satan hath desired to have *you*, that he may sift *you*, as wheat; but I HAVE PRAYED FOR THEE that thy faith fail not; and thou being once converted, CONFIRM THY BRETHREN."*

The meaning of these words is obvious and clear even to the dullest capacity. In reward for their fidelity in remaining with Him throughout all His bitter trials and temptations, the Saviour promises to establish a vast spiritual, but yet visible kingdom upon earth, in which they are to be princes and judges,—"sitting upon thrones and judging the twelve tribes of Israel;"—that is, all its subjects throughout the world. But a visible kingdom cannot be set up without a visible king, or Primate. Hence, He directs His eyes to Peter, to whom He had already, in the presence of the other Apostles, explicitly promised this high dignity. Penetrating through the darkness of the future, He discovers that Peter will temporarily yield to temptation, and, in an evil hour, deny his divine Lord and Master. His solicitude is awakened in behalf of His principal disciple,—the Rock upon which His Church is to be built. *All* the apostles were "to be sifted as wheat;" yet for Peter *alone*† does He pray that "his faith may fail not;" and upon Peter *alone* does He lay the solemn command, that "being once converted, he should CONFIRM HIS BRETHREN."

How explain all this, but in the hypothesis that Chris

---

* St. Luke xxii: 28–32.

† This is still more clear from the original Greek text; in which the *you*, in the first part of the passage is plural, and refers to all the Apostles; whereas the object of Christ's prayer, as well as of His command to confirm the brethren, are denoted by the singular pronouns *thee* and *thou*.

really meant to constitute Peter the visible head of His Church, and the Primate among his brethren of the apostolic college? In any other explanation it has no meaning whatever.

Finally, My Dear Brethren, when the proper time had arrived for the full organization of the Church; when Christ had already accomplished the redemption by His death upon the cross, and had fully confirmed the truth of His Religion by the splendid miracle of His resurrection; when He was on the eve of leaving this earth, bidding a last farewell to his sorrowing disciples, and returning to the bosom of His Father who had sent Him; we find Him fully redeeming the promises which He had already made, by actually constituting Peter the chief visible pastor of all that vast and united sheepfold, of which He was yet to remain the great invisible Shepherd, and "Prince of pastors." The occasion was most solemn and interesting; it was after the miraculous draught of fishes, and the affecting repast that followed it, when Jesus manifested Himself to His disciples for the third time after His resurrection. Peter, Thomas, James, John, and several other apostles or disciples were present; and their hearts were filled with unspeakable reverence, and they glowed with burning love towards their risen Lord and Master, with whom they were sitting at table, perhaps for the last time. The repast over, the following affecting dialogue took place between Christ and Peter:

"Jesus saith to Simon Peter: Simon, (son) of John, lovest thou me *more than these?* He saith to him: yea, Lord, thou knowest that I love thee. He saith to him: FEED MY LAMBS.* He saith to him again: Simon, (son) of John, lovest thou me? He saith to him: yea, Lord, thou knowest that I love thee. He saith to him: FEED MY LAMBS. † He saith to him the third time: Simon, (son) of John, lovest thou me? Peter

* Βοσχε τα Αρνια μου.

† Ποιμαιν τα προβατα μου.—The Vulgate here reads AGNOS—*lambs*; but the sense is the same. The Greek word Ποιμαιν, means *to rule, to govern;* hence Homer calls the princes, Ποιμενες λαων—*rulers of the people.—Passim.*

was grieved, because he said to him the third time,—lovest thou me? And he said to him: Lord thou knowest all things; thou knowest that I love thee. He said to him: FEED MY SHEEP."*

Who is so blind as not to see that Christ here actually constituted Peter the supreme and universal pastor over his entire flock, including both the lambs and the sheep? Does He make any limitation whatever? Does He exempt any portion of the whole flock from his supervision and control? What type could even He have selected more suitable for conveying the idea of the most ample spiritual power conferred on His favored Apostle? What is more docile, united, and tractable, than a flock of sheep? Who has more unlimited authority than a shepherd over his sheepfold? To *feed* a flock, is to govern and control all its movements; and the word used in the original Greek text clearly implies this. This is, moreover, the ordinary Scriptural import of the term. Thus David, king as he was, is styled *the shepherd* of God's people.† Thus, again, the mighty king Cyrus is called the *shepherd* of God.‡ And it is for this very reason that Christ himself is called the great Shepherd of the one Sheepfold.§

Will you tell me, that this power was given to Peter merely as the foreman and representative of the apostolic band, and that Christ really meant to impart it, through him, to the other Apostles?—I answer, that this is a groundless assumption, wholly unwarranted by the text, and clearly opposed to its obvious meaning and drift. Christ addresses Peter *only*, by name, and in his individual capacity. He singles him out from the other Apostles who were present, and, to indicate His intention to impart to him some special power over the rest, He asks him emphatically: "lovest thou me *more than these*" (other Apostles)?

You will tell me, that Christ required this triple declaration of love from Peter, merely to repair the scandal given

* St. John, xxi: 15–17. † Ezekiel, xxxiv. Read the whole chapter. ‡ See Isaiah, xliv: 28. § St. John, x.

by his previous triple denial. This, too, is little better than an assumption; the Scriptures, the Protestant's *only* rule of faith, say no such thing. But allow it to be true; it is still certain, and is even admitted by this very interpretation, that Christ gave this universal power to Peter in His personal character; to that very Peter who had thrice denied Him, and to no other. Thus the basis of our argument remains in all its strength, and its force is not only not diminished, but rather increased.

From all these Scriptural evidences, it is manifest, My Beloved Brethren, that Christ did institute a Primacy, and that He did constitute Peter the first incumbent of that office. Reason, analogy, and the precedent set by God Himself in the Old Testament, naturally led us to expect this feature in the spiritual government instituted by Christ for His Church. A great number of minor circumstances and incidents recorded in the New Testament, all pointed to Peter as the first Primate; and made it already clear, that if he was not to be invested with that dignity, no other certainly was. The explicit and solemn promises of Christ, on two different occasions, still direct us to Peter, and strengthen the conviction before entertained. The persuasion amounts to absolute certainty, when we find Christ, under the most impressive and affecting circumstances, fully redeeming His promise, and actually intrusting His whole flock to the spiritual charge of His great Apostle. The evidence is thus cumulative and complete, and no one can resist it, without shutting his eyes to the clearest light of truth, and virtually rejecting the Scriptures themselves.

Thus, the first proposition in regard to the Primacy,—that Christ actually instituted that office,—may be viewed as fully established. In the next Lecture, with the grace of God and your kind indulgence, I will proceed to establish the second and third propositions above stated; which, you will remember, consist of the two assertions:—that Christ intended the Primacy to be a perpetual institution in His Church; and that the Roman Catholic Church alone is in possession of this important element of government.

30

Whatever may be your own particular religious views on this subject, please lend me your patient attention, while I will proceed to spread out before you such a portion of the evidence establishing these two great truths as the narrow limits of one Lecture will allow.

May God vouchsafe to bestow His holy grace upon us all, My Beloved Brethren, that, after centuries of separation and confusion, we may all at length be conducted back again to that blessed Unity of faith and love which characterized *your* ancestors, as well as mine, for fifteen centuries, before all these dissensions arose among Christians! May we, like they, be united by clinging to the Chair of Peter. May God's grace and light, without which we can do nothing, lead us all to this quiet haven of rest, where we may be united as brethren around the same holy altar, and may have but one heart and one soul, like the first Christians; through Jesus Christ, our common Lord and Master. Amen.

LECTURE XII.

CHURCH GOVERNMENT—THE PAPACY—THE NINTH EVIDENCE OF CATHOLICITY (CONCLUDED).

The Roman Church—Its early fame—Recapitulation of preceding Lecture —The second proposition stated and proved—The third proposition— Already virtually admitted by our opponents—A cloud of witnesses— Why Rome was selected as the seat of the Primacy—St. Peter at Rome and first Roman bishop—The chair of Peter—The Roman episcopacy and Primacy not incompatible—The alleged silence of the New Testament—Roman Pontiffs always viewed by Christian antiquity as the successors of St. Peter—The testimony of the first three centuries— The cases of Popes St. Victor and St. Stephen—The ancient patriarchates—The first eight general councils—The sixth canon of Nice—The Isidorian Decretals—Testimonies of ancient Greek and Latin fathers— The opponents of the Papacy, ancient and modern—Alleged abuses of the Papacy—Its uncompromising character—The charge of persecution —Balancing accounts—Temporal power of the Popes—Their prohibiting divorces and rebuking powerful tyrants—Charge that the Papacy is despotic repelled—The nature of Church Government under the Papacy—Appeals to prejudice and passion—The true issue—Recapitulation—The Ninth Evidence of Catholicity—A fuller definition of the Church.

" First I give thanks to my God through Jesus Christ for you all ; because your faith is spoken of in the whole world."—ROMANS, 1 : 8.

IN these terms of high eulogy did the glorious Apostle of the gentiles speak of the Church of Rome, nearly eighteen hundred years ago. His heart was filled with holy joy, and his tongue broke forth into a canticle of praise to God, when he heard on all sides the most glowing accounts of the faith of the Romans. He had not yet visited the imperial city of the Cæsars; * and the foundations of the

---

* His Epistle to the Romans was written about twenty-four years after the ascension of Christ, or about the year 58. He informs us himself, in this epistle, that he had not yet been to Rome, but was very desirous of visiting that city. Chapter i., verses 10, 11.

Church there, the fame of which had already been sounded forth in the whole world, had been laid by other hands than his own. Who built up that flourishing Church, so famous from its very infancy? Whence its importance in all subsequent ages of Christian history? And why do we now, after the lapse of eighteen centuries, still look up to it, and speak of it, with the reverence, and in the terms of praise, with which it was looked up to and spoken of by the whole world in the days of St. Paul? I shall endeavor to answer these questions in the course of the present Lecture. I beg of you to dismiss all preconceived opinions, and to give me an impartial and attentive hearing.

You will recollect, that, in the preceding Lecture, I rested the whole evidence in favor of the Primacy on the establishment of three consecutive propositions involving plain questions of fact: first, that Christ instituted a Primacy of power and jurisdiction in his Church; second, that he wished it to be perpetuated therein to the end of the world; and third, that the Roman Catholic Church alone has this element of government. The first proposition, I trust, I have already proved by establishing the Primacy of St. Peter. I proceed now to unfold the evidence in support of the other two.

II. CHRIST INTENDED AND WISHED THAT THE PRIMACY INSTITUTED BY HIMSELF SHOULD BE PERPETUATED IN HIS CHURCH TO THE END OF THE WORLD.

This proposition need not detain us long. It is proved by precisely the same species of evidence by which we establish the permanency and perpetuity of baptism, of the holy eucharist, of the preaching of the gospel, and of all the other institutions of Christianity. The Church was to continue to the end of time just such as Christ established it; unchanged in all its substantial elements and parts. A Church which does not correspond in all its institutions with that founded by Christ, would be a human, not a divine Church; at least not *the* Church of Christ. The addition or subtraction of a single doctrine or institution would adulterate its purity, and thereby mar its integrity.

Our adversaries cannot deny the soundness of this principle; in fact, they generally admit it and speak a great deal about restoring the Church to its primitive purity, and making it precisely such as it came originally from the hands of Christ. Discard this principle, and you at once break off all connection between the original Church of Christ, and any Church of the present day claiming to be that Church; and you thus virtually renounce Christianity itself, and plunge into the gulf of infidelity.

Besides, there are, if possible, much stronger reasons for maintaining the perpetuity of the Primacy, than there exist for asserting that of any other original institution of Christ: for this is a primary element of the Church, essential to its well-being and to its very existence. Without it, the Church could not possibly have remained in its original oneness and integrity, even for one century after the death of the Apostles. It would have been broken up into fragments, and its institutions would have been scattered to the winds. It would have been left like an army without a general, a navy without an admiral, a kingdom without a ruler, a sheepfold without a shepherd. Divisions, schisms, rebellions, would have started up on all sides; and there would have been no remedy to the ever increasing evil. The sheepfold would have been dispersed or devoured by ravenous wolves, lurking within it in the garb of sheep. While the Apostles lived, their commanding authority and personal inspiration might have secured unity and quelled religious insurrection; after their death what but a divinely instituted Primacy, generally recognized as still existing in all its pristine vigor, could have secured that good, or averted this crying evil?

This is precisely the view taken by all the ancient Christian fathers who had occasion to allude to the subject. Thus St. Cyprian, the holy martyr-bishop of Carthage, in the middle of the third century, lays it down as an undoubted principle universally received in his time, that the Primacy was instituted by Christ for the purpose of securing unity to His Church: "That He (Christ) might manifest unity, He ordained by His own authority, that its origin should begin with one single individual (Peter)."* Thus also, St. Jerome, writing against the heretic Jovinian, in the fourth century, says expressly: "One among the twelve is chosen, that, a head being constituted, the occasion of schism might be taken away."†

Surely, My Brethren, the danger of schism greatly increased after the death of the Apostles; and, therefore, if Christ deemed the Primacy necessary for the Church during their lifetime, He must have judged it still more necessary afterwards; and must consequently have willed its perpetuation to the very end of time. In proportion as the Church would extend its empire over the nations, and the number of its children would increase, in the very same ratio would the importance and necessity of this great restraining and conservative principle become more apparent and more strikingly evident to all. Christ foresaw, too, that in the course of time the fervor of His disciples would gradually cool down, and their faith would become more and more impaired in vividness and vigor:—are we then to say that, with this clear foresight, He made no permanent provision fully adequate to meet the ever increasing danger to unity? If we indulge in so unworthy a thought, we virtually deny His wisdom and goodness; and thereby reject not only His divinity, but His divine mission itself. Therefore, the second proposition may be considered as fully established, and I pass at once to the third.

III. THE ROMAN CATHOLIC CHURCH ALONE HAS THE PRIMACY ORIGINALLY INSTITUTED BY JESUS CHRIST IN THE PERSON OF ST. PETER.

This, too, is equally manifest with the two preceding propositions. No other Christian denomination even *claims*

---

* "De Unitate Ecclesiæ;" a golden treatise, in which, reasoning against the heretics of his day, he takes precisely the same Catholic ground which we now occupy, while arguing against Protestants.

† "Unus inter duodecim eligitur, ut capite constituto schismatis tolleretur occasio.—ADVERSUS JOVIN. LIB. i: c. 14.

to have a Primacy; they all unanimously agree in discarding it as unnecessary, and as no part of the original revelation made by Jesus Christ. If, then, the two propositions
already established be admitted as true, all the denominations alluded to, have virtually, if not even positively, un-
churched themselves, and cut themselves off from Christ,
by the act of separation from the only Church on the
face of the earth which claims to possess and retain this
original institution of Christianity. If the Roman Catholic
Church has not the Primacy, what other church, I ask, has
it? If it be not found in the Roman Church founded by
St. Peter, and praised by St. Paul, in what other church or
episcopal see is it to be found? No other see nor church
certainly ever claimed, or even now claims, to have this
element of government.

Here I might rest the argument; but I will go a step
further, and present a rapid analysis of the mass of evidence by which the claim of the Roman see to the Primacy
is triumphantly sustained. Supposing the divine institution of the Primacy, and the will of Christ that it should
be perpetuated in the Church, this claim rests upon an
historical *fact;* which must be proved, like every other
'fact,—by the weight of testimony. And, as I trust to convince you, we have, in support of it, a cloud of witnesses
of unexceptionable authority and unimpeachable veracity,
scattered throughout all the ages of Christianity, and presenting an unbroken chain of testimony reaching back
from our own days to those of the Apostles themselves.
No one can resist its force who is not prepared to reject all
human testimony, and with it all history.

1. As we have already proved, St. Peter was the divinely
appointed Primate of the whole Church, and he was, by
the will of Christ, to transmit this Primacy to successors
who were to perpetuate it to the end of the world:—where
was he to locate his primatial see? Which of all the cities
on the face of the earth was to become the favored metropolis of Christendom? Glance for an instant at the
map of the world, as it was constituted immediately after

the day of Pentecost; and you will discover at once that
he could scarcely have selected for this purpose any other
city than Rome. Constantinople was not yet in existence.
Jerusalem lay on the extreme eastern border of the Roman
empire, which was manifestly to become the principal
domain of Christianity. Alexandria, Antioch, Ephesus,
Smyrna, were all too far east to be chosen as this great
Christian center; at least such was the case after the
amazing extension of the gospel, even before the middle
of the first century.*

Rome alone, the greatest city then in existence, and
occupying a central position easy of access; Rome, the metropolis of that vast empire which bestrode the earth, the
great heart of the world, the pulsations of which were felt
at its most remote extremities; Rome, to which all the
civilized nations looked up as to a mistress, and with which
they were necessarily thrown into daily communication
and contact; Rome alone was the appropriate seat of the
Primacy. The Primate established here might have facilities for extending the gospel, for holding intercourse with
the most distant people, and for governing the Church
spread over the whole earth, which he could possess in no
other location. Rome was, then, the very city which·
seemed to be designated by Providence for the see of St.
Peter; and we would naturally expect to find this great
Prince of the Apostles locating himself there.

2. Accordingly, we find that St. Peter did remove to
Rome, and did fix his episcopal and primatial see in that
city. All Christian antiquity bears evidence to this great
fact of Church history. It is attested by St. Clement, St.
Ignatius, and Papias, bishop of Hieropolis,—all of them
immediate disciples of the Apostles,—in the first century;

* It is a remarkable fact, that during the first seven years after the day
of Pentecost, St. Peter selected Antioch for his see, this being as yet the
most important and the most central city in Christendom; but that when
Christianity was extended farther westward, he removed his see to Rome.
This fact is attested by many ancient writers of undoubted authority.

by St. Irenæus, Dionysius of Corinth, Tertullian, and Cajus, a Roman priest, in the second; by St. Cyprian and Origen, in the third; by Eusebius, the father of Church history, St. Epiphanius, St. Jerome, St. Optatus of Milevi, St. Pacian, St. Augustine, St. John Chrysostom, and an ever-increasing host of other witnesses, in the fourth, fifth, and following centuries.*

To say that all these witnesses were deceived in regard to a public and notorious fact known to the whole world, or that they all conspired to deceive us, would amount to an absolute historical skepticism. Many learned Protestant writers, such as Blondel, Cave, Grotius, and even John Calvin himself, have not ventured to deny the fact. Cave says: "We intrepidly affirm with all antiquity, that Peter was at Rome, and for some time resided there. . . . All, both ancient and modern, will, I think, agree with me that Peter may be called bishop of Rome in a less strict sense (!), inasmuch as he laid the foundations of this Church, and rendered it illustrious by his martyrdom." †

3. That he was really bishop of Rome, in the strictest sense of the term, and that he died bishop of Rome, is proved by the self-same evidence alleged above to establish the fact of his having visited Rome. If he was not the first bishop of Rome, who was? Does antiquity point to any other individual as filling that office during St. Peter's lifetime? History is wholly silent on this subject; and it is surely both illogical and absurd to assume an historical fact without one particle of evidence to sustain it, nay against all evidence. Whilst St. Peter was at Rome, was it not natural that he should take upon himself the episcopal

---

* See all their testimonies, and those of many others, given in full in Archbishop Kenrick's splendid work on the Primacy, chap. v., and *passim*: this work exhausts the whole subject of the Primacy. The American reader is also referred to the American edition of Eusebius, b. II., c. xiv: p. 63, 64.

† Sæculum Apostol. S. Petrus.—Quoted by Archbishop Kenrick, ibid. p. 79.

government of that Church? Who else would have ventured to assume this office, while he was present?. St. Paul?—But the Roman Church had been already founded, and its episcopal see established and filled, years before St. Paul visited the city, as he himself attests in the first chapter of his Epistle to the Romans. St. Peter, as the voice of all ancient Church history proclaims, had already preached the Gospel there, and had fully organized the Church. Was St. Paul to disturb the existing order of things, and to occupy a chair already filled by that great Apostle whom Christ had appointed the Rock upon which His Church should be built, and to whom He had given in charge His entire flock, sheep as well as lambs? Certainly not.

St. Paul may, indeed, be called one of the founders of the Roman Church, and he is so designated by many ancient writers; because he preached the gospel there, had great weight of authority as the chosen Apostle of the gentiles, and made many additional converts: but not one of them all calls him bishop of Rome, at least in the strict sense in which they give St. Peter that title. They all call the Roman See the *Chair of Peter;** none of them call it the *Chair of Paul.*

4. Nor tell me that St. Peter's being bishop of Rome was incompatible with his apostolic office, which made his mission and labors as wide as the world, and thereby.prevented him from settling down in any particular place. This is nothing but a mere sophism, as shallow as it is trite. Could not St. Peter, while residing at Rome, hold constant communication with the whole world? Was there any location where he would be likely to see more people from distant regions, and to have greater facilities for discharging his apostolic office? Was he bound, in order to fulfill this office, to be perpetually in motion? Again, did his being Roman bishop, necessarily confine him entirely to the city? Could he not make frequent excursions to other

---

* Cathedra Petri.

adjoining or distant places? Is not St. James universally recognized as the first bishop of Jerusalem, without any detriment whatever to his apostolic charge? The whole objection is based upon a very strange confusion of ideas in reference to the respective characters of the episcopal and apostolic offices. The latter is merely more ample than the former; it does not exclude, but rather includes it, as the greater does the less. Hence there is obviously no incompatibility whatsoever between the two. The present bishop of Rome, like all his predecessors, actually combines both offices in his own person; and it is surely competent to reason from a fact to its possibility.

Still more weak and futile is the objection often urged against the visit of St. Peter to Rome, and his death there, from the alleged silence of the New Testament on the subject. The New Testament does not tell us that St. Peter went to Rome or died there; therefore he did not go to Rome nor die there!—But does the New Testament inform us whither he went, or where he died? If from its silence on his death at Rome, you infer that he did not die there, from its total silence as to his death, I might, with the same reason, infer that he did not die at all! Who does not see that this is a merely negative argument, which proves nothing?—especially when we can oppose to it a mass of positive testimony clearly establishing the fact. The New Testament gives us but little information on the lives of the Apostles during the last years of their career. The Acts of the Apostles, where we would naturally look for such information, are almost entirely taken up, after the twelfth chapter, with an account of St. Paul's missionary travels; and the interesting narrative stops suddenly short about four years before his death. Are we to conclude from this silence, that St. Paul, too, did not die at Rome, contrary to the unanimous voice of Christian antiquity? No one but a child would reason thus.

But is it quite certain that there is no mention in the New Testament of St. Peter's visit to the imperial city?

He concludes his First Epistle in these words: " The Church which is *in Babylon*, elected together, saluteth you; and (so doth) my son Mark," &c.* Where was this *Babylon*, from which he wrote his epistle? Babylon the great of the Assyrians had long since fallen; and Babylon in Egypt was a very insignificant place, which no ancient historian tells us St. Peter ever visited. It is highly probable, then, that he wished to designate pagan Rome by this name, which appears to have been a common practice with the early Christians. Thus it is almost certain that St. John, in his Apocalypse, depicts the vices and predicts the fall of pagan Rome, under the mystic appellation of *Babylon*. Papias, a disciple of the Apostles, expressly informs us that St. Peter wrote his epistle from Rome, calling it Babylon.†

It is, then, wholly certain that St. Peter visited Rome, that he was the first bishop of Rome, and that he died bishop of Rome. If we do not admit these three facts, we are at full liberty to reject every thing contained in history; for there are no historical facts more public, more notorious, or more fully attested. No one ever dreamed of denying them for the first thirteen hundred years of the Christian era; and no man of any pretensions to learning will venture to question them at the present day, unless he be entirely blinded by prejudice.

5. While St. Peter was bishop of Rome, the episcopacy of the Roman see and the Primacy of the Church were united in the same individual; at his death, they continued so united in his successors to the Roman episcopacy. The bishops of Rome were considered by all Christian antiquity as sitting in the CHAIR OF PETER, as occupying THE PLACE OF PETER; and, therefore, as his regular successors in the Primacy. Thus St. Cyprian tells us, that Cornelius was

---

* I Peter, v: 18.

† See also Eusebius — Church history; B. II, c. xv. For a full and triumphant demonstration of Peter's residence, death, and episcopacy at Rome, see Fogginio — De Romano D. Petri Itinere et Episcopatu; 1 vol. 4to.

chosen bishop of Rome, when "the place of Fabian, that is, THE PLACE OF PETER was vacant."* In a letter to the Roman Pontiff Cornelius, speaking of certain African schismatics, the same father says: "A false bishop having been ordained for them by heretics, they venture to set sail and carry letters from schismatical and profane men to the CHAIR OF PETER and the PRINCIPAL, OR RULING CHURCH, WHENCE SACERDOTAL UNITY HAS ARISEN; nor do they reflect that they are Romans, whose faith is extolled by the Apostle, to whom perfidy can have no access."†

St. Cyprian in this does but re-echo the universal sentiment of his age, and he speaks the language of all his predecessors and contemporaries. I have already given you, on this subject, the splendid testimonies of Tertullian and St. Irenæus, in the second century. I have already had occasion to state the remarkable fact, that no less than four ancient Christian writers,—St. Irenæus, Eusebius, St. Optatus of Milevi, and St. Augustine,—not to mention the ancient catalogue of Liberius,‡—men writing at different times, in different places, and without any mutual understanding or collusion whatsoever; all nevertheless agree in furnishing us with a list of Roman bishops from St. Peter down to the times at which they severally wrote, and likewise in attaching to that unbroken succession precisely the same importance as we now claim for it in our arguments with modern dissenters.§ By all of them, and by a host of other ancient fathers, the Roman See, or the Chair of Peter,

---

* Epistola LV. ad Antonianum.

† Epist. ad Cornelium LIX. The terms *Cathedra principalis* and *Ecclesia principalis*, properly denote a *ruling chair* or CHURCH, as Archbishop Kenrick well observes. The imperial edicts were often styled *jussiones principales*. "Primacy, &c." p. 88, note.

‡ Supposed by Pearson and other learned men to be as old as the fourth century, and to have been drawn up under the pontificate of Liberius, or about the year 354. See Archbishop Kenrick, ibid. p. 81.

§ See the Eighth Lecture, p. 218, 219. Tertullian and other ancient writers also frequently refer to the same argument based upon the succession in the chair of St. Peter.

was unanimously viewed as the MOTHER CHURCH, the ROOT
of all other churches, and as the ROCK upon which Christ
had built his Church.

6. Our dissenting brethren are in the habit of looking
up with reverence to the faith and practice of the Christian
Church during the first three centuries of its existence.
This they generally regard as the period of primitive
purity, when the Church, bleeding at every pore under the
rod of a protracted and relentless persecution, still continued faithful to the doctrines of the Apostles and of Christ.
If, then, it can be clearly shown, that during this period
the Christian world generally acknowledged the Primacy
of the Roman Pontiffs, they will surely not object to the
authority. Now this can be proved by evidence satisfactory to every unprejudiced mind; notwithstanding the well
known fact, that, owing to the violence of the persecutions
and other causes, most of the documents belonging to the
epoch in question are no longer extant. To this period, as
you all know, belong St. Irenæus, Tertullian, and St. Cyprian, whose words you have already heard. A very learned and excellent living writer, thoroughly versed in the
fathers, and as moderate as he is erudite, gives the following comprehensive summary of the evidences in favor of the
Roman Primacy, furnished by the facts and documents of
Church history previous to the first general council of Nice
in 325. I extract it entire, because it is as accurate as it is
condensed; though, as will be perceived, it embodies some
things already stated.

" Faint they (the evidences in favor of the Primacy) may
be one by one, but at least they are various, and are drawn
from many times and countries, and thereby serve to illus-
trate each other, and form a body of proof. Thus St.
Clement, in the name of the Church of Rome, writes a
letter to the Corinthians, when they were without a bishop;
St. Ignatius of Antioch addresses the Roman Church, and
it only out of the churches to which he writes, as 'the
Church which has the first seat in the place of the country
of the Romans;' St. Polycarp of Smyrna betakes himself

to the bishop of Rome on the question of Easter; the heretic Marcion, excommunicated in Pontus, betakes himself to Rome; Soter, bishop of Rome, sends alms, according to the custom of his Church, to the churches throughout the empire, and in the words of Eusebius, 'affectionately exhorted those who came to Rome, as a father his children;' the Montanists of Phrygia come to Rome to gain the countenance of its bishop; Praxeas, from Africa, attempts the like, and for a while is successful; St. Victor, bishop of Rome, threatens to excommunicate the Asian churches; St. Irenæus speaks of Rome as 'the greatest Church, the most ancient, the most conspicuous, and founded and established by Peter and Paul,' appeals to its tradition, not in contrast indeed, but in preference to that of other churches, and declares that 'in this Church, every church, that is, the faithful from every side, must meet, or agree, together,—*propter potiorem principalitatem.*'* 'O Church, happy in its position,' says Tertullian, 'into which the Apostles poured out, together with their blood, their whole doctrine!' The presbyters of St. Dionysius, bishop of Alexandria, complain of his doctrines to St. Dionysius of Rome; the latter expostulates with him, and he explains. The emperor Aurelian leaves 'to the bishops of Italy and of Rome' the decision, whether or not Paul of Samosata shall be dispossessed of the see-house at Antioch; St. Cyprian speaks of Rome as 'the See of Peter and the principal Church, whence the unity of the priesthood took its rise, . . . whose faith has been commended by the Apostle, to whom faithlessness can have no access;" St. Stephen refuses to receive St. Cyprian's deputation, and separates himself from various churches of the East;† Fortunatus and Felix, deposed by St. Cyprian, have recourse to Rome; Basilides, deposed in Spain, betakes himself to Rome, and gains the ear of St. Stephen. Whatever objections may be

---

* "On account of its greater principality or headship." *Principalitas* is derived from *princeps*—a prince, a ruler.

† Or merely *threatened* to do so, as is more probable.

made to this or that particular fact, and I do not think any valid ones can be raised, still, on the whole, I consider that a cumulative argument rises from them in favor of the active and doctrinal authority of Rome."*

7. We are often told, that, in the two cases of Popes St. Victor and St. Stephen, referred to in the above quotation, large portions of the Church protested against their official acts as an usurpation ; and that, of course, those holy Pontiffs were not then viewed as holding the Primacy. But where is the evidence for this assertion, or for the inference drawn from it ? Is there one document in the history of those times which sustains either, or makes either even so much as probable ? Not one. Neither St. Irenæus, who expostulated with Pope St. Victor, and endeavored to dissuade him from excommunicating the Asiatic churches, nor St. Cyprian, who differed from St. Stephen on the subject of re-baptizing those who had been baptized by heretics, ever once thought of questioning the Primacy of those Pontiffs, or their *right* to excommunicate particular churches for obstinate non-conformity. It was only the *exercise* of the right that they deprecated.

And it is not a little remarkable, that in both these cases, the decisions of the Pontiffs were sustained by the whole Church : Easter was kept, even by the Asiatic churches, just as St. Victor had decided that it should be kept; and persons baptized by heretics were not re-baptized, as St. Stephen had determined in accordance with ancient tradition. Thus the whole Church of the second and third centuries practically sanctioned the principle that Rome held the spiritual Primacy. Two Roman Pontiffs of those centuries respectively boldly step forward, and by an alleged prerogative of their office, decide two important questions of discipline or doctrine ; there is at first some resistance to their decision,—not to their *claim*,—in certain churches of Asia and Africa; nothing daunted, they openly announce

---

* An "Essay on the Development of Christian Doctrine;" by John Henry Newman. Introduction, p. 17, 18.

their intention to cut off from the communion of the Church all the refractory; the opposition gives way and breaks down under the menace, and the whole Church, both in the east and in the west, comes forth to the rescue, unanimously rallies around the successors of St. Peter, and confirms their decisions! Does not all this look like a solemn recognition of the Primacy in the second and third centuries of the Church?

8. According to the generally received and well known discipline of the primitive Church, Christendom was divided into three great patriarchates, which ranked respectively as follows: Rome, the first; Alexandria, the second; and Antioch, the third. Rome was the first, because founded by St. Peter, and because therein was perpetuated the authority of St. Peter's Primacy; Alexandria was the second, chiefly because founded by St. Mark, the cherished disciple of St. Peter; Antioch was the third, mainly because it had been the See of St. Peter before his removal to Rome.* This was the order uniformly recognized and observed in the early Church, at least until near the close of the fourth century; and principally for the very reasons indicated. Every Church historian is well acquainted with these facts.

The Church of Constantinople had certainly no importance whatever, certainly no pre-eminence, during this whole period. It had been founded by no apostle nor immediate disciple of the Apostles; its bishops were dependent on the Archbishops of Heraclea.† Things continued in this state, until the second general council,‡ convened at Con-

---

* The patriarchate of Jerusalem, as we have already stated, (in Lecture VIII,) was of later origin.

† These and some of the preceding and following facts, have been already referred to in a note appended to the Eighth Lecture, giving an account of the origin of the Greek schism. But it is deemed expedient here to repeat them in a different connection, in order to make it easier for the reader to follow the line of illustration and argument here traced out.

‡ In itself it was merely a council of the Greek Church; but it is reckoned a general council, because its doctrinal decisions were confirmed by one held about the same time at Rome, under Pope Damasus.

stantinople in the year 381; when an attempt was made, under imperial influence, to disturb the existing order, by giving to the Constantinopolitan bishops the *second* place after those of Rome, on the ground that Constantinople was the "new Rome." *   The Roman Pontiffs and the western Church never approved of this attempted innovation; still less did they sanction the daring ambition which, in the council of Chalcedon,—or rather after its legitimate sessions had closed and the legates of the Roman See had departed, —enacted the famous canon that gave the see of Constantinople *equal* power with that of Rome. †   This decision of the Greek bishops was directly opposed to their own solemn declarations made during the legitimate sessions of the council, in which they had said: "Peter hath spoken by the voice of Leo;" and "We all see that, before all things, *the Primacy* and the principal honor should, *according to the canons*, be confirmed to the most beloved Archbishop of Rome."‡   These were the first indications of that towering ambition in the Constantinopolitan bishops, which finally severed the Unity of the Church, and brought incalculable evils in its train.

To say that the order of precedency above described resulted merely from the respective magnitude and importance of the various cities in which the principal sees were located, is to assume without proof what is directly opposed to all the facts and principles of Church History. That those cities were originally selected by the Apostles in consequence of their importance and favorable position, may be the fact; that they derived all their ecclesiastical importance from these circumstances of a merely temporal nature, and not from the high character of their respective founders, is nothing better than a mere assumption.

9. It might easily be shown, that the first eight general councils, though all held in the East, and composed chiefly

---

* See the third canon of this council, in Labbæi—Concilia, &c.

† Canon xxviii.

‡ Sessio vel Actio xvi.   Labbæi Concil.

of Greek bishops, distinctly recognized the Primacy of the
Roman See. I have just quoted the testimony of the great
council of Chalcedon, composed of about six hundred Greek
bishops. In the sixteenth session of this council, Paschasi-
mus, one of the legates of the Roman See, read the sixth
canon of the first general council of Nice with this introductory clause: "THE ROMAN SEE HAS ALWAYS HELD THE
PRIMACY."* The assembled prelates did not deny, but
rather sanctioned the genuineness of the quotation, nor did
they question its truth;—a conclusive evidence that they
recognized the Primacy of Rome, and an important circumstance, inasmuch as that clause has since disappeared
from the modern collections of the Nicene canons. That
it was a part of the sixth canon as currently received in
the fourth century, is still farther apparent from a decree
of the emperor Valentinian against St. Hilary of Arles, in
which distinct allusion is made to it, as a standing law
of the universal Church.†

With this introductory clause, the sixth canon of Nice is
manifestly in favor of the Roman Primacy. But even
without it, the canon plainly says nothing against the
principle; for it merely enacts that the see of Alexandria
shall have patriarchal or metropolitan rights over its
immediate dependencies, *similar* to those held by that of
Rome over the churches under its more immediate control.
This is certainly not opposed to the idea of a Primacy; for
it does not touch this question at all, even remotely.‡ The
primatial prerogatives of the Roman Pontiffs are entirely
distinct from their patriarchal and metropolitan rights;
though they all co-exist in the same incumbent of the
Roman See.

10. It has often been said by the enemies of the Primacy,

---

* Ἡ Ἐκκλησια Ρωμης Παντοτε Ειχε τα Πρωτεια. See Cabassutius, Notitia
Ecclesiastica, p. 108, seqq.

† See Cabassutius, *ibid.*, p. 111, Edit. Lugduni, 1702; in one volume,
folio.

‡ See Archbishop Kenrick on the Primacy, and Natalis Alexander, in a
special dissertation on the subject—Historia Ecclesiastica—Sæculum iv.

that the rights of the Roman See, as claimed and exercised
for many centuries past, rest almost entirely on the spurious Decretals circulated some time in the eighth century,
by an obscure individual, calling himself Isidore Mercator,
or Peccator.* This trite objection, like almost every thing
else that has been alleged against the Catholic Church, has
been already made and triumphantly refuted at least a
thousand times; and I am astonished at the confidence with
which it is constantly reproduced by every bold declaimer
against the Papacy. Is it to be believed that one obscure
and insignificant compiler of spurious canons could have
succeeded in completely revolutionizing the public sentiment of the Church in regard to the Primacy? That all
the bishops throughout the world would have submitted
tamely to essential innovations in Church government, on
authority so very slender?

It is, moreover, a notorious fact, that the Isidorian col
lection is mainly and almost entirely made up of extracts
from the fathers and from the decrees of councils belonging to the first five centuries of the Church. Does the
mere error of criticism, consisting in falsely ascribing many
of those ancient documents to the Popes of the first three
centuries, really affect their substance, or destroy their
weight as evidence of the faith and practice of the early
Church on this subject?

Again, can it be shown that the spurious Decretals gave
to the Roman Pontiffs a single prerogative or right which
the latter had not claimed and *exercised* for centuries before
they made their appearance? The history of the first centuries had afforded many precedents of those very rights
which are said to have been introduced for the first time;
such as: "the judgments of all bishops, the holding of all
councils, and a right to hear appeals from all ecclesiastical
judgments."† The annals of Church History clearly prove,
that the earlier Roman Pontiffs had often actually exercised

---

* So very obscure that his real name is not known with certainty.

† These are the three alleged heads of innovation, as given by the Rev.
Dr. Palmer in his "Compendious Ecclesiastical History;" p. 103, 104,
American Edition, with notes by Bishop Whittingham.

all these prerogatives. Is it not a well known fact, for instance, that Popes Liberius, Julius I., and Innocent I. actually received and acted upon appeals made to them, from the judgments of eastern bishops, by St. Athanasius and St. John Chrysostom, patriarchs respectively of Alexandria and Constantinople? About the middle of the fourth century, Pope Julius wrote to the Arian bishops who had condemned St. Athanasius, in these emphatic terms: "Were you ignorant, that *it was customary* that we should be written to *first, that hence the first decision might issue?*" And the Greek Church historian, Sozomenes, says, speaking of this letter of the Pontiff: "There was a SACERDOTAL LAW, that those things should be held *null and void*, which were done *against or without the sanction of the Roman Bishop.*"*

Moreover, the legates of the Roman See successfully insisted in the great council of Chalcedon, held in 451, that Dioscorus, patriarch of Alexandria, should be excluded from its deliberations, "Because he had *presumed and dared* to celebrate a general synod without the authority of the apostolic see, WHICH NEVER HAD BEEN ALLOWED, NEVER HAD BEEN DONE?"† Finally, the council of Sardica, held in the year 347, under Pope Julius I., expressly enacted that appeals should be made to Rome in all difficult matters regarding bishops.‡ All these undoubted facts of early Church History, and many more of the same kind which I am compelled to omit, clearly prove to the satisfaction of every impartial mind, that the Isidorian Decretals really effected no innovation whatever in Church government, so far at least as the substantial rights of the Primacy are concerned.

11. Were I not afraid, My Dear Brethren, of trespassing too long upon your time, and of presuming too much upon

---

* Histor. Ecclesiast. Lib. III. c. x.

† Quia præsumpsit et ausus est synodum generalem facere sine auctoritate Sedis Apostolicæ, QUOD NUNQUAM LICUIT, NUNQUAM FACTUM EST. Concil. Chalced. Act. I. Labbæi, etc.

‡ See the third and fourth canons of this council, apud Labbæi Concil. It was held in great reverence by the ancient Church, and was viewed as a sort of appendix to the general council of Nice.

Y

your patience, I might bring forward many other strong and conclusive testimonies from Christian antiquity in favor of the Roman Primacy. A volume might be written composed entirely of such evidence, selected from the works of eminent writers who flourished in all the successive ages of the Church, from the death of the last Apostle down to the present time. This chain of testimony unites us to the ancient Church almost as strongly as does the chain of succession in the Roman See itself. I must content myself with four or five additional testimonies of the ancient fathers, selected almost at random from an immense mass of evidence of the same kind. Hear what St. Cyril, patriarch of Alexandria, in the fifth century, says on this subject, writing against the Nestorians:

"That this is so, I will produce, as an ample witness, the most holy Cælestine, THE ARCHBISHOP OF ALL THE WORLD, and the father and patriarch of the great Rome, who himself thrice exhorted you by letters to desist from that mad blasphemy, and you obeyed him not. . . . . . . All, *by divine right*, bow the head to Peter, and the princes of the world obey him, as they would the Lord Jesus. We also, who are members, ought to adhere TO OUR HEAD, THE ROMAN PONTIFF AND APOSTOLIC SEE." *

Let us hear another Greek father and patriarch of the same age,—Juvenal of Jerusalem,—discoursing in the general council of Ephesus, held in the year 431, against the Nestorian heresy : †

"It was the duty of John, the most reverend bishop of Antioch, considering this holy, great, and general synod, to come without delay, and clear himself of those things which are laid to his charge, before the Apostolic See of Rome, which is with us here; and to show obedience, and to do honor to the Apostolic Holy Roman Church of God, by which the church of Antioch must be directed and judged, AS CUSTOM, DERIVED FROM THE APOSTOLIC RULE AND TRADITION, PARTICULARLY REQUIRES."

---

* In Encom. in S. Mariam—Opp. Tom. V. Pars V. § 11.　　† Actio iv.

These splendid testimonies of the eastern, or Greek Church, are re-echoed in language equally strong by the fathers of the West. Hear St. Optatus of Milevi, in his reasoning against the schismatical Donatists of Africa, in the fourth century:

" *You cannot deny*, that St. Peter, the chief of the Apostles, established an episcopal Chair at Rome: this Chair was one, that all others might preserve Unity by the union they had with it; so that whosoever sets up a chair against it, should be a schismatic and an offender. It was then in this one Chair, WHICH IS THE FIRST MARK OF THE CHURCH, that St. Peter first sat; to St. Peter succeeded Linus, and after him others till Damasus, who is now our colleague: by whose means all the churches of the world are united with us in the same communion, keeping correspondence by circular letters."*

Again, mark the language in which another Latin father, the great and learned St. Jerome, addresses this same Pope Damasus, the contemporary and colleague of St. Optatus; —the passage occurs in a letter written to the Pontiff from the deserts of Syria:

"I am following no other than Christ, united to the communion of your holiness, that is, TO THE CHAIR OF PETER. I know that the Church is founded upon THIS ROCK. Whosoever eateth the Lamb out of this House is a profane man. Whosoever is not in the Ark shall perish by the flood. But forasmuch as being retired into the desert of Syria, I cannot receive the sacrament at your hands, I follow your colleagues, the bishops of Egypt. I know not Vitalis; I do not communicate with Meletius; Paulinus is a stranger to me: HE THAT GATHERETH NOT WITH YOU, SCATTERETH."†

Finally, listen to St. Augustine, the great luminary of the Church in the fifth century; and mark the emphatic language he employs to express his sense of the importance to be attached to the doctrinal decisions of Rome in matters

---

* De Schismate Donatist. Lib. II.
† Epist. xiv. ad Damasum. Opp. Tom. iv.

of controversy. The two African councils, whose decisions,
he says, had been sent to Rome to be confirmed by Pope
Innocent I., were those of Milevi and Carthage, both held
against the Pelagian heresy, in the year 416.

"The decisions of the two councils having been already
sent to the Apostolic See, the rescripts have come thence.
THE CAUSE IS NOW FINISHED;—would to God that the error
may also have an end!"*

12. You would almost imagine, My Dear Brethren, that
you were listening to eulogies of the Papacy, delivered in
earnest and impassioned language, by some modern Roman
Catholic; while really you have been hearing the words of
the greatest men and brightest ornaments of the Christian
Church in the fourth and fifth centuries. The voice which
you have heard so loudly proclaiming the Roman Primacy
comes to you, not from Rome itself, nor even from Italy,
but from Alexandria, from Jerusalem, from Africa, from the
burning deserts of Syria. It comes precisely from these
remote parts of the world, where one would naturally
suppose that the Papacy was least known and had least
influence.

If the time permitted, I might very easily extend this
testimony; and I might exhibit to you Spain and Gaul, and
the most distant parts of the west, uniting with Africa in
the South and Asia in the East, in bearing evidence to
the Roman Primacy, and in re-echoing throughout the
Christian world the splendid eulogy which St. Paul had
pronounced on the faith of the Romans. This faith has
ever been that of the great body of Christendom; it has
always "been spoken of in the whole world," from the days
of St. Paul down to the present time. The breath of heresy
has never tainted its purity. Christ himself had uttered
the solemn promise: "THOU ART PETER, AND UPON THIS
ROCK I WILL BUILD MY CHURCH, AND THE GATES OF HELL
SHALL NOT PREVAIL AGAINST IT." All Church History is a

---

* Causa finita est;—utinam finiatur error! Sermo ii.—alias cxxxi.—
No. 10. Tom. x. p. 95. Edit. Paris—1586.

faithful commentary on this emphatic and divine declaration and prophecy; and if there were nothing else to prove the divinity of Catholic Christianity, besides the marked fulfillment of this promise, in the wonderful preservation of St. Peter's See through all the changes and revolutions of time, this striking and undeniable fact alone would almost suffice to establish it beyond a doubt.

You will tell me that the Roman Primacy has been called in question and opposed in all ages of the Church. I know and admit the fact. But by whom? By errorists, schismatics, and separatists, of every varying shade of opinion; —never by the great body of Christians. The thousand and one discordant heresies which have at various times troubled the peace of the Church, from the first dawn of Christianity down to the present day, have all risen up unanimously against the Primacy, and have moved heaven and earth to compass its destruction. From Simon Magus down to Alexander Campbell, all of them have hated St. Peter and his successors with an undying hatred. But as St. Peter quelled the pride and defeated the wicked impostures of Simon Magus, * so have his successors, with the divine blessing and aid, also fully succeeded in defeating the mischievous devices of all subsequent heresiarchs. Nearly all of these have long since descended to the tomb, and along with them most of the crude and heterogeneous systems of which they were the authors. The Papacy has stood, and it still remains; not in a state of weakness, or decay, but clothed in all its pristine vigor, and blooming with all the freshness of eternal youth! It has survived all its most bitter enemies in the past; with the blessing of God, it will also outlive those who have risen up against it

---

* The account given by Eusebius of the manner in which St. Peter, "that powerful and great apostle, who by his courage took the lead of all the rest, was conducted to Rome against this pest of mankind," and of his brilliant success in undeceiving those who had previously erected a statue at Rome in honor of the magician, is very interesting, and well worthy of perusal. See Book II., chapters xiii. and xiv. American Translation, pp. 62, 63, 64.

32

in the present age. If it could have been put down, the
powerful and combined hosts who, in past ages, successively marshalled their strength against it, would certainly
have effected its overthrow. If all their joint efforts proved
abortive; if they but destroyed themselves by dashing
against that ROCK upon which Christ built His Church,
instead of succeeding in removing it from its place or in
breaking it into pieces; then must we conclude, that this
ROCK is firm, immovable, indestructible even as Christ foretold. History has no voice and it conveys no lesson, if it
does not teach this plain truth.

Would to God, My Beloved Brethren, that all would at
length learn and profit by this impressive teaching of
Church History! Would to God, that some modern Christians, instead of wasting their valuable time and throwing
away their otherwise commendable zeal and energy, in the
vain and fruitless attempt to destroy the Papacy, would
unite with the great body of Christians of all ages and
nations in sustaining it, and in hearing its voice! Would
to God, that, instead of heeding the discordant clamor of
the ancient heretics against the Roman Primacy, they
would but listen to the reverent language of all the true
children of the Church, scattered over the ages of the past!
Then would all religious discord and heart-burning cease
for ever, and union and love, the distinctive virtues of Christianity, would again reign on the earth. Christians would
not then be severed from Christians; but all would unite in
the one faith, all would kneel at the one altar, all would
pour out their souls in the one solemn worship, and all
would rally around the one Chair of Peter! This is the
great center of unity, the great conservative element of
Christianity. With it, all is unity and harmony; without
it, all is confusion and anarchy. The religious history of
past ages, and the universal experience of all Christendom,
have fully attested this great truth.

But how acknowledge an authority which has been so
fearfully abused in times past; which has been so often
marked by towering ambition and the usurpation of tem-

poral power; which has been ever uncompromising, relentless, and tyrannical in its course and policy; and which
has been, moreover, so often stained with the blood of its
opponents! How bend to a Primacy which condemns all
who oppose its teachings; which has never changed its
principles; and which even professes that it will not and
cannot change them! This is a hard saying; and who can
hear it!

Alas! My Brethren, all this is little better than idle
clamor and prejudice; a mere appeal to worldly interests
and passions, against an authority divinely established and
clearly recognized by the vast majority of Christians for
eighteen centuries. Most of these accusations against the
Papacy are either wholly unfounded in point of fact, or are
greatly exaggerated by prejudice; while those of them
which are true, instead of furnishing an argument against
the divine origin and character of the Papacy, present one
strongly in its favor.

To begin with the charges last referred to;—is not the
unchanging and unyielding course of the Papacy, and its
uncompromising hostility to all heresies and innovations,
whether in ancient or in modern times, one very striking
evidence of its consistency, and of the truth upon which it
is firmly based? Is it not the essential character of truth
to be unchangeable, and ever the same in all succeeding
ages? Does truth,—can it,—ever compound with error?
Does it ever flatter those whom it believes to be in the
wrong? Is it carried about "by every wind of doctrine?"
Does it trim its sails to every popular breeze? Does it
heed the voice of clamor and opposition? Does it shift its
principles to suit the times? Did Christ, the eternal Truth,
act upon this time-serving policy? Did He not always,
on the contrary, bear testimony against error in all its
forms; and was He not nailed to the cross for His uncompromising advocacy of the truth? And is not this very
feature in His life one of the most striking evidences of
His divinity? If so, why should not a precisely similar
quality in the Papacy be as convincing an argument in

favor of its divine institution and character? Is it not, in one word, the most glorious trait in the Papacy, that it has, in all ages, constantly and unflinchingly borne evidence against all new errors opposed to the old truths of which it was the divinely appointed guardian?

But the Papacy has persecuted, and it would still persecute, if it had the power.—It now has the power, to a greater or less extent, in Italy, in France, in Austria, in Bavaria, in Hungary, in Bohemia, in Belgium, in Spain, in Portugal, and in many other places; yet it does not persecute religious dissenters in any of these countries. How, then, insist on the assertion, that it would still persecute, if it had the power to do so? Is it fair to charge upon the Papacy religious persecutions that grew out of an order of things which has long since ceased to exist, and for which it was never fairly accountable? Does the Catholic Religion, of which the Papacy is the visible head, contain any principle of faith which leads to religious persecution? It does not; as has been often and clearly proved by many of our standard writers.*

But are the Protestant sects themselves free from the reproach of persecution? Have they not persecuted, not only Catholics, but even their own brethren, almost whenever and wherever they have had the power to do so? Is not this strikingly true particularly of one or two leading sects in our own country, which have ever been the loudest in their denunciations of the Papacy? If so,—and it *is* so,—let them first wipe off the stain from their own skirts, before they point it out on those of the Papacy; let them "cast the beam out of their own eye," before they begin to clamor about "the mote in the eye of their neighbors!" Protestantism, in its brief and fitful career, has shed at least as much blood in the hallowed name of Religion, as

---

* Among others, see Milner's "Letters to a Prebendary;"— Letter V.,— in which this subject is treated at length. See also the "Oral Discussion" between the Rev. John Hughes (now Archbishop Hughes, of New York) and the Rev. John Breckinridge. Question I.

have those professing the faith of the Catholic Church
during its long and eventful history of eighteen centuries!
We may, then, fairly balance the account; and we ought,
as Christians, to dismiss the odious subject of persecution
altogether and for ever. Thank God! better days have
dawned upon us. A more moderate spirit has gone forth
over the Christian world.* Persecution for conscience' sake
has, to a great extent, ceased. It has gone down to the
tomb;—there let it remain.

But the Papacy invested itself with temporal power;
and, in the middle ages, it claimed the right to depose
princes and to absolve their subjects from the oath of allegiance.—Be it so; what then? Was this accession of temporal power ever viewed as an *essential* prerogative of the
Papacy? Or was it not considered merely as an *accidental*
appendage; the creature of peculiar circumstances? Are
there any examples of such alleged usurpations during the
first ten centuries of its history?. Has this power been
exercised, or even claimed, by the Roman Pontiffs, for the
last three centuries?† If these two facts are undoubted,—
as they certainly are,—then how maintain that a belief in
the Papacy involves a recognition of its temporal power?
The latter was certainly never a *doctrine* of the Catholic
Church. If it was, where is the proof; where the Church
definition that made it a doctrine? Five leading Catholic
universities, when officially called on by Mr. Pitt, prime
minister of Great Britain, solemnly and unanimously dis-
claimed this opinion, and maintained the contrary.‡ Did

---

* No thanks are, however, due to Protestantism for this change; for
it can be *proved* that Protestants continued to persecute much longer than
Catholics.

† I believe that the last instance of the kind on record is that of Pope
Sixtus V., in the time of Queen Elizabeth. But the English Catholics
did not pay any attention to the claims set up by this Pontiff. They
fought as bravely and as cheerfully against the Spaniards as did the
English Protestants themselves. This occurred nearly three hundred
years ago.

‡ The universities of the Sorbonne, Louvaine, Doway, Alcala, and Sala-
manca. The appeal to them was made by Mr. Pitt in 1788, at the time

the Catholic Church, did the Popes ever rebuke them for
the disclaimer? Do not Catholics all over the world now
almost unanimously disclaim it; and are they the less
Catholic for this? I fearlessly assert,—and I do it ad-
visedly,—that there are very few Catholics at the present
day who do not reject this opinion; that there are still
fewer who maintain it; and that it is not defended, at least
publicly, even in Rome itself! Such being clearly the case,
is not all this clamor about the temporal power of the
Popes a mere stale device,—a conjuring up of a phantom
in the past, for the purpose of frightening persons of weak
nerves into a hatred of the Papacy?

Besides, were the Popes fairly responsible for the exercise of a power, which was really thrust upon them by the
imperative circumstances of the middle ages? When all
society was in a state of transition and chaos; when civil
and social rights were vague and undefined; when *might*
and *right* were almost synonymous terms; when the strong
oppressed the weak, and the weak had no means of casting
off the heavy yoke which bowed them down to the dust;
when the fierce Moloch of feudalism, ever rapacious and
blood-thirsty, was daily demanding new victims; when a
wasting border warfare was spreading desolation over all
Europe:—when things were in this dreadful state, who
can blame the Roman Pontiffs for having rushed to the
rescue of bleeding humanity? Were they to remain calm
and unconcerned spectators of such accumulated horrors,
when they, and they alone, had the remedy in their own
hands? Would they have been held blameless by posterity,
if they had not, under such circumstances, struck at least
one blow for oppressed liberty, and one blow against
tyranny enthroned in high places? Theirs was the only
power then universally recognized and respected; theirs
was the only voice which could be heard amidst the din

---

the Catholic question was agitating Great Britain. See the answers of
the universities in Butler's "Book of the Roman Catholic Church, ' Appendix, p. 287–8. Edit. Baltimore, 1834.

of arms, and the uproar and confusion of society;—should
that power lie dormant, and that voice remain silent?

They were appealed to by princes arrayed against each
other, and by the people oppressed by their princes. They
were universally recognized as the fathers of Christendom;
their powerful influence was invoked on all sides; they
were called on to act as mediators and pacificators in almost
every great and difficult social emergency;—did they do
wrong to hearken to the strong appeal thus made on all
sides for their powerful interposition to shield the weak
against the strong, to protect suffering virtue against despotic vice? Did they do wrong in resisting powerful tyrants, and in telling the oppressed people that they were
free to cast off the odious yoke of an intolerable despotism?
If they did, then were our forefathers also wrong in declaring us *absolved* from the oath of allegiance to the king
of Great Britain! In both cases, the principle contended
for was precisely the same.

Or did the Popes of the middle ages act improperly in
prohibiting divorces, and in thereby protecting the rights
of feeble and unprotected woman? Did they do wrong in
boldly rebuking powerful kings and emperors for their
avarice and brutality? What other authority could have
opposed an effectual barrier to the exactions and lusts
of the latter? But they undertook to depose some refractory princes. I wish from my heart that they had
deposed many more of them than they actually did; it
would have been all the better for humanity, and for
LIBERTY! The general voice of Christian Europe, which
had been indebted to them mainly for all its social improve-
ments, then gave them the power to do so; and they did
well to exercise this prerogative, so long as popular consent would continue to vest it in their hands, and to bestow
upon them a sort of universal protectorate over Christian
society. No one at all acquainted with the peculiar history
of the middle ages, unless he be a secret lover of tyranny,
can have any other sentiment or wish than this.

But, you will farther object, even the spiritual autho-

rity of the Papacy, held by all Roman Catholics as a
doctrine of faith, is boundless in its extent, and therefore
absolute and tyrannical in its very nature: the Catholic
theory of Church government making the Church one vast
irresponsible monarchy, to whose decisions all must bow.
Here is another grievous misapprehension and exaggeration; another unworthy appeal to popular prejudice and
passion against the Papacy. The spiritual power of the
Popes is, indeed, ample enough to meet every emergency;
it is large and stringent enough to secure unity of faith and
obedience among all Christians: it was instituted for this
very purpose. Christ made no exception or limitation
whatever, when he gave to St. Peter the charge of feeding
and governing His entire flock; He certainly made none,
when He said to him: "And to thee I will give the keys
of the kingdom of heaven; and *whatsoever* thou shalt bind
upon earth, it shall be bound also in heaven; and *whatsoever* thou shalt loose upon earth, it shall be loosed also in
heaven."

Still, this spiritual power is not boundless in the sense
of the objection; it is bounded by its very nature and the
objects for which it was established; it cannot travel out
of its appropriate sphere of spiritual and religious matters;
it is powerful within this sphere, outside of its province it
is powerless. Its exercise is also variously restrained by
precedent, by tradition, by the acts of councils, by the well
known and generally received principles of the Church.
Never was there a power more tenacious of precedent,
more cautious in its official acts, more strongly opposed to
all innovation, more slow to decide on weighty questions.
Even its most relentless enemies have freely awarded it
this praise. The slowness and cautious wisdom of the
Roman court are proverbial the world over.

But this doctrine makes the Church a monarchy, and it is
therefore opposed to republican principles.—This is another
sophism, and another appeal to mere popular prejudice.
If the government of the Church is a species of spiritual
monarchy, we should bear in mind that it was so con-

stituted by Christ himself, who alone is responsible for its
organization. And we are even simple enough to believe,
that Christ knew what form of government was best calculated to secure the important objects which He had in
view in founding His Church. If He thought proper to
appoint ONE to govern and control the whole body of His
Church, we are not disposed to find fault with Him for so
doing; but, on the contrary, we rather admire and applaud
His divine wisdom. Surely, a mere democracy, especially
one without some head or chief executive to restrain and
control its action, would have been very ill-suited to a
Church which was to embrace all nations, and to exist in
all time. Never has the world witnessed such a system
of government; it could not subsist for one year, even in
a most circumscribed territory. Strike out the office of
our own chief executive, and what would become of our
cherished republic? And yet this is precisely the system
of Church government which seems best to please the
fancies of our adversaries! They hold that the Church is
a radical democracy; in which every one is to think and
do as he pleases, without being restrained by any one
visible head!

The truth is, the Church of Christ is totally different,
both in its nature and in its objects, from every other organized society on earth; and therefore it is fair to infer
that it should have a form of government different from
any other established for merely human purposes. It
should have a government that would not clash with any
other, but be compatible with all,—with monarchies, with
aristocracies, with democracies; as well as with those in
which these three elements are found blended together in
equal or unequal proportions. A Christian might be a good
citizen of every civil government, and yet not cease for all
that to be a good Christian. The wisdom of Christ seemed
to require this characteristic, in the form of Church government established by Himself for all times and for all places.

Accordingly, we find that this is precisely the case. The
Catholic form of Church government has elements in com-

mon with almost all systems of civil polity: in its general
complexion, however, it is totally different from them all;
while its ends are immeasurably above those contemplated
by any of them.   It is an elective monarchy, with some elements of aristocracy and democracy.   The humblest subject
of the Church is eligible to the highest offices within its
gift; many of the Roman Pontiffs, as well as a very great
number of the cardinals and bishops,—its spiritual aristocracy,—have been and are still often selected from the
lowest walks of life.

Almost every thing is done in the Catholic Church
through deliberative assemblies, either local or general;
and the Church presents the oldest as well as the best
models for such assemblies.   The Pope himself has his regular counsellors, by whose opinions he is mainly governed
in the exercise of the Primacy.   All the business of the
Roman court is transacted in such deliberative bodies, composed of *congregations*, or standing committees of cardinals.
Here every question is fully discussed and settled only after
the most mature examination; after which it is referred to
the Pontiff for his final decision on its merits.   Who then
will say that our Church government is merely an absolute
and unlimited monarchy?   Is it not wholly absurd and
puerile to cry out against the danger to popular institutions
from a government thus essentially *spiritual* in its whole
character and in all its acts, and checked and controlled,
at every step of its exercise, by so many wise safeguards?

That Catholics can be good citizens of every civil government on earth, is proved from the fact, that there is nothing
in their whole theory or practice of Church government
opposed to that of any other; and from the other well
known fact, that they have been good citizens of every
government under which they have lived,—and they have
lived under all kinds of government which have ever existed.   It is one strange evidence of the perversity and
blindness of popular prejudice in our regard, that, whereas,
in England and in Europe, Catholics have been often
held up to public odium as the enemies of monarchy, in

this country, they are represented as the secret enemies of republicanism! And this, too, in the face of the notorious fact, that they were certainly the first who gave to the breeze the banner of universal freedom, both civil and religious, in North America.*

When will this unworthy and unchristian mode of warfare against our Church be discontinued? When will Christians who love Christ, and cherish His holy institutions, cease to employ the mere arms of the flesh against His holy Church? If the Catholic Church be not the Church of Christ; if the Papacy be not of divine institution, our opponents should surely be able to establish the fact without seeking to arouse popular prejudice, and without pandering to mere human passions. Truth never was promoted by such means; these are the usual weapons of error. Christ, too, was accused of being an enemy to Cæsar, and a sower of sedition among the people: and He was nailed to the cross under the influence of a popular excitement lashed into fury by precisely such calumnies as these. And we may surely be content to walk in His footsteps, and to share in His opprobrium in this as in other respects!

All the popular objections against the Papacy, which I have thus far endeavored very briefly and summarily to answer, are, My Beloved Brethren, really beside the great question at issue between us and our separated friends. That question is,—not whether the Papacy may be or has been abused,—but whether it be itself of divine institution? The best things may be occasionally abused; and it is obviously not fair to argue from the abuse to the thing itself. Such a mode of reasoning would disprove the Bible, the Christian Religion,—every thing that is great and good; for what is there that corrupt man will not, or may not abuse!

The real question, then, is simply one of fact; and its solution, as I have already said, depends upon the decision of three other questions, involving likewise plain matters

* See Bancroft's History of the United States, vol. i., Maryland; and other writers on American history, *passim.*

of fact: 1. Did Christ establish a Primacy? 2. Did He wish it to continue in His Church to the end of time? 3. Has the Roman Catholic Church, and it alone, this divinely constituted and perpetually preserved Primacy?

In this and the previous Lecture, I have labored, and I hope not wholly without success, to answer all these questions, by proving the three affirmative propositions which they involve. The conclusion is inevitable:—that the Roman Catholic Church alone is the true Church;—because it alone has or even claims to have an essential principle and element of government, impressed upon the Church by Christ himself, and intended by Him to be perpetual therein.

THIS IS THE NINTH EVIDENCE OF CATHOLICITY.

From what has been said in this and the foregoing Lectures, in regard to the nature, objects, and qualities of the Church, we may now be prepared for, a fuller and more adequate definition of it than that which was given in the second Lecture of this course. The Church may then be defined:

A VISIBLE SOCIETY OF MEN, BOUND TOGETHER BY THE PROFESSION OF THE SAME CHRISTIAN FAITH, A COMMUNION IN THE SAME SACRAMENTS AND WORSHIP, AND A SUBJECTION TO THE SAME BODY OF LAWFUL PASTORS, ESPECIALLY TO THE ROMAN PONTIFF, THE SUCCESSOR OF ST. PETER IN THE PRIMACY.*

May God, who made the light shine forth out of darkness, vouchsafe to us the guidance of His Holy Spirit, that we may be enabled to lay aside all undue prejudice, and may all meet together and live harmoniously in this great family of Christians, by reverently hearing and humbly obeying the voice of that first pastor, to whose charge His divine Son committed the entire flock; through Christ our Lord! Amen.

---

* This definition is that of Liebermann, with some slight modifications. Institutiones Theologicæ—Tom. ii: p. 196. Brixiæ, 1881.

LECTURE XIII.

SIX OTHER EVIDENCES.

Recapitulation—Other evidences—Whence did Protestants derive the
Bible?—A special providence to account for its preservation, akin to
the tenet of Infallibility—Furnishing a satisfactory account of the
Bible—Settling its canon—And proving its inspiration—The Religion of the Bible—What interpretation of it is consistent and uniform?—Who accepts *all* its doctrines?—And in their plain and natural
sense?—Extreme unction—Which interpretation is more conformable
to the genius of Christianity—Doctrinal mysteries—Things hard to
flesh and blood—Immutability of doctrine—Losing England—Chinese
Rites—Union of all the sects against Catholicity—Its source and principles—Estimated by analogy and by Scriptural principles—Leading
features of the anti-Catholic crusade in this country—An honorable
exception—The Protestant ministry a lucrative profession—The fifteenth
and last Evidence of Catholicity.

*" Dearly beloved, believe not every spirit ; but try the spirits whether they be
of God: because many false prophets are gone out into the world. . . . They are
of the world ; therefore of the world they speak, and the world heareth them.
We are of God. He that knoweth God, heareth us ; he that is not of God
heareth us not:* BY THIS WE KNOW THE SPIRIT OF TRUTH, AND THE SPIRIT
OF ERROR."—I ST. JOHN, iv: 1, 5, 6.

In the preceding Lectures, My Beloved Brethren, I endeavored briefly to develop some of the general evidences
of Catholicity. And those of you who have favored me
with your attention throughout the course, will, I trust,
have come to the conclusion, that the Roman Catholic
Church can present at least very strong claims to be the
identical Church which Christ established, and against
which He solemnly promised that the gates of hell should
not prevail. In the present Lecture I intend to submit
to your consideration some other arguments, which will go
far to establish the same position. Most of these are,
indeed, more or less directly contained in the general
evidences already presented, or they may be inferred from

them; still, they are deemed of sufficient importance to merit a separate consideration. I entreat you, to weigh them with serious attention, in the presence of that God who is to judge us all, knowing the all-important interests involved in the conclusion to be reached. I exhort you, in the words of the inspired Apostle, to "prove all things, and to hold that which is good."*

I. The first of these additional evidences may be stated as follows:

The Roman Catholic Church alone has preserved the Bible; she alone can give a consistent and satisfactory account of it; she alone could settle its canon; she alone can prove its inspiration;

Therefore, the Catholic Church has the most valid claim to be considered the true Church of Christ.

The conclusion is inevitable, if the facts from which it is derived can be established; and that they can be proved, will appear from the following very plain considerations.

1. The Catholic Church alone has preserved the Bible.

The children of the reformation have always prided themselves on their love for the Bible. The Bible! the Bible alone! has been ever their motto and watchword. They profess to have restored the Christian Religion to its primitive purity and simplicity, by bringing it back to the true Bible standard. Their great war-cry against the Catholic Church has constantly been, that she is the sworn enemy of the Bible, that she keeps it from the people, because she feels that it testifies against her doctrines and her worship. Now the question naturally arises: whence did Protestants receive that very Bible about which they make so much noise? This question must be answered, not by mere declamation, but by plain and satisfactory historical facts, before they can make good their position,— that they are the peculiar friends, and that the Catholic Church is, and has ever been, the special enemy of the Bible.

Whence, then, I ask emphatically, did Luther, Calvin,

_____
*I Thess. v: 21.

and the other founders of Protestantism, obtain the Bible? Was an angel sent down from Heaven to place it in their hands? They advanced no such claim. Did they receive it immediately from the hands of Christ and His Apostles? But they came into the world full fifteen hundred years too late for this. From the Greek church?—But this is plainly opposed to the facts of the case, for the Greek church lay fully a thousand miles away from the first theater of the reformation; and the early reformers had no communion with it whatsoever. Besides, as I have elsewhere said, the Greek church still continues to agree with the Roman Catholic on almost every point in which Protestants differ from the latter. In regard to the Bible, particularly, the Greeks have always received it and held it precisely as the Catholic Church, including those books which Protestants have been pleased to call *apocryphal.* When the German Protestants, about fifty years after the origin of the reformation, attempted to enter into communion with the Greek church, the latter rejected their overtures with pious indignation and horror, and reprobated their distinctive doctrines more strongly even than they had been condemned at the council of Trent. * There-

---

* All the efforts of the early Protestants to win over the Greek church to their party proved utterly fruitless. Melancthon's letter to the patriarch of Constantinople, enclosing the confession of Augsburg, was treated with silent neglect or contempt. The success of the Protestant theologians of Tubingen with Jeremias the Constantinopolitan patriarch was no better. He openly declined all communion with them, and cut short the correspondence, by begging them not to write to him any more on the subject. This took place between the years 1576 and 1581. (See Mosheim, Hist. Eccles. Sæc. xvi. sect. iii. p. 1, c. 2.) The Calvinists succeeded, by bribery and intrigue, in intruding a certain Cyril Lucaris into the see of Constantinople, in the year 1621; but he was soon hurled from it with indignation by the Greek bishops; and this ambitious partisan of Calvinism was, at their instance, put to death by order of the Turkish emperor, in the year 1636. The confession of faith previously drawn up by him, which savored strongly of Calvinism, was condemned, in the most stringent terms, by Greek councils held at Constantinople under the subsequent patriarchs, Cyril and Parthenius, and also by a council held

fore, Protestants cannot truly or consistently claim to have
received the Bible, or, in fact, any thing else, from the
Greek church.

The question, then, returns in all its force: Whence did
the reformers obtain their Bible? Plainly and obviously
from the Roman Catholic Church, from which they separated; from that Church, against which they protested
with so much energy as the great apostasy and the mystic
Babylon of the Apocalypse! From that Church, which
they blindly accused of having corrupted the Word of God,
of having been sullied with superstition and idolatry, of
having been stained with the blood of God's saints, of
having ever been the sworn enemy of the Bible itself!

This Church had faithfully kept the Bible for fifteen centuries before Protestantism was heard of; she had labori-
ously transcribed it thousands of times before the invention
of the art of printing; she had translated it into different
languages, had watched over its safety, had guarded it with
parental solicitude, amidst storm and revolution, amidst fire
and flood, amidst change and persecution; she had pressed
it to her bosom as a treasure of priceless value; her children
had repeatedly shed their blood rather than surrender it,
or expose it to the least danger of profanation. * And
yet is she constantly held up as the enemy of the Bible!
Protestants received it from her hands, and then fiercely
assailed her as its greatest enemy ! ! They received it from
her, and then openly charged her with having basely and

---

at Jerusalem in 1672, under the patriarch Dositheus. These facts are all
known to every reader of ecclesiastical history; and they will not be denied. They prove conclusively that what is above stated in the text is
strictly true, and that there never has existed any sympathy between the
Greek schismatics and the Protestant sects.

* Under the fiery ten years' persecution of Diocletian and his three
bloody colleagues, hundreds of Christians willingly laid down their lives
rather than give up the sacred books. So also, during the northern invasions, and the revolutions of the middle ages, the first thing always
thought of by the monks, who were then the principal transcribers of the
Bible, was to transport the sacred volume to the mountains or to some
other place of safety, at the first approaches of danger.

impiously corrupted the Religion which it teaches! They quietly and willingly received the very foundation, and what they viewed as the *only* foundation of their faith, on her sole authority; and then they discarded her authority as to the superstructure of faith built up thereon! The Catholic Church had corrupted every thing else in Christianity,—doctrines, morals, sacraments, worship,—she had not laid violent hands on the Bible, but had preserved it, and handed it down to them in all its integrity! She might, indeed, have easily corrupted the sacred text, and, according to the Protestant view of the subject, she had every motive to do so, in order to make it sustain her doctrines. Yet she did not even attempt any thing of the kind, during the long centuries that she was its sole guardian, and had exclusive control over its destinies.

But you will say, God watched specially over the integrity of the Bible, while He permitted the Church to corrupt every thing else, and to go herself to utter ruin. How sustain this paradoxical assertion? Is it not plainly a mere assumption? Does the Bible itself, your *only* rule of faith, contain any divine promise to this effect? If it does, produce at once the testimony; but this you certainly cannot do, for the obvious reason that no such promise is recorded in the Bible. If it does not, then are you bound at once to give up the assertion, as wholly unsupported by your only rule of faith.

What! God, through an interposition of His special providence, would guard the integrity of the Bible, of itself a mere dead letter; and, at the same time, He would permit His Church, its authorized and *living* expounder, and the teacher of the nations appointed by Himself, to go astray, and to mislead the world for centuries! He would work a miracle to preserve the Bible, which He had never specially pledged Himself to preserve; and yet He would do nothing to redeem His reiterated, positive, and solemn promises to preserve the Church!* The Bible, when rightly.

---

* See these promises in the Lecture on Infallibility, Lecture IX.

33 *

understood, is infallible, and to guard its infallibility by
preserving it in its pristine integrity, God works a special
miracle of His providence; while the Church,—"the house
of the living God, the pillar and ground of the truth,"—is
quietly allowed by this same providence to become corrupt
to its very center, and to be, for many centuries, "the pillar
and ground" of *error*, and of every abomination! The Bible
to which not one in ten thousand could possibly have access
during the first fourteen centuries of the Christian era,* was
miraculously preserved; but the Church, which all were
bound by divine command to hear and obey, and whose
voice was necessarily the sole guide of the Christian world
during this protracted period, was permitted to go to ruin,
and thereby to become totally unfit for the high mission
with which it had been entrusted by Christ! O consistency!
thou art indeed rarely found among the partisans of error!

2. The Roman Catholic Church alone can give a consistent and satisfactory account of the Bible.

This is manifest from what has been already said in
support of the preceding proposition. The Protestant may
indeed trace back the history of the Bible to the date of
the reformation; beyond this epoch he can not consistently
go. All beyond this is involved in doubt and uncertainty.
The history of Christianity, and consequently that of the
Bible, during the first fifteen centuries, is for him full of
perplexities and darkness. He can not hope to see his
way clearly through the darkness which, according to his
theory, brooded over the world, from the early ages of
Christianity up to the rise of the reformation. In the
attempt to traverse this portion of history, he must walk
in a land overshadowed for him by heavy clouds, and full
of inexplicable mysteries. How will he then be able to
overleap this frightful chasm of fifteen centuries in his
religious history? How prove that the Bible itself has not
been swallowed up with primitive Christianity in this

---

* Till the invention of printing, about the middle of the fifteenth century. See the Third Lecture.

yawning abyss, which had swallowed up every thing else? How will he do it, but by calling to his aid that venerable Church against which he protests with all his might? But where is his consistency in invoking her kind assistance to rescue him from difficulties growing out of the rejection of her authority? How accept the hand of a Mother against whom he has openly rebelled, and whom he yet persists in denouncing as a traitress to Christ and to His holy Religion?

The Catholic Church alone, My Dear Friends, can furnish us with a consistent and satisfactory history of that Bible which we all prize so much. She alone can tell us a plain, straightforward, and unvarnished tale in regard to its origin and uninterrupted transmission from the apostolic days to our own times. She alone can unfold its entire history; and she alone can unravel all the otherwise insuperable difficulties of its text, growing out of thousands of different readings in its various translations into different languages. She needs no adventitious aid for this purpose; her simple testimony is all-sufficient; the history of the Bible is an essential part of her own history. The inspired volume was handed down from generation to generation along with her other institutions: it was ever held as her written constitution, which she prized as dearly as she did her own life, and of which she was the divinely appointed guardian and expounder. Her public and official acts, in every succeeding age, are its best and only authentic commentary. If her account of the Bible be not consistent and satisfactory, no other certainly is, or can be; for there is obviously no other worthy the name. Hence this point is settled; and we may proceed at once to the next.

3. The Roman Catholic Church alone can satisfactorily settle the canon of the Bible.

This proposition need not detain us long, as I have already dwelt on it at some length, in a previous Lecture.* Protestants *now* agree with us in regard to the canon of

---

* In the Third Lecture of this series.

the New Testament, though some of the early reformers
rejected many of its books, on the alleged ground that they
were not originally received by the Church.* They still,
however, persist in rejecting as apochryphal several books
of the Old Testament; chiefly on the ground that they were
not admitted into the Jewish canon, compiled under Esdras,
before those books were written! The synagogue does not
receive them as inspired books; but the *whole* Christian
Church received them unanimously, both in the east and
in the west, for more than a thousand years previous to
the reformation: but our dissenting brethren are pleased to
prefer the merely *negative* authority of the Jewish, to the
positive authority of the Christian Church!

Where is the consistency in this? If the Christian
Church be deemed fully competent to decide on the canon
of the New Testament, by what process of reasoning is her
competency denied for settling that of the Old Testament?
For our own part, we are content, with the great St. Augustine, to prefer the authority of that venerable Church
which Christ founded, and which He expressly commanded
all His followers to hear, to that of a dispensation of mere
types and shadows, which has long since passed away.
And we are also fully content with the reasoning which
induced this brilliant luminary of the ancient Church to
sustain the truth of the next proposition, which I will now
proceed to state; and which made him utter the memorable
words, already quoted: "But I would not believe the
gospel, if the authority of the Catholic Church did not
move me to do so."

4. The Catholic Church alone can prove the inspiration
of the Bible.

I have nothing to add to the proofs already furnished
in support of this proposition in the previous Lectures;†

---

* As, for example, the Epistle to the Hebrews, the Epistle of St. James,
the Second and Third of St. John, the Second of St. Peter, that of St.
Jude, and the Apocalypse or Revelations of St. John.

† In the Third and Ninth Lectures of this course; to which the reader
is respectfully referred.

which I shall, of course, consider as sufficiently established.

The four propositions laid down at the beginning of this argument, are thus, I hope, satisfactorily proved; and the conclusion derived from them is plain:—that the Catholic Church alone can justly claim to be the true Church of Christ; even in the Protestant view, which makes the whole of Christianity to consist in the Bible alone.

THIS IS THE TENTH EVIDENCE OF CATHOLICITY.

II. The next evidence will throw additional light upon the one last presented, to which it is nearly akin. It is this:

That Church alone can be the true Church of Christ, which alone is, and has been, consistent and uniform in the interpretation of the Bible;

But the Roman Catholic Church alone is, and has been, consistent and uniform in the interpretation of the Bible;

Therefore the Roman Catholic Church alone is, or can be, the true Church of Christ.

The first, or *major* proposition, is almost self-evident. The Bible contains the Religion of Christ only in so much as it is rightly understood and interpreted. Misunderstand and pervert its legitimate meaning, and it no longer exhibits the Religion of Christ, but only the fancies of your own brain. Now, the Religion of Christ, as contained in the Bible, is obviously consistent in all its parts, and uniform in its very nature; therefore no Church can possibly hold the true Religion of Christ, which does not adopt a consistent and uniform system of Bible interpretation.

All that I have to do, then, to complete the argument, is to prove the second, or *minor* proposition: that is, to show that the Catholic Church has always adopted a consistent and uniform interpretation of the Bible, and that no other church, at least no Protestant church, has done this.

1. As to consistency in Bible interpretation, it is certain that Protestants can lay no valid claim to its possession. Their whole religious systems are, in fact, little better than a sad jumble of glaring inconsistencies and contradictions.

In addition to the inconsistencies above pointed out, I will here briefly allude to a few others. The Protestant discards all Church authority in determining the meaning of Scripture, and substitutes for it the private judgment of each individual. This is the cardinal principle of Protestantism. Yet there is scarcely a denomination in this country which has not its church articles and confessions of faith, setting forth the doctrines which, the sect professes to believe, are fairly deducible from the Bible; and to which all its members must subscribe, else they fall under what is called church discipline!* That is, every one is to read and interpret the Bible for himself; still he must take care to interpret it according to the tenets of the sect to which he belongs! Is this consistent?

Again, the Protestant professes to hold nothing which cannot be clearly proved from the Bible; yet all the Protestant sects do certainly believe many things which are not contained therein. They all hold the inspiration of St. Mark and St. Luke, and that of the other writers of the New Testament;† the correctness of the Protestant canon of the Bible; and the substantial accuracy of king James' translation:‡ yet all these things are certainly not contained, either directly or indirectly, in the Bible itself; and they involve, too, what are admitted to be fundamental and essential principles of faith!

Moreover, all Protestants profess great reverence for the Christian Sunday, or Lord's day, which they improperly call the *Sabbath*;§ and this is deemed by them a vital and

---

* The reformers, or Campbellites, and perhaps one or two other minor sects, are an exception to this remark; they cry out against creeds, for the reason I have indicated in the text. But let them grow a little *older*, and probably they will change their opinion in this respect;—if they have not indeed already began to exhibit symptoms of a change.

† I should, perhaps, except the Unitarians, the Quakers, and perhaps, one or two other ultra sects.

‡ Except the Baptists and Campbellites, who are diligently engaged in getting up a new version more conformable to their peculiar views; but the argument in the text will apply equally to their forthcoming translations.

§ Except the Seventh Day Baptists, a very small sect.

fundamental point. Now where is the Scriptural warrant
for keeping the *first* day of the week, or Sunday, instead of
the *seventh* day, or Saturday, as God expressly commanded
in the old law,—and this, too, in one of the ten commandments? Surely, if the Bible contain every thing appertaining to the Religion of Christ, it should furnish some
account of this change; but it contains nothing of the
kind.* Again, the vast majority of Protestants admit the
validity and lawfulness of infant baptism, though the Bible
certainly contains nothing from which alone it can be conclusively inferred;—especially if you admit the generally
received Protestant notion that baptism is not necessary to
salvation.

Finally, have not most of the American Protestant sects
many things in their worship, for which they can plead no
warrant of Scripture? Where, for instance, is the Scriptural authority for "mourners," for "anxious seats," for
their peculiar manner of "getting Religion," and for other
curious things connected with what are called "revivals of
Religion?" I ask again, are our separated brethren consistent in believing and practicing so many things not
contained in their *only* rule of faith,—the Bible?

The Catholic Church, on the contrary, is consistent
throughout her whole system of Bible interpretation. Her
principles of Church authority and tradition throw a broad
and steady light on the sacred page, clearing up its difficulties, removing its obscurities, and supplying its omissions.
Here there is no clashing of opposing principles, no assumption of what cannot be proved by the rule itself, no
inconsistency in the method of interpretation. The va-
garies of private judgment are restrained by the divinely
established principle of hearing the Church. In this system, every thing in the Bible or concerning the Bible, is

* Those Scriptural passages which are sometimes alleged for this purpose
are wholly inconclusive. The meeting on the first day of the week for
collecting alms, or even for religious worship, does not prove the change
alluded to. Do not our Protestant brethren often hold religious meetings
on other days than Sundays?

clear and satisfactory; outside of it all is vagueness and uncertainty.

2. We come now to the question of uniformity in Bible interpretation. Christ certainly established but one Religion, and the Bible obviously contains but one. To say that it contains more than one Religion, were little short of blasphemy; for it would amount to the assertion that the Holy Ghost, who inspired the sacred volume, is Himself the Author of inconsistencies and contradictions! And this is true, whether the contradictions be in matter deemed of smaller, or in those considered of greater importance; for the Holy Ghost cannot contradict Himself in small any more than He can in great things.

Now it is a notorious fact, that Protestants have extracted from the Bible more than a hundred contradictory systems of Religion; and that these systems are always shifting and multiplying, the older ones giving way to those which are new. On the other hand, it is equally notorious, that the Catholic Church finds in it but one Religion; and that this one Religion has been always the same and unchangeable. In view of these undeniable facts, which of the two systems, I ask, should be presumed to have adopted the uniform and true method of Bible interpretation? No reasonable Christian can pause long for an answer; it rises up spontaneously to the mind of every one who reflects but for a moment on the subject. The blessed Saviour has Himself laid down the golden rule by which the question may be easily settled: "By their fruits ye shall know them." The fruits of the Protestant system have been; and are, endless contradictions and variations of creeds, those of the Catholic, have ever been divine unity and consistent uniformity.

Therefore, it is apparent that the Roman Catholic Church alone has adopted a consistent and uniform system of Bible interpretation. Then she alone has the Religion of the Bible. Then she alone is the true Church of Christ.

THIS IS THE ELEVENTH EVIDENCE OF CATHOLICITY.

III. But I will go a step farther, and maintain her claim

to be the only true Church of Christ, on the two following grounds; which, if they can be sustained, will show still more clearly that she alone really holds the one true Religion of the Bible:—

1. The Catholic Church alone really accepts the doctrines of the Bible, in the plain, natural, and obvious sense of the inspired record.

2. She alone accepts *all* the doctrines of the Bible.

1. The Catholic Church is not called on, by her religious system, to torture the sacred text into strange and unnatural meanings, unwarranted by its obvious drift and language; she accepts the Scriptural doctrine just as the text declares it, without turning either to the right or to the left. It is enough for her, that Christ, or His inspired apostles have declared a doctrine in plain and explicit language; she stops not to inquire how far it may be comprehensible to human reason, or palatable to human sense; she humbly bows at once to the divine authority, and reverently believes without farther inquiry.

Thus, when Christ says, "This *is* my body; This *is* my blood;" she instantly believes Him, and says, without a moment's hesitation: "Yes, O Lord, it *is* thy holy body, it *is* thy sacred blood." She would shudder at the bare thought of contradicting the Saviour, by saying that it *is not* His body, it *is not* His blood, but only a mere figure of them without the reality. She would tremble at the idea of virtually joining with the perverse Jews and incredulous disciples, who exclaimed: "How can this man give us his flesh to eat?"—and, "This is a hard saying, and who can hear it?" *

Again, when Christ says to the body of his first ministers: "Whose sins you shall forgive, they are forgiven them; and whose sins you shall retain, they are retained;"† and, "Whatsoever you shall bind upon earth, it shall be bound in heaven, and whatsoever you shall loose upon earth, it shall be loosed in heaven;"‡—she

---

* St. John, vi: 52, and following.   ‡ St. Matt., ch. xviii.
† St. John, ch. xx.
84

accepts His language in its plain and obvious meaning,
and fully carries it out in her doctrine and practice.
When Christ says: "If he will not hear the Church, let
him be to you as a heathen and a publican;"* she reverently bows to His authority, and recognizes at once the
divine command, without one word of opposition. And
when He uttered the promise: "Upon this rock I will
build my Church, and the gates of hell SHALL NOT prevail against it;"†—she believes that He meant precisely
what He said, and that He was fully able to redeem His
pledge.

This illustration might be extended to many other
things; but these will suffice to explain and establish the
fact or principle here contended for. It is plain that the
Catholic Church alone, of all the modern claimants to be
the one true Church of Christ, interprets the Bible just as
it reads, and according to its plainest and most natural
signification. She alone practically adopts the sound
canon of interpretation, that a passage should be expounded
in its literal and obvious sense, unless there be very strong
and satisfactory reasons for expounding it otherwise; and,
among these reasons, she does not reckon the mere incom-
prehensibility of the doctrine stated, or the circumstance
of its being "hard to flesh and blood."

2. But she alone actually receives *all* the doctrines of the
Bible. This follows in part from what has been already
said; and it will appear still more clearly from what will
be said in the development of the next evidence. For the
present I will be content with instancing only one plain
Scriptural doctrine or institution, contained in the following
remarkable passage of the New Testament: "Is any man
sick among you? Let him bring in the priests‡ of the
Church, and let them pray over him, ANOINTING HIM WITH
OIL IN THE NAME OF THE LORD; and the prayer of faith

---

* St. Matt. ch. xviii.   † St. Matt. xvi.

‡ In the Protestant Bible it is *the elders;* but this is not material to the
argument; as, in any case, the ministers of the church are clearly meant.

shall save the sick man; and the Lord shall raise him up; *and if he be in sins, they shall be forgiven him.*"*

Now, which of all the Protestant sects complies with this solemn injunction of an inspired apostle? Which of them thinks it necessary, or even advisable, to anoint the sick man with oil, and to pray over him, in order that "if he be in sins they may be forgiven him?" You will tell me, perhaps, that this was a mere Jewish rite, long since abolished. But where is the proof? Does the Bible any where say so? What? An inspired apostle enjoin a mere Jewish rite! But, you will insist, that this is not an important, or at least a necessary observance?—Again I ask, where is the proof? I receive nothing without proof, and I must have proof, too, from your *only* rule of faith, the Bible. Do you profess to know what is important or necessary better than did St. James? Does not this same inspired writer say in this very epistle: "Whosoever shall keep the whole law, but offend in one (point,) is become *guilty of all?*"† And how can Protestants be certain that they do not fall under this strong denunciation, persisting as they do in the transgression of a commandment clearly laid down by the Apostle himself; a commandment which was deemed of binding force among all the Christians who lived on the earth for the first fifteen hundred years of the Church; and which is at present viewed in the same light by the Greek church, the oriental sects, the Roman Catholic Church,—in short, by *four-fifths* of the Christian world? With this fact staring them in the face, how can our Protestant brethren be certain that they have the *whole* Religion of that Bible of which they talk so much? Let them look to it in time.

It may, then, be set down as a position clearly established, that the Roman Catholic Church alone accepts the doctrines of the Bible in their plain, natural, and obvious sense; and that she alone accepts all those doctrines. The inference is

---

* St. James, v: 14, 15.   † St. James, ii: 10.

clear and necessary—that she alone is the true Church of
Jesus Christ.

THIS IS THE TWELFTH EVIDENCE OF CATHOLICITY.

IV. I go still farther, and maintain that the doctrines
which the Catholic Church derives from the Bible are much
more comformablo to the genius of Christianity, and therefore much more likely to be the true doctrines of that
sacred book, than are those alleged to have been drawn
from it by the Protestant sects. I can not, of course, go
now into a minute and detailed comparison, which it would
require a volume to institute;—even if it were possible
to ascertain with precision what each of the Protestant
denominations now really believes and teaches. I must
confine myself to some of the more general characteristics
of the Catholic and Protestant systems.

No Christian will deny that the Religion of Christ is a
supernatural dispensation; that is, a system of truths, moral
and doctrinal, entirely *above* the *natural* order of things.
It is supernatural in its origin, supernatural in its ends,
and it must be supernatural in its very nature and in all
its parts. It rests entirely upon the revelation made to
mankind by Christ Jesus; it contemplates the reconciliation
of sinful man with his offended Creator, the sanctification
of his soul, his union with God in time and throughout
eternity. All its doctrines and institutions must, then, be
worthy of this divine origin, and be eminently calculated
to promote these high ends: they must bear, stamped upon
them, the unmistakable impress of the incomprehensible
Deity; and they must necessarily war against human pride
and passion. This consideration naturally leads us to expect to find the Christian Religion marked by two distinctive elements: mysteries in its doctrines, and things hard
to flesh and blood in its morals and institutions.

If, even in natural things coming fairly under the range
of the senses, we are surrounded by mysteries which we
can not fathom; if the real causes of most of the phenomena
of nature are entirely hidden from our view, and we are
able to pronounce only on the palpable facts: how much

more should we expect this in things entirely above the natural order, and so far removed, by their very nature, from the reach of the senses? If we cannot explain the visible works of God, how can we hope to understand those which are invisible? If we cannot fathom the nature and mind of man, how can we hope to fathom the nature and counsel of God?

Again, we know, from the past history of the world and by our own sad experience, that the human heart is corrupt and prone to evil; and that it cannot be kept from vice or be made to incline to virtue, but by doing constant violence to its own natural inclinations. Man left God and lost himself, by following his own appetites and indulging a rebellious pride: he must be reclaimed and brought back to God by a contrary process;—by making war on his evil propensities, resisting the inclinations of flesh and blood, and humbling himself before God. Hence the Christian Religion could not lead man back to his Creator, without embodying the essential features of mortification, self-denial, and humiliation. And hence, reasoning *à priori*, we would naturally expect to find these among the most prominent characteristics of the Christian system.

Accordingly, we find, My Beloved Brethren, that this antecedent probability is fully sustained by the facts. Christianity, as taught by Jesus Christ and His inspired Apostles, is a system full of incomprehensible mysteries, and of things very humbling to human pride and very painful to nature. No one can deny this, who reads the New Testament through with a simple and upright mind and heart. The whole system is based upon three great incomprehensible mysteries; the Trinity, the Incarnation, the Atonement: and the influence of these three leading principles is strongly felt throughout all its parts. Again,—two of these mysteries,—the Incarnation and the Atonement, show forth, in an eminent degree, the humiliation of soul, and the spirit of self-denial and of sacrifice, which prevade all Christianity.

It is, then, obvious that no religious system can possibly

34 *   2 A

be the Religion of Christ, which does not accept and fully
carry out these principles: that is, which does not exhibit
Christianity as a collection of doctrinal mysteries, and of
moral principles and observances embodying the spirit of
self-sacrifice, humiliation, and mortification.

All that we have to do, then, My Beloved Brethren, in
order to ascertain which is the true Religion of Jesus Christ,
is to inquire whether Catholicity or Protestantism is more
conformable to the genius and spirit of these undeniable
principles, or carries them out more consistently and
thoroughly. The question is thus reduced to a plain matter
of fact, easily investigated by even the lowest capacity.

1. And first, let us apply the test in regard to mysteries. Those Protestant denominations which call themselves
evangelical agree, indeed, in admitting as fundamental the
mysteries of the Trinity, the Incarnation, and the Atonement. But do they not stop here? Do they carry out this
principle of mysteries through the entire Christian system?
Do they not evidently incline to the rejection of almost all
mysterious doctrines beyond these three, and to assert that,
while the foundations of Christianity are deeply mysterious
and hidden away in the unsearchable counsels of God, its
superstructure is entirely plain and comprehensible to
human reason? Is it not deemed by them a strong, if not
an insuperable objection to a particular doctrine, that it is
above the reach of reason? Do they not constantly allege
against many of the mysterious doctrines which were held
by *all* Christians for the first fifteen centuries, and which
are still held by the vast majority of Christendom, as an
essential portion of the original Christian revelation, the
very same objections which are urged by the Unitarian
and the deist against the three mysteries just named, and
against all mysteries and all supernatural revelation? In
a word, is there not, even among evangelical Protestants, a
manifest tendency to reject mysteries, merely because they
are mysteries?

A few obvious examples will prove that this is the case.
The Catholic Church, in common with all the old Churches,

and with four-fifths of modern Christendom, proposes to the belief of Christians, as an essential part of the original revelation, the doctrine of the real presence and transubstantiation; and the Protestant cries out that it is a mystery, that it is incomprehensible, absurd, impossible; and that, therefore, it should be at once rejected. The Catholic Church, under the same high sanction, proposes the doctrines of priestly absolution, of a perpetual visible sacrifice, of sacramental efficacy in conferring grace; and the Protestant objects to all of these on a similar ground. In these instances, it is not a little remarkable, that the difficulty and mysteriousness of. the doctrine are the chief objections in the way of its reception; the *fact* of its revelation, and the testimony brought forward in support of this fact, are deemed comparatively unimportant, or they occupy only the back-ground of the picture.

The plainest and most explicit language of Scripture must bend before this all-pervading disposition to reject whatever is mysterious in Religion; and it is now often deemed almost a sufficient motive for rejecting a doctrine, to exclaim with the unbelieving disciples of the Gospel, — "This is a hard saying, and who can hear it?" The Unitarian seizes up with avidity the self-same principle, and levels it against all Christian mysteries; while the deist carries it still farther, and rejects every thing supernatural, and revelation altogether! And it is a striking circumstance in Protestant history, that this downward tendency has been steadily developing itself, and growing stronger and stronger with each successive generation ever since the time of the reformation; until at last it has already withdrawn from the ranks of "evangelical" Protestantism more than half of its original members, and now threatens to annihilate every thing mysterious in the Christian system! What is Protestantism in Germany, in Switzerland, in France, and even, to a greater or less extent, in England and America, but an empty rationalism or a barren unitarianism? Who, with these palpable facts before him, will deny that the natural tendency of Protestantism is towards rationalism and infidelity? And, such being obviously the case, who can believe, for a moment, that it is conformable to the genius of Christianity, or that it is, or can be, the true Church of Christ?

2. It is the same, or even worse, in regard to that essential characteristic of the Christian Religion, which consists in moral principles and observances painful to human nature or humbling to a corrupt heart. Protestantism, with its two cardinal principles of uncontrolled private judgment in matters of faith, so very flattering to human pride; and of justification by faith *alone* without works, so soothing to the corrupt heart naturally averse to painful works; has virtually done away with the cross of Jesus, and with the spirit of self-denial and bodily mortification which necessarily grow out of its doctrines. Christ said: " If any one will come after me, *let him deny himself, take up his cross*, and follow me ;"* Protestantism virtually says to its followers: " If you would be disciples of Christ, deny yourself nothing beyond what is openly criminal, reject all the crosses and sufferings not imposed on you by God himself against your own choice, eschew fasting, corporal maceration, humble obedience to the will of others, and all such *popish* superstitions ;—and thus you will best follow Christ! He has done every thing; He has left you nothing to do but to *believe* and trust in His abounding mercy !" Is it upon any other principle than this, that such painful and humiliating Catholic doctrines and observances, as confession, satisfaction, fasting, bodily inflictions, retirement from a guilty world, celibacy, and humble obedience to Church authority, are so constantly rejected and so frequently sneered at by our separated brethren? What is there, in fact, in Protestantism, that is specially opposed to human inclinations, or to the innate pride of the human heart? And what is there in Catholicity, which does not declare open war against the whole army of the passions?

These reflections might be easily extended to much

---

* St. Matthew, xvi.

greater length; but I must hasten on. What has been already said is deemed sufficient to prove: 1st, that the genius of Christianity necessarily requires a belief in mysteries, not only as lying at its foundation, but as pervading its entire system; and in painful institutions and observances of a similar nature and extent; and 2dly, that the Roman Catholic Religion alone carries out these principles to their legitimate results and fullest extent; while Protestantism either stops half way, or rejects them altogether. The conclusion is inevitable:—that the Roman Catholic Religion alone is conformable to the spirit and letter of that taught and established by Christ; and that therefore the Roman Catholic Church alone is, or can be, the true Church of Christ. '

THIS IS THE THIRTEENTH EVIDENCE OF CATHOLICITY.

V. But there is yet another essential characteristic of Christianity which only the Roman Catholic Church exhibits, and upon which I intend to base another argument to establish her identity with the primitive Church of Christ. I allude to immutability of doctrine, and inflexibility of purpose in maintaining the truth once ascertained and decided on.

The Protestant sects can obviously lay no claim to the possession of this fixedness of doctrine; their whole history from the date of the reformation down to the present time, has been a history of perpetual changes and variations. Protestantism has not remained stationary for one year, or even for one day. Each successive generation has witnessed the appearance of new confessions of faith, of new sects, of new doctrines, and of new *discoveries* in Religion! New religions start into existence almost daily; and so very unsettled has all religious faith become, that many Christians now-a-days would almost seem to be practically of the opinion, that that religious system is the *truest* which is the *newest!* Is this picture at all exaggerated? Is not every light and shade of it unfortunately but too true to nature.

And yet, My Dear Christian Friends, truth is one, inflexible, unchangeable. No one can deny this. All truth has this essential character; none more so than that which cometh directly from God. Can it be, then, I earnestly ask you, that Protestantism is the Religion of the Bible; the one true, unchangeable Religion of Jesus Christ, taught by the Man-God, and sealed with His precious blood? Can it be, that what is avowedly a mass of crude and inconsistent speculations, and of ever-changing opinions, is that one original Religion of God, based on the revelation made through Christ our Lord? No; the very idea is revolting; it implies a horrid blasphemy; it cannot be seriously entertained by any logical mind. Protestantism cannot possibly be the Religion of Christ; it bears stamped on its brow all the marks of a merely-human institution, embodying the natural results of erring human reason and of seductive human passions. This brand can be removed only by removing the system itself.

2. A spectacle precisely contrary to this presents itself to our view in the Catholic Church. She does not change her doctrines with every change of human opinion; she does not say one thing to-day, and another thing to-morrow; but, like her divine Founder, she "IS YESTERDAY, TO-DAY, AND THE SAME FOREVER."* Her system is not made up of a hundred incompatible and contradictory elements; it is one in its nature, and the same every-where that it has been at all times. She can not tolerate dissent within her own bosom; those who will not comply with the divine command,—"Hear the Church;"—and who will not submit humbly to her authority, must go out from her;—she will have no disobedient children, no wrangling, no sects within her "ONE FOLD OF THE ONE SHEPHERD."

While the details of her discipline may vary to suit times and places, her doctrines are unchangeable; because she holds these to be the revelation of God, which she has no mission to change, nor even to modify. She would not sacrifice one of her principles even to gain the whole world.

---

* Hebrews, xiii: 8.

She lost England, because she would not yield nor compromit her doctrine in regard to the indissolubility of Christian marriage. Christ had said: "What God hath joined together, let no man put asunder;"* and she did not feel at liberty to contravene His command, even though her Pontiffs were sagacious enough to apprehend, in view of the ungovernable temper and headlong passions of Henry VIII., that in consequence of her inflexible firmness, England would be torn from her communion.

I will furnish here another evidence of her unyielding adherence to principle. She lost China in the eighteenth century, because she could not and would not sanction the Chinese Rites; which, after mature deliberation, she ascertained to be superstitious, if not idolatrous. Her enemies charge these same odious qualities on her own worship; she refuted the foul calumny by setting her condemnation on those Rites; which some of her most learned and pious missionaries nevertheless believed harmless, or at most as only an expression of exaggerated reverence for the illustrious dead, but which she, after long examination, believed to be wholly inadmissible. Her decision on this subject was made, too, at the very crisis of the Chinese mission, when her prospects in China were the brightest; and she was well aware, while making it, that it would arouse a feeling of indignation from one end of the empire to the other, and would probably result,—as it did result,—in a bitter and bloody persecution. Yet did she persist in her inflexible purpose of never compromising THE TRUTH, of which she was the divinely appointed witness and guardian. She determined to do right, and was content to leave the consequences in the hands of God, whose organ she was.

Who does not see, in the perpetual variations and endless contradictions of Protestantism, on the one hand; and in the steadfastness, inflexibility, and uniform and consistent course of Catholicity, on the other, a plain and palpable

---

* St. Matthew, xix: 6.

evidence that the former is not, and that the latter is, the true Religion of Jesus Christ.

AND THIS IS THE FOURTEENTH EVIDENCE OF CATHOLICITY

VI. The fifteenth evidence grows naturally out of this. For this very unchangeableness of doctrine and inflexibility of purpose, the Catholic Church is now, and has ever been, cordially hated by all the sects. Whatever may be their own intestine disputes and heart-burnings, these all rise up in arms against her, accuse her of an exclusive and intolerant spirit, and declaim against her as not adapted to the spirit and wants of the age, and as being averse to the march of improvement. They all unite in railing against her as an institution which is already antiquated and obsolete; and in making it a matter of grave accusation against her that she will not change, or, as they choose to express it, *reform.* They can not brook the idea that she alone should remain unchangeable, while every thing else is changing around her. But they do not pause to reflect, that, while they prefer this charge, they are really, without intending it, bestowing upon the Catholic Church the greatest possible eulogy. For to say that a Religion does not, will not, can not change, is equivalent to saying, that it has at least one essential and prominent characteristic of divine truth.

This union of all the Protestant sects against the Catholic Church is as notorious as it is remarkable. It is *notorious;* for every one who has glanced at their history must have observed the fact, that how much so ever they may differ among themselves, they all bury their private feuds, and, from the high-church Episcopalian down to the Unitarians and Universalists, they unite to a man, and make common cause, either openly or by silent sympathy, whenever it is question of attacking the Catholic Church. It is *remarkable;* for they unite on but few other points having reference to Religion. We naturally ask for a satisfactory explanation of this strange phenomenon. To us, it presents a very strong evidence that the Catholic Church is right, and that the Protestant sects are all wrong. Whether we reason from analogy, or from the leading principles of Christianity, we can explain the phenomenon on no other hypothesis.

1. History presents us with many examples of precisely similar unions of merely human sects or parties against the *truth*; it does not furnish us with one single example of a union of various *true* religious sects against *error*. Thus all the sects of Judaism,—the Scribes, the Pharisees, the Herodians,—buried their mutual differences, and united as one man against Jesus Christ,—"the way, and THE TRUTH, and the life."* Thus also, Pilate and Herod, from being bitter enemies, became fast friends, when it was question of attacking and crucifying the blessed Saviour. Thus, all the old sects constantly united together against the great body of Christians, or the Catholic Church. The same remarkable fact pervades all Church History, from the numerous heresies which started up under the eyes of the Apostles themselves down to those of our own days.†

The hundred discordant sects of the first four centuries hated Catholicity as unanimously and as cordially as do the hundred discordant sects of the present day. And they did so for precisely the same reason;—because the Catholic Church condemned them, and because it would not sanction their errors, either in whole or in part. They imagined too, that, by their joint opposition and their perpetual clamor, they would succeed in silencing her voice and in accomplishing her destruction. Vain imagination! They have all long since descended to the tomb, after having respectively run their fitful career of error; the Catholic Church has subsisted, in unimpaired energy and ever increasing strength, to the present day. So also, the numerous sects of the sixteenth century fancied that they were on the eve of blotting out the very name of the Catholic Church from the face of the earth; still she has bravely

---

* St. John, xiv: 6.

† For a very learned and able analysis of testimony on this subject in the fourth and fifth centuries, see Dr. Newman's recent work, "On the Development of Christian Doctrine;" p. 116, seqq.

stood her ground, and has survived their combined assaults.
She saw the beginning of all the sects; she has already
lived to see the end of most of them; and she will as certainly live to see the end of all those which yet remain.

Thus, if we examine this union of the sects against
Catholicity by the light of history and by the principles of
analogy, we are not at all surprised at it. We feel that
Solomon was right when he said, "There is nothing new
under the sun;" and we necessarily conclude that this circumstance is a strong additional evidence that Catholicity
is right, and that Protestantism is wrong.

2. This conclusion will be greatly strengthened, My Dear
Brethren, if we farther examine this remarkable phenomenon by the light of certain Christian principles clearly laid
down in the Bible, and accepted by all Christians. One of
these principles is, that God is love;—that Christianity, His
noblest work, is based upon love;—and that hatred comes
not from God, but from the great enemy of God and man,—
Satan. Now, what is the basis of this union of the Protestant sects against the Catholic Church? Is it love, or is it
hatred? If it be love, then, I ask, what love, and amongst
whom? Amongst the sects themselves?—But they obviously have no particular love for one another. They
mutually differ, dispute, and wrangle so long as they are
left to themselves; they often lose even common Christian
charity in the ardor of their mutual controversies;—they
are pacified, and they begin to love one another, only when
the battle-cry is raised against Catholicity! Love towards
Catholics or the Catholic Church?—But this is manifestly
not the motive of their opposition. It comes from another
principle altogether;—from a deep and settled and abiding
hatred. This consideration is as true as it is painful. I
wish, from the bottom of my heart, it were not so; but I can
not change the *facts;* and these give evidence of hatred
rather than of love.

If the opposition of the sects grew out of love towards
Catholics and a charitable zeal to reclaim them from dangerous error, would it, I ask, be marked by the bitter and

ferocious spirit which has so often distinguished it, and never, perhaps, more so than in our own days? Would the persons and character of Catholics be so often denounced from the pulpit and the press? Would Catholics be so constantly held up to public odium, as unpatriotic and dangerous citizens? Would maddening appeals be made to the blind passions of the multitude; and would the ignorant and the vicious be let loose upon them to burn down their convents, their schools, their libraries, and their churches? Would men, calling themselves ministers of the God of peace and love, be found leaving their appropriate sphere of Christian benevolence and meekness, and descending into the arena of worldly contention to fan the blaze of popular fury? Would the Catholic priesthood be so constantly held up to public execration as consisting of impure and wicked men, and this on mere foul suspicion? Would the virtue of Catholic females be assailed with unworthy insinuation, because, in common with three-fourths of Christendom, they choose to go to confession, believing this to be a divine institution obligatory on all? Would reverend ministers think proper to deliver lectures against Catholicity with doors closed against females, in order that they might not be restrained by the decency imposed by the presence of the latter?—thus clearly implying, that what is not good enough for ladies' ears, is quite good enough for the house of the living God, and for the utterance of His ministers!!

Does all this, and much more of the same kind to which allusion might be made, spring from true Christian zeal and charity? Compare these public and notorious *facts* with the following graphic picture of charity drawn by an inspired apostle; and then you will be able to judge of what spirit those are who do these things: "Charity is patient, is kind; charity envieth not, dealeth not perversely, is not puffed up, is not ambitious, seeketh not her own, is not provoked to anger, *thinketh no evil*, rejoiceth not in iniquity, but rejoiceth with the truth; beareth all things, believeth all things, hopeth all things, endureth all things."* Are not the characteristics of the warfare carried on during the last few years in this country against Catholics the exact reverse of all these qualities of true charity? Let the impartial Christian answer this question.

Again, it is a cardinal principle of Christianity, admitted by all and embodied in one of the commandments, that "We shall not bear false witness against our neighbor." Now, I ask, is this sacred principle observed by those who are foremost in the modern crusade against our Church? Do the leaders in this movement adhere strictly to *truth* in their representations of Catholic doctrine? Do they represent our principles fairly and honestly, or do they not, on the contrary, constantly misrepresent and pervert them, thrusting upon us, as our own, doctrines of their own coining, which we abhor at least as much as they do themselves? Do they allow us the benefit of our own standards, and of our own repeated explanations and declarations of our real sentiments and principles? Are we treated by them with even that common decency,—to say nothing of fairness and honesty,—which is willingly extended to the veriest criminal that ever was arraigned at the bar of justice? Is it not a lamentable fact, that, while deists and atheists are judged by their real sentiments as set forth and explained by themselves; Catholics only, who constitute the vast numerical majority of Christendom, and who can justly plead that they belong to the Church of all ages and of all nations, are denied this privilege of the most common justice, and are judged, not by their real doctrines, but by the misrepresentations of their enemies?

Is it not a remarkable fact, that Catholics *only* are so often attacked by abuse, calumny, and unblushing forgery? That they *only* are assailed by such atrocious libels and impostures as Maria Monk's impure and notoriously false "Awful Disclosures," as "Six Months in a Convent," as "Rosamond Culbertson's" lascivious adventures, as Eugene

---

* I Corinthians, xiii: 4, 7.

Sue's " Wandering Jew," as Michelet's wicked and deistical
" Spiritual Direction,"—and a thousand slanderous books
of the same wicked character? And is it not an implied
homage to Catholic truth, that the Church cannot be
assailed, with any prospect of even apparent success, by
means less foul and more fair than these?

Truly is it an immortal honor to her, that so many of her
adversaries thus openly league with avowed infidels and
notorious miscreants in order to effect her destruction.
If she were the false and idolatrous Church that she is
represented to be, could not her enemies prove it without
resorting to falsehood and calumny, and without extending
the right hand of fellowship to such infidels as Sue, Quinet,
Michelet, and Voltaire? Does not this mode of warfare
indicate rather a blind and perverse hatred, than an enlightened zeal or a true Christian charity? And if hatred
be its animating principle, how can this opposition be said
to grow out of a zeal for the truth, or for the honor of that
God who is charity itself? Does it not savor rather of the
great adversary of God and men; of that dark and atrocious embodiment of hatred, who knows not what charity
is, and who is doomed never to feel its softening influence?

I do not here speak, My Dear Brethren, of all those who
are opposed to the Catholic Church ;—God forbid. Among
our adversaries we reckon many sincere men who condemn
the spirit which directs all this unhallowed crusade as
much as we do ourselves. The great body of Protestants, I
verily believe, are well disposed and charitable, but they
are misled by the devices of their preachers, whose obvious
interest it is to keep up the popular prejudice against the
Catholic Church. The Protestant ministry has become a
regular business and *trade* in this country, as much so
almost as any other profession ; and it is, perhaps, withal
as *lucrative* as any other!

The Protestant parsons of the Anglican church in
England receive more money annually than all the other
ministers of all other denominations put together, the world

35 *

over !* In this country too, the seven thousand Protestant
ministers receive annually an immense sum of money from
their generous and confiding congregations, not only for
foreign missions and other benevolent enterprises, but also
for their own comfortable support.† And it has often been
remarked, that those among them who have been the
loudest and boldest in their denunciations of the Catholic
Church, have often been precisely the ones who have attained to the greatest eminence *in their profession*, and have,
in consequence, been promoted to the fattest livings !

This singular feature in our religious condition may
greatly aid us in explaining their zeal against Catholicity.
If the Catholic Church should prosper, their *profession*
would be almost at an end, and their means of living would
be greatly abridged, if not wholly cut off! I do not mean
to imply, that this is the case with all the Protestant ministers, even with all those who have joined the crusade
against Catholicity; but I think that every impartial man
will agree with me that many among them are more or
less influenced by these unhallowed motives: — whether
consciously or unconsciously, God only can judge; and to
His judgment I leave them!

Had they a true and enlightened Christian zeal against
error and vice, might they not find sufficient exercise for
it in denouncing the infidelity, irreligion, and immorality,

---

* The annual income of the Anglican establishment falls little short of
FORTY MILLIONS OF DOLLARS !

† Setting down the average annual salary of the American Protestant
preachers at $800,—a very moderate calculation,—their total annual
income would amount to more than TWO MILLIONS OF DOLLARS ! This is,
probably, much below the sum they actually receive, without taking into
the account their income from missions, agencies, and other sources. In
this heavy amount are they bound to their respective sects, and induced
to war against Catholicity ! Their own *comfortable* support, as well as
that of their *wives* and *children*, is deeply involved in the issue. The
latter consideration—their having families dependent for support on their
exertions—while it explains the largeness of the amount they annually
receive, may also serve to account for the ardent zeal manifested by many
of them against the old Church !

which are, alas! stalking forth amongst us in the full light of day, almost unchecked and unrebuked? Would not the eradication of these crying and ever-increasing evils be a much more appropriate object for their holy *alliances, associations, leagues,* and *secret societies* loving darkness rather than the light, than the vain attempt to destroy the Catholic Church, from which, nevertheless, they have derived, along with the Bible itself, all the religious principles which they still possess! Why treat with gentleness and charity open infidels and indifferentists, and direct all their efforts to the destruction of the only Church which can connect them with the apostolic days? Why aid unbelievers in removing the only solid foundation of Christian faith? Is this consistent? Is it *Christian?* *

From all these considerations, it is manifest that the

---

* During the late Presidential contest, the Protestant ministers became generally strong political partisans, and made their pulpits resound with impassioned political harangues, often verging on the wildest fanaticism. They thus exhibited Protestantism as being plainly of "the earth, earthly." In the North, they generally threw themselves with ardor into the ranks of the Free-soilers; while in the South a very large proportion—probably the great majority of them—became clamorous partisans of that light-shunning and most despicable of all political factions — the Know Nothings. In fact, it may be said, without exaggeration, that throughout the Union they constituted the chief strength and were the very bone and sinew of the two great wings of the opposition to the national party, which achieved so signal a triumph in the election of Mr. Buchanan. The weapon which they wielded with most vigor and success in the struggle, was bitter denunciation of the Catholic Church and of its members. While proscribing Catholics as the enemies of free institutions, and boasting that they were the accredited champions of liberty, they were all the time inflicting a mortal stab on freedom, by aiming to disfranchise their Catholic fellow-citizens! The American people did not, however, become the dupes of an hypocrisy so shallow; they rose up in their might and taught the preachers a lesson which may be profitable to them in the future! While seeking to destroy the Catholic Church, they came well nigh ruining themselves! One thing they have proved to every impartial mind—that Protestantism is not the work of God, but a mere creature of circumstances, and an index of current human feelings and passions.

union of the Protestant sects against the Catholic Church, based, as it is, upon the principle of hatred rather than upon that of love, and often carried out, too, by means the most reckless and unhallowed, affords one of the strongest and most palpable proofs, that the Catholic Church alone is the one true Church of Jesus Christ; and that Protestantism, on the contrary, is the result of that same spirit of pride and revolt which robbed heaven of one-third of its inhabitants, which drove our first parents from the earthly paradise, and which has been constantly at work in the world ever since. This spirit has been always and everywhere the same. It nailed Jesus to the cross; and it now seeks to crucify His pure and immaculate Spouse,— THE CHURCH.

THIS IS THE FIFTEENTH EVIDENCE OF CATHOLICITY; and the last which I shall present to your consideration in these Lectures.

May God vouchsafe us His holy grace, that we may all see His truth alike; and that, dismissing all pride and passion, we may humbly and lovingly embrace it! May Christ grant that we may learn and prize the test of divine truth laid down by His beloved disciple in my text: "He that knoweth God, heareth us; he that is not of God, heareth us not: BY THIS WE KNOW THE SPIRIT OF TRUTH AND THE SPIRIT OF ERROR!" Amen.

LECTURE XIV.

RECAPITULATION—THE PARALLEL—CONCLUSION.

Becoming little children for Christ's sake—Faith a gift of God, vouchsafed only to the humble—Object of this concluding Lecture—Drawing
scattered lights to a focus—Rapid analysis of the evidences contained
in the thirteen previous Lectures—St. Augustine's reasons for being a
Catholic—Our own still more ample and conclusive—THE PARALLEL
between the two lines of reasoning in support of Christianity and
Catholicity—Prophecies of the Old and New Testaments—Ancient
types and figures fulfilled in the Catholic Church alone—Miracles—
Rapid propagation of Christianity—Its beneficial influence on morals—
The number of its martyrs—Its stability and permanency—No infidels
among Christians in Catholic times—But many now in Christendom—
Appeal—Conclusion—Prayer.

*"At that time Jesus answered, and said: I give thanks to thee, O Father,
Lord of heaven and earth, because thou hast hid these things from the wise and
prudent, and hast revealed them to little ones: Yes, Father, for so it hath
seemed good in thy sight!"*—ST. MATTHEW, xi: 25, 26.

*"Amen, I say to you, unless you be converted and become as little children,
you shall not enter into the kingdom of heaven."*—ST. MATTHEW, xviii: 3.

IN these two remarkable passages, My Beloved Brethren,
our divine Lord and Master lays down a principle, which,
though of vast and paramount importance, is not sufficiently
attended to by Christians in these days of boasted enlightenment and progress. The precious gift of faith, with the
light which it throws upon the things of God in this world,
and the kingdom of heaven, which is its reward in the
next, is promised only to those who are willing to school
their proud natures into the simplicity, humility, and docility of little children. Not to the wise and prudent ones
of this world; not to those who are puffed up with their
own conceits, and who think themselves wiser and better
than other men; not to those who spurn to be taught and

2 B   (417)

to obey; but to those who have a meek and lowly and
tractable spirit, is the knowledge of the truth promised in
this world, and its bright and glorious and eternal reward
in the next.

"*Every one* that exalteth himself shall be humbled; and
he that humbleth himself shall be exalted:"* and "God
resisteth the proud, and giveth grace to the humble:" † —
contain but different and emphatic expressions of the self-
same cardinal principle of Christianity. An humble appreciation of ourselves, a lowly estimate put upon our own
lights, a willingness to be taught, and an inclination to
obey; these are the essential dispositions which we should
bring to the all-important inquiry into religious truth.
Without them, we can not hope to obtain the blessing of
God, or to come to a knowledge of his Saving truth through
divine faith.

Alas! My Beloved Friends, that, after the lapse of
eighteen centuries since the establishment of the Christian
Religion, it should still be a matter of inquiry among
Christians,—Which is the true Religion of Christ? Alas!
that, after all the lights which history, experience, and the
express teaching of Christ and His inspired apostles have
thrown upon the subject, it should still be found by many
difficult to ascertain which, among all the modern claimants
to that high honor, is really that one Church which Christ
established and commanded all to obey, under the awful
penalty of being reckoned with heathens and publicans!
But it is even so.

Christ surely made His truth sufficiently plain to all;
and originally it was certainly no difficult problem to find
out where and by whom that truth was taught. Whence,
then, the difficulty to which I have just alluded? It can
have come from no other source than the unbridled pride
of the human heart, setting itself up against the teaching
of God, and obscuring with its dark clouds the traits of his
clearest and noblest work. If all Christians had the hu-

* St. Luke, xiv: 11.   † St. James iv: 6.

mility and docility of little children, religious controversies
would cease at once and altogether; because all would then
readily agree in accepting the one original truth as revealed by God. Can we reasonably hope for this blessed
result? We can, at least, with Abraham, "hope against
hope;" and we can do, with the divine light and assistance,
whatever lies in our power to bring about so blissful a
consummation.

This is what I have feebly, but, I trust, honestly endeavored to do in the course of these Lectures, which I must now
bring to a close. I have presented successively to your consideration FIFTEEN EVIDENCES, or arguments, to show that
the Roman Catholic Church has the very strongest claims to
be that identical Church which Christ established, and which
He sealed with His precious blood. Whatever you may
have thought of the force of each of these evidences taken
separately, I think that those among you who have given
me a patient hearing throughout the entire course, will have
come to the conclusion that, when taken together, they
furnish a cumulative argument in favor of the position,
which is very strong, if not wholly conclusive. And that
you may be able, at a single glance, to estimate the force of
the whole argument, I intend, in this concluding Lecture,
rapidly to review the ground we have passed over together,
to point out its principal landmarks, and to recall and render
familiar to you, as far as may be, the many objects of interest which it has successively unfolded to our view. I
bespeak your undivided attention, while I thus endeavor to
draw to a focus the various scattered lights which God may
have shed upon your minds, in the progress of these very
imperfect Lectures.

1. I started out, as you will recollect, with some considerations to prove the obligation of religious inquiry,
and to unfold the spirit and manner in which it should
be conducted in order to produce a good result. I then
proceeded to lay down a few general preliminary ideas
on the nature and properties of the Christian Religion,
and on its relation to the Church of Christ. I endeavored

to show that the Religion of Christ is not a mere theory, nor a mere science, to be learned and defined by human reason: but that it is a *positive* institution, depending solely, for its origin, for its nature, for all its parts, on the will of Christ, its divine Founder: and hence, that all we have to do in order to ascertain its nature, is to inquire into the *fact* of the revelation of Christ, which is to be ascertained and proved, like every other fact—by testimony. I then showed, that, among the essential qualities of this Religion, are the four following: that it is one, is clearly defined in all its parts, is obligatory on all mankind, and is therefore easily discoverable by all. I next proceeded to show that the Church is a visible and divinely organized body of men, instituted by Christ to be the perpetual guardian and witness to the world of this one Religion; and that, therefore, the essential office of the Church is to maintain the Religion of Christ in its original purity and integrity, and to apply its benefits to mankind, to the end of the world.

2. These preliminaries settled, I passed at once to the examination of the momentous question: Which, of all the Christian Churches now in existence, is that one original Church of Christ, established by Him for the high mission just indicated? As a first step towards coming to a right conclusion on this point, I placed the religious inquirer along with the eleven apostles to whom our divine Lord, in His farewell address on Mount Olivet, imparted the wonderful commission to teach and to baptize all nations; and I made him listen reverently with them to the sacred pledge Christ gave on that most solemn occasion, that He would be with them when preaching, teaching, and baptizing "*all days even to the consummation of the world.*" What was the *method* ordained by Christ for fulfilling this commission? Who has fulfilled it, by the actual conversion of the nations to Christianity? These were the important questions which naturally rose to the mind of the sincere inquirer. No church which has not fulfilled the commission, and in the manner divinely appointed, can surely claim to be the Church of Christ; for He wished and intended that His

Church, and His only, should carry out this magnificent purpose for bringing all nations to the foot of His cross. Now the method ordained by Christ for achieving this glorious result was, *preaching* and *teaching* by an authorized ministry sent by Himself, and sustained by His presence; not *writing*, of which He nowhere breathes one syllable. Therefore the Church which alone has adopted this Rule of Faith, is the only one which can lawfully claim to be His Church; but the Catholic Church alone has invariably followed this Rule; therefore the Catholic Church alone can claim to be the true Church of Christ. This was the first evidence.

3. Again, all history proclaims the fact, that *no nation* has ever been converted from heathenism to Christianity but by authorized ministers acting in communion with, and deriving their mission from the great body of Christians, or from the Catholic Church ; and that *all the nations* which have been so converted, have been gathered into the one Christian fold by the Catholic Church alone. Therefore, the Catholic Church alone has actually carried out the intentions of Christ; and she alone has, in all ages, proved herself to be His lawful Spouse by her marvelous fruitfulness in bringing forth spiritual children to Him : then, she alone can rightly claim to be His Church. This was the second evidence.

4. Moreover, she alone claims to have been blessed in all the successive ages of her history with visible and unmistakable signs of the divine presence and protection, in an uninterrupted continuation of miraculous interpositions in her behalf, as the brilliant and divine seals of her apostleship. Christ had promised these miraculous gifts as the accompaniment of the commission, without any limitation whatever, either as to time or place; He was GOD, and He had both the power and the will to fulfill His promise; He did fulfill it; all other Christian denominations have the candor to acknowledge that He did not fulfill it *in them* : the Catholic Church claims that it has been fulfilled in her ; she makes good her claim by an array of evidence extending throughout all the ages of her history, based upon

testimony which will bear the most rigid scrutiny, and which cannot be rejected without sapping the foundations of all historical faith :—therefore, she alone is proved to be the lawful, and in fact, the only heir to the divine promise of miraculous gifts; then, she alone is the true Church of Christ. This was the third evidence.

5. The argument might have been left on its own merits, as thus far exhibited. But I went still farther than this. Christ impressed upon His Church certain bold and prominent qualities; certain clear, unmistakable, and distinctive *marks* or characteristics, by which it might be known at a glance, and might be easily distinguished from every other society. These characteristics grow out of its very nature and divine origin; they are inseparable from it; they can be found in no other society on earth, whether civil or religious. Among these, I placed in the first rank two, which are the most palpable, and which are indissolubly connected together,—Unity and Catholicity; each of them threefold in its nature, extension, and objects : and I showed, by an array of facts which will not be denied nor even contested, that the Catholic Church alone can even seriously claim to be in possession of both these attributes. From this notorious fact, viewed in connection with the express will of Christ in regard to the qualities by which He wished His Church to be always distinguished, I necessarily inferred that the Catholic Church alone is His Church. This was the fourth evidence.

6. Another distinctive characteristic of the true Church is Sanctity, both in the tendency of its doctrines and institutions to promote holiness, and in the practical fruits thereof which it was to gather in great abundance among mankind. This Sanctity consists in disengagement from the flesh and the world, and in devotedness to heavenly things and to God : in fully entering into the sacrificial spirit of the atonement, in crucifying the flesh with its vices and concupiscences, in trampling under foot the world with all its fascinating allurements, and in "taking the wings of the dove, flying away, and being at rest" in the bosom of God.

I endeavored to show that the Catholic alone adopts the loftiest standard of holiness; that she alone dearly prizes the evangelical counsels of holy poverty, immaculate chastity, and humble obedience; that she alone exhorts those of her children who feel themselves called to a higher perfection, to sever entirely and for ever the chains that bind them to the world with its three all-pervading concupiscences, mentioned by St. John the beloved disciple; that in her communion alone is the loftiest type of Sanctity practicable; that the Protestant sects all laugh at these things as above human strength, and as a dangerous snare to human weakness; that the Catholic Church alone has produced saints, properly so called; and that the Protestant communions have virtually given up even the claim, by sneering at the bare idea of saints, and by acknowledging, what is clearly the fact,—that they have never produced any worthy the name: that, therefore, the Catholic Church alone has the distinctive characteristic of Sanctity; and that, of course, she alone can claim to be the true Church of Christ. This was the fifth evidence.

7. Still another of these essential characteristics is an Antiquity which goes back, by uninterrupted ministerial succession, to the days of the Apostles themselves, and to the date of the commission originally given to them, as the first incumbents of the ministerial office. I showed, by historical facts which cannot be gainsaid, that, while none of the Protestant denominations can follow their history farther back than the reformation, the Catholic Church alone can trace hers to the Apostles and to Christ Himself: that, to the Protestant, all Church History beyond the days of Luther and Calvin is involved in darkness and is a puzzling enigma; while, to the Catholic alone, it is familiar ground, clear and intelligible·in all its outlines and landmarks: and that the Catholic alone can prove his connection with the apostolic days by. his communion with a venerable line of chief bishops, coming down in regular and unbroken succession from St. Peter,—the great leading Apostle, whom Christ made the ROCK upon which He was

to build that Church against which the gates of hell should
not prevail; whereas Protestants either candidly and openly
discard the idea of an apostolic succession altogether, as
wholly untenable in their position, or virtually give it up,
by the evident lameness and inconsistency of their attempts
to derive it from that great Catholic Church against which
they protest with all their might, and which, in its turn,
discards and unchurches them as rebellious children. I
showed, moreover, that even apart from the question of the
ministerial succession, the Catholic Church is plainly and
historically as old as Christianity itself; that Protestants
cannot prove that she has ever changed, because they
have never been able to show *when, where, by whom*, and
under what circumstances, the alleged change took place;
that they sadly disagree among themselves in assigning the
date of what they are pleased to call *the apostasy*; and that
hence, in common honesty, they should give up the charge
altogether. This was the sixth evidence.

8. But, to prove still farther how utterly groundless is
the stale accusation, that the Catholic Church, once the true
Church of Christ, fell away from her original purity or
violated her original integrity, I appealed to the explicit,
repeated, and solemn promises of Christ, that He would be
with her teaching and baptizing all days even unto the
consummation of the world; that the gates of hell should
not prevail against her, built as she was upon a rock; and
that the Holy Ghost should teach her all truth and abide
with her forever: and also to the emphatic declaration of
St. Paul, that she is the pillar and ground of truth, and the
immaculate Spouse of Christ, without spot, or wrinkle, or
blemish, subject to the divine Bridegroom *in all things*.
From these reiterated declarations and promises, one of
two things clearly followed: either that Christ was not
God, or even a Prophet of God, because He either could
not or would not redeem His own pledges, nor verify the
sayings of His inspired Apostle; or that His Church was
infallible in doctrine and morals: there is no escape from
the dilemma. Therefore, if the Catholic Church was ever

the true Church of Christ, she is so still. And this was the seventh evidence.

9. But, even apart from the divine promises just alluded to, history proclaims, with a hundred voices, that the Catholic Church is the favored child of heaven, and the cherished object of God's special interposition and protection. Her trials and her triumphs in all ages; her brilliant and glorious victories over combinations of causes which have swept away all other institutions possessed of much more natural strength and worldly wisdom than she; her repeated and signal triumphs in the midst of those great emergencies and crises when every thing boded her ruin:— these bold and prominent outlines of her history present a commentary on the divine promises in her behalf, written by the finger of God Himself, and in characters so clearly marked and so legible that no one can possibly misread or mistake them. History avers that she is wholly indestructible; therefore she is not a human, but plainly a divine institution. This was the eighth evidence presented to your consideration.

10. The ninth evidence was still more fully drawn out in two successive Lectures.* It consisted in a comparison of the various forms of Church government now adopted among the several Christian communions, with that originally instituted by Christ himself; and in the inquiry which naturally grew out of this comparison,—which of all these systems of ecclesiastical polity comes the nearest to the original divine type. The question was first stated in general, and the decision was made to rest upon the outlines of Church government, as plainly laid down in the New Testament. From this divine source it clearly appeared: that Christ conferred full spiritual powers, not only *ministerial* but also *gubernatorial*, on a certain body of men chosen by Himself, and upon none others; that these men were organized into three distinct but subordinate orders,— bishops, priests, and deacons,—corresponding respectively with the apostles, the seventy-two disciples, and the

---

* Lectures xi. and xii.

36 *

seven deacons of the New Testament, and carrying out the type of the three orders in the Aaronitic priesthood; that to this body of men, thus organized by Himself, He imparted full and plenipotentiary powers, legislative, judicial, and executive in Church matters; and that finally, He wished and intended, that this order of Church government should be perpetuated in regular ministerial succession, through legitimate channels, to the very end of time. I then briefly showed that the Catholic Church alone accepts these principles in all their length and breadth and extension; and that she alone, therefore, has the original type of Church government; and, of course, that she alone can claim to be the true Church of Christ.

But this argument, clear and irresistible as it appeared to my own mind, opened to our view so many subordinate or collateral issues into which the general plan of these Lectures forbade me to enter in detail, that I did not reckon it as a distinct evidence of Catholicity; but left it to its own intrinsic merits, as they might be appreciated by each one of my hearers.

But there is another essential and distinctive feature of Church government which the Catholic Church alone avowedly possesses; and which, if it can be once established to be of divine origin and imperative obligation on all Christians, at once settles the question,—Which is the true Church of Christ? I allude to the Primacy, that great center of Unity and conservative principle of Church government, and consequently of the Church itself. I proved these three facts: that Christ established a Primacy in the person of Peter; that He wished it to be perpetuated in His Church to the end of time; and that it has been so perpetuated in the line of Roman Pontiffs, in the Catholic Church, and in this Church alone. The inference was plain and necessary:— that, such being the case, the Catholic Church alone can claim to have the original and divine type of Church government; and that, then, she alone can claim to be the true Church of Christ. This was the ninth evidence.

11. The remaining six evidences, compressed into the last

Lecture, must be so fresh in the memory of those among you who honored me with your attention, that I need scarcely recapitulate them. Suffice it to say, that I endeavored to prove the identity of the Catholic Religion with that contained in the Bible, by these six considerations: 1, The Catholic Church alone preserved the Bible for the first fifteen centuries; she alone can give a straightforward and consistent account of it; she alone can settle its canon and prove its inspiration: 2, She alone is consistent and uniform in its interpretation: 3, She alone really follows its meaning in the plain, natural, and obvious sense; and she alone accepts *all* its doctrines, without turning either to the right hand or to the left: 4, She alone derives from it doctrines and institutions which are the most conformable to its genius and scope, such as mysteries in faith, and things hard to flesh and blood in practice; while her Protestant adversaries either stop half-way, or reject these mysterious and painful dispensations altogether: 5, She alone has ever been inflexible and uncompromising in the advocacy of the truth "once delivered to the saints;" while all the sects are changing their ground every day: and 6, She alone has been always honored with the combined opposition of all sectarians and errorists and deists in every age and country, our own not excepted; she alone is the "sect every-where spoken against;" she alone is persecuted and nailed to the cross with her blessed Founder and Bridegroom; she alone is hated according to Christ's express prediction, by men who "think they do God a service" "by calumniating her, and saying all manner of evil against her falsely."

12. If these last six evidences, in conjunction with the nine preceding ones, do not convince you that the Catholic Church is the only true Church on the face of the earth, then you must be very incredulous indeed, and very hard to be persuaded of things the most obvious and palpable. You must be far more keen-sighted, or much less logical, than was, perhaps, the greatest genius that ever wrote on Christianity, or illumined the Catholic Church with his brilliant talents. St. Augustine was converted to Catho-

licity on grounds even less striking and less comprehensive
than those above alleged. Listen to him in the following
passage, in which he assigns to the Manicheans, whose sect
he had abandoned, the many strong reasons which made
him thank God for having become a firm believer in the
Catholic Church; and you cannot fail to remark that all
these reasons have been embodied in the evidences spread
out before you in these Lectures, and many more besides,
either growing out of them, or more or less different from
them. St. Augustine says:

"In the Catholic Church, not to speak of that most pure
wisdom, to the knowledge of which few spiritual men attain in this life so as to know it even in its least measure,
as men indeed, yet without any doubt, (for the multitude of
Christians are safest, not in understanding with quickness,
but in believing with simplicity;) not to speak of this
wisdom, which ye do not believe to be in the Catholic
Church,* there are many considerations which most sufficiently hold me in her bosom. I am held by the consent of
peoples and nations ;† by the authority which began in
miracles,‡ was increased by charity, and made steadfast by
age ;§ by that succession of priests from the chair of the
apostle Peter, to whose feeding the Lord, after His resurrec-
tion commended His sheep, even to the present episcopate;||
lastly, by the very title of *Catholic*, which, not without
cause, hath this Church alone, amidst so many heresies, obtained in such sort, that, whereas all heretics wished to be
called Catholics, nevertheless to any stranger who asks how

* Precisely as modern Protestants do not understand or appreciate the
wisdom or sanctity of the Catholic Church at the present day.

† The Unity and Catholicity of the Church.

‡ The proof from miracles, of the continuation of which down to his
day, St. Augustine, as I have shown, is an express witness.

§ The apostolical antiquity of the Church, and her strength increased by
age, in spite of all the trials she had to encounter in her eventful history.

|| The apostolic succession, traced, precisely as we trace it, through the
line of Roman Pontiffs who have successively occupied the Chair of Peter,
down to "the present episcopate" in Pius IX.

to find a *Catholic* Church, no one would dare to point to his
own conventicle (*basilica*) or house.* These dearest bonds,
then, of the Christian name, so many and so great, rightly
hold a man in belief in the Catholic Church, even though,
by reason of the slowness of our understanding or our
deserts, truth hath not yet shown itself to us in its clearest
tokens. But among you, who have none of these reasons
to invite and detain me, I hear but the sound of the
promise of truth; which truth, verily, if it be so manifestly
displayed that there can be no mistake about it, is to be
preferred to all those things by which I am held in the
Catholic Church; but if it is *promised* alone, and not produced, no one shall move me from that faith which by so
many and great ties bind my mind to the Christian
Religion." †

It is clear, My Beloved Friends, that the great St. Augustine viewed Catholicity and Christianity as identical. His
"mind was bound to the *Christian* Religion," by the very
same motives which "most sufficiently held him in the
bosom of the Catholic Church." In his vast and luminous
intellect, Catholicity and Christianity stood or fell together;
the same proofs which established the one, also established
the other; they were as much identical, in point of reason
and argument, as they were in point of fact and of history.‡

I shall endeavor briefly to develop this idea of the great
African doctor; and, by a rapid comparison of the two parallel lines of evidence traced out by the Christian and by
the Catholic apologist to prove Christianity and Catholicity,
shall attempt to show that they are both substantially the
same; and that no one can therefore, logically or con-

---

* Who does not see here, that the heretics of the fifth century resorted
to precisely the same devices, and with exactly the same meager success,
as do the sectarians of our own days! Truth has always been the same,
and so has error.

† Contra Epistolam Manichæor. 5.

‡ The reader will here recall to his mind the famous saying of St.
Augustine, already quoted above: "But I would not believe the Gospel,
unless the authority of the Catholic Church moved me to do so."

sistently, be a Christian without being likewise a Catholic.
Nearly all of the evidences scattered through the preceding Lectures look to this great conclusion : and all that
I have to do, in closing them, is to endeavor to concentrate
them upon this one cardinal point.

What are the principal evidences of Christianity as set
forth by its champions? They may be comprised under
the six following heads :

1. The prophecies of the Old and New Testaments fulfilled
in Christ and His Religion; 2, The wonderful miracles
wrought by Christ and His apostles to prove His divine mission and the truth of His doctrine; 3, The astonishing and
evidently preternatural propagation of Christianity, by instruments and means, humanly speaking, wholly inadequate
to the purpose, and in the midst of the most adverse and
unpropitious circumstances; 4, The wonderful effects it produced on the moral condition of the world, so far as mankind
came under its beneficial influence; 5, The thousands of
martyrs who willingly and cheerfully shed .their blood in
its defense; and 6th, Its permanency and indestructibility
under the action of causes which would have destroyed any
merely human institution, and which actually did destroy
institutions naturally much stronger than itself. Under
these six heads may be classed almost all the arguments
brought forward by the Christian apologist in defense of
Christianity.

Now, I maintain that all these evidences combine, with
equal force and conclusiveness, to sustain Catholicity. This
will sufficiently appear from a very summary analysis of
the arguments already produced in these Lectures in support
of the Catholic Church, with such modifications and additional reflections as the comparison I am now instituting
may seem to require.

1. And first, in regard to the evidence derived from prophecy. As may be easily gathered from what I have already
incidentally said on this subject,* no Christian denomina-

* In many of the preceding Lectures, and particularly in that on the
Unity and Catholicity of the Church, Lecture VI.

tion that ever existed, except the Catholic, comes up fully
to the lofty standard and realizes the sublime imagery of
ancient prophecy. In no other have all the nations of
the earth been blessed, according to the prophetic promises
made to Abraham, Isaac, and Jacob; in no other can all
the nations and peoples of the world be invited to praise the
Lord, as David so often does in his divine and prophetic
Psalms; in no other are fulfilled those splendid prophecies
of Isaiah, Solomon,* and other ancient seers, in regard to
the abundant peace, glorious prosperity, and perfect unity
of Christianity; in no other, in fine, are realized the many
ancient predictions in relation to the perpetual duration
of that glorious kingdom over which Christ was to reign
forever. Take away the Catholic Church, and all these
prophecies remain unfulfilled, or they mean nothing; admit
Catholicity, and they are all clear, determinate, easily understood, and perfectly accomplished. This must be almost
self-evident to every calm and reflecting mind.

But, besides the prophecies of the Old, there are those
also of the New Testament; and the evidence drawn
from the latter is as striking in favor of Catholicity as
that derived from the former. The Catholic Church alone,
as I hope I have already fully shown, fulfills the oft-
repeated and solemn predictions of Christ in regard to the
universal extension, the unity, sanctity, perpetual duration,
and infallibility of that Church which He built on a
rock, and against which He promised that "the gates of
hell should not prevail." She alone has actually fulfilled
His prophetic intentions, according to their letter and
their spirit; has adopted the rule of faith established by
Him; has actually taught all the nations; has fully realized
His sublime purpose of gathering all His followers into
"the ONE FOLD under the ONE SHEPHERD." No other Christian denomination has made even a plausible attempt
to do all this. No other even apparently comes up to the
lofty type of His Church, as He foresaw and predicted

---

* In his Canticles, where He says of the Church, among other things:
"ONE is my dove; my perfect one is but ONE." Cant. vi: 8.

that it should be. Therefore, no other adequately fulfills the prophecies of the New Testament.

Again, there is found, scattered through the Old Testament, a great number of prophecies, less strictly such, consisting of *things* rather than of *words;*—of types and figures foreshadowing the future condition of the Christian Church in its government, in its worship, and in its distinctive characteristics. These, too, find their complete and perfect fulfillment in the Catholic Church, and in her alone. I have not time here to go fully into an argument which would require more than a whole Lecture for its complete development. But the following brief summary will be sufficient for my present purpose.

.St. Paul often adverts to the argument derived from the types and figures of the Jewish dispensation. Thus, in his epistle to the Hebrews, which is a tissue of such illustrations, he lays down the general principle, that "the law (of Moses) had a *shadow* of the good things to come;"* and, in his first epistle to the Corinthians, speaking of some facts and incidents in the Jewish history, he says: "Now, all these things happened to them *in figure;* and they are written for our correction, upon whom the ends of the world are come."† It is fair, then, to infer the character of the new dispensation from the types, "shadows," and "figures" of the old. Many of those types, indeed, as St. Paul shows in his epistle to the Hebrews, find their fulfillment in the person of Christ: but there are yet many others which clearly point to His mystical body, the Church; and which, in fact, can be explained in no other way.

This is particularly true of the ecclesiastical polity and peculiar worship developed under the Mosaic dispensation. Glancing at that divinely appointed, but temporary system of Religion, we find, among its distinguishing characteristics, the following: a *priesthood* divinely ordained, consecrated with solemn ceremonies,‡ and organized into three perpetual orders under one visible head, who was also the

---

* Hebrews, x: 1. † I Corinthians, x: 11. ‡ See Leviticus, viii, etc.

supreme judge of all religious controversies; an order of
visible *sacrifices* of various kinds, offered up upon the altar
in the temple of Jerusalem; a gorgeous and splendid *ceremonial*, defined by God himself in its most minute details;
an *external worship*, with its appliances of religious vest-
ments, of lights, of incense, of holy water,* of purifications,
and of many other religious emblems; an *ark of the covenant*, preserved always in the temple, containing the mystic
manna and other significant types; a *visible presence* of
God in His own chosen holy of holies, speaking from His
own Mercy-Seat, overshadowed by the wings of the mysterious cherubim; a *temple* ornamented, by God's own direction, with a number of religious images and representations;
the Breads of Proposition, or the Shew-Breads, ever re-
posing within the sanctuary; a *mystic candlestick*, with its
seven branches bearing the *seven* emblematic lights;† a
regular round of *public anniversary festivals, fasts, and celebrations;* finally, a *unity* among all the members of the true
Church scattered over Judea,‡ in the profession of the one
faith, in the practice of the one worship, and in obedience
to the one visible head,— the high-priest.

Where, My Beloved Brethren, do you find, among Christians, the counterpart and anti-type of all these characteristic institutions of the old law? They are certainly nowhere to be found among the Protestant sects;—for these
all agree in rejecting, as superstitious, all those emblems of
worship which would best tally with those divinely appointed by God under the ancient dispensation. They are
realized only in the Catholic Church, whose whole system
of worship and Church government alone corresponds
exactly, in all its parts, with that ancient, divine, and

---

* See Numbers, v: 17; Leviticus, xi: 82; and *passim.*

† Viewed by many of the ancient fathers as emblematic of the seven
lights of the Christian Church,—the seven sacraments.

‡ The Samaritans were, indeed, schismatics; but they were condemned
by God, and delivered over to a reprobate sense, for this very offense;—
an impressive warning to all who follow their example.

eminently typical order of things, established by God himself as a preparation for the Gospel.

It would seem, indeed, that the Catholic Church had taken those venerable ordinances of God as the heavenly model of her own sublime ceremonial and priesthood; and that she alone had fully complied with the divine injunction originally given to Moses, as a rule he was to follow in completing all things necessary for the Jewish worship: "Look, and make (it) according to the pattern which was shown thee on the mount."* Protestants do not surely attend sufficiently to this, when they sneer so much at the Catholic worship.

2. In regard to the evidence from miracles, the Catholic apologist can plead in favor of his Church, not only those recorded in the New Testament, but those likewise wrought in every succeeding age of the Church, for its propagation and vindication. As I have already sufficiently developed this argument in a separate Lecture,† it will not be necessary to dwell any longer upon it here.

3. I may make a similar remark with respect to the brilliant evidence founded on the rapid propagation of Christianity, against all human probability, and under circumstances which would have destroyed, at its very birth, any system not manifestly divine in its origin and character. The Catholic gives a yet wider scope, and imparts a more conclusive character to this argument; by showing that this wonderful extension of the Gospel was not confined to the first period of its history, but went steadily on, under the auspices of his Church *only*, during all the succeeding ages of Christianity. He can prove, by irrefutable historical evidence, that the moral miracle presented in the first propagation of Christianity by twelve poor, unlettered fishermen or peasants of Judea, was often renewed at subsequent epochs of Church History, and under circumstances, too,

---

* Exodus, xxv: 40. Inspice et fac secundum exemplar quod tibi menstratum est in monte.

† Lecture V.

when every human probability was strongly opposed to
such results;—that, at the very time when every thing
seemed to bode ruin to the Church, she put forth her
greatest energies and achieved her most brilliant victories.
This I have also shown at some length in previous Lectures.*

4. In relation to the argument derived from the beneficial
moral effects of early Christianity on those who were brought
under its influence, I trust I have already shown, in the
Lecture on the Sanctity of the Church,† that those same
fruits of holiness were gathered in all subsequent ages of the
Church, in almost, if not quite, as great abundance as during
the period of primitive fervor. Scandals, indeed, there
were; great and deplorable scandals, over which, though
they had been predicted by her divine Founder, the Church
ceased not to weep: but there were also great and brilliant
examples of virtue and Christian heroism, which consoled
her in her affliction, and amply proved the divine potency
of her institutions in reforming the morals of a corrupt
world. No one can examine with impartiality the history
of the Catholic Church, especially during the middle ages,
without coming to the conclusion, that whatever amount
of civilization, of refinement, of elevation and purity of
morals we now boast of possessing, is fairly traceable to
her beneficial influence on society, and to her constant and
ever victorious contests with vice in high places. So incontestable is this great truth, that even Protestants, with all
their bitter prejudices against our Church, have freely admitted it, and have had the candor openly to avow their
conviction.‡

5. In regard to the Christian evidence based on the great
number of martyrs who died in its defense, the Catholic
Church can present it in her own favor with still greater
force, than can the Christian advocate in vindication of
Christianity. She alone can fairly claim the whole army

---

* Lectures IV. and X.   † Lecture VII.
‡ See, among other Protestant writers, Guizot's "Lectures on Civilisa-
tion in Modern Europe;" and Voigt's "Life of Gregory VII."

of Christian martyrs who shed their blood in the first three
centuries;—for she alone carefully guards their tombs in
the catacombs, she alone reverences their memory in stated
anniversary festivals, and she alone has reared their monuments. She can add to their number the vast multitude of
martyred heroes who died in her defense in all subsequent
ages of her history. What country is there in the wide
world, which is not purpled with the blood of her missionaries? What age is there in her history, in which a vast
multitude of her children, both men and women, were not
ready at any moment to accept, if not even to court, the
crown of martyrdom? Have her members in latter ages
degenerated from the noble devotedness and heroism of
their ancestors in the early times?

Look at the history of Catholic missions in heathen lands
during the last three centuries; follow the Catholic missionaries into the East Indies, into Japan, into China, into
the West Indies, into the remotest recesses of North and
South America, into the most distant islands of Oceanica;
mark their disinterested labors, their privations, their
sufferings, their death for Christ; and then lay your hands
upon your hearts, and tell me candidly, whether the
Catholic Church of this latest period has not rivaled, in
zeal and in the spirit of martyrdom, the Catholic Church
of the first three centuries. Look at the immense number
of Christian converts in Japan, who willingly suffered
death rather than trample upon the cross in denial of their
faith;* glance at the history of the apostolic labors of
the Jesuit missionaries among the Indian tribes of North
America, and the glorious martyrdom of many among their
number, as so eloquently set forth by our own historian,
Bancroft;† and then tell me, whether the Catholic Church
be not still fruitful in martyrs, and whether she cannot lay

---

* The Dutch Protestant traders were accused, probably with sufficient
reason, of having suggested this impious test to the heathen authorities of
Japan, in order to exclude the Catholic Portuguese from the trade of that
empire!

† Bancroft's History of the United States, Vol. III. ch. xx.

in a valid claim to the evidence based upon their number and heroism.

6. The stability and perpetuity of Christianity, in spite of obstacles which would have destroyed any merely human institution, is the last, and certainly one of the strongest evidences of its divine origin and character. The Catholic Church can plead this evidence in her own behalf with at least equal force and conclusiveness. She, too, has survived all the terrible assaults of time, of revolution, of fierce denunciation, of open vituperation and calumny, of conspiracies for her destruction from within and from without; all the combined efforts of wicked men, and of infuriate demons, for full eighteen centuries. She has come victorious out of every struggle and is as fresh and vigorous now, as when first she entered upon her career of trial and suffering! Her most powerful enemies have all perished, while she still remains, with no symptoms of decay or even decline. She alone has continued changeless amidst all the vicissitudes of human affairs around her. How explain this singular phenomenon? You cannot explain it by any principle of mere human philosophy; you must resort to the teachings of a higher Wisdom. Christ has explained it in two simple but very plain declarations: "Upon this rock I will build my Church, and the gates of hell SHALL NOT PREVAIL against it;" "Heaven and earth shall pass away, but MY WORD shall not pass away."

You will remember, that I devoted three separate Lectures to the development of this important argument; in the first of which I treated of the Antiquity and Apostolicity, in the second, of the Infallibility, and in the third, of the Trials and Triumphs, of the Church.* And I confidently leave it to the decision of all those who heard those Lectures, whether the Catholic argument, drawn from the stability and permanency of the Church, be not at least as strong as the Christian evidence derived from the same source. Take away the Catholic Church from

---

* Lectures VIII., IX., X.

history, and the very basis of this evidence in favor of Christianity is entirely removed, and the whole evidence falls to the ground of itself.

Thus have I endeavored, My Dear Brethren, to convince you, by a rapid glance at the two lines of reasoning traced out by the respective champions of Christianity and Catholicity, that the self-same arguments which prove the former also prove the latter, and even with redoubled force.

If this be the case, the conclusion is plain :—that the two systems are strictly and logically identical, and that you cannot rationally admit the one, without at the same time admitting the other. Then, there is no rational or logical medium between Catholicity and infidelity; between a *full* admission or a *total* rejection of Christianity. For the first fifteen hundred years of the Christian era, the two systems were identical in point of fact; for if the Catholic was not then the Christian Religion, the true Religion had totally disappeared from the face of the earth. The identity is as much a matter of fact now, as it was then; for neither system has suffered any change. Therefore this identity still exists in point of fact, as well as of reason and evidence.

The argument is still farther strenghtened by the remarkable fact in Church History, notorious to every one, that, so long as Catholicity held full and undivided sway over the minds of Christians there were no infidels—at least no organized bodies of infidels—within the boundaries of Christendom. Those who admitted Catholicity never once seriously thought of denying Christianity. Has it been so during the last three centuries,—since the boasted emancipation of the human mind from the thraldom of the Catholic principle, by the reformation? Alas! My Brethren, has not infidelity stalked abroad over Christendom with an unblushing front, and with an air of confidence and of open triumph? Have not men's minds, bewildered by the endless divisions and glaring inconsistencies of Protestantism, been often drawn into the yawning gulf of total unbelief? How are we to explain the alarming progress of infidelity

RECAPITULATION. **439**

among us, but by the instinctive feeling of intelligent and logical minds, that there is no rational medium between Catholicity and a total rejection of all revelation?

Is it not also true, that the strongest arguments against Christianity have been those precisely which have been leveled against Catholicity? How else did Voltaire and the other French infidels of the eighteenth century attack the Christian system? What other weapons are employed by their modern French disciples, Michelet, Sue, and Quinet? These men all instinctively felt, and they still feel, that Christianity cannot be destroyed, so long as that Church shall remain which was built upon A BOOK, and which was always the bulwark of—nay fully identified with—that divine system of Religion.

CONCLUSION.

I must now bring to a close these imperfect Lectures. I am aware of having in the course of them used plain and strong language, to express plain and strong truths. But I am conscious, too, that I have had no intention to offend or to wound, or even to deal harshly with, the religious feelings or prejudices of my opponents. Deeply and thoroughly persuaded of the divine origin and infallible truth of Catholicity, I have endeavored to impart a portion of my own conviction to those who honestly and sincerely differ from the Catholic Church.

How far I may have succeeded, you will best judge. But I entreat you diligently to examine and carefully to weigh the evidences which I have here labored to spread out before you. Brethren, time is short, eternity is never ending. "What doth it profit a man, if he gain the whole world, but lose his own soul?" In a few short years, we shall all have to appear at the dread bar of Christ, to give a rigorous account of our faith as well as of our works. Let us, then, be humble; let us pray; let us inquire; let us find out the truth; let us embrace it at once; let us live according to its requirements; that we may all be found acceptable on that fearful day of account!

May God grant, My Beloved Brethren, that all controversy may entirely cease among Christians; that the deplorable divisions of Christianity may be finally healed; that a blessed and glorious union may again reign throughout Christendom; and that we may all again meet in worship around those venerable altars at which our forefathers so reverently bowed down: in order that being united here below, as a band of brothers, we may all be re-united in heaven round the altar of the Lamb, and may mingle our voices in that swelling and eternal anthem of praise and adoration which is there poured forth by all the redeemed; through Jesus Christ, our blessed Lord and Saviour.   Amen.

THE END.